LEGAL MEDICINE 1986

LEGAL MEDICINE 1986

CYRIL H. WECHT,
M.D., J.D., Series Editor

Former Coroner, Allegheny County (Pittsburgh), Pa.; Clinical Adjunct Professor of Pathology, University of Pittsburgh Schools of Medicine and Dental Medicine; Adjunct Associate Professor of Epidemiology, University of Pittsburgh Graduate School of Public Health; Adjunct Professor of Pathology and Legal Medicine, Duquesne University School of Pharmacy; Adjunct Professor of Law, Duquesne University School of Law; Director, Pittsburgh Institute of Legal Medicine; Past President, American Academy of Forensic Sciences; Past President, American College of Legal Medicine.

PRAEGER

New York
Westport, Connecticut
London

ISBN 0-275-92551-X
ISSN 0197-9981
Library of Congress Catalog Card No. 80-647751

Library of Congress Catalog Card Number: 80-647751
ISBN: 0-275-92551-X
ISSN: 0197-9981

First published in 1986

Praeger Publishers, 521 Fifth Avenue, New York, NY 10175
A division of Greenwood Press, Inc.

Printed in the United States of America

The paper used in this book complies with the Permanent Paper Standard issued by the National Information Standards Organization (Z39.48-1984).

10 9 8 7 6 5 4 3 2 1

Contents

Contributors

Dale H. Cowan, M.D., J.D. Oncology Services, Inc., Garfield Heights, Ohio

Abdullah Fatteh, M.D., Ph.D., LL.B., F.R.C.P., F.C.L.M. Director, Broward Family Practices Associates, Plantation, Florida; Clinical Assistant Professor, Department of Family Medicine, University of Miami

Faiz Fatteh. Student, Plantation, Florida

Naaz Fatteh. Student, Plantation, Florida

Bernard J. Ficarra, M.D., Sc.D., LL.D. Director of Medical Legal Research, Ficarra Foundation, Oyster Bay, New York

Marvin H. Firestone, M.D., J.D., F.C.L.M. Marvin Firestone and Associates, Boulder, Colorado

Harold L. Hirsh, M.D., J.D., F.C.L.M. Clinical Assistant Professor of Medicine, Howard University College of Medicine, Washington, D.C.; Professorial Lecturer, George Washington University National Law Center

Edward V. Norton, J.D. Attorney, Ann Arbor, Michigan

Martin L. Norton, M.D., J.D. Professor of Anesthesiology; of Counsel; University of Michigan Hospitals

C. K. Parikh, B.S., M.B., D.P.H. Medicolegal Consultant, Bombay, India; former Honorary Professor of Forensic Medicine and Toxicology, Bombay University

Stephen Poljak. Duquesne University School of Law, Pittsburgh, Pennsylvania

John T. Rago. Duquesne University School of Law, Pittsburgh, Pennsylvania

Harry Rein, J.D., M.D., F.C.L.M. Physician and lawyer in private practice, Orlando, Florida

Stewart R. Reuter, M.D., J.D. Professor and Chairman, Department of Radiology, The University of Texas Health Science Center, San Antonio, Texas

S. Sandy Sanbar, M.D., Ph.D., J.D., F.C.L.M. Clinical Assistant Professor, University of Oklahoma Health Sciences Center

Robert Schur, J.D. Associate in the firm of Marvin Firestone and Associates, Boulder, Colorado

Charles L. Winek, Ph.D., D.A.B.F.T. Director and Chief Toxicologist, Allegheney County Department of Laboratories; Professor of Toxicology, Duquesne University

Preface

This year's volume once again establishes an annual sequence of publication for *Legal Medicine*, for which I am indebted to Mr. William Day, Medical/Life Sciences Editor, of Praeger Publishers.

As in past years, I have attempted to bring together a variety of chapters dealing with interesting, relevant, and timely medical-legal subjects. From AIDs and the Bhopal tragedy to thermography and surrogate motherhood, this book covers a wide gamut of material that all professionals interested and involved in medico-legal events and new developments should find informative and helpful. A special effort has been made to include discussions that are both pragmatic and philosophical, so that *Legal Medicine 1986* can be used as a reference in the office and courtroom, or as an academic text for legal medicine classes in medical and law schools.

I should like to express my appreciation to all the contributing authors for their excellent papers and unstinting cooperation. I am grateful to my personal secretary, Maribeth Blettner, for her special attention to this project, and to Bill Day for his cooperation and assistance.

Cyril H. Wecht

AIDS: An Exhaustive Review of Medical and Legal Aspects

Abdullah Fatteh, M.D., Ph.D., LL.B., F.R.C.P., F.C.L.M., Faiz Fatteh, and Naaz Fatteh

INTRODUCTION

The acquired immune deficiency syndrome (AIDS) is a medical malady identified in recent years. This disease, popularly described as the "gay plague," has acquired the status of the most virulent epidemic of the century. With over fifteen thousand cases already reported, and with an additional twenty thousand 20,000 cases by midsummer 1986 predicted, the disease has created mass hysteria. Sufferers and scientists alike are perplexed about almost every aspect of the disease as intensive investigation has raised many questions and provided few concrete answers. The precise cause of this complex disease still remains a matter of speculation; the scenario of the etiology keeps changing, and the therapeutic measures are far from satisfactory. The worst aspect of the disease is that all of the research has had no impact on its prognosis.

The world literature is flooded daily with publications containing new information. Two of us (F. F. and A. F.) attempted a brief review discussing the medical and legal aspects of this disease.[1] That review was based on the study of papers published in 1982–84.[2-19] However, with the tremendous inpouring of new data during the last few months it seems important to incorporate this information and present a broader, more exhaustive review of this entity. Perhaps it would be appropriate to stress that by press time a considerable amount of additional information will be forthcoming. Therefore, this review has the limitation of being up to date only until the end of the year 1985.

In this paper an attempt is made not only to present the medical aspects of the disease but also to discuss a variety of complex legal questions.

DEFINITIONS

The Centers for Disease Control (CDC) in Atlanta have defined AIDS as "a disease, at least moderately predictive of a defect in cell-mediated immunity, occurring in a person with no known cause for diminished resistance to that disease."

Although it is suspected that the onset of the disease in the United States probably occurred in the late seventies, surveillance for AIDS was not initiated in the United States until June 1981. At that time the CDC established for the purposes of surveillance a definition that demands two criteria:

1. The presence of a reliably diagnosed disease at least moderately predictive of cellular immunodeficiency;
2. The absence of an underlying cause for the reduced resistance to the disease.

The Conference of State and Territorial Epidemiologists approved a set of resolutions in June 1985 and recommended amendments to the above case definition of AIDS for national reporting:

1. In the absence of the opportunistic diseases required by the current case definition, any of the following diseases will be considered indicative of AIDS if the patient has a positive serologic or virologic test for human T-lymphocyte virus (HTLV–III/LAV):
   a. disseminated histoplasmosis (not confined to lungs or lymph nodes), diagnosed by culture, histology, or antigen detection;
   b. isosporiasis, causing chronic diarrhea (more than one month), diagnosed by histology or stool microscopy;
   c. bronchial or pulmonary candidiasis, diagnosed by microscopy or by presence of characteristic white plaques grossly on the bronchial mucosa (not by culture alone);
   d. non-Hodgkin's lymphoma of high-grade pathologic type (diffuse, undifferentiated) and of B-cell or unknown immunologic phenotype, diagnosed by biopsy;
   e. histologically confirmed Kaposi's sarcoma in patients who are sixty years old or older when diagnosed.
2. In the absence of the opportunistic diseases required by the current case definition, a histologically confirmed diagnosis of chronic lymphoid interstitial pneumonitis in a child (younger than thirteen years of age) will be considered indicative of AIDS unless test(s) for HTLV–III/LAV are negative.
3. Patients who have a lymphoreticular malignancy diagnosed more than three months after the diagnosis of an opportunistic disease used as a marker for AIDS will no longer be excluded as AIDS cases.
4. To increase the specifity of the case definition, patients will be excluded as AIDS cases if they have a negative result on testing for serum antibody to HTLV–III/LAV, have no other type of HTLV–III/LAV test with a positive result, and do not have a low number of T-helper lymphocytes or a low ratio of T-helper to T-suppressor lymphocytes. In the absence of test results, patients satisfying all other criteria in the definition will continue to be included.[51]

EPIDEMIOLOGY

United States

Since the identification of a few initial cases in 1981 there has been an exponential rise in the number of reported cases. At the time of this writing more than fifteen thousand cases have been reported by the CDC. According to this organization the number of victims is doubling every six months. The estimates indicate that a person in the general population has one chance in 62,000 of being afflicted by this grave disease. The epidemic is spreading worldwide. It is estimated at this time that approximately one million Americans may have been exposed to the AIDS virus. It is impossible to predict what percentage of those infected will actually develop the disease. Nevertheless, it can be stated that the virus can remain latent for months and years before causing symptoms. Therefore, persons infected five or more years ago may still develop the disease.

Most of the known cases have occurred in large cities. The analysis of the first three thousand reported cases indicates that 44.9 percent of the cases occurred in New York, 22.3 percent in California, 7.0 percent in Florida, 6.3 percent in New Jersey, and the remaining 19.5 percent in other states. The small town of Belle Glade in South Florida has the dubious distinction of having the highest rate of incidence in the world.

The striking feature of the disease is its age distribution. Over 90 percent of the patients are young, between the ages of twenty and fifty, and half of these are between twenty and thirty. Males predominate; more than 93 percent of all patients are males. Of the first three thousand cases reported, 58.9 percent were whites, 26.4 percent blacks, 14.4 percent Hispanics, and 0.3 percent members of other groups. Strikingly, there were only eight patients of Asian origin in the first three thousand cases.[21]

A vast majority of AIDS cases in the United States (about 73 percent) has occurred in homosexual or bisexual men. Intravenous drug abusers account for close to 16 percent of the cases, and Haitians for 5.5 percent. Persons with hemophilia account for approximately 1 percent of the cases. AIDS is now the leading cause of death in hemophiliacs; uncontrollable bleeding, which was the leading cause until now, has taken second place.

Of the afflicted Americans, 43 percent are known to have died. The CDC data show that 16 percent die within three months of diagnosis, 23 percent within six months, 35 percent within one year, 57 percent within two years, and 81 percent within three years of the onset of the disease.

Europe and Other Countries

By the end of 1984 a total of 762 cases of AIDS were reported to the World Health Organization (WHO).[22] This number has risen to 1,226 cases as of June 30, 1985.[52] The highest rates of AIDS cases per million population occurred in

Belgium and Switzerland. The incidence of cases in seventeen European countries is documented in Table 1.

Of the total of the 1,226 patients, 626 (51 percent) have died. The figures show that of the patients diagnosed one year ago, 61 percent have died; of those diagnosed three years ago, 83 percent have died.

Of the 1,226 cases, 1,011 (82 percent) occurred in Europe, 36 (3 percent) in the Caribbean Islands, 141 (12 percent) in Africa, and the remaining 38 (3 percent) elsewhere.[52]

The distribution of the cases in Europe with reference to the risk factors is as follows: total cases 1,011, male homosexual or bisexual 809, hemophilia patient 38, intravenous drug abuser 48, bisexual or homosexual intravenous drug abuser 15, transfusion recipient without other risk factors 20, and unknown risk factors 74.

TRANSMISSION OF AIDS

The transmission of AIDS is probably through sexual contacts (anal, vaginal, or oral), blood transfusions, use of contaminated needles (by drug users), intimate contacts (skin infection), saliva, and semen or urine. It is also possibly transmitted by the mother to the fetus in her womb. The specific means of transmission of the virus causing AIDS are similar to those for hepatitis type B. The best evidence for transmission of AIDS through blood products is the finding that AIDS occurred in a small number of hemophilia patients receiving large amounts of Factor VIII. This indicates that the infectious agent is most likely to be present in blood. However, it may also be present in other body fluids. The most common means of transmission is sexual activity especially with multiple anonymous sexual partners.[23] AIDS is also believed to be transmitted by heterosexual sexual contact. Transmission of HTLV–III/LAV from heterosexual men to their female sexual partners has also been well established.[52] There is also evidence to support the occurrence of bidirectional heterosexual transmission—male to female and female to male. Recent reports indicate the possibility of transmission of AIDS through contact with tears and through the use of serum proteins for the treatment of cancers.[53, 54] As of the end of November 1985, the HTLV–III that has been associated with AIDS has been isolated from peripheral blood, bone marrow, plasma, saliva, semen, lymph nodes, brain, cerebrospinal fluid, and tears.[55] It is equally important to note that AIDS can be transmitted from persons who show only mild symptoms and who have not been compromised by opportunistic diseases.[24]

INCUBATION PERIOD

With changing times it appears that the incubation period is lengthening. In October 1984 we reported that the incubation period was thought to be six months to two years. In May 1985 the CDC epidemiologist Dale N. Lawrence stated

TABLE 1. Cases of AIDS in Europe

Country	Number of cases reported by end of 1984	Number of cases reported by end of June 1985	Rate per million population
France	260	392	7.0
Federal Republic of Germany	135	220	3.6
United Kingdom	108	176	3.1
Belgium	65	99	10.0
Netherlands	42	66	4.6
Switzerland	41	63	9.7
Denmark	34	48	9.4
Spain	18	38	1.0
Sweden	16	27	3.3
Italy	14	52	0.9
Austria	13	18	2.4
Greece	6	9	0.9
Finland	5	6	1.2
Norway	5	11	2.6
Czechoslovakia	0	0	0.0
Iceland	0	0	0.0
Poland	0	0	0.0

that an infected person can harbor the virus for 14.2 years before his disease becomes clinically evident. He indicated that the mean incubation period for the virus is 5.5 years. This prolonged incubation period indicates that the disease was widespread in homosexuals long before it was identified and that it may remain concealed in the heterosexual population for years.[20]

RISK FACTORS

The analysis of the cases in the United States allows for the identification of several groups that are at increased risk for developing AIDS. The important high-risk groups are:

1. Homosexual men;
2. Intravenous drug abusers;
3. Patients with hemophilia;
4. Patients who have received blood from infected donors.

As has been mentioned earlier, homosexuals account for the majority of AIDS cases. This high percentage has been attributed to homosexual AIDS victims' extreme promiscuity and abuse of drugs. It has been shown that homosexual men with AIDS have more anonymous sexual encounters, engage more frequently in anal sex, use illicit drugs more often, and have had more sexually transmitted diseases than homosexual males without AIDS.[23, 25, 26] Significant statistics regarding homosexual risk factors also include a number of other factors such as exposure to feces, semen, and rectal trauma. The sexual practices of homosexuals undoubtedly are the single greatest cause for the high incidence of AIDS in them.

The next population likely to be at high risk of contracting the disease may be heterosexual men and women with multiple sex partners and persons whose sex partners are members of the four principal AIDS risk groups. The reports of high seroconversion rates and even the development of disease in sex partners of the four high-risk groups indicate that AIDS can be transmitted sexually by both men and women. It is also thought that heterosexual men may be at an added risk with their contacts with female prostitutes. Conversely, women who are steady partners of men with AIDS or of men in high-risk groups have increased risk of contracting AIDS. These facts suggest that in the future AIDS may become more common in heterosexuals than in homosexuals.

Another associated factor is the use of nitrite inhalants as aphrodisiacs and as muscle relaxants to facilitate anal sex. Nitrite inhalants are thought to be associated with the onset of Kaposi's sarcoma. Also, these reportedly immunotoxic drugs are used almost exclusively by homosexuals and so may help explain in part why such a high percentage of the AIDS cases fall into this category.

The second most common victim of AIDS (17 percent) is the intravenous drug user. These patients, often heroin and cocaine addicts, transmit the AIDS virus by sharing used needles. They are known to pump their own blood in and out of the syringe being used. Female partners of the drug abusers are also at an added risk.

Hemophiliacs are the third largest risk group. The problem of AIDS in hemophiliacs seems to be linked to two methods of treatment of hemophilia. Lyophilized concentrate and cryoprecipitate are two products used in the treatment of hemophilia, and they are obtained from pools of plasma from a large number of donors (up to 5,000 in the case of lyophilized concentrate and up to 20 in cryoprecipitate).[27]

The fourth largest risk group consists of individuals who have received blood from infected donors. The first such reported case occurred in an infant who received blood from a person who was known to have developed AIDS. Curran and his workers have reported eighteen transfusion-associated cases in the United States.[28] Every one of these patients developed *Pneumocystis carinii* pneumonia. A few of them received blood from the same donor.

After AIDS was first recognized, Haitians were considered a high-risk group. The large number of Haitians with AIDS led researchers to consider in them such risk factors as homosexuality, heterosexual promiscuity, use of unsterilized needles by doctors, malnutrition, and the widespread occurrence of parasitic infections and antimicrobial agents. As a result of these researches, Haitians were recently removed from the list of high-risk groups by the CDC. This is because apart from the incidental high incidence of AIDS in Haitians, no scientific evidence was available to justify their inclusion in the risk groups.

ETIOLOGY OF AIDS

The hypotheses attempting to explain the etiology of AIDS change almost every day. One fact remains unchanged: in AIDS there is a nearly complete breakdown of a person's natural immune system. When the immune system breaks down, the victims become prey to cancers and to infections that a normal healthy individual would be able to fight off. Several opportunistic infections have been reported in patients with AIDS. These are reviewed in the section dealing with the pathology of AIDS.

Some of the older theories explaining the causation of AIDS are:

1. A virus transmitted sexually, through the skin or by parasites, destroys the body's natural immune system.
2. Overexposure to sperm from many sources may play a part in the suppression of the immune system.
3. The immune system is crippled after repeated infections by sexually transmitted diseases such as syphilis, gonorrhea, and herpes.

In recent months viral etiologies have received the greatest attention. The viruses that are implicated in the etiology of AIDS are:

1. Human T-lymphotropic virus type III (HTLV–III), lymphadenopathy-associated viruses (LAV), and AIDS-associated retrovirus (ARV);
2. Cytomegalovirus (CMV);
3. Epstein-Barr virus (EBV).

The researchers from France and the United States support the hypothesis that AIDS is caused by HTLV-retrovirus. This virus has been variously named. Gallo and his associates call it HTLV–III.[29] Barré-Sinoussi and his co-workers call it LAV, and Levy and his team describe it as ARV.[30, 31] Whether these three are one and the same virus is not known. The works of Popovic and Gallo indicate that HTLV–III was isolated from 36 percent of adult AIDS patients, 37 percent of juvenile AIDS patients, 87.5 percent of "pre-AIDS" patients, and none of the 115 heterosexual controls.[32, 33] Additional observations made by these researchers and their associates have revealed that the antibodies to HTLV–III are present in 87.8 percent of AIDS patients, 78.6 percent of "pre-AIDS" patients, 26.6 percent of homosexual men without AIDS, 60 percent of intravenous drug abusers, and 0.5 percent of normal controls.[34]

Further studies have shed more light on the viral etiologies. A recent study by Redfield and his group has shown frequent transmission of HTLV–III among spouses of patients with AIDS-related complex and AIDS.[35] They showed this with a study of seven married males and five spouses who had HTLV–III infection. They also evaluated eleven children and found only one fourteen-month-old child seropositive for antibody to HTLV–III. They suggest that the HTLV–III can be transmitted by repeated heterosexual contacts and that a close household contact to patients with AIDS-related complex or AIDS is not an efficient mechanism for virus transmission.

Another recent study deals with the isolation of LAV and the detection of LAV antibodies from the United States patients with AIDS.[36] This study provides support for the etiologic association of LAV and AIDS.

The CMV antibodies have been found in 80 to 95 percent of AIDS patients compared with 50 percent in the general population. CMV has been cultured from the urine of homosexual men but not from the urine of heterosexual men. There is also evidence that the CMV infections can be transmitted sexually. EBV has also been implicated. Antibodies from EBV have been found in very high concentrations in a group of AIDS patients.

PATHOLOGY OF AIDS

The pathologist, just the same way as the clinician, should be acutely aware of the diverse pathological patterns that AIDS can create. He must be at the center of all the complexities of the disease. The clinical pathologist should be able not only to comply with the requests for ordered tests but also to guide the clinicians toward a more rewarding investigation of a patient.

AIDS patients are susceptible to a variety of infections: viral, protozoal, fungal, and bacterial. The viral agents, discussed elsewhere, are capable of causing an array of pathological conditions such as pneumonia, esophagitis, entercolitis, hepatitis, shingles, lymphoma, encephalitis, leukoencephalopathy, and retinitis. The protozoal infestations could produce pneumonia, entercolitis, cholecystitis, and encephalitis. The *Pneumocystis carinii* pneumonia is, of course, the most common of all the infections. The fungi could cause thrush, esophagitis, pneumonia, and meningitis, and the bacterial infections could result in lymphadenitis, pneumonia, hepatosplenomegaly, and pancytopenia.

In addition to the above pathological manifestations, AIDS causes Kaposi's sarcoma and primary central nervous system lymphoma and may be related to other lymphomas and to squamous cell carcinoma of either the oral cavity or the anus.

Recent research indicates that the AIDS virus affects T-helper lymphocytes and brain cells. Infection of the central nervous system results in multifocal rarefaction of neutrophils, microglial nodules, and perivascular infiltrates of white matter with relative sparing of gray matter.[43] Vacuolar myelopathy of the spinal cord with myelin swelling and fluid within the sheath is also caused by AIDS virus.

A study of fifteen brains of individuals with AIDS and encephalopathy has shown the presence of HTLV–III DNA in five brains and viral-specific RNA in four.[44]

Autopsy on a Case of AIDS

The autopsy on a case of AIDS should be done as soon as possible after death. The pathologist and those assisting him in the autopsy, as well as other observers, should take special precautions of wearing double gloves, protective eyewear, masks, caps, gowns, waterproof apron, and shoe coverings. Great care should be exercised in preventing injuries from the instruments. The tissues retained for histological studies should be formalin-fixed immediately and labeled with biohazard tags. After the autopsy, the table and the instruments used should be adequately decontaminated.

There have been no reports of the transmission of HTLV–III virus as a result of an autopsy. However, one can expect the possibility of autopsy-related transmission of AIDS with increasing numbers of autopsies on AIDS victims. In a recent publication Mass has described precautions that a pathologist can take while performing an autopsy on an AIDS case.[56]

SIGNS AND SYMPTOMS OF AIDS

AIDS can present itself in a variety of ways.

The symptoms and signs will depend on whether the disease is caused by the opportunistic infections or is a neoplastic disease. In general, the most common symptoms are fatigue (70 percent), fever (49 percent), and night sweats (44 percent). These symptoms persist for weeks or months. Some patients (28 percent) lose weight. Diarrhea is also a frequent complaint.

The signs or symptoms associated with Kaposi's sarcoma and/or *P. carinii* pneumonia are dyspnea, skin lesions, fever, weight loss, lymphadenopathy, diarrhea, and oral thrush. The other important symptoms are malaise, anorexia, fatigue, muscle aches, painful adenopathy, night sweats, decreased libido, sinusitis, diffuse alopecia, and arthralgias.

The fever following opportunistic infections is either intermittent or continuous with an afternoon or nocturnal pattern. Physical activity produces spikes of fever with profuse sweating.

The central nervous system involvement can produce headaches, stiff neck, slow thought, impaired concentration, slow motor and verbal performances, impaired intellect, confusion, disorientation, change in behavior, loss of vision, depression, and even seizures.

The cutaneous manifestations could include rashes (maculopapular or diffuse), dermatitis or eczema, tinea versicolor or staphyloccal impetigo, facial erythema, and postherpetic hypopigmentation (weeping lesions or scarring). If the victim has Kaposi's sarcoma, he may have dark blue or purple-brown plaques or nodules, most commonly on the lower extremities.

The respiratory symptoms and signs consist of dyspnea, nonproductive or productive cough, chest pain, rhonchi, rales, and tachypnea.

The gastrointestinal infection in homosexual men has earned the name of "gay bowel syndrome." The gastrointestinal manifestations may range from oral thrush to proctitis. Diarrhea and weight loss are common. Sore throat and mouth ulcers could be associated with dysphagia. Likewise, esophagitis would cause dysphagia; enteritis would result in diarrhea, abdominal cramps, and bloating; proctocolitis would be associated with diarrhea and lower abdominal pain; and anorectal pain and mucopurulent discharge may result from AIDS proctitis.

A common feature of the disease is the enlargement of lymph glands in the neck or groin. The size and consistency of the glands are variable. They may be soft, fluctuating, and tender. In about 26 percent of patients, there is also enlargement of the liver and the spleen. The spleen is usually soft and moderately enlarged in the febrile stage, but in established AIDS cases it may be large and firm.

In children with immune deficiency, the clinical picture consists of anemia (hypochromic microcytic), infections, failure to thrive, hepatosplenomegaly, recurrent febrile episodes, thrush, and eczemalike rash.

EVALUATION OF A CASE OF AIDS

The most important aspect of the evaluation of a patient suspected to have AIDS is history taking. The physician should take great pains in eliciting a full history with particular emphasis on sexual activity and the sequential development of the symptoms.

The initial investigations must include chest X rays, chemistry profile with electrolytes, complete and differential blood counts, platelet count, and sedimentation rate. The clinician should carry out other investigations that may throw additional light on the possibility of the existence of this disease. For instance, he could order an anti-HBc test to detect possible AIDS infectivity in the blood. This blood test is positive in 90 percent of the victims of AIDS and in only 5 percent of the general population. Other investigations may include the biopsy of the skin lesions, fungal studies, and immunologic tests. A summary of the abnormal laboratory tests is presented in Table 2. Of course, the viral studies as detailed elsewhere must be carried out.

The physician should refer the patient to an appropriate place for further investigations if his office or the nearby hospital is not equipped to carry out the investigations. In an outpatient setting the physician should advise his patient to come for regular medical evaluations and treatment.

If the patient is admitted to the hospital, appropriate consultants should be summoned. For instance, if there are neurological symptoms or signs the services of a neurologist should be requested so that additional investigations such as CAT scans of the brain and lumbar puncture are done. A gastroenterologist may be needed for possible endoscopy, sigmoidoscopy, or colonoscopy. An infectious

Table 2. Abnormal Laboratory Tests in AIDS

Laboratory test	Result
T-helper cells (T4)	↓ ↓ ↓
T4/T8 ratio	↓ ↓
Total cells (T11)	↓
IgG	↑
Hepatitis B core AB (anti-HBc)	+
Skin tests for PPD, histo, candida, dermatophytin, mumps	↓ ↓
Lymphoblastic transformation PHA, Con A, and PWM	↓ ↓
Natural killer cell cytotoxicity	↓
Circulating immune complexes	Normal or ↑
Total hemolytic complement activity	↑

disease specialist may be needed for a variety of infections, and a pulmonary consultant for bronchoscopic evaluation. The suspicion of AIDS in a child will require a consultation with a pediatrician possessing good insight in the field of AIDS.

AIDS ANTIBODY TESTS

Since the Department of Health and Human Services, Public Health Service Section, of the Food and Drug Administration declared in a letter to all physicians in the United States that HTLV–III virus causes AIDS, rapid moves have been made to prepare a test for detecting HTLV–III antibodies. The test uses ELISA (enzyme-linked immunosorbent assay) technology.[37] This test detects HTLV–III antibodies. It is not a test for AIDS, but it is an important development for screening suspected cases, donated blood, and plasma for antibodies to HTLV–III virus. The test may give false positive results. If HTLV–III antibody is detected in an asymptomatic person it could mean an infection with the virus has occurred without clinical evidence of the disease. Of those individuals positive for HTLV–III antibody, only a few develop AIDS.

In instances where HTLV–III antibody is detected in blood and plasma donors the Public Health Service recommends additional testing with the Western blot technique.[38] This technique allows identification of antibodies to proteins of specific molecular weight. It is less sensitive than the ELISA test but is more specific when positive.

All persons accepted as donors should be informed that their blood or plasma will be tested for HTLV–III antibody. They should be informed that their test results will be kept confidential except for medical or public health purposes.

Since the ELISA test is not for AIDS because it may be false positive, and since it raises numerous questions, the CDC, Food and Drug Administration, Alcohol, Drug Abuse and Mental Health Administration, National Institutes of Health, and Health Resources and Services Administration have jointly prepared recommendations for an individual likely to have an HTLV–III infection.[39] These are reproduced here:

1. The prognosis for an individual infected with HTLV–III over the long term is not known. However, data available from studies conducted among homosexual men indicate that most persons will remain infected.
2. Although asymptomatic, these individuals may transmit HTLV–III to others. Regular medical evaluation and follow-up is advised, especially for individuals who develop signs or symptoms suggestive of AIDS.
3. Refrain from donating blood, plasma, body organs, other tissue, or sperm.
4. There is a risk of infecting others by sexual intercourse, sharing of needles, and possible exposure of others to saliva through oral-genital contact or intimate kissing. The efficacy of condoms in preventing infection with HTLV–III is unproven, but the consistent use of them may reduce transmission.
5. Toothbrushes, razors, or other implements that could become contaminated with blood should not be shared.
6. Women with a seropositive test, or women whose sexual partner is a seropositive, are themselves at increased risk of acquiring AIDS. If they become pregnant, their offspring are also at increased risk of acquiring AIDS.
7. After accidents resulting in bleeding, contaminated surfaces should be cleaned with household bleach freshly diluted 1:10 in water.
8. Devices that have punctured the skin, such as hypodermic or acupuncture needles, should be steam sterilized by autoclave before reuse or should be safely discarded. Whenever possible, disposable needles and equipment should be used.
9. When seeking medical or dental care for intercurrent illness, these persons should inform those responsible for their care of their positive antibody status so that appropriate evaluation can be undertaken and precautions taken to prevent transmission to others.
10. Testing for HTLV–III antibody should be offered to persons who may have been infected as a result of their contact with seropositive individuals (e.g., sexual partners, persons with whom needles have been shared, infants born to seropositive mothers).

TEST KITS AND CONTROVERSIES

There is no doubt that the ELISA tests for HTLV–III antibody can be useful screening procedures to help reduce or eliminate the risk of transmitting AIDS in donor blood.[40] The Department of Health and Human Services and the Food and Drug Administration have given license to Abbott Laboratories to market AIDS antibody test kits. This laboratory began shipping the kits to blood banks on March 2, 1985, at a charge of $2.00 and $3.00 apiece.

The previous research has indicated that the ELISA test is capable of picking up a high percentage of those truly positive for AIDS antibody.[41] The sensitivity and specificity reports from four companies are:

DuPont: 97.4 percent sensitivity and 99.3 percent specificity;

Electro-Nucleonics: 99.6 percent sensitivity and 99.7 percent specificity;

Litton: 99.5 percent sensitivity and 95.6 percent specificity;

Travenol: 99.5 percent sensitivity and 95.6 percent specificity.

Despite its apparent usefulness, the ELISA test has created serious controversies. This is mainly because the test gives false negative results in 5 percent of AIDS patients. Another important fact is that an initial testing of the sera of 17,000 blood donors showed 0.6 percent positive, but a repeat test to eliminate error reduced the percentage to 0.21 percent. The figure of 5 percent false negative suggests that 1,000 donors from each month's one million tested will be true positive and therefore about 50 contaminated units of serum will pass the screening process each month.[42]

Further, the estimates from the initial trials with the kits indicate that over 2,000 donors will be reported to physicians. The physicians will not be able to render any advice as to prognosis in these donors without further confirmations.

The test is also likely to raise medico-legal questions concerning confidentiality. The notation of positive results of the donors in their medical records may result in job discrimination and may affect their insurability if the results are released to the parties requesting them. For these reasons gay rights groups have called for the boycott of the test.

Despite these problems the testing for HTLV–III virus is becoming increasingly common. At the present time the Public Health Service recommends screening of all donated plasma and blood for HTLV–III antibody. The screening recommendations go beyond testing of the high-risk groups. Since September 1985 the criteria for testing include "any man who has had sex with another man since 1977" and every man who has had even a single homosexual experience.[57] The Public Health Service also recommends that the HTLV–III antibody testing be done to screen blood and serum from donors of organs, tissues, or semen intended for human use.[58] Even the United States Department of Defense has decided to screen all military personnel for antibodies to the HTLV–III.[59]

PREVENTION AND TREATMENT OF AIDS

Prevention of AIDS

Several organizations such as the National Gay Task Force, the National Hemophilia Foundation, the American Red Cross, the American Association of Blood Banks, and the American Association of Physicians for Human Rights have issued statements on prevention and control of AIDS. All organizations, physicians, public, and the press should share responsibility in disseminating available information on AIDS. The following recommendations should be followed by persons or organizations concerned. These will greatly help in controlling and preventing AIDS:

1. A person experiencing symptoms of AIDS should seek medical advice as soon as possible so that the physician can take a full history, perform a complete examination, carry out laboratory tests, and render appropriate advice.
2. Physicians should adhere strictly to medical indications for transfusions.
3. Blood collection centers should adopt strict screening procedures to eliminate donors with a probability of transmitting AIDS.
4. Infants born to mothers from groups at high risk for AIDS should be carefully screened by physicians.
5. Every proven or suspected case of AIDS should be reported to the CDC.
6. Male homosexuals involved in extensive sexual activity should use condoms during sexual activity. In addition, mutual manual masturbation of involved partners without contact with semen may be substituted for anal or oral sex.
7. Additional recommendations made by the CDC and the Public Health Service of the U.S. Department of Health and Human Services detailed elsewhere should be carefully implemented.

Prevention of Possible Spread of HTLV–III/LAV Virus from Tears

Since the virus has been isolated from the tears of patients with AIDS, the following preventive measures should be taken.[53]

1. Professionals performing eye examinations or other procedures involving contact with tears should wash their hands immediately after a procedure.
2. Instruments coming in contact with external surfaces of the eyes should be disinfected.
3. Contact lenses used in trial fittings should be disinfected between each fitting.

Prevention of Risk of AIDS to Health and Other Workers

In December 1984 a British nurse developed symptoms of AIDS after she stuck her finger with a needle on a syringe that contained blood from an AIDS patient. As a result of this unique case, the CDC made a study, prior to the summer of 1985, of AIDS risk to health workers and came to a conclusion that no AIDS cases have resulted from caring for 9,000 AIDS patients in the United States. However, since then Weiss and his associates have documented one HTLV–III positive health worker whose apparent exposure was through puncture wounds from needles used to draw blood from AIDS patients.[60] Even though no cases have been reported in dentists and doctors as a result of the treatment of AIDS, almost all dentists in Florida and many physicians are refusing to treat AIDS patients.

Although the risk is small, physicians, nurses, and laboratory personnel caring for AIDS patients should take the following steps to prevent exposure:

1. Discard the needles rather than recapping them;
2. Locate the disposal containers near the patient;
3. Use nonpenetrable plastic disposal containers;
4. Dispose of blades and other sharp objects immediately after they are used in patient care.

As time passes it is becoming increasingly clear that more detailed preventive advice is needed, not just for health care workers but also for all persons at the workplace. This gap has been filled with the publication of two important articles summarizing the recommendations for preventing transmission of infection with HTLV–III in the workplace.[65, 66] The articles address persons providing health care, those providing personal services and preparing and serving food and beverages, as well as those persons in settings such as offices, schools, factories, and construction sites. The documents do not recommend routine HTLV–III/LAV antibody screening for the groups addressed because AIDS is not spread by casual contact. The recommendations in the articles further state that "food service workers known to be infected with AIDS should not be restricted from work unless they have another infection or illness for which such restriction should be warranted."

Treatment of AIDS

Treatment of the patient with AIDS can be divided as follows:

1. Treatment of opportunistic infections;
2. Treatment of Kaposi's sarcoma;
3. Psychosocial care.

Treatment of Opportunistic Infections

The infections in AIDS patients are caused by viruses (CMV, herpes simplex, herpes zoster, EBV, poxvirus and polyoma virus), protozoa (*Pneumocystis carinii, Toxoplasma gondii, Cryptosporidium, Entameba histolytica,* and *Giardia lamblia*), bacteria (*Mycobacterium avium-intracellulare* and *Mycobacterium tuberculosis*), and fungi (*Candida* species and *Cryptococcus neoformans*).

Recent literature, summarized in the *American Medical News* (May 3, 1985) and *Medical World News* (March 11, 1985), has discussed drugs that attack the AIDS virus: they either kill the virus or inhibit its growth. Each drug acts by interfering with the replication of the AIDS virus HTLV–III.

The drugs that offer promise are:

Suramin: a drug used against parasitic disease that blocks the infectivity and replication of the virus.

HPA–23: also inhibits viral replication by inhibiting the reverse transcriptase enzyme.

Phosphonoformate: acts the same way as HPA–23 does. It has persistent antiviral activity.

Ribavirin: causes suppression of the replication of HTLV–III in cultured T-cells.

Alpha interferon: has worked well in the treatment of influenza and herpes zoster and CMV infections and appears effective in treating retroviruses.

Amsanycin: reduces virus infectivity and inhibits reverse transcriptase activity.

The latest update on the use of anti-AIDS agents such as suramin, ribavirin, HPA–23, and azidothymidine shows variable results.[61] Each of the above drugs has a limitation in that none can consistently cure AIDS. Perhaps the real breakthrough will come from a vaccine that may protect the population against AIDS. In the meantime, prevention is presently the only available means for combating the AIDS epidemic.

Treatment of Kaposi's Sarcoma

The drugs most useful in the therapy of Kaposi's sarcoma are vinblastine, actinomycin, IRCF, bleomycin, DTIC, and BCNU.

Psychosocial Treatment

Despite the agonizing turmoil that AIDS has created in its victims and their contacts, perhaps the least attention has been paid to the psychosocial aspects of this disease. The chance of potential development of disease, uncertainty about its cause, lack of knowledge of effective treatment, and poor prognosis combine to cast a shadow of doom. The disease evokes intense fears in the sufferers, populations at risk, and the worried well.

The disease is so widely publicized that the patients, and their friends and families are usually well informed. This publicity, however, also results in patients being ostracized by society. Physical contact with them is avoided and social contact reduced. The patients experience job discrimination and are stigmatized as lepers. Instances of difficulty in gaining entry to churches, schools, and other public institutions are increasingly heard of.

The nature of the disease and the social reactions invariably create serious psychological problems in these patients. They suffer from anxiety, headaches, loss of recent memories, guilt, social isolation, personality change, demoralization, and depression. Their psychosocial functioning is impaired. Some patients suffer from insomnia, and some entertain thoughts of suicide. The autopsy data have shown neuropathological abnormalities in nearly two-thirds of AIDS patients. These changes cause dementia in 40 percent of the patients, and some develop full-blown incapacity. With such a state of mind in the sufferer there is no doubt that he is in need of psychosocial care. Such care should be organized to cover the following aspects:

1. Education of patients and their families and friends on the medical aspects of the disease;
2. Plans for referral of the patient to an appropriate center capable of management of specific medical problems;
3. Continuous psychological counseling to sustain the morale of the patient and to deal with his specific psychological problems;
4. Organization of hospital services to provide tertiary care and plans to deal with the dying patient and the grief of the family and friends;
5. Plans for crisis intervention for suicidal patients;
6. Plans for dealing with AIDS anxiety in the worried well.[46]

The primary care physician must assume a pivotal position in such plans. He is probably in the best position to provide psychological counseling. His major goal should be to maximize the quality of the patient's life. In dealing with these patients the value of compassion cannot be overemphasized. The physician should not only deal with the symptoms of anxiety, depression, and so on but should also counsel the patient carefully on his wish for sexual activity and the rights of the persons he may infect.

LEGAL ASPECTS OF AIDS: ISSUES AND ACTIONS

A variety of medico-legal questions can be raised in relation to the entity of AIDS. Several legal battles are already erupting in courts on the medico-legal issues arising out of this disease. In view of the stigma, modes of transmission, emotional factors, and unanswered questions of the etiology of the disease, and most of all, the conflict between the individual's civil rights and the public health needs of the nation, a great number of legal actions are anticipated. The following cases represent some of the legal issues.

In Broward County, Florida, two men were fired from their county jobs for having the disease. The county wrote to one of the fired employees, "There is no factual dispute regarding the reason for your termination. Upon confirming that you were diagnosed as having Acquired Immune Deficiency Syndrome (AIDS), the county took the position that in order to protect its employees and members of the public with whom you would come in contact in the performance of your job functions, your future employment would pose a potential risk to others."[47]

The employee has quite rightly appealed to the Florida Commission on Human Relations on the grounds of unlawful employment discrimination. Since it is established that AIDS is not communicated through casual contacts, the county's decision appears unfair and discriminatory. The *Morbidity and Mortality Weekly*

Report of the CDC (January 11, 1985) indicated that no cases have been documented to occur "through such common exposures as sharing meals, sneezing or coughing, or other casual contacts."[39]

The following two cases deal with civil rights of children.[64]

In New Jersey a superior court judge has rendered a judgment that may be important. He has turned down a request from the state attorney general to order a school to admit to classes a five-year-old child with AIDS.

In another pending litigation in New York City, two school boards have challenged the city's right to have experts review cases and recommend whether a child with AIDS should be allowed to attend regular classes.

In Michigan, a former employer of an insurance man took out a $100,000 life insurance policy before firing him. The man died from AIDS, and his employer is trying to collect $100,000. However, the contractor for the insurance company has filed a $5,000,000 suit against the former employer of the deceased AIDS victim claiming discrimination on the grounds that the insured employee had been fired after the employer deduced homosexuality and development of AIDS in the deceased insured.[48]

A physician, an infectious disease specialist, in Manhattan's Greenwich Village received an eviction notice from his landlord because most of his patients were AIDS victims. The doctor decided to fight the eviction and establish that AIDS is not transmitted by casual contact. He produced stacks of affidavits from medical authorities, proved his point, and won the case.[49]

In Britain the government has taken stiff measures. There the magistrates are given the authority to put AIDS patients in hospitals, detain them there forcefully if the patients try to leave, and take all steps to protect the public from coming into contact with the AIDS victims' dead bodies.[50]

The city of Los Angeles has taken quite the opposite action. The Los Angeles City Council has enacted a law that prevents employers, employment agencies, and labor unions from firing or refusing to hire people with AIDS. Segregation of AIDS sufferers at work is also banned. Restaurants and schools are not allowed to deny entry, and doctors as well as dentists are prohibited from refusing to treat victims. Also, the insurance companies cannot refuse to write health or life coverage or raise premiums of victims.

In view of the likelihood of increasing numbers of medico-legal and social complaints the following situations are worth a brief discussion:

1. *Actions against Hospitals:* The victim undergoing the investigations and treatment, or his family, may initiate an action against the hospital on the grounds of malpractice in the event of failure to make proper diagnosis or mishaps in the management of the patient. The treating physician and other staff members may be joined in the action by the patient. Also, hospital staff members contracting the disease may claim that the disease was acquired from AIDS patients cared for in the hospital. Additional liability questions involve assuring the patient a proper source of blood, giving reasonable alternatives, and giving an informed consent.
2. *Liability on the Basis of Blood Transfusion:* Extreme care is necessary in selecting

blood donors. Inadequate screening of a donor has resulted in the past in the development of hepatitis in the recipient. This has given rise to legal actions. On the same basis, the transmission of AIDS may result from blood transfusions. In the United States, by August 15, 1985, 194 cases of possible transfusion associated AIDS had been reported to the CDC, infants accounting for 10 percent of the cases.[62] Liability claim would involve the blood banks, laboratories, and hospitals. Such liability involves the issues of selecting suitable donors, fulfilling testing requirements, and adhering to standards of practice.

3. *Issues of Civil Rights:* As stated above, the victims of AIDS are often treated as "untouchables." The AIDS antibody tests will further complicate the dilemma. A thorny problem will be the question of how the society should deal with the individuals who are found to carry antibodies to HTLV–III. No test is available to determine which of the individuals who are antibody positive are also infectious. In dealing with nearly a million people who are potentially infectious, the society will have to balance the affected persons' civil rights against the public health needs of the unaffected general population.

   Children who are HTLV–III positive may face social discrimination. The parents of well or unaffected children may demand separate schools for their offspring. Fortunately, the American Academy of Pediatrics has advanced recommendations that could ease the existing confusion and controversy.[63]

   a. Since no child has been known to have contracted AIDS in schools or day-care centers, most children and adolescents with AIDS should be allowed to attend school with the approval of their physician.
   b. Children with AIDS who lack control of their body secretions, have a tendency to bite others, or have open sores should be placed in more restricted school settings.
   c. Screening of all school children for AIDS should not be undertaken.

The National Education Association has asserted that "children with AIDS should not be barred from classes without case review by panels that include the child's parents, health experts and school officials." It has also said that if there is a "reasonable cause" to believe that the student or an employee might be infected with AIDS, the school should be able to require that person to undergo a medical evaluation.

4. *Inheritance Problems:* The family members of some AIDS victims feel so strongly about the stigma of the disease that they disown the victim. Such disowning of the victim by his parents is bound to create questions and perhaps legal actions about inheritance.

The medical facts presented and the legal questions raised above make it abundantly clear that there is a need to crystallize the measures that would help prevent the spread of the disease among contacts. The following precautionary steps would not only help the patient and the contacts medically but would also reduce the chances of liability actions.

Liability of the Hospital

From the time a patient with AIDS or suspected to have AIDS is admitted to the hospital, a multitude of liability-creating mishaps can occur if proper protocol is not followed. The liabilities can arise from the development of disease in the nursing staff, physicians, other patients, physical and respiratory therapists, laboratory staff, and, in fact, any person coming in close contact with the patient. To reduce or eliminate the chances of spread of disease to contacts, the hospital should publish guidelines for various departments. These guidelines should include specific advice on all matters as follows:

1. *Reporting of the Patient:* The attending physician or the infection control nurse should report the patient to the local or state health department. They, in turn, will report to the Centers for Disease Control.
2. *Emergency Room Precautions:* The emergency room staff, as well as the teams of paramedics and rescue squads dealing with a case of AIDS, should be advised to take precautions that are usually taken for patients requiring isolation. They should also be advised to use disposable equipment. If cardiopulmonary resuscitation is to be administered, disposable respiratory equipment should be used. They should also follow the advice rendered to the laboratory staff for handling blood, sputum, body fluids, excretions, and secretions.
3. *Admission to Isolation Room:* A private room should be used for a patient with AIDS. If the patient is coughing or sneezing, or there are strong social and emotional factors, these are further grounds for isolation. Also, he must not be allowed to share a room with a patient who is an impaired host with a potential for susceptibility to opportunistic infection, or who may be harboring opportunistic infection that may be transmitted to the patient with AIDS.
4. *General Precautions*
   a. Appropriate signs should be put on the room door regarding the use of mask and gloves, handwashing, and so on.
   b. All persons from different departments who are likely to come in contact with blood, tissues, body fluids, excretions, and secretions or articles potentially contaminated by these substances should follow the advice outlined below for the laboratory staff.
   c. The use of gowns is recommended for those who are likely to come in contact with blood, sputum, body fluids, excretions, or secretions. Masks must be worn by all coming in contact with a coughing patient or an intubated patient whose throat is being suctioned. Such a patient must also wear a mask if he has to be transported to another area of the hospital.
   d. When there is a likelihood of splatter of blood, fluids, or secretions, eyewear should be used. This may occur during surgery or other procedures such as bronchoscopy, endoscopy, and so on.
   e. The linen used by the AIDS patient should be double-bagged as per isolation procedures, and all disposable items should be considered infectious and disposed of as such.
   f. Hands must be washed before and immediately after contact with the patient with AIDS, even if gloves are worn.
   g. The room occupied by the AIDS patient should be cleaned daily and after discharge in the same way as an isolation room.
5. *Patient's Anonymity:* For social and emotional reasons, it is important to maintain the patient's anonymity. The diagnosis of AIDS carries a stigma; hence, every effort

should be made by the hospital staff to preserve the confidentiality of all information on the patient.

6. *Reporting of the Death:* Should a patient with AIDS die, this fact should be reported to the local or state health department. In some jurisdictions, it is mandatory to report the death of an AIDS patient to the local medical examiner or coroner.
7. *AIDS and the Hospital Employees:* All job applicants diagnosed to have been suffering from AIDS must be seen by their personal physicians or the hospital physician to determine if they are free of transmitting infection and not at risk for contracting an infection before they are hired. An employee with asymptomatic AIDS should be assigned work in an area where there is no direct patient contact. Such an employee may be allowed to take part in cardiopulmonary resuscitation courses but should not be allowed to practice mouth-to-mouth resuscitation on the manikins.[18]

Liability of Pathology Laboratories

Blood from the victims of AIDS is bound to be handled by the technicians in the pathology laboratory. These technicians may endanger themselves if they sustain wounds accidentally with sharp instruments contaminated with potentially infectious materials or if their open skin lesions come in contact with the material from AIDS victims. If such a worker develops AIDS, he or she may consider the laboratory liable. The laboratories should, therefore, have the staff rigidly follow precautions. Every laboratory should prepare a list of precautions to be followed by the technicians. They should be advised as follows:

1. Wear gloves when handling blood from suspected cases of AIDS.
2. Wash hands thoroughly if you come in contact with blood.
3. Do not handle a blood container if it is contaminated by blood on its outside or if it is cracked or leaking.
4. Follow the procedures of disposal of infectious waste rigidly to get rid of materials from possible or probable cases of AIDS.
5. Put used needles in puncture-resistant containers for proper disposal.
6. Label all specimens with a biohazard label.
7. Be ultracareful in preventing accidental injuries.
8. Do not work with any materials from a suspected or proven case of AIDS if you have open wounds or sores on your body.

Liability of Blood Banks

Blood transfusion is one of the important modes of transmission of AIDS. Therefore, it is very important for blood banks to screen the donors. They must take a meticulous history to identify persons at high risk of developing AIDS, examine them, and, if necessary, carry out laboratory investigations. They must rigidly comply with the FDA recommendations. This way, they will be able to eliminate potential legal liability. The Public Health Service recommendations for donated blood use are:

1. Screen all plasma and blood for HTLV–III antibodies.
2. Do not use any blood or plasma that is reactive for HTLV–III antibody for transfusion or for use in manufacturing injectable products.
3. Notify the donor only upon a positive result from a second ELISA test or Western blot and refer the donor to a physician for evaluation.
4. Keep positive test results confidential.[57]

Treatment-Related Liability

A clinic in Freeport, Bahamas, treats cancer patients with serum proteins. Samples of serum proteins used there have been tested, and eight out of eighteen vials have been repeatedly found to be reactive for HTLV–III antibody.[54] It is clear, therefore, that some of the patients receiving serum protein injections may develop AIDS, making the Freeport clinic legally liable.

Liability of Physicians

Physicians could be involved in legal liability situations in a variety of ways as follows:

1. Malpractice in the management of the patient;
2. Failure to obtain proper consultation or provide proper referral;
3. Inadequate investigations and/or error in diagnosis;
4. Failure to obtain informed consent, offer alternate treatments, and describe the risks and benefits when blood or plasma transfusion is given;
5. Abandonment of the patient suffering from AIDS.

U.S. Department of Defense Policy and HTLV–III

Legal questions will be raised by some of the 2.1 million men and women now serving in the military who will be required to be tested for HTLV–III antibody.

1. Would the department maintain confidentiality?
2. Would the policy be construed as a screening process to keep homosexuals out of a military career?
3. Would the seropositive employees receive unemployment benefits?
4. Would career servicemen at high levels lose their hard-earned professional status?

Health Care Workers and Their Legal Remedies

The risk of nosocomial HTLV–III transmission is low, but it is known to occur through percutaneous exposure. Despite rigid and appropriate policies and employee education, accidents will occur. Such an accident could result in HTLV–III infection in a health care worker. What compensation is the health care worker entitled to?

Liability of Attorneys

There are many facets to the legal aspects of AIDS. Government and professional organization policies change almost every day. The attorneys assisting the hospitals, laboratories, and medical personnel are required to counsel them on legal matters. If they fail to keep up with the current state of the art in the field of legal questions arising from AIDS, they may themselves be targets of legal actions.

THE FUTURE

There are still many unknowns about AIDS.

One thing is certain: there will be a continuing increase in the number of cases of AIDS in the coming years. However, precise epidemiological projections of future incidence of AIDS are almost impossible to make. This is because there are probably several hundred thousand virus-infected people in the United States and the world. Some of these are bound to develop the life-threatening illness. And it can be predicted that thousands more will die from AIDS in the years to come. Also, as has been pointed out earlier, the heterosexuals may outnumber homosexuals in contracting AIDS. This creates a grim situation. It appears very likely that AIDS will remain with us as a significant threat for decades.

The diagnostic test for AIDS is not in sight at this time. The ELISA test is perhaps the first step toward the eventual goal. In view of the diversity of medical conditions that AIDS creates it seems unlikely at this time that a foolproof test will be forthcoming soon that could provide all answers.

A major development in the coming months will be concern about the meaning of the ELISA test. HTLV–III tests are going to open a new Pandora's box. Probing questions are going to be raised by physicians before they know how to interpret the results and by patients and contacts before they are fully educated about the positive and negative test results.

The lack of sufficient data concerning the etiology of the disease makes it even more difficult to prognosticate on therapeutic measures. If the viral etiology is established more antiviral drugs will go through laboratory and clinical trials, and hopefully one or more will be effective against AIDS virus.

The preparation of the Salk vaccine quickly ended the threat of polio, and at the time of this thirtieth anniversary of the announcement of the polio vaccine, one would hope that an AIDS vaccine will be developed soon to wipe out this complex biological riddle.

In the meantime, persons infected with the AIDS virus and those having full-blown AIDS will have to live on hope. Those persons who are infected with the virus and have not developed the disease will have to seek lifetime medical evaluations to monitor their immune status and receive treatment to keep the virus in check. This is because the infection with the virus as detected by the HTLV–III antibody test is, unfortunately, irreversible.

With further research, AIDS will not remain the "captain of the men of death."

The legal issues are going to be extremely complex and varied. The authors predict that AIDS will be responsible for more legal actions in the next several years than any other disease has been. The suits will be filed against federal, state, and local governments and against hospitals, blood banks, laboratories, physicians, dentists, churches, schools, insurance companies, and even attorneys. A majority of the suits are likely to be on the basis of discrimination, apparent or real, perceived by AIDS patients. The actual resolution of legal conflicts is going to be extremely complicated because of the changing knowledge about the disease. Perhaps the most interesting aspect of the legal battles will be appeals; initial decisions made by the courts with the current body of knowledge may be very different from the initial decisions made in the past with the then existing knowledge. One can only hope that the resolution of complexities of the disease will make it possible to have no conflicts and no legal issues. In the meantime, AIDS is going to cause increasing medical and legal turmoil.

REFERENCES

1. Fatteh, F., and A. Fatteh. 1984. "Medical and Legal Aspects of Acquired Immune Deficiency Syndrome (AIDS)." *Scalpel and Quill, The Bulletin of the Pittsburgh Institute of Legal Medicine* 18 (3, October):1–24.

2. Drew, W. L., L. Mintz, R. C. Miner, M. Sands, and B. Ketterer. 1981. "Prevalence of Cytomegalovirus Infection in Homosexual Men." *The Journal of Infectious Diseases* 143 (2, February):5–11.

3. Follansbee, S. E., D. F. Busch, C. B. Wofsy, D. L. Coleman, J. Gullet, G. P. Aurigemma, T. Ross, K. W. Hadley, and W. L. Drew. 1982. "An Outbreak of *Pneumocystis Carinii* Pneumonia in Homosexual Men." *Annals of Internal Medicine* 96(1):20–32.

4. Friedman-Kien, A. E., L. J. Laubenstein, P. Rubinstein, E. Buimovici-Kien, N. Marmor, R. Stahl, I. Spigland, K. S. Kim, and S. Zolla-Pazner. 1982. "Disseminated Kaposi's Sarcoma in Homosexual Men." *Annals of Internal Medicine* 96(1):3–12.

5. Public Health Service, U.S. Department of Health and Human Services. 1983. *Morbidity and Mortality Weekly Report, Centers for Disease Control,* 33 (8, March 4).

6. Oleske, J. M., and A. B. Minnefor. 1983. "Acquired Immune Deficiency Syndrome in Children." *Pediatric Infectious Disease* 2 (2, March):40–50.

7. Overby, L. R. 1983. "AIDS: A New and Deadly Disease." *Hepatitis Forum,* Abbott Laboratories Diagnostics Division (March):1–15.

8. *Physicians' Washington Report* 6 (12, June 1983).

9. Pitchenik, A. E., M. A. Fischl, G. M. Dickinson, D. M. Becker, A. M. Fournier, M. T. O'Connell, R. M. Colton, and T. J. Spria. 1983. "Opportunistic Infections and Kaposi's Sarcoma among Haitians: Evidence of a New Acquired Immunodeficiency State." *Annals of Internal Medicine* 98 (3, March): 25–40.

10. Poon, M. C., A. Landay, E. F. Prasthofer, and S. Stagno. 1983. "Acquired Immunodeficiency Syndrome with *Pneumocystis Carinii* Pneumonia and *Mycobacterium Avium-Intracellulare* Infection in a Previously Healthy Patient with Classic Hemophilia." *Annals of Internal Medicine* 98 (March):14–18.

11. Rubinstein, A., M. Sicklick, A. Gupta, L. Bernstein, N. Klein, E. Rubinstein, I. Spigland, L. Fruchter, N. Litman, H. Lee, and M. Hollander. 1983. *JAMA* 249 (17, May 6):3–18.

12. Small, C. B., R. S. Klein, G. H. Friedland, B. Moll, E. E. Emeson, and I. Spigland. 1983. "Community-Acquired Opportunistic Infections and Defective Cellular Immunity in Heterosexual Drug Abusers and Homosexual Men." *The American Journal of Medicine* 74 (March):58–72.

13. Sonnabend, J., S. S. Witkin, and D. T. Purtilo. 1983. "Acquired Immunodeficiency Syndrome, Opportunistic Infections, and Malignancies in Male Homosexuals." *JAMA* 249 (17, May 6):31–38.

14. Stahl, R. E., A. Friedman-Kien, R. Dubin, M. Marmor, and S. Zolla-Pazner. 1982. "Immunologic Abnormalities in Homosexual Men: Relationship to Kaposi's Sarcoma." *The American Journal of Medicine* 73 (August):23–29.

15. Viera, J., E. Frank, T. J. Spira, and S. H. Landesman. 1983. "Acquired Immune Deficiency in Haitians: Opportunistic Infections in Previously Healthy Haitian Immigrants." *The New England Journal of Medicine* 308 (3, January):101–11.

16. Volberding, P., M. A. Conant, R. B. Stricker, and B. J. Lewis. 1983. "Chemotherapy in Advanced Kaposi's Sarcoma: Implications for Current Cases in Homosexual Men." *The American Journal of Medicine* 74 (April):64–76.

17. *The Infection Reporter* 1 (2 February, 1984).

18. Ebbesen, P., R. J. Biggar, and M. Melbye, eds. 1984. *AIDS: A Basic Guide for Clinicians*. Copenhagen: Munksgaard International Publishers Ltd.

19. J. E. Conte, W. K. Hadley, and M. Sandy. 1983. "Special Report: Infection Control Guidelines for Patients with Acquired Immunodeficiency Syndrome (AIDS)." *The New England Journal of Medicine* 316 (2, September 22): 740.

20. "The AIDS Circle Widens." *Medical World News*. May 13, 1985.

21. Allen, J. R. 1984. "Epidemiology: United States." In *AIDS: A Basic Guide for Clinicians,* ed. P. Ebbesen, R. J. Biggar, and M. Melbye. Copenhagen: Munksgaard International Publishers Ltd.

22. Public Health Service, U.S. Department of Health and Human Services. 1985. "Update: Acquired Immunodeficiency Syndrome—Europe." *Morbidity and Mortality Weekly Report, Centers for Disease Control,* 34 (11)

23. Jaffe, H. W., K. Choi, P. A. Thomas, H. W. Haverkos, D. M. Auerbach, M. E. Guinan, et al. 1983. "National Case-Control Study of Kaposi's Sarcoma and *Pneumocystis Carinii* Pneumonia in Homosexual Men: Part I, Epidemiologic Results." *Annals of Internal Medicine* 99:145–151.

24. Amman, A. J., M. J. Cowan, D. W. Wara, P. Weintrub, S. Dritz, H. Goldman,

et al. 1983. "Acquired Immunodeficiency in an Infant: Possible Transmission by Means of Blood Product Administration." *Lancet* 1:956–958.

25. Marmor, M., A. E. Friedman-Klein, L. Laubenstein, R. D. Byrum, D. C. William, S. D'onofrio, et al. 1982. "Risk Factors for Kaposi's Sarcoma in Homosexual Men." *Lancet* 1:1083–1087.

26. Ebbesen, P., M. Melbye, R. J. Biggar. 1984. "Sex Habits, Recent Diseases and Drug Use in Two Groups of Danish Male Homosexuals." *Arch. Sex Behaviour* 13:291–300.

27. Desforges, J. F. 1983. "AIDS and Preventive Treatment in Hemophilia." *New England Journal of Medicine* 308:94–95.

28. Curran, J. W., D. N. Lawrence, H. Jaffe, J. E. Kaplan, L. D. Zyla, and M. Chamberland. 1984. "Acquired Immunodeficiency Syndrome (AIDS) Associated with Transfusions." *New England Journal of Medicine* 310:69–75.

29. Gallo, R. C., S. Z. Salahuddin, M. Popovic, et al. 1984. "Frequent Detection and Isolation of Cytopathic Retroviruses (HTLV–III) from Patients with AIDS and at Risk for AIDS." *Science* 224:500–503.

30. Barré-Sinoussi, F., J. C. Chermann, F. Rey, et al. 1983. "Isolation of a T-lymphotropic Retrovirus from a Patient at Risk for Acquired Immune Deficiency Syndrome (AIDS)." *Science* 220:868–871.

31. Levy, J. A., A. D. Hoffman, S. M. Kramer, J. A. Landis, J. M. Shimabukuro, and L. S. Oschiro. 1984. "Isolation of Lymphocytopathic Retroviruses from San Francisco Patients with AIDS." *Science* 225:840–842.

32. Popovic, M., M. G. Sangadharan, E. Read, and R. C. Gallo. 1984. "Detection, Isolation and Continuous Production of Cytopathic Retroviruses (HTLV–III) from Patients with AIDS and Pre-AIDS." *Science* 224:497–500.

33. Gallo, R. C., S. Z. Salahuddin, M. Popovic, G. M. Shearer, M. Kaplan, B. F. Haynes, T. J. Palker, et al. 1984. "Frequent Detection and Isolation of Cytopathic Retroviruses (HTLV–III) from Patients with AIDS and at Risk for AIDS." *Science* 224:500–503.

34. Sarngadharan, M. G., M. Popovic, L. Bruch, J. Schupback, and R. C. Gallo. 1984. "Antibodies Reactive with Human T-lymphotropic Retroviruses (HTLV–III) in the Serum of Patients with AIDS." *Science* 224:506–508.

35. Redfield, R. R., P. D. Markham, S. Z. Salahuddin, M. G. Sarngadharan, A. J. Bodner, T. M. Folks, W. P. Ballou, D. C. Wright, and R. C. Gallo. 1985. "Frequent Transmission of HTLV–III among Spouses of Patients with AIDS-related Complex and AIDS." *JAMA* 253(11):1571–1573.

36. Barré-Sinoussi, F., U. Mathur-Wagh, F. Rey, F. Brun-Vezinet, S. R. Yancovitz, C. Rouzioux, L. Montagnier, D. Mildvan, and J. C. Chermann. 1985. "Isolation of Lymphadenopathy-Associated Virus (LAV) and Detection of LAV Antibodies from U.S. Patients with AIDS." *JAMA* 253(2):1737–1739.

37. Sarngadharan, M. G., M. Popovic, L. Bruch, J. Schupback, and R. C. Gallo. 1984. "Antibodies Reactive with Human T-Lymphotropic Retroviruses (HTLV–III) in the Serum of Patients with AIDS." *Science* 224:506–508.

38. Darrow, N. W., H. W. Jaffe, E. Braff, et al. 1984. "Acquired Immunodeficiency Syndrome (AIDS) in a Cohort of Homosexual Men." Presentation at 24th Interscience Conference on Antimicrobial Agents and Chemotherapy, Washington, D.C.

39. Public Health Service, U.S. Department of Health and Human Services. 1985. "Provisional Public Health Service Inter-agency Recommendations for Screening Donated

Blood and Plasma for Antibody to the Virus Causing Acquired Immunodeficiency Syndrome." *Morbidity and Mortality Weekly Report Centers for Disease Control* 34 (1, January 11).

40. *JAMA* 253 (1985): 221–225.

41. "Use of AIDS Antibody Test May Provide More Answers." 1985. Medical News. *JAMA* 253(12):1699.

42. "Countdown for HTLV–III Referrals." *Medical World News,* p. 13, March 25, 1985.

43. "AIDS Virus Casts Another Shadow." *Medical World News,* p. 13, May 13, 1985.

44. Shaw, G. M., et al. 1985. "HTLV–III Infection in Brains of Children and Adults with AIDS Encephalopathy." *Science* 227:177–182.

45. Kovacs, J. A., and H. Masur. 1984. "Treatment of Opportunistic Infections." In *AIDS: A Basic Guide for Clinicians,* ed. P. Ebbesen, R. J. Biggar, and M. Melbye. Copenhagen: Munksgaard International Publishers Ltd.

46. Nichols, S. E., and D. G. Ostrow, eds. 1984. *Psychiatric Implications of Acquired Immune Deficiency Syndrome.* Clinical Insights Monograph Series. Washington, D.C.: American Psychiatric Press.

47. *American Medical News,* Feb. 15, 1985.

48. *American Medical News,* March 15, 1985.

49. Kirchner, M. 1985. "The Doctor Who Refused to Be Bluffed by Bigots." *Medical Economics* (February 18), p. 223.

50. *American Medical News,* April 5, 1985.

51. Public Health Service, U.S. Department of Health and Human Services. 1985. *Morbidity and Mortality Weekly Report, Centers for Disease Control* 34(25, 26).

52. Public Health Service, U.S. Department of Health and Human Services. 1985. *Morbidity and Mortality Weekly Report, Centers for Disease Control* 34(37, 38).

53. Public Health Service, U.S. Department of Health and Human Services, 1985. *Morbidity and Mortality Weekly Report, Centers for Disease Control* 34(34).

54. *JAMA* 254 (1985):1139.

55. *JAMA* 254 (1985): 2867.

56. Mass, A. E. 1985. "AIDS Autopsy Precautions." *Pathologist* (November), p. 20.

57. *FDA Drug Bulletin* 15 (3, October 1985).

58. CDC, FDA, ADAMHA, NIH, HRSA. 1985. "Provisional Public Health Service Interagency Recommendations for Screening Donated Blood and Plasma for Antibody to the Virus Causing Acquired Immunodeficiency Syndrome." *Morbidity and Mortality Weekly Report, Centers for Disease Control* 34(5, 6, 7).

59. *American Medical News,* November 1, 1985.

60. Weiss, S. H., et al. 1985. "HTLV–III Infection among Health Care Workers, Association with Needle-Stick Injuries." *JAMA* 254:2089.

61. *JAMA* 254 (1985):2521.

62. Peterman, T. A. 1985. "Transfusion-Associated Acquired Immunodeficiency in the United States." *JAMA* 254:2913.

63. *JAMA* 254 (1985):2865.

64. *American Medical News,* October 25, 1985.

65. Public Health Service, U.S. Department of Health and Human Services. 1985. *Morbidity and Mortality Weekly Report, Centers for Disease Control* 34(45).

66. Public Health Service, U.S. Department of Health and Human Services. 1985. *Morbidity and Mortality Weekly Report, Centers for Disease Control* 34 (43, 45).

Medico-Legal Aspects of the Bhopal Tragedy

C. K. Parikh, B.S., M.B., D.P.H.

On the night of December 2, 1984, leakage of methyl isocyanate (MIC) from the Union Carbide plant produced a gruesome tragedy in Bhopal, India. Measured by the dimensions of mortality, morbidity, and pain suffered by the victims, this tragedy was worse than the "yellow-red rain" that struck the Hmong tribesmen of Laos a few years ago. MIC is described in the Union Carbide manual as an "extremely hazardous chemical," a poison against which stringent precautions must be observed to eliminate any possibility of human contact. It was this substance, used by Union Carbide to manufacture pesticides, that vaporized in Bhopal's midnight air, resulting in the largest industrial disaster in the history of the world.

A complete analysis and commentary of the Bhopal tragedy would need to include the following factors: (1) MIC, (2) the plant at Bhopal, (3) the accident, (4) the safety systems that failed, (5) other failures, (6) effects of MIC leakage, (7) treatment of the victims and prognosis, (8) disposal of the dead and related problems, (9) legal aspects, and (10) comments.

METHYL ISOCYANATE

MIC is a fairly stable liquid below 27°C. It has a pungent but sweetish smell. It has a boiling point of 37°C. It is highly volatile and inflammable. Its vapors are denser than air and cause acute and chronic toxicity in living organisms. It reacts vigorously with water, including moisture, alkaloids, and many solvents, and hence requires storage under completely inert conditions. Its reactivity is due to its electrophilic, that is, electron-deficient, carbon center, which reacts strongly with electron-rich nucleophiles, such as water, alkali, alcohol, and so on. It is generally stored to a purity of 99.5 percent; up to 0.1 percent of phosgene is permitted as an impurity.

MIC is an ideal industrial raw material for a wide range of products, varying from simple carbamates (pesticides) to polyurethane formulations like adhesives and plastics. The carbamate pesticides are effective against several insect pests causing economic crop losses. There is practically no doubt about their beneficial role under judicious use. However, the raw product MIC is one of the deadliest of toxic chemicals and can kill in very small doses when ingested, inhaled, or when absorbed through the skin. The threshold limit value (TLV) for MIC, as regards the maximum permissible limit for industrial workers, is only one-fiftieth of one part per million (ppm). For hydrogen cyanide, it is 10 ppm, and for phosgene, one-tenth of a million.

The toxicity of MIC is due to its two actions, (1) the irritant action of the vapor at the biophysical level and (2) the carbamylation action at the biochemical level. The vapor causes intense irritation of the skin, eyes, and mucous membranes. When inhaled, it causes irritation of the pulmonary alveoli resulting in pulmonary edema in acute cases and fibrosing alveolitis in chronic ones. Carbamylation inactivates various substrates, and if this effect is allowed to continue, chronic deterioration follows. For example, damage to the highly specialized alveolar membrane would lead to widespread systemic effects far out of proportion to the applied dose. In addition, carbamylation of purine and pyrimidine bases in nucleic acids can result in mutagenesis.

THE PLANT AT BHOPAL

The Union Carbide factory at Bhopal was allowed to be established at a distance of one kilometer from the railway station. At this facility, MIC was stored in three double-walled stainless steel tanks (610, 611, and 619) buried mostly underground to prevent leakage from the tanks and to protect the tanks from the effects of rising temperatures in the tropical summer. The tanks were connected to a refrigeration system to keep the highly volatile gas in liquid form. The tanks were also equipped with thermostats, valves, and other devices to warn when the temperature of the chemical exceeded 37°C, at which temperature liquid MIC is instantaneously converted into lethal gas. If the temperature of the gas should rise further, the gas would expand, leading to an increase in the pressure in the tank. Should the pressure in the tank build up, a relief valve would vent the gas to prevent rupture of the tank.

In case a tank ruptured, the plant had two safety devices that would operate automatically. The first one was a scrubber that would neutralize the lethal gas by treating it with caustic soda. In the event the scrubber failed, there was another mechanism, the flare tower, which would ignite and burn off the gas in the air, rendering it innocuous before much harm was done.

MIC was being used in the plant to produce relatively toxic pesticides known as Sevin and Temik. It is commonly known that carbon monoxide, chlorine, carbonyl chloride (commonly known as phosgene), and the cyanide group are intermediate products of the pesticide manufacturing process at one stage or the other. All these substances are highly poisonous unless they are in the form of complex ions. In the pesticide manufacturing plant, the workers are exposed to these chemicals at one stage or the other and consequently suffer from their harmful effects depending on the exposure. Singly or in combination, these chemicals have been used in war to annihilate troops.

When the manufacturing process is a continuous one, as in this case, and follows a flow sheet, small leakages are common.

No effective measures were devised to cover issues like control of habitation near the plant, freighting of poisonous materials, effective safety training for the involved personnel, and effective legal safeguards for operators translated down to procedures. Some of the safety systems did not exist at the plant, and those that existed were not in working order. The victims of this failure bear mute witness to the inadequacy of the safety systems that existed at the plant and the need for additional effective safety systems. This is all the more regrettable inasmuch as technique are actually available that do enable the design and the implementation of such effective systems, and these are in use in the similar Union Carbide plant at Charleston, West Virginia, in the U.S.A.

THE ACCIDENT

On Sunday, December 2, 1984, about 75 of the 950 employees were on duty on the shift that was to end at 10:45 P.M. At about 10:15 P.M., a supervisor on duty who was new to the MIC unit asked an operator to wash the inside of a length of piping near the MIC tank. This is a time-consuming procedure because (1) the pipes have to be washed out thoroughly and (2) a metal sheet known as a slip blind is required to be inserted near the safety valve to seal off the rest of the system from the pipe being washed lest the safety valve leak and allow water to enter the tank. Should water enter the tank, it would result in a dangerous chemical reaction converting liquid MIC into a gas that might escape with fatal consequences.

When the operator connected the water pipe to the pipe that was required to be washed, he possibly did not insert the slip blind, and this led to the avoidable accident. The absence of a slip blind allowed water to leak into MIC storage tank 610. It resulted in the evolution of a lot of gas, thereby increasing the equipment pressure, liberating considerable heat, and raising the temperature. Thus, a potentially violent chemical reaction, unknown to the new shift, was already under way in MIC storage tank 610 when the new shift came on duty at 10:45 P.M.

The sequence of events that took place can be reconstructed as follows:

10:15 P.M.: A new supervisor asks an operator to wash the inside of a length of piping near the MIC tank. The operator connects the water hose pipe to the pipe to be washed without inserting the slip blind. Water enters the MIC storage tank 610 and triggers a potentially violent chemical reaction. The shift ends at 10:45 P.M., and a new set of operators goes on duty. The new shift is unaware of the impending danger from the chemical reaction well under way.

11:00 P.M.: The pressure in MIC tank 610 has risen from the normal 3 pounds per square inch to 10 pounds per square inch. As the manufacturing process was in operation, the pressure in tank 611 was deliberately increased by injecting nitrogen into it to transfer the MIC to the pesticide unit. The new set of operators, when they see the high pressure in tank 610, believe that the pressure in this tank has also been deliberately increased by the earlier shift to transfer the MIC to the pesticide unit. They have no inkling of the violent chemical reaction under way and the impending danger therefrom.

11:30 P.M.: The rising pressure and temperature in tank 610 results in a leak of the gas causing irritation of the eyes among the operating staff in the utility area. The operators ignore the leak because minor leaks in the plant are common.

11:45 P.M.: The operators around the MIC unit (usually unaffected by minor leaks) also experience irritation of the eyes, suspect a leak, and report it to the production assistant. Almost at the same time, the MIC control room operators report that the pressure in tank 610 is abnormally high and is still rising.

12:15 A.M.: The production assistant and an operator check tank 610 to find that the rupture disk, a device that bursts when the pressure reaches 40 pounds per square inch, has already burst. The next checkpoint, a safety valve, has also met with the same fate.

12:30 A.M.: The flow of water washing the pipe is hurriedly turned off, but it is already too late to save the situation. A violent chemical reaction with a rise in equipment pressure and liberation of considerable heat converting liquid MIC into lethal gas is already in active progress, and even the concrete bed in which tank 610 lies shows large cracks, testifying to the intensity and magnitude of the reaction.

1:00 A.M.: Untreated MIC vapor is seen escaping through the nozzle of the 33–meter-high vent line into Bhopal's cool midnight air and continues to escape until all the 40 tons in tank 610 are emptied shortly before 3:00 A.M. Since 0.1 percent phosgene is permitted as an impurity, when the 40 tons of MIC vaporize, 40 kilograms of phosgene also escape simultaneously.

The vapors pass over the towns of Jaiprakash and Chhola, just outside the walls of the plant, leaving hundreds dead during their sleep. Next to be enveloped is the railway station, where a number of beggars taking shelter against the night chill meet with the same fate. In a few minutes, an additional few hundred are dead and many more are gravely ill. The vapors continue to spread their lethal effects across a 25–square-mile area of the city covering the shops, streets, temples, and lakes. The wind is stationary and the night air cool, allowing the vapors to settle on the earth with their disastrous consequences, immediate and remote. The vapors have a concentration more than 100 times the stipulated safety level.

Crowds of people, hardly able to see from intense irritation of the eyes, run helter-skelter toward uncontaminated air and in the process stumble into one another in darkness. Others simply collapse on the road in the stampede. Still others who have inhaled fumes die hours later from pulmonary irritation, after having reached what they thought to be a safe zone. On Monday, December 3, 1984, the death toll is 500, and on Friday, December 7, 1984, it is more than 2,500 with about 3,000 critically ill. By the weekend, numbers have no meaning, for no one can tell how many from the population who have survived the exposure will eventually die. Roughly, the fatalities are in proportion to the distance from the source of exposure and concentration of the gas. The death toll varies from about 25 percent within a one-kilometer radius to about 1 percent at a five-kilometer radius. As for the affected persons, over 150,000 are treated at Bhopal's Hamidia hospital and the various clinics in the city.

THE SAFETY SYSTEMS THAT FAILED

The sorry state of affairs at the plant is highlighted by a report prepared in mid-1982 by three American experts who studied the plant's safety measures and equipment. The report says, "The plant represents either a higher potential for serious accident or more serious consequences if an accident should occur"—words that have proved all too prophetic.

All the safety systems designed to prevent an accident actually failed when they were most needed. Some of the systems were under repair and others not functioning. For reasons of safety, a minimum of two safety devices should be in perfect working order when the MIC unit is in operation.

The systems that failed are (1) the vent gas scrubber, (2) the flare tower, (3) the water curtain, (4) the refrigeration system, and (5) the spare tank.

The vent gas scrubber: The scrubber was shut down for maintenance. Its function is to detoxify the lethal MIC vapors by spraying them with caustic soda solution. If the scrubber was in working condition, MIC vapors should have passed through the scrubber and escaped through the vent line as a relatively harmless gas.

The flare tower: This is a 30–meter-long vertical pipe designed to burn toxic gases high in the air and consequently prevent any danger to the public from gas leakage. A pilot flame is kept constantly burning to ignite any gas that escapes through the tower. This flare tower could not be used because a length of piping was corroded and awaiting replacement.

The water curtain: The plant is equipped with a system of water outlets that can shoot a jet of water about 12 to 15 meters high in the air to drop like a curtain around sensitive areas where gas leaks are possible. Water knocks down MIC vapors to form either dimethyl urea or trimethyl biuret depending on the quantity of water. These are comparatively harmless compounds. The water curtain was turned on shortly after 1:00 A.M. but was ineffective because it was designed to reach a height of only 12 meters, while MIC was escaping at a height of 33 meters.

The refrigeration system: The MIC storage tanks are connected to a 40–ton refrigeration system that uses Freon 22 to keep the coolant salt solution at between − 15°C and − 10°C. The coolant circulates around the tank and keeps the liquid MIC under 15°C, though its ideal storage temperature is 0°C. The refrigerant Freon 22 had been removed for use elsewhere; therefore, the MIC tank 610 could not be cooled to slow down the reaction when the gas escaped in the air with its disastrous consequences.

The spare tank: Of the three tanks (610, 611, and 619) in the MIC unit, tank 619 was kept empty as required to meet with any emergency such as the present one. A pipe did connect tank 610 to 619 through a suction pump. If only the valves had been opened—and this takes only three minutes—the buildup of pressure in tank 610 would have moved the liquid MIC into tank 619, allowing some breathing time to effect other measures of safety. In the confusion that prevailed, the valves were not opened, and the gas escaped in the air until tank 610 was empty.

OTHER FAILURES

The plant was furnished with only one manual backup alarm system instead of the four-stage alarm system required in the United States. The plant also lacked the computerized early warning and fail-safe system used in the U.S. factory.

To make matters worse, a critical panel in the control room had been removed, perhaps for maintenance, thus preventing the leak from showing up on the monitors. The plant had a system of walkie-talkies to inform higher authorities should any emergency occur at the plant. The system is operative around the clock but was not used.

The plant had two sirens: a loud continuous one for the public and a muted one over the public address system for factory workers. Although it was known that MIC was escaping in huge quantities, endangering public safety, the public siren was not put on until around 1:00 A.M., and then only for a few minutes. Then it was put off for an hour till 2:00 A.M., when it was sounded once again. However, it was already too late then.

The staff position was also unsatisfactory. Initially, when work on the MIC plant was commenced, only science graduates with a diploma in engineering were taken as operators, and were subjected to six months' theoretical training followed by on-the-job training. This requirement, however, was relaxed later on. Operators without any science or engineering background were recruited, and they were not subjected to any effective training; the number of staff had been cut on grounds of economy; and there was no maintenance supervisor on the night shift.

EFFECTS OF MIC LEAKAGE

Bhopal is a city with a population of 672,000, of whom over 150,000 have been treated for the effects of gas leakage at the Hamidia hospital and other clinics.

All 750 beds of the hospital were fully occupied, and many patients were kept on the floor. The army had set up 60 tents, which became instant wards for 20 people each. Even six days after the accident, patients were arriving at the Hamidia hospital at the rate of one per minute. While the Indian Council of Medical Research is funding a long-term research project to follow up the victims and the results of such study will be available in due course, the immediate observations on the victims have shown the following symptomatology.

MIC is highly irritating to the skin, eyes, and mucous membranes. Victims dying within 48 hours complained of acute irritation of the eyes, severe burning in the throat, chest pain, and labored breathing. Death was due to pulmonary edema. The disaster struck hardest at children and old people whose lungs were either too small or too weak to withstand the poison.

Subacute cases and those who survived for five to six days experienced the original symptoms of exposure in addition to fever, cough with expectoration, often bloody, and neurological effects that included motor weakness, paralysis in some cases, convulsions, coma, and cerebral edema leading to death.

Those who survived for over a week developed delayed symptoms such as shivering, dry mouth and throat, hemoptysis, dyspnea, jaundice, weakness of limbs, and death due to exhaustion.

Those who survived more than a week developed symptoms referable to parenchymal degeneration of vital organs and died due to what can be described as aftereffects from mild exposure.

Personnel engaged to look after the victims during hospitalization complained of easy fatigue and substantial weakness after moderate exertion.

About 10 percent of the victims attending the clinics have reported psychiatric symptoms such as anxiety, depression, sleep disturbances, gas phobia, and a feeling of helplessness. A notable finding is the apprehensiveness of children. A number of families in the affected area are unable to cope with the stress of day-to-day life.

Another notable finding of the medical survey pertains to women. Of the 198 women examined by the team, 100 had gynecological symptoms. The main complaint was "excessive vaginal discharge." According to the survey report, 29 of the 38 pregnant women in December 1984 reported abortion in their first or second trimester. A common feature in 17 pregnant women examined by the medical team was anemia. The women also reported reduced fetal movements. There have since been two cases of birth of deformed babies. The deformities were similar in nature. While it cannot be conclusively stated that the deformities are due to MIC exposure, the available evidence implicates MIC as a causative or contributory factor. According to the survey team, the growth of the fetus in the uterus in the gas-affected women is not normal, and it is possible that some agents are present in the body that are causing abnormality in the growth of the fetus. Stillbirths are relatively more common.

Among the surveyed children living within a distance of 1.5 to 2 kilometers from the Union Carbide factory, the respiratory system was found to be affected in 50 percent of cases. The X-ray findings indicated an abnormal condition in 67 percent of the cases.

MIC affects growth as well as heredity of garden plants and standing crops in the area within the gas spread. Cattle have also perished in large numbers.

Serious biochemical changes have been observed in the survivors. Glutathione, a chemical found in all animal tissues, is very important for oxidation reactions and aids the body cells to fight and nullify the toxicity of many compounds. A number of survivors have been found to have alarmingly reduced levels of glutathione, making them very vulnerable to a wide range of toxins and infections.

Chemical analyses of the blood of the victims have revealed the presence of MIC, cyanide ions, and monomethylamine. Carbamylation of the hemoglobin molecule has been detected. Hemoglobin is thus deprived of its capacity to clear carbon dioxide from the tissues, and its oxygen-carrying capacity is reduced with the result that recurrent and continued respiratory problems due to tissue anoxia are frequent among survivors even weeks after mild exposure.

The average thiocyanate level in the blood of Bhopal victims is 2.6 ppm as against 0.9 ppm in the blood of a control group in Bombay. High thiocyanate level in blood is known to be one of the causes of goiter. The thiocyanate level in water of the upper lake, the main source of water supply to Bhopal, when tested in March 1985, has been 4 ppm. It has been 3 ppm in the lower lake and 2 ppm in filtered water. As compared to this, the thiocyanate level of the tap water in Bombay is 0.8 ppm. High thiocyanate level in Bhopal water can affect the functioning of the thyroid gland among its users.

Fish appear to have a certain amount of tolerance to MIC. However, ingestion of such fish would result in toxicity to human beings.

At postmortem, all victims showed effects of severe irritation of the eyes (whitening), nose, trachea, and bronchi. Characteristic appearances were seen in the lungs. Victims who died within 48 hours had lungs two to three times their normal weight. The lungs were filled with fluid, causing the equivalent of death by drowning. Those who died in the next 48 hours had pink blood. Victims dying five days after the accident had dark red blood, heavily congested organs, and toxic necrosis of the gastrointestinal mucosa. Victims dying thereafter showed parenchymatous degeneration of vital organs (brain, heart, lungs, liver, kidneys) due to tissue anoxia. The autopsy teams inhaled gases trapped inside the bodies and suffered from gas poisoning, also.

TREATMENT AND PROGNOSIS

The treatment is purely symptomatic. It consists of administration of hydrocortisone against inflammation, bronchodilators against difficulty in breathing, antibiotics (tetracycline and ampicillin) against lung infection, eyedrops against eye irritation and corneal ulcers, and oxygen when required to combat respiratory failure. The use of sodium thiosulfate has proved beneficial. Victims tend to make better use of their oxygen intake, which results in a feeling of marked improvement in their condition. Nonetheless, they cannot expect to regain their original health: many survivors will suffer from emphysema, asthma, bronchitis, and even fibrosing alveolitis. Those whose lungs are badly affected will eventually die of respiratory failure despite treatment. Those who have endured whitening of their eyes will never regain their sight. MIC affects the central nervous system, and this increases the chances of permanent mental retardation. Goiter and malfunctioning of the thyroid are distinct possibilities in those who continue to use water with high thiocyanate content. The poisoning may result in necrobiosis of the liver and other vital organs. Toxic irritation of gastrointestinal mucosa would lead to persistent diarrhea, vomiting, and abdominal pain. Like many other agrochemicals, as a long-term effect, MIC may turn out to be a carcinogenic and mutagenic agent.

DISPOSAL OF THE DEAD AND RELATED PROBLEMS

Some distance away from the tents intended to shelter the victims for treatment, the army had set up a morgue. The patrols in the city brought the dead bodies to the morgue for identification and disposal according to their religious customs. The sheer numbers of the dead prevented individual identification, and the threat of an epidemic made it necessary to simply identify the bodies either as Hindu or Muslim for disposal purposes. Hindus were cremated, and Muslims were buried.

The traditional method for Hindu cremation is one pyre for one body. However, because the victims were too numerous and the firewood too scanty, five or six corpses, each wrapped in a cotton shroud and covered with flowers, had to be placed on one pyre. The pyres burnt continuously for several days.

Likewise, Muslims were also buried in groups. Rescue workers dug up graves, fifteen feet wide and six feet long. Each grave accommodated eleven corpses. Shortage of space for graves resulted in the opening of old tombs, displacing bones of the dead buried over a hundred years ago.

A related problem was the removal and disposal of a number of birds and animals killed by the gas. They clogged the city's streets and houses and posed a real danger of cholera. Vultures and dogs roamed through the piles of rotting flesh, and rats ran about them, awakening fears of bubonic plague. A sickly stench of decay emanated continuously from the bloated carcasses. The army removed them with cranes. The walls of several houses had to be broken open because it was impossible to pull out bloated buffaloes (a bloated buffalo looks like an elephant) from the narrow doors. The carcasses were disposed of five kilometers away in a pit three meters deep over one acre of land. As a precautionary measure, to prevent toxic gases from bursting the bloated carcasses, considerable quantities of salt, bleaching powder, lime, and caustic soda were evenly spread in the pit.

LEGAL ASPECTS

While the exact legal position will not be known until the cases filed in the various courts are decided, some predictions can be drawn.

American Courts

Under American law, in all likelihood, the operation of the Union Carbide plant to manufacture methyl isocyanate would be classified as an ultrahazardous activity, and the company would be strictly liable for direct injury and damage, without the need for proof of fault or negligence. Ultrahazardous enterprises are described as unusual or unnatural uses of land operations such as industrial plants or dynamite sites or nuclear energy systems, which necessarily involve, by their character, extreme danger to nearby persons and the surrounding environment, and in which no amount of care can entirely eliminate the risk of explosion or leakage. The ultrahazardous enterprise liability is an accepted law for such industries. This rule of law recognizes that the world cannot be made risk-free, and the incentive to prevent loss or limit the extent of damage in an extremely remote but generally predictable explosion, leakage, or other accident does not lie in personal injury suits. The recovery for personal injury is thus made a cost of operations and is paid from insurance or self-insurance and from disaster coverage provided by reinsurance with large carriers. Since negligence need not be proved, the company cannot avoid or defend the suit by showing that it did everything that was technically possible to prevent the accident or that the accident was caused by the negligence of other contractors or suppliers.

An important question is the problem of jurisdiction—whether any action can or should be brought in an American court.

1. The American courts may exercise their jurisdiction over the issues of compensation and punitive damages on the grounds that:
   a. Union Carbide is a United States citizen, and it is subject to United States processes for acts it directly authorized.
   b. The main causes of the accident are inadequate design and engineering and excessive economic measures regarding staff and safety procedures. Safety systems such as those employed in the Union Carbide facility at Virginia would have been adequate.
   c. Without American investigative procedures, it is not possible to uncover all the facts pertaining to the disaster. Vital records required for evidence are in the United States.
   d. It is necessary to employ sophisticated techniques to process mass disaster litigation. Such experience is not available in India. It is available in the United States, the abode of the parent company.
   e. The enlightened administration of the United States would like to see that justice is done to the victims who worked for an American enterprise.
   f. The U.S. administration may desire to protect the interest of foreign citizens employed by American enterprises in other countries.

2. Since the accident occurred on Indian soil, American courts may entertain claims on behalf of only those victims whose dependents/relations are in America. Others may have to file their claims in Indian courts.
3. The American parent company may be held liable if it is established that there was a design defect. If it is proved that the accident was due to poor maintenance, the Indian company will be mainly liable; the parent U.S. company may not be able to claim total immunity.

Indian Courts

1. There is no specific law or statute in India under which compensation can be claimed. A civil suit can be filed under the law of torts (civil wrongs). There is case law to go by. The amount of compensation is decided by the judge on the basis of the nature and extent of injury, the expense incurred in treatment, loss of earning capacity, and pain suffered. The compensation awarded is according to Indian standards and is much less than what is awarded by American courts.
2. There is no provision for punitive damages in Indian law. American courts normally award punitive damages in accident and negligence cases to compensate the victim adequately.
3. In the Indian company, civil claims can be made against officers in charge of administration, while criminal prosecution can be launched against officers directly in charge of maintenance. Under section 304–A of the Indian Penal Code, the maximum punishment for culpable homicide not amounting to murder is two years. Under section 304, a conviction of culpable homicide through negligence will result in a life term.

One issue is clear, however. If claims are filed in Indian courts, the American attorneys cannot recover a large portion of each award as a contingent fee for professional legal services. Such a system of recovery is not allowed in India on ethical grounds, and the possibility that an exception may be made in this specific case seems remote.

COMMENTS

The disaster in Bhopal is the latest in a series of major industrial mishaps in the world. It holds out lessons that have much to do with basic human concerns for safety, various standards, and good sense. Certain minimum safety standards should be legally enforced:

1. Plants using hazardous substances/chemicals should be located away from population centers. Escape plans should be devised for full-scale evacuation in the event of a disaster.
2. Trucks used to transport chemicals should be strong enough to survive a rollover without breaking open, and tank cars a derailment.
3. The air in the plant should be automatically monitored to detect leakages, and leakages should be effectively dealt with by crack emergency teams.

4. Once built, the plant should be maintained according to rigorous standards of safety specifically laid down to meet the relevant requirements.
5. Safety systems should be reviewed from time to time by company officials, insurance companies, and outside consultants.
6. A continuing safety education program for workmen by means of training films, classroom lessons, and on-the-job training should be a regular feature.
7. The plant should provide adequate facilities for prevention and detection of industrial medical hazards. Medico-legal expertise should be utilized for victim investigation—identification of bodies, and determination of cause, manner, and circumstances of death. Measures should be devised to handle mass casualties in the event of a disaster.
8. Developing countries should remember that large multinational chemical concerns would like to locate their hazardous chemical factories on their soil to benefit from cheap labor and lax laws and to escape stringent regulations in their own country. They should insist on similar safety standards and comparable compensation given to their counterparts in the parent company.

If these lessons are not learned, accidents will continue to occur, and social advancement will be appreciably hampered.

REFERENCES

1. The description of the factory and the sequence of events of the disaster are based on observations by the representative of *India Today* who visited the site personally, as reported in *India Today,* December 31, 1984.

2. The symptomatology and postmortem findings are based on the observations and follow-up studies by medical officers who treated and followed up the patients in the various hospitals and clinics in Bhopal and elsewhere and who actually performed the autopsies.

3. The various scientific data as regards chemistry, toxicology, and effects of MIC are based on the information as given in the Union Carbide manual and the releases by various scientific organizations like the Indian Council of Medical Research, New Delhi; the Indian Toxicology Research Center, Lucknow; and the survey teams comprising 21 medical specialists and laboratory technologists sponsored by the Citizens Relief and Rehabilitation Committee in Collaboration with the Voluntary Health Association of India in New Delhi and Bhopal.

4. The concept of ultrahazardous enterprise liability is based on the information provided by William J. Curran in the Law Medicine Notes in the *New England Journal of Medicine,* October 24, 1985, pp. 1068–1070.

It is my pleasure to acknowledge these sources and the help derived therefrom.

Drug and Chemical Blood Level Data 1986

Charles L. Winek, Ph.D., D.A.B.F.T.

This chapter represents an update of the continuing tabulation of drug and chemical blood level data. Although other lists have been prepared, they represent attempts at duplicating this present list. It is always a compliment to be copied. The present list was published originally in *Clinical Toxicology*.[1] As additional blood level data became available, updated lists were published in the *Modern Drug Encyclopedia,*[2] Goth's pharmacology text,[3] and Wecht's *Legal Medicine,*[4] as well as several forensic references.[5, 6, 7]

Two important considerations make it necessary to update the list of drug levels. The first is the introduction of new therapeutic agents, and the second is improved analytical techniques that enable a more accurate representation of the drug or chemical concentration. This would be expected with the improved sensitivity of analytical technology.

This list is intended as a ready reference, and the levels must be interpreted taking into consideration the usual and many factors that can affect blood level data. Please note that the present list gives blood level data using a double unit system. That is, the concentration of drug or chemical is presented in mg%, a unit usually used by forensic pathologists and toxicologists, and mcg/ml, a unit usually used by clinical laboratories. These units are explained below.

DEFINITION OF BLOOD LEVELS

Winek[1] has divided drug blood levels into therapeutic, toxic, and lethal categories. These are defined as follows:

Therapeutic Blood Level: The concentration of drug present in the blood (its serum or plasma) following therapeutically effective dosage in humans. With some drugs, the major metabolite may be pharmacologically active as well. The concentration of metabolite is added to the drug concentration to obtain the total therapeutic level.

Toxic Blood Level: The concentration of drug or chemical present in the blood (its serum or plasma) that is associated with serious toxic symptoms in humans.

Lethal Blood Level: The concentration of drug or chemical present in the blood (its serum or plasma) that has been reported to cause death, or is so far above reported therapeutic or toxic concentrations that one can judge that it might cause death in humans.

UNITS

Since levels are reported by various laboratories in different units, it will be helpful to know how to convert from one unit to another. The following paragraph explains the conversion.

Mg% (milligram percent) is equal to mg/dL (milligram/deciliter); μg/ml (microgram/milliter) is equal to mg/L (milligram/liter). Multiply the mg% level by 10 to obtain ug/ml. Divide the mg% level by 100 to obtain mg/ml (or multiply mg/ml by 100 to convert to mg%). Divide the μg% level by 100 to obtain μg/ml (or multiply ug/ml by 100 to convert to μg%).

The best reference to date that explains the significance of drug and chemical blood levels is the book by Baselt.[8]

REFERENCES

1. Winek, C. L. 1970. "Laboratory Criteria for the Adequacy of Treatment and Significance of Blood Levels." *Clinical Toxicology* 3(4):541–549.

2. Winek, C. L. Contributor to the *Modern Drug Encyclopedia,* 9th, 10th, 11th, and 12th editions. R. R. Donnelley Company, New York.

3. Winek, C. L. 1984. Contributor to *Medical Pharmacology* by A. Goth, 11th edition. St. Louis: C. V. Mosby Company.

4. Winek, C. L. 1973. Contributor to *Legal Medicine 1973,* ed. C. H. Wecht. New York: Appleton-Century-Crofts.

5. Winek, C. L. 1977. Contributor to *Forensic Medicine* (in three volumes). Philadelphia: W. B. Saunders Co.

6. Winek, C. L. 1981. Contributor to *Forensic Sciences* (in three volumes), ed. C. H. Wecht. New York: Matthew Bender.

7. Winek, C. L., and F. M. Esposito. Contributors to *Forensic Sciences.*

8. Baselt, R. C. 1982. *Disposition of Toxic Drugs and Chemicals in Man,* 2nd edition. Davis, Calif.: Biomedical Publications.

Table 1. Drug and Chemical Blood Level Data 1986

DRUG	Therapeutic or Normal		Toxic		Lethal	
	mg%	mcg/ml	mg%	mcg/ml	mg%	mcg/ml
A						
Acetaminophen (Tylenol)	1.0-2.0	10.0-20.0	15.0 +	150 +	16.0 +	160 +
Acetazolamide (Diamox)	1.0-1.5	10.0-15.0	------	------	------	------
Acetohexamide (Dymelor)	2.1-5.6	21.0-56.0	------	------	------	------
Acetone	------	------	20.0-30.0	200-300	55.0 +	550 +
Acetylsalicylic Acid (Salicylate) [normal usage]	2.0-10.0	20.0-100	15.0-30.0	150-300	50.0 +	500 +
Acetylsalicylic Acid [for rheumatoid arthritis]	2.0-25.0	20.0-250	------	------	------	------
Alcaine (Proparacaine)	------	------	------	------	1.5 +	15.0 +
Aldrin	0.00015	0.0015	0.00035 +	0.0035 +	------	------
Alphaprodine (Nisentil)	0.087-0.1	0.87-1.0	------	------	------	------
Alprazolam (Xanax)	0.02	0.2	------	------	------	------
Aluminum	0.013	0.13	------	------	------	------
Aminophylline (Theophylline)	1.0-2.0	10.0-20.0	3.0-4.0	30.0-40.0	5.0-25.0	50.0-250
Amitriptyline (Elavil)	0.005-0.02	0.05-0.2	0.05 +	0.5 +	0.2-2.0	2.0-20.0
Amitriptyline [plus metab. nortriptyline]	0.012-0.025	0.12-0.25	0.05 +	0.5 +	------	------
Ammonia	0.05-0.17	0.5-1.7	------	------	------	------
Amobarbital (Amytal)	0.1-0.5	1.0-5.0	1.0-3.0	10.0-30.0	1.3-9.6	13.0-96.0
Amoxapine (Asendin)	0.001-0.021	0.01-0.21	------	------	0.295 +	2.95 +
Amoxapine [plus metab. 8-OH amoxapine]	0.02-0.04	0.2-0.4	------	------	------	------
Amphetamine	0.003	0.03	0.05 +	0.5 +	0.1 +	1.0 +
Amytal (Amobarbital)	0.1-0.5	1.0-5.0	1.0-3.0	10.0-30.0	1.3-9.6	13.0-96.0
Anaprox (Naproxen)	2.6-6.9	26.0-69.0	------	------	------	------
Anileridine (Leritine)	------	------	------	------	0.09 +	0.9 +
Aniline	------	------	------	------	0.63 +	6.3 +
Antabuse (Disulfiram)	0.25	2.5	------	------	------	------
Antipyrine	0.5-2.0	5.0-20.0	------	------	------	------
Aralen (Chloroquine)	0.001-0.04	0.01-0.4	------	------	0.3-9.9	3.0-99.0
Arsenic	0.0-0.002	0.0-0.02	0.1 +	1.0 +	0.9-1.5	9.0-15.0
Asendin (Amoxapine)	0.001-0.021	0.01-0.21	------	------	0.295 +	2.95 +
Aspirin [as salicylate]	2.0-10.0	20.0-100	15.0-30.0	150-300	50.0 +	500 +
Ativan (Lorazepam)	0.002-0.024	0.02-0.24	0.03-0.06	0.3-0.6	------	------
Atromid (Clofibrate)	12.2	122	------	------	------	------
Atropine	0.0035-0.02	0.035-0.2	------	------	0.02 +	0.2 +
Aventyl (Nortriptyline)	0.005-0.015	0.05-0.15	0.05 +	0.5 +	1.3 +	13.0 +
B						
Barbital	1.0	10.0	6.0-8.0	60.0-80.0	10.0 +	100 +
Barbiturates (Short Acting)	0.1	1.0	0.7 +	7.0 +	1.0 +	10.0 +

DRUG	Therapeutic or Normal		Toxic		Lethal	
	mg%	mcg/ml	mg%	mcg/ml	mg%	mcg/ml
B						
Barbiturates.............. (Intermediate)	0.1-0.5	1.0-5.0	1.0-3.0	10.0-30.0	3.0 +	30.0 +
Benadryl.................. (Diphenhydramine)	0.001-0.01	0.01-0.1	0.5 +	5.0 +	1.0 +	10.0 +
Benemid.................... (Probenecid)	10.0-20.0	100-200	------	------	------	------
Benzedrex.................. (Propylhexedrine)	0.001	0.01	------	------	0.2-0.3	2.0-3.0
Benzene....................	------	------	0.0 +	0.0 +	0.094 +	0.94 +
Benzphetamine............. (Didrex)	0.0025-0.05	0.025-0.5	0.05 +	0.5 +	------	------
Benztropine................ (Cogetin)	------	------	0.0048 +	0.048 +	------	------
Bethanid................... (Bethanidine)	0.002-0.05	0.02-0.5	------	------	------	------
Bethanidine................ (Bethanid)	0.002-0.05	0.02-0.5	------	------	------	------
Bismuth....................	1.0-2.0	10.0-20.0	10.0 +	100 +	------	------
Boron......................	0.08	0.8	4.0 +	40.0 +	5.0 +	50.0 +
Brethine................... (Terbutyline)	0.0007	0.007	------	------	0.004 +	0.04 +
Bromide....................	0.3-30.0	3.0-300	50.0-150	500-1500	200 +	2000 +
Brompheniramine........... (Dimetane)	0.0008-0.0015	0.008-0.015	------	------	------	------
Bupivacaine................ (Marcaine)	0.022-0.345	0.22-3.45	1.0 +	10.0 +	------	------
Butabarbital.............. (Butisol)	0.1-0.5	1.0-5.0	1.0-3.0	10.0-30.0	3.0 +	30.0 +
Butalbital................ (Sandoptal)	0.1	1.0	0.7 +	7.0 +	1.3-2.6	13.0-26.0
Butaperazine.............. (Repoise)	0.002-0.069	0.02-0.69	------	------	------	------
Butazolidine.............. (Phenylbutazone)	1.6-15.0	16.0-150	20.0 +	200 +	40.0 +	400 +
Butisol.................... (Butabarbital)	0.1-0.5	1.0-5.0	1.0-3.0	10.0-30.0	3.0 +	30.0 +
C						
Cadmium....................	0.00001-0.0002	0.0001-0.002	0.005 +	0.05 +	------	------
Caffeine...................	0.2-1.0	2.0-10.0	------	------	10.0 +	100 +
Carbamazepine............. (Tegretol)	0.4-1.2	4.0-12.0	1.5 +	15.0 +	------	------
Carbital................... (Carbromal) [as bromide]	0.6	6.0	40.0-125	400-1250	128-245	1280-2450
Carbocaine................. (Mepivicaine)	0.028-0.55	0.28-5.5	1.0 +	10.0 +	5.0 +	50.0 +
Carbon Monoxide............ [hemoglobin saturation]	1.0 %sat.	------	15.0-35.0 %sat.	------	50.0 + %sat.	------
Carbon Tetrachloride.......	------	------	2.0-5.0	20.0-50.0	10.0-20.0	100-200
Carbromal.................. (Carbital) [as bromide]	0.6	6.0	40.0-125	400-1250	128-245	1280-2450
Carisoprodol.............. (Soma)	1.0-4.0	10.0-40.0	3.0-5.0	30.0-50.0	11.0 +	110 +
Catapres................... (Clonidine)	0.00003-0.00015	0.0003-0.0015	------	------	------	------
Celontin................... [as N-desmethylmethsuximide]	1.0-4.0	10.0-40.0	4.0 +	40.0 +	------	------
Chlor-Trimeton............ (Chlorpheniramine)	0.0017	0.017	2.0-3.0	20.0-30.0	------	------

Table 1. (*cont.*)

DRUG	Therapeutic or Normal		Toxic		Lethal	
	mg%	mcg/ml	mg%	mcg/ml	mg%	mcg/ml
C						
Chloral Hydrate............ [as trichloroethanol]	0.2-1.2	2.0-12.0	10.0 +	100 +	25.0 +	250 +
Chloramphenicol............ (Chloromycetin)	1.0-2.0	10.0-20.0	------	------	------	------
Chlordane..................	0.0001	0.001	0.00025 +	0.0025 +	0.17-0.4	1.7-4.0
Chlordiazepoxide........... (Librium)	0.1-0.3	1.0-3.0	0.5 +	5.0 +	2.0 +	20.0 +
Chlormezanone.............. (Trancopal)	0.25-0.88	2.5-8.8	------	------	------	------
Chlormycetin............... (Chloramphenicol)	1.0-2.0	10.0-20.0	------	------	------	------
Chloroform.................	2.0-5.0	20.0-50.0	7.0-25.0	70.0-250	39.0 +	390 +
Chlorophen................. (Chlorphentermine)	0.032	0.32	------	------	------	------
Chloroprocaine............. (Nesacaine)	0.2-0.4	2.0-4.0	------	------	------	------
Chloroquine................ (Aralen)	0.001-0.04	0.01-0.4	------	------	0.3-9.9	3.0-99.0
Chlorothiazide.............	0.6	6.0	------	------	------	------
Chlorpheniramine........... (Chlor-Trimeton)	0.0017	0.017	2.0-3.0	20.0-30.0	------	------
Chlorphentermine........... (Chlorophen)	0.032	0.32	------	------	------	------
Chlorpromazine............. (Thorazine)	0.001-0.05	0.01-0.5	0.1-0.2	1.0-2.0	0.3-1.2	3.0-12.0
Chlorpropamide............. (Diabenese)	3.0-36.7	30.0-367	20.0-75.0	200-750	------	------
Chlorprothixene............ (Taractan)	0.004-0.03	0.04-0.3	0.04-0.08	0.4-0.8	------	------
Chlorthalidone............. (Combipress)	0.021-0.14	0.21-1.4	------	------	------	------
Cimetidine................. (Tagemet)	0.05-0.45	0.5-4.5	------	------	------	------
Citanest................... (Prilocaine)	0.1-0.5	1.0-5.0	------	------	------	------
Clofibrate................. (Atromid)	12.2	122	------	------	------	------
Clonapin................... (Clonazepam)	0.0005-0.012	0.005-0.12	------	------	------	------
Clonazepam................. (Clonapin)	0.0005-0.012	0.005-0.12	------	------	------	------
Clonidine.................. (Catapres)	0.00003-0.00015	0.0003-0.0015	------	------	------	------
Clorazepate................ [as N-desmethyldiazepam]	0.01-0.26	0.1-2.6	0.5 +	5.0 +	------	------
Cocaine....................	0.012-0.047	0.12-0.47	0.025+	0.25+	0.09-31.0	0.9-310
Codeine....................	0.003-0.012	0.03-0.12	------	------	0.16 +	1.6 +
Cogentin................... (Benztropine)	------	------	0.0048 +	0.048 +	------	------
Colbenemid................. (Colchicine)	0.00003-0.003	0.0003-0.03	------	------	------	------
Colchicine................. (Colbenemid)	0.00003-0.003	0.0003-0.03	------	------	------	------
Combipress................. (Chlorthalidone)	0.021-0.14	0.21-1.4	------	------	------	------
Compazine.................. (Prochlorperazine)	------	------	0.1 +	1.0 +	0.5 +	5.0 +
Copper.....................	0.1-0.15	1.0-1.5	0.54 +	5.4 +	0.25-6.3	2.5-63.0

*DRUG	Therapeutic or Normal		Toxic		Lethal	
	mg%	mcg/ml	mg%	mcg/ml	mg%	mcg/ml
C						
Coumadin (Warfarin)	0.1-0.118	1.0-1.18	------	------	------	------
Cresol	------	------	------	------	12.0 +	120 +
Cyanide	0.015	0.15	------	------	0.5 +	5.0 +
Cyclizine	0.003-0.03	0.03-0.3	0.076 +	0.76 +	1.5 +	15.0 +
Cyclobenzaprine (Flexeril)	0.0003-0.0036	0.003-0.036	------	------	------	------
Cyclopropane	8.0-18.0	80.0-180	------	------	------	------
D						
Dalmane (Flurazepam)	0.00005-0.0028	0.0005-0.028	0.02 +	0.2 +	0.05-1.7	0.5-17.0
Dantrium (Dantrolene)	0.1-0.3	1.0-3.0	------	------	------	------
Dantrolene (Dantrium)	0.1-0.3	1.0-3.0	------	------	------	------
Darvon (Propoxyphene)	0.005-0.02	0.05-0.2	0.03-0.06	0.3-0.6	0.08-0.2	0.8-2.0
DDT	0.0013	0.013	------	------	------	------
Demerol (Meperidine)	0.007-0.08	0.07-0.8	0.5	5.0	0.5 +	5.0 +
Depakene (Valproic Acid)	5.0-10.0	50.0-100	20.0 +	200 +	------	------
Desipramine (Norpramine)	0.001-0.03	0.01-0.3	0.05 +	0.5 +	1.0-2.0	10.0-20.0
Desyrel (Trazodone)	0.07-0.16	0.7-1.6	------	------	------	------
Dextromethorphan	0.00018	0.0018	------	------	------	------
Diabenese (Chlorpropamide)	3.0-36.3	30.0-363	20.0-75.0	200-750	------	------
Diamox (Acetazolamide)	1.0-1.5	10.0-15.0	------	------	------	------
Diazepam (Valium)	0.002-0.2	0.02-2.0	0.5-2.0	5.0-20.0	2.0 +	20.0 +
Diazepam [metab. N-desmethyldiazepam]	0.002-0.18	0.02-1.8	------	------	------	------
Diazoxide (Hyperstat)	1.5-2.0	15.0-20.0	10.0 +	100 +	------	------
Dichloromethane (Methylene Chloride)	------	------	------	------	28.0 +	280 +
Dicumarol	0.8-5.9	8.0-59.0	7.0 +	70.0 +	------	------
Didrex (Benzphetamine)	0.0025-0.05	0.025-0.5	0.05 +	0.5 +	------	------
Dieldrin	0.00015	0.0015	0.015-0.03	0.15-0.3	------	------
Diethylpropion (Tenuate)	0.0007-0.02	0.007-0.2	------	------	0.54 +	5.4 +
Diflunisal (Dolobid)	0.9-9.0	9.0-90.0	------	------	60.3 +	603 +
Digitoxin	0.0003-0.0039	0.003-0.039	------	------	0.032 +	0.32 +
Digoxin	0.00006-0.0002	0.0006-0.002	0.00021-0.0009	0.0021-0.009	0.0015 +	0.015 +
Dilantin (Phenytoin/Diphenylhydantoin)	1.0-2.0	10.0-20.0	2.0-5.0	20.0-50.0	10.0 +	100 +
Dilaudid (Hydromorphone)	0.0008-0.0032	0.008-0.032	------	------	0.01 +	0.1 +
Dimetane (Brompheniramine)	0.0008-0.0015	0.008-0.015	------	------	------	------
Dimethyltryptamine	0.0001-0.01	0.001-0.1	------	------	------	------
Dinitro-O-Cresol	------	------	3.0-4.0	30.0-40.0	7.5 +	75.0 +
Diphenhydramine (Benadryl)	0.001-0.01	0.01-0.1	0.5 +	5.0 +	1.0 +	10.0 +

Table 1. *(cont.)*

DRUG	Therapeutic or Normal		Toxic		Lethal	
	mg%	mcg/ml	mg%	mcg/ml	mg%	mcg/ml
D						
Diphenoxylate.............. (Lomotil)	0.001	0.01	------	------	------	------
Diphenylhydantoin.......... (Dilantin)	1.0-2.0	10.0-20.0	2.0-5.0	20.0-50.0	10.0 +	100 +
Disopyramide.............. (Norpace)	0.2-0.6	2.0-6.0	0.7 +	7.0 +	2.6 +	26.0 +
Disulfiram................. (Antabuse)	0.25	2.5	------	------	------	------
Divinyl Oxide.............	------	------	------	------	70.0 +	700 +
Dolobid.................... (Diflunisal)	0.9-9.0	9.0-90.0	------	------	60.3 +	603 +
Dolophine.................. (Methadone)	0.001-0.11	0.01-1.1	0.2 +	2.0 +	0.4 +	4.0 +
Dopram..................... (Doxapram)	0.27-0.52	2.7-5.2	------	------	------	------
Doriden.................... (Glutethimide)	0.2-1.2	2.0-12.0	1.0-8.0	10.0-80.0	3.0-10.0	30.0-100
Dothiepin.................. (Prothiaden)	0.0017-0.042	0.017-0.42	------	------	0.11-2.0	1.1-20.0
Doxapram................... (Dopram)	0.27-0.52	2.7-5.2	------	------	------	------
Doxepin.................... (Sinequan)	0.003-0.017	0.03-0.17	0.05-0.2	0.5-2.0	1.0 +	10.0 +
Doxepin.................... [plus metab. N-desmethyldoxepin]	0.01-0.025	0.1-0.25	0.05 +	0.5 +	------	------
Duranest................... (Etidocaine)	0.05-0.15	0.5-1.5	------	------	------	------
Dymelor.................... (Acetohexamide)	2.1-5.6	21.0-56.0	------	------	------	------
Dyphilline.................	0.65-1.43	6.5-14.3	------	------	------	------
E						
Elavil..................... (Amitriptyline)	0.005-0.02	0.05-0.2	0.05 +	0.5 +	0.2-2.0	2.0-20.0
Endrin.....................	0.0003	0.003	0.003 +	0.03 +	------	------
Ephedrine..................	0.01	0.1	------	------	------	------
Ethanol.................... [Toxic represents Legal intoxication]	------	------	100 +	1000 +	350 +	3500 +
Ethchlorvynol.............. (Placidyl)	0.05-0.8	0.5-8.0	2.0-10.0	20.0-100	15.0 +	150 +
Ethinamate................. (Valmid)	0.5-1.0	5.0-10.0	------	------	10.0-20.0	100-200
Ethosuximide............... (Zarontin)	4.0-10.0	40.0-100	15.0 +	150 +	25.0 +	250 +
Ethyl Chloride.............	20.0-30.0	200-300	------	------	40.0 +	400 +
Ethyl Ether................	90.0-100	900-1000	------	------	140-189	1400-1890
Ethylene Glycol............	------	------	150 +	1500 +	200-400	2000-4000
Etidocaine................. (Duranest)	0.05-0.15	0.5-1.5	------	------	------	------
F						
Feldene.................... (Piroxicam)	0.085-1.35	0.85-13.5	------	------	------	------
Fenfluramine............... (Pondimin)	0.004-0.03	0.04-0.3	0.02-0.09	0.2-0.9	0.6-1.5	6.0-15.0
Fenoprofen................. (Nalfon)	1.4-6.6	14.0-66.0	------	------	71.0 +	710 +
Fentanyl................... (Sublimaze)	0.001-0.01	0.01-0.1	------	------	------	------
Flexaril................... (Cyclobenzaprine)	0.0003-0.0036	0.003-0.036	------	------	------	------

DRUG	Therapeutic or Normal		Toxic		Lethal	
	mg%	mcg/ml	mg%	mcg/ml	mg%	mcg/ml
F						
Flexin...................... (Zoxazolamine)	0.3-1.3	3.0-13.0	------	------	------	------
Fluoride....................	0.05	0.5	------	------	0.2 +	2.0 +
Fluothane................... (Halothane)	2.2-26.0	22.0-260	------	------	20.0 +	200 +
Fluphenazine................ (Prolixin)	0.00009-0.0017	0.0009-0.017	------	------	------	------
Flurazepam.................. (Dalmane)	0.00005-0.0028	0.0005-0.028	0.02 +	0.2 +	0.05-1.7	0.5-17.0
Flurazepam.................. [plus metab. N-desalkylflurazepam]	0.00005-0.018	0.0005-0.18	------	------	------	------
Furadantin.................. (Nitrofurantoin)	0.18	1.8	------	------	------	------
Furosemide.................. (Lasix)	0.1-1.0	1.0-10.0	2.0 +	20.0 +	------	------
G						
Glutethimide................ (Doriden)	0.2-1.2	2.0-12.0	1.0-8.0	10.0-80.0	3.0-10.0	30.0-100
Gold........................ (Sodium Aurothiomalate)	0.3-0.8	3.0-8.0	------	------	------	------
Guanethidine................ (Ismelin)	0.001	0.01	------	------	------	------
H						
Halcion..................... (Trriazolam)	0.001	0.01	------	------	------	------
Haldol...................... (Haloperidol)	0.0006-0.001	0.006-0.01	0.005-0.05	0.05-0.5	------	------
Haloperidol................. (Haldol)	0.0006-0.001	0.006-0.01	0.005-0.05	0.05-0.5	------	------
Halothane................... (Fluothane)	2.2-26.0	22.0-260	------	------	20.0 +	200 +
Hexachlorophene............. (Phisohex)	0.0003-0.065	0.003-0.65	------	------	3.5 +	35.0 +
Hydralazine.................	0.02-0.09	0.2-0.9	------	------	------	------
Hydrochlorothiazide......... (Hydrodiuril)	0.007-0.045	0.07-0.45	------	------	------	------
Hydrocodone.................	0.002	0.02	------	------	------	------
Hydrodiuril................. (Hydrochlorothiazide)	0.007-0.045	0.07-0.45	------	------	------	------
Hydrogen Sulfide............	------	------	------	------	0.092 +	0.92 +
Hydromorphone............... (Dilaudid)	0.0008-0.0032	0.008-0.032	------	------	0.01 +	0.1 +
Hydroxychloroquine.......... (Plaquenil)	0.0045-0.021	0.045-0.21	------	------	6.1 +	61.0 +
Hydroxyzine.................	0.008	0.08	1.3 +	13.0 +	3.9 +	39.0 +
Hyoscine.................... (Scopolamine)	0.00003	0.0003	------	------	------	------
Hyperstat................... (Diazoxide)	1.5-2.0	15.0-20.0	10.0 +	100 +	------	------
I						
Ibuprofen................... (Motrin)	0.5-4.9	5.0-49.0	10.0-70.0	100-700	------	------
Imipramine.................. (Tofranil)	0.001-0.013	0.01-0.13	0.05-0.15	0.5-1.5	0.2 +	2.0 +
Imipramine.................. [plus metab. Desipramine]	0.015-0.025	0.15-0.25	------	------	------	------
Inderal..................... (Propanolol)	0.001-0.034	0.01-0.34	0.2 +	2.0 +	0.8-1.2	8.0-12.0

Table 1. *(cont.)*

DRUG	Therapeutic or Normal		Toxic		Lethal	
	mg%	mcg/ml	mg%	mcg/ml	mg%	mcg/ml
I						
Indocin.................... (Indomethacin)	0.05-0.3	0.5-3.0	0.6+	6.0+	------	------
Indomethacin.............. (Indocin)	0.05-0.3	0.5-3.0	0.6+	6.0+	------	------
Ionamin.................... (Phentermine)	0.009	0.09	------	------	------	------
Iron.......................	0.065-0.175	0.65-1.75	0.6 +	6.0 +	2.0-5.0	20.0-50.0
Ismelin.................... (Guanethidine)	0.001	0.01	------	------	------	------
Isopropanol...............	------	------	150 +	1500 +	------	------
Isordil.................... (Isosorbide Dinitrite)	0.0003-0.0018	0.003-0.018	------	------	------	------
Isosorbide Dinitrate....... (Isordil)	0.0003-0.0018	0.003-0.018	------	------	------	------
K						
Kemadrin................... (Procyclidine)	0.008-0.063	0.08-0.63	------	------	0.78 +	7.8 +
Ketamine...................	0.02-0.63	0.2-6.3	------	------	------	------
L						
Lasix...................... (Furosimide)	0.1-1.0	1.0-10.0	2.0 +	20.0 +	------	------
Lead.......................	0.0-0.03	0.0-0.3	0.13 +	1.3 +	0.11-0.35	1.1-3.5
Leritine................... (Anileridine)	------	------	------	------	0.09 +	0.9 +
Levoprome.................. (Methotrimeprazine)	0.002-0.014	0.02-0.14	------	------	------	------
Levorphanol...............	------	------	------	------	0.08-0.27	0.8-2.7
Librium.................... (Chlordiazepoxide)	0.1-0.3	1.0-3.0	0.5 +	5.0 +	2.0 +	20.0 +
Lidocaine..................	0.15-0.5	1.5-5.0	0.9-1.4	9.0-14.0	2.5 +	25.0 +
Lindane....................	0.0001	0.001	0.05 +	0.5 +	------	------
Lithium....................	0.42-0.97	4.2-9.7	0.139+	1.39+	3.47+	34.7 +
Lomotil.................... (Diphenoxylate)	0.001	0.01	------	------	------	------
Lopressor.................. (Metoprolol)	0.002-0.034	0.02-0.34	------	------	------	------
Lorazepam.................. (Ativan)	0.002-0.024	0.02-0.24	0.03-0.06	0.3-0.6	------	------
Loxapine................... (Loxitane)	0.001-0.003	0.01-0.03	------	------	0.77 +	7.7 +
Loxitane................... (Loxapine)	0.001-0.003	0.01-0.03	------	------	0.77 +	7.7 +
LSD........................	------	------	0.0001-0.0004	0.001-0.004	------	------
Ludiomil................... (Maprotiline)	0.005-0.035	0.05-0.35	0.045-0.08	0.45-0.8	0.2-1.3	2.0-13.0
Lysergic Acid Diethylamide. (LSD)	------	------	0.0001-0.0004	0.001-0.004	------	------
M						
Magnesium..................	1.5-6.6	15.0-66.0	9.0-13.0	90.0-130	------	------
Manganese.................. [in serum]	0.00008-0.00026	0.0008-0.0026	0.46 +	4.6 +	------	------
Maprotiline................ (Ludiomil)	0.005-0.035	0.05-0.35	0.045-0.08	0.45-0.8	0.2-1.3	2.0-13.0
Marcaine................... (Bupivacaine)	0.022-0.345	0.22-3.45	1.0 +	10.0 +	------	------
MDA........................ (Methylenedioxyamphetamine)	------	------	------	------	0.41-1.0	4.1-10.0
Mefenamic Acid............. (Ponstel)	0.03-2.0	0.3-20.0	1.1-14.8	11.0-148	------	------

DRUG	Therapeutic or Normal		Toxic		Lethal	
	mg%	mcg/ml	mg%	mcg/ml	mg%	mcg/ml
M						
Mellaril........ (Thioridazine)	0.01-0.26	0.1-2.6	0.5 +	5.0 +	0.1-1.8	1.0-18.0
Mepiridine........ (Demerol)	0.007-0.08	0.07-0.8	0.5-	5.0-	0.5 +	5.0 +
Mephenesin........ (Myanesin)	0.3-1.0	3.0-10.0	------	------	------	------
Mephenytoin........ [plus N-desmethylmephenytoin]	1.5-4.0	15.0-40.0	5.0 +	50.0 +	------	------
Mepivacaine........ (Carbocaine)	0.028-0.55	0.28-5.5	1.0 +	10.0 +	5.0 +	50.0 +
Meprobamate........	0.3-2.6	3.0-26.0	6.0-10.0	60.0-100	14.0-35.0	140-350
Mercury........ (inorganic)	------	------	0.018-0.062	0.18-0.62	0.04-2.2	0.4-22.0
Mercury........ (organic)	0.0-0.008	0.0-0.08	0.02 +	0.2 +	0.06 +	0.6 +
Mesantoin........ [plus N-desmethylmephenytoin]	1.5-4.0	15.0-40.0	5.0 +	50.0 +	------	------
Mesoridazine........ (Serentil)	0.01-0.11	0.1-1.1	------	------	0.3 +	3.0 +
Metformin........	0.1-0.4	1.0-4.0	4.5-7.0	45.0-70.0	------	------
Methadone........ (Dolophine)	0.001-0.11	0.01-1.1	0.2 +	2.0 +	0.4 +	4.0 +
Methamphetamine........	0.001-0.005	0.01-0.05	0.06-0.5	0.6-5.0	1.0 +	10.0 +
Methanol........	------	------	20.0 +	200 +	89.0 +	890 +
Methaqualone........ (Quaalude)	0.04-0.8	0.4-8.0	1.0-3.0	10.0-30.0	0.5 +	5.0 +
Methazolamide........ (Neptazane)	4.0	40.0	------	------	------	------
Methocarbamol........ (Robaxin)	2.6-4.1	26.0-41.0	------	------	------	------
Methotrimeprazine........ (Levoprome)	0.002-0.014	0.02-0.14	------	------	------	------
Methoxyfluorane........ (Penthrane)	3.0-20.0	30.0-200	------	------	------	------
Methsuximide........ [as desmethylmethsuximide]	1.0-4.0	10.0-40.0	4.0 +	40.0 +	------	------
Methyldopa........	0.1-0.75	1.0-7.5	1.0 +	10.0 +	------	------
Methylene Chloride........ (Dichloromethane)	------	------	------	------	28.0 +	280 +
Methylenedioxyamphetamine.. (MDA)	------	------	------	------	0.4-1.0	4.0-10.0
Methylfentanyl........ (China White)	------	------	------	------	0.0002-0.0011	0.002-0.011
Methylphenidate........ (Ritalin)	0.001-0.006	0.01-0.06	0.08 +	0.8 +	0.23 +	2.3 +
Methyprylon........ (Noludar)	0.5-1.5	5.0-15.0	3.0-6.0	30.0-60.0	10.0 +	100 +
Metoprolol........ (Lopressor)	0.002-0.034	0.02-0.34	------	------	------	------
Mianserin........	0.001-0.016	0.01-0.16	0.011-0.05	0.11-0.5	0.01-0.26	0.1-2.6
Milontin........ (Phensuximide)	0.4-1.4	4.0-14.0	8.0-15	80.0-150	------	------
Morphine........	0.01	0.1	------	------	0.005-0.4	0.05-4.0
Motrin........ (Ibuprofen)	0.5-4.9	5.0-49.0	10.0-70.0	100-700	------	------
Myanesin........ (Mephenesin)	0.3-1.0	3.0-10.0	------	------	------	------
Mysoline........ (Primidone)	0.2-1.9	2.0-19.0	5.0-8.0	50.0-80.0	10.0 +	100 +

Table 1. *(cont.)*

DRUG	Therapeutic or Normal		Toxic		Lethal	
	mg%	mcg/ml	mg%	mcg/ml	mg%	mcg/ml
N						
N-acetylprocainamide.......	0.2-1.2	2.0-12.0	1.6 +	16.0 +	------	------
N-desalkylfluazepam........ [metab of Fluazepam]	0.001-0.014	0.01-0.14	------	------	------	------
N-desmethyldiazepam........ [from Clorazepate]	0.01-0.26	0.1-2.6	0.5 +	5.0 +	------	------
N-desmethyldiazepam........ [metab of Diazepam]	0.002-0.18	0.02-1.8	------	------	------	------
Nalfon..................... (Fenprofen)	1.4-6.6	14.0-66.0	------	------	71.0 +	710 +
Naloxone................... (Narcan)	0.001	0.01	------	------	------	------
Naproxen................... (Anaprox)	2.6-6.9	26.0-69.0	------	------	------	------
Narcan..................... (Naloxone)	0.001	0.01	------	------	------	------
Nardil..................... (Phenylzine)	0.0001-0.0002	0.001-0.002	------	------	0.15 +	1.5 +
Navane..................... (Thiothixene)	0.001-0.01	0.01-0.1	------	------	------	------
Nembutal................... (Pentobarbital)	0.1-0.3	1.0-3.0	0.5 +	5.0 +	1.0-16.9	10.0-169
Neo-Synephrine............. (Phenylephrine)	0.003	0.03	------	------	------	------
Naptazane.................. (Methazolamide)	4.0	40.0	------	------	------	------
Nesacaine.................. (Chloroprocaine)	0.2-0.4	2.0-4.0	------	------	------	------
Nickel.....................	0.011	0.11	------	------	------	------
Nicotine...................	0.001-0.005	0.01-0.05	1.0 +	10.0 +	0.5-5.2	5.0-52.0
Nisentil................... (Alphaprodine)	0.087-0.1	0.87-1.0	------	------	------	------
Nitrofurantoin............. (Furandantoin)	0.18	1.8	------	------	------	------
Nitroprusside.............. [as thiocyanate]	0.6-2.9	6.0-29.0	------	------	------	------
Nitrous Oxide..............	29.0-44.0	290-440	------	------	35.0 +	350 +
Noctec..................... [as trichloroethanol]	0.2-1.2	2.0-12.0	10.0 +	100 +	25.0 +	250 +
Noludar.................... (Methyprylon)	0.5-1.5	5.0-15.0	3.0-6.0	30.0-60.0	10.0 +	100 +
Nordiazapem................ (N-desmethyldiazepam)	0.01-0.26	0.1-2.6	0.5 +	5.0 +	------	------
Norflex.................... (Orphenadrine)	0.003-0.085	0.03-0.85	0.2 +	2.0 +	0.4-0.8	4.0-8.0
Norpace.................... (Disopyramide)	0.2-0.6	2.0-6.0	0.7 +	7.0 +	2.6 +	26.0 +
Norpramin.................. (Desipramine)	0.001-0.03	0.01-0.3	0.05 +	0.5 +	1.0-2.0	10.0-20.0
Nortriptyline.............. (Aventyl)	0.005-0.015	0.05-0.15	0.05 +	0.5 +	1.3 +	13.0 +
Novocain................... (Procaine)	0.02-1.3	0.2-13.0	2.1 +	21.0 +	------	------
O						
Orinase.................... (Tolbutamide)	4.3-9.6	43.0-96.0	------	------	64.0 +	640 +
Orphenadrine............... (Norflex)	0.003-0.085	0.03-0.85	0.2 +	2.0 +	0.4-0.8	4.0-8.0
Oxalate....................	0.2	2.0	------	------	1.0 +	10.0 +

DRUG	Therapeutic or Normal		Toxic		Lethal	
	mg%	mcg/ml	mg%	mcg/ml	mg%	mcg/ml
O						
Oxazepam.................. (Serax)	0.015-0.14	0.15-1.4	0.2 +	2.0 +	------	------
Oxycodone................. (Percodan)	0.001-0.01	0.01-0.1	0.02-0.5	0.2-5.0	------	------
Oxyphenbutazone........... (Tandearil)	1.1-11.8	11.0-118	------	------	------	------
P						
Pancronium................ (Pavulon)	0.009-0.1	0.09-1.0	------	------	0.16 +	1.6 +
Papaverine................	0.025-0.4	0.25-4.0	------	------	------	------
Para-methoxyamphetamine.... (PMA)	------	------	------	------	0.1 +	1.0 +
Paradione................. (Paramethadione)	0.11-0.5	1.1-5.0	------	------	------	------
Paraldehyde...............	2.0-33.1	20.0-332	20.0-40.0	200-400	50.0 +	500 +
Paramethadione............ (Paradione)	0.11-0.5	1.1-5.0	------	------	------	------
Paraquat..................	------	------	0.85 +	8.5 +	3.5 +	35.0 +
Parathion.................	------	------	------	------	0.05-3.4	0.5-34.0
Parnate................... (Tranylcypromine)	0.005	0.05	------	------	------	------
Pavulon................... (Pancronium)	0.009-0.1	0.09-1.0	------	------	0.16 +	1.6 +
PCP....................... (Phencyclidine)	------	------	0.0007-0.024	0.007-0.24	0.1-0.5	1.0-5.0
Pentachlorophenol.........	------	------	------	------	4.6 +	46.0 +
Pentazocine............... (Talwin)	0.003-0.1	0.03-1.0	0.2-0.5	2.0-5.0	0.3 +	3.0 +
Penthrane................. (Methoxyflurane)	3.0-20.0	30.0-200	------	------	------	------
Pentobarbital............. (Nembutal)	0.1-0.3	1.0-3.0	0.5 +	5.0 +	1.0-16.9	10.0-169
Pentothal................. (Thiopental)	0.1-4.2	1.0-42.0	0.7 +	7.0 +	1.0-40.0	10.0-400
Percodan.................. (Oxycodone)	0.001-0.01	0.01-0.1	0.02-0.5	0.2-5.0	------	------
Perphenazine.............. (Trilafon)	0.00004-0.003	0.0004-0.03	0.1 +	1.0 +	------	------
Phenacetin................	0.01-2.0	0.1-20.0	3.0 +	30.0 +	------	------
Phencyclidine............. (PCP)	------	------	0.0007-0.024	0.007-0.24	0.1-0.5	1.0-5.0
Phendimetrazine...........	0.002-0.024	0.02-0.24	------	------	------	------
Phenelzine................ (Nardil)	0.0001-0.0002	0.001-0.002	------	------	0.15 +	1.5 +
Phenmetrazine............. (Preludin)	0.004-0.024	0.04-0.24	------	------	0.4 +	4.0 +
Phenobarbital.............	1.0-4.0	10.0-40.0	4.0-6.0	40.0-60.0	8.0 +	80.0 +
Phenol....................	------	------	------	------	9.0 +	90.0 +
Phensuximide.............. (Milontin)	0.4-1.4	4.0-14.0	8.0-15.0	80.0-150	------	------
Phentermine............... (Ionamine)	0.009	0.09	------	------	------	------
Phenylbutazone............ (Butazolidin)	1.6-15.0	16.0-150	20.0 +	200 +	40.0 +	400 +
Phenylephrine............. (Neo-Synephrine)	0.003	0.03	------	------	------	------
Phenylpropanolamine........	0.005-0.01	0.05-0.1	------	------	4.8 +	48.0 +
Phenytoin................. (Dilantin)	1.0-2.0	10.0-20.0	2.0-5.0	20.0-50.0	10.0 +	100 +

Table 1. *(cont.)*

DRUG	Therapeutic or Normal		Toxic		Lethal	
	mg%	mcg/ml	mg%	mcg/ml	mg%	mcg/ml
P						
Phisohex (Hexachlorophene)	0.0003-0.065	0.003-0.65	------	------	3.5 +	35.0 +
Phosphorous (Adult)	2.0-4.8	20.0-48.0	------	------	------	------
Phosphorous (Children)	4.0-7.0	40.0-70.0	------	------	------	------
Piroxicam (Feldene)	0.085-1.35	0.85-13.5	------	------	------	------
Placidyl (Ethchlorvynol)	0.05-0.8	0.5-8.0	2.0-10.0	20.0-100	15.0 +	150 +
Plaquenil (Hydroxychloroquine)	0.0045-0.021	0.045-0.21	------	------	6.1 +	61.0 +
PMA (Para-methoxyamphetamine)	------	------	------	------	0.2-0.4	2.0-4.0
Polythiazide (Renese)	0.2-0.7	2.0-7.0	------	------	------	------
Pondimin (Fenfluramin)	0.004-0.03	0.04-0.3	0.02-0.09	0.2-0.9	0.6-1.5	6.0-15.0
Ponstel (Mefanamic Acid)	0.03-2.0	0.3-20.0	1.1-14.8	11.0-148	------	------
Prazepam	0.001-0.004	0.01-0.04	------	------	------	------
Preludin (Phenmetrazine)	0.004-0.024	0.04-0.24	------	------	0.4 +	4.0 +
Prilocaine (Citanest)	0.1-0.5	1.0-5.0	------	------	------	------
Primidone (Mysoline)	0.2-1.9	2.0-19.0	5.0-8.0	50.0-80.0	10.0 +	100 +
Probenecid (Benemid)	10.0-20.0	100-200	------	------	------	------
Procainamide (Pronestyl)	0.4-0.8	4.0-8.0	1.0 +	10.0 +	2.0 +	20.0 +
Procaine (Novocain)	0.02-1.3	0.2-13.0	2.1 +	21.0 +	------	------
Prochlorperazine ((Compazine)	------	------	0.1 +	1.0 +	0.5 +	5.0 +
Procyclidine (Kemadrine)	0.008-0.063	0.08-0.63	------	------	0.78 +	7.8 +
Prolixin (Fluphenazine)	0.00009-0.0017	0.0009-0.017	------	------	------	------
Promazine (Sparine)	------	------	0.1 +	1.0 +	0.5 +	5.0 +
Promethazine	0.0003-0.0023	0.003-0.023	------	------	------	------
Pronestyl (Procainamide)	0.4-0.8	4.0-8.0	1.0 +	10.0 +	2.0 +	20.0 +
Proparacaine (Alcaine)	------	------	------	------	1.5 +	15.0 +
Propoxyphene (Darvon)	0.005-0.04	0.05-0.4	0.03-0.06	0.3-0.6	0.08-0.2	0.8-2.0
Propoxyphene [plus metab. norpropoxyphene]	0.02-0.19	0.2-1.9	0.25-1.2	2.5-12.0	0.3-4.7	3.0-47.0
Propanolol (Inderal)	0.001-0.034	0.01-0.34	0.2 +	2.0 +	0.8-1.2	8.0-12.0
Propylhexedrine (Benzedrex)	0.001	0.01	------	------	0.2-0.3	2.0-3.0
Prothiaden (Dothiepin)	0.0017-0.042	0.017-0.42	------	------	0.11-2.0	1.1-20.0
Protriptline (Vivactil)	0.007-0.038	0.07-0.38	0.05-0.2	0.5-2.0	0.1 +	1.0 +

DRUG	Therapeutic or Normal		Toxic		Lethal	
	mg%	mcg/ml	mg%	mcg/ml	mg%	mcg/ml
P						
Psuedoephrine............. (Sudafed)	0.05-0.077	0.5-0.77	------	------	1.9 +	19.0 +
Pyribenzamine............. (Tripelennamine)	0.006	0.06	------	------	1.0 +	10.0 +
Q						
Quaalude.................. (Methaqualone)	0.04-0.8	0.4-8.0	1.0-3.0	10.0-30.0	0.5 +	5.0 +
Quinidine.................	0.03-0.6	0.3-6.0	1.0 +	10.0 +	3.0-5.0	30.0-50.0
Quinine...................	0.17-0.97	1.7-9.7	1.0 +	10.0 +	1.2 +	12.0 +
R						
Rantidine................. (Zantac)	0.0036-0.0094	0.036-0.094	------	------	------	------
Ranese.................... (Polythiazide)	0.2-0.7	2.0-7.0	------	------	------	------
Repoise................... (Butaperazine)	0.002-0.069	0.02-0.69	------	------	------	------
Restoril.................. (Temazepam)	0.04-0.09	0.4-0.9	------	------	------	------
Ritalin................... (Methylphenidate)	0.001-0.006	0.01-0.06	0.08 +	0.8 +	0.23 +	2.3 +
Robaxin................... (Methocarbamol)	2.6-4.1	26.0-41.0	------	------	------	------
S						
Salicylate................ (Acetylsalicylic Acid) [normal usage]	2.0-10.0	20.0-100	15.0-30.0	150-300	50.0 +	500 +
Salicylate................ [for rheumatoid arthritis]	2.0-25.0	20.0-250	------	------	------	------
Sandoptal................. (Butalbital)	0.1	1.0	0.7 +	7.0 +	1.3-2.6	13.0-26.0
Scopolamine............... (Hyoscine)	0.00003	0.0003	------	------	------	------
Secobarbital.............. (Seconal)	0.1-0.5	1.0-5.0	0.3 +	3.0 +	0.5-5.2	5.0-52.0
Seconal................... (Secobarbital)	0.1-0.5	1.0-5.0	0.3 +	3.0 +	0.5-5.2	5.0-52.0
Serax..................... (Oxazepam)	0.015-0.14	0.15-1.4	0.2 +	2.0 +	------	------
Serentil.................. (Mesoridazine)	0.01-0.11	0.1-1.1	------	------	0.3 +	3.0 +
Sinequan.................. (Doxepin)	0.003-0.017	0.03-0.17	0.05-0.2	0.5-2.0	1.0 +	10.0 +
Sodium Aurothiomalate...... (Gold)	0.3-0.8	3.0-8.0	------	------	------	------
Soma...................... (Carisoprodol)	1.0-4.0	10.0-40.0	3.0-5.0	30.0-50.0	11.0 +	110 +
Sparine................... (Promazine)	------	------	0.1 +	1.0 +	0.5 +	5.0 +
Stelazine................. (Trifluoperazine)	0.05-0.2	0.5-2.0	0.12-0.3	1.2-3.0	0.3-0.8	3.0-8.0
Strychnine................	------	------	0.2 +	2.0 +	0.28-1.2	2.8-12.0
Sublimaze................. (Fentanyl)	0.001-0.01	0.01-0.1	------	------	------	------
Sudafed................... (Pseudoephedrine)	0.05-0.077	0.5-0.77	------	------	1.9 +	19.0 +
Sulfadiazine..............	8.0-15.0	80.0-150	------	------	------	------
Sulfaquanidine............	3.0-5.0	30.0-50.0	------	------	------	------
Sulfanilamide.............	10.0-15.0	100-150	------	------	------	------
Sulfioxazole..............	9.0-10.0	90.0-100	------	------	------	------

Table 1. (*cont.*)

DRUG	Therapeutic or Normal mg%	Therapeutic or Normal mcg/ml	Toxic mg%	Toxic mcg/ml	Lethal mg%	Lethal mcg/ml
S						
Surmontil................ (Trimipramine)	0.001-0.03	0.01-0.3	------	------	0.87-1.2	8.7-12.0
T						
Tagamet.................... (Cimetidine)	0.05-0.45	0.5-4.5	------	------	------	------
Talwin..................... (Pentazocine)	0.003-0.1	0.03-1.0	0.2-0.5	2.0-5.0	0.3 +	3.0 +
Tandearil.................. (Oxyphenbutazone)	1.1-11.8	11.0-118	------	------	------	------
Taractan................... (Chlorprothixene)	0.004-0.03	0.04-0.3	0.04-0.08	0.4-0.8	------	------
Tegretol................... (Carbamazepine)	0.4-1.2	4.0-12.0	1.5 +	15.0 +	------	------
Temazepam.................. (Restoril)	0.04-0.09	0.4-0.9	------	------	------	------
Tenuate.................... (Diethylpropion)	0.0007-0.02	0.007-0.2	------	------	0.54 +	5.4 +
Terbutyline................ (Brethine)	0.0007	0.007	------	------	0.004 +	0.04 +
Tetrachloroethylene........	------	------	------	------	0.45-4.4	4.5-44.0
Tetrahydrocannabinol.......	0.0-0.019	0.0-0.19	------	------	------	------
Thallium...................	0.0-0.008	0.0-0.08	0.1 +	1.0 +	0.05-1.1	0.5-11.0
Theophylline............... (Aminophylline)	1.0-2.0	10.0-20.0	3.0-4.0	30.0-40.0	5.0-25.0	50.0-250
Thiocyanate................	8.0-14.0	80.0-140	------	------	------	------
Thiocyanate................ [from nitroprusside]	0.6-2.9	6.0-29.0	------	------	------	------
Thiopental................. (Pentothal)	0.1-0.42	1.0-4.2	0.7 +	7.0 +	1.0-40.0	10.0-400
Thioridazine............... (Mellaril)	0.01-0.26	0.1-2.6	0.5 +	5.0 +	0.1-1.8	1.0-18.0
Thioridazine............... [plus metab. mesoridazine]	0.03-0.4	0.3-4.0	------	------	------	------
Thiothixene................ (Navane)	0.001-0.01	0.01-0.1	------	------	------	------
Thorazine.................. (Chlorpromazine)	0.001-0.05	0.01-0.5	0.1-0.2	1.0-2.0	0.3-1.2	3.0-12.0
Tigan...................... (Trimethobenzamide)	0.1-0.2	1.0-2.0	------	------	------	------
Tin........................	0.012-0.014	0.12-0.14	------	------	------	------
Tocainide.................. (Tonocard)	4.0-10.0	------	------	------	------	------
Tofranil................... (Imipramine)	0.001-0.013	0.01-0.13	0.05-0.15	0.5-1.5	0.2 +	2.0 +
Tolbutamide................ (Orinase)	4.3-9.6	43.0-96.0	------	------	64.0 +	640 +
Tolectin................... (Tolmetin)	3.7	37.0	6.0 +	60.0 +	------	------
Tolmetin................... (Tolectin)	3.7	37.0	6.0 +	60.0 +	------	------
Toluene....................	------	------	------	------	1.0 +	10.0 +
Tonocard................... (Tocainide)	0.4-1.0	4.0-10.0	------	------	------	------
Trancopal.................. (Chlormezanone)	0.25-0.88	2.5-8.8	------	------	------	------
Tranxene................... [as N-desmethyldiazepam)	0.01-0.26	0.1-2.6	0.5 +	5.0 +	------	------
Tranylcypromine............ (Parnate)	0.005	0.05	------	------	------	------

DRUG	Therapeutic or Normal		Toxic		Lethal	
	mg%	mcg/ml	mg%	mcg/ml	mg%	mcg/ml
T						
Trazodone.................. (Desyrel)	0.07-0.16	0.7-1.6	------	------	------	------
Triazolam.................. (Halcion)	0.001	0.01	------	------	------	------
Tribromoethanol............	------	------	------	------	9.0 +	90.0 +
Trichloroethane............	------	------	------	------	10.0-100	100-1000
Trichloroethanol........... [from Chloral Hydrate]	0.2-1.2	2.0-12.0	10.0 +	100 +	25.0 +	250 +
Trichloroethylene..........	------	------	0.1-9.0	1.0-90.0	0.3-11.0	3.0-110
Tridione................... (Trimethadione)	1.0-3.0	10.0-30.0	------	------	------	------
Trifluoperazine............ (Stelazine)	0.05-0.2	0.5-2.0	0.12-0.3	1.2-3.0	0.3-0.8	3.0-8.0
Trilafon................... (Perphenazine)	0.00004-0.003	0.0004-0.03	0.1 +	1.0 +	------	------
Trimethadione.............. (Tridione)	1.0-3.0	10.0-30.0	------	------	------	------
Trimethobenzamide.......... (Tigan)	0.1-0.2	1.0-2.0	------	------	------	------
Trimipramine............... (Surmontil)	0.001-0.03	0.01-0.3	------	------	0.87-1.2	8.7-12.0
Tripelennamine............. (Pyribenzamine)	0.006	0.06	------	------	1.0 +	10.0 +
Tubocurarine...............	0.004-0.6	0.04-6.0	------	------	------	------
Tylenol.................... (Acetaminophen)	1.0-2.0	10.0-20.0	15.0 +	150 +	16.0 +	160 +
U						
Uric Acid..................	3.0-7.0	30.0-70.0	------	------	------	------
V						
Valium..................... (Diazepam)	0.002-0.2	0.02-2.0	0.5-2.0	5.0-20.0	2.0 +	20.0 +
Valium..................... [with metab. N-desmethyldiazepam]	0.002-0.18	0.02-1.8	------	------	------	------
Valmid..................... (Ethinamate)	0.5-1.0	5.0-10.0	------	------	10.0-20.0	100-200
Valproic Acid.............. (Depakene)	5.0-10.0	50.0-100	20.0 +	200 +	------	------
Vivactil................... (Protriptyline)	0.007-0.038	0.07-0.38	0.05-0.2	0.5-2.0	0.1 +	1.0 +
W						
Warfarin................... (Coumadin)	0.1-1.18	1.0-11.8	------	------	------	------
X						
Xanax...................... (Alprazolam)	0.02	0.2	------	------	------	------
Xylene.....................	------	------	------	------	0.3-4.0	3.0-40.0
Z						
Zantac..................... (Rantidine)	0.0036-0.0094	0.036-0.094	------	------	------	------
Zarontin................... (Ethosuximide)	4.0-10.0	40.0-100	15.0 +	150 +	25.0 +	250 +
Zinc.......................	0.068-0.13	0.68-1.3	------	------	------	------
Zoxazolamine............... (Flexin)	0.3-1.36	3.0-13.6	------	------	------	------

Implantable Cardiovascular Devices: Medico-Legal Aspects

S. Sandy Sanbar, M.D., Ph.D., J.D., F.C.L.M.

INTRODUCTION—HUMAN BIOTECHNOLOGY

Implantation of artificial devices in humans has not only significantly prolonged life but also dramatically improved the quality of life for many people.

Artificial implantable human medical devices have developed in part due to advances in microcomputer technology. A vital component of an artificial computerized implant is its microprocessor, a highly sophisticated informational network that functions much like a brain. Information storage in microprocessors may take the form of read-only memory (ROM) or random-access memory (RAM), which can be both written to or read from. By utilizing very-large-scale integrated (VLSI) circuitry, it is possible for many functions or modes to be incorporated onto a single highly miniaturized chip.

The clinical application of microcomputer advances to human biotechnology and specifically the development of sophisticated implantable medical devices has been accompanied by a multitude of attendant medical problems, complications, duties, and responsibilities on the part of both the manufacturer and the health care provider.

This chapter presents an overview of recent advances in implantable medical devices and describes the medical, legal, ethical, and economic aspects of implantable permanent pacemakers.

OVERVIEW OF IMPLANTABLE MEDICAL DEVICES

During the past two decades, medical biotechnology has successfully utilized microcomputers to develop a variety of implantable therapeutic medical devices

FIGURE 1. Artificial ear comprised of an external microcomputer (below) that drives the cochlear implant (above).

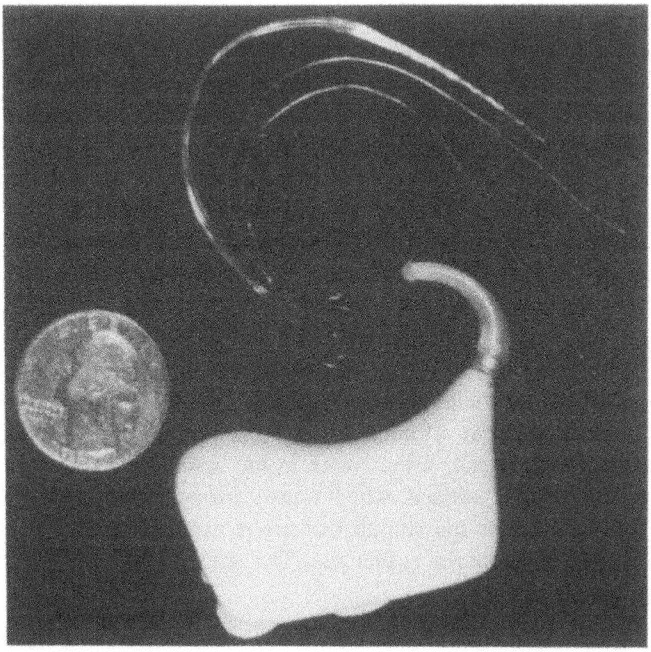

that are presently at various stages of development. Their therapeutic objectives have been to remedy human organ system deficiencies of the ears and eyes and of the endocrine, nervous, genital, musculoskeletal, and cardiovascular systems.

Among the noncardiovascular medical devices developed are the following.

Artificial Cochlea (Ear)

Substantial progress has been made in the production of a cochlear prosthesis for the deaf (see Figure 1). Investigators have known for years that if the auditory nerve is electrically stimulated by an electrode in the cochlea some deaf persons will typically hear a tone. In this situation the auditory nerve conveys signals to the brain and is fully functional. The deafness is due solely to nonfunctional transducers, the "hair cells," which cannot stimulate the auditory nerve. Using an artificial implantable cochlea, deafness can be remedied to a large degree.

There are, however, three basic problems with cochlear prostheses that have not yet been fully resolved. The first involves the electrode that stimulates the auditory nerve. The cochlea, or inner ear, determines the pitch and intensity of incoming sound, stimulating different groups of nerve endings for different pitches. To enhance sound perception and to present a full range of tones to the patients, the new generations of implants will use a linear array of electrodes to stimulate the auditory nerve rather than the single electrode now in use, which cannot access different pathways in the auditory nerve.

The second problem with present cochlear implants deals with the code for stimulating the auditory nerve. Incoming sounds must be broken down into their component frequencies, and signals must be sent to appropriate electrodes on the cochlear membrane so that the brain can differentiate pitch and form an accurate and clear image of incoming sound. Although a lot of work has been done by researchers, the best way to encode these signals has yet to be found.

The third problem deals with the external component of the artificial cochlea. Researchers are seeking to produce a small enough package that could be worn behind the ear of the patient and would house the microcomputer components of the implant.

Artifical Retina (Eye)

Compared with the artificial ear, the artificial eye is extremely intricate. The first step in developing an artificial eye is determining the appropriate method of electrostimulation of the visual cortex in the brain. To achieve this, a complicated silicon retina is utilized, which transforms optical images into electrical signals. The latter create the stimuli that are transmitted to and interpreted by the visual cortex of the brain as pictures. The artificial retina is presently in its developmental stages.

Implantable Infusion Pumps

Microcomputer-controlled infusion pumps have been implanted in patients for continuous infusion of hormones, nutrients, electrolytes, and medications.

Patients with chronic pain due to cancer or other disorders are being effectively treated with controlled, continuous pump infusion of pain-relieving medications.

Some diabetics are being treated with implanted insulin infusion pumps. An insulin infusion button, called a subcutaneous peritoneal access device (SPAD), is presently being tested in humans and may eventally be used in conjunction with an insulin infusion pump.

To date, real-life programmable implantable medication systems contain an "open-loop" pump, that is, the unit dose senses nothing within the human body but dispenses medications as programmed. The next generation of implantable pumps will include "closed-loop" systems, which have many capabilities including sensing, dispensing, and responding to varying physiologic needs and treatment of disorders such as hypertension (Figure 2).

Spinal Cord (Nervous System) Stimulator

During the past fifteen years, neurosurgeons have utilized external spinal cord stimulators to alleviate chronic intractable pain due to "failed" back surgery,

FIGURE 2. Programmable miniature insulin infusion pump.

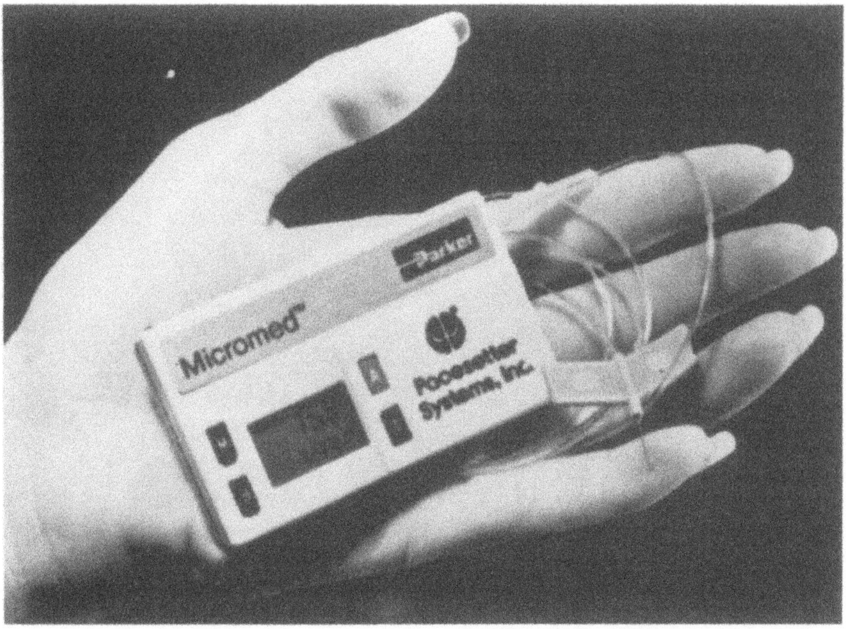

ischemic pain, adhesive arachnoiditis, and peripheral deafferentation syndromes. A recent development is the internal Itrel Spinal Cord Stimulation System (Medtronics, Inc., Minneapolis). This is a totally implantable pulse generator, similar to a pacemaker, which is programmable to effectively stimulate the spinal cord and successfully relieve pain (Figure 3). The implant weighs 37 grams. Among its complications are lead dislodgment, ineffective stimulation and insufficient pain relief, infection, soreness and burning at the implant site, and radicular stimulation.

Penile Prostheses

Penile prostheses are among the more widely used implants (Figure 4). They are mainly mechanical and include:

1. The Small-Carion semirigid cylindrical rods;
2. The Finney semirigid adjustable rod with a soft silicon hinge;
3. The Jonas silicon-silver malleable paired rods;
4. The Scott inflatable polyurethane implant with pump;
5. The Mentor inflatable polyurethane implant with pump.

In the developmental stages are implantable nerve stimulation devices, which conceivably could stimulate the autonomic nerves that control erection. Individ-

FIGURE 3. Spinal Cord Stimulator with generator (left) and console programmer (right) by Medtronics, Inc.

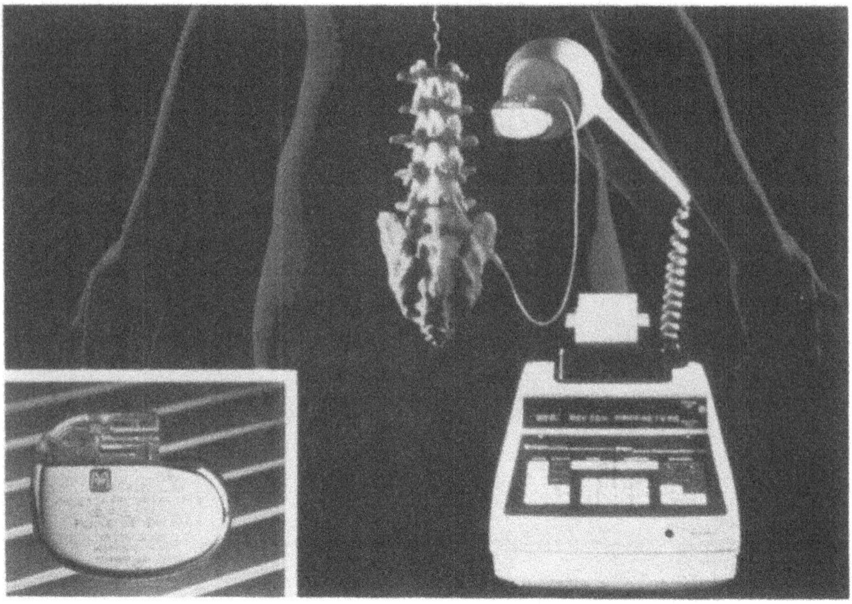

uals who might benefit from nerve stimulation have a neurogenic basis for their impotence rather than an ischemic (or circulatory) cause.

Erectaid, a tumescence assist device, is a new external penile prosthesis that will be marketed for an estimated cost of $150 to $200, compared with $8,000 to $10,000 for surgery for a penile implant.

Musculoskeletal Devices

Until two decades ago, the development of artificial limbs was limited to cosmetic devices. Newer prostheses include electromyogenic- (EMG-) controlled limbs. The Utah Arm, designed by Dr. Stephen Jacobson, is a very good example of an EMG-controlled limb. Its cost, about $15,000, has limited its widespread adoption. Present models of the Utah Arm utilize sophisticated analog circuitry to control the arm's movements in all directions. The system must monitor a large number of parameters to realize the arm's limited motion. Low-amplitude cutaneous EMG-control signals have to be emitted first, then transmitted, amplified, integrated, filtered, and finally returned with the response that is appropriate for the situation.

Future directions include the development of artificial devices for leg amputees and paraplegics. Additionally, custom-made artificial prosthetics for human limbs and other body parts will become available using computer-assisted design and

FIGURE 4. Inflatable Penile Prosthesis (Scott).

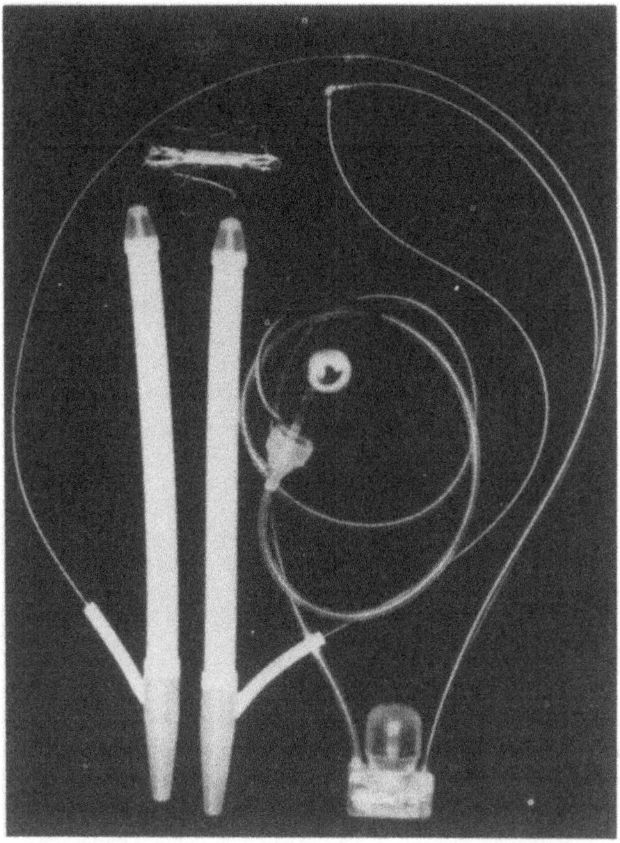

manufacturing in lieu of the "one size fits all" prosthetics, for example, the hip prothesis.

Among the cardiovascular devices developed for implant in humans are the following.

Heart Assist Devices

The development of the bulky heart-lung machine in 1953 marked the beginning of a new era of heart assist devices.

Presently available invasive devices that assist the circulation fall in to one of these categories:

1. *Direct Assistance:* This method utilizes a ventricular balloon. Temporary improvement in systemic perfusion is accomplished by synchronous balloon pulsation with the ventricle.

FIGURE 5. Novacor model IIIA pump.

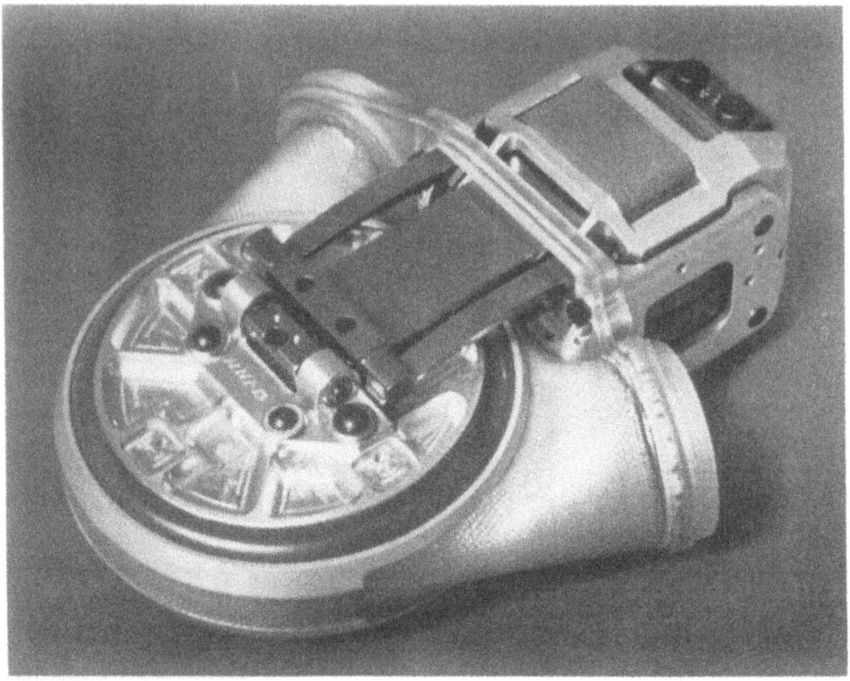

2. *Series Assistance (or Counterpulsation):* The heart workload is diminished by this approach, which is aimed at reducing systolic pressure and increasing diastolic pressure. An example of this approach is invasive counterpulsation. In particular, the intra-aortic balloon pump, used first in 1953, is presently the most commonly used mechanical circulatory or heart assist device. The balloon pump may produce up to a 20 percent increase in cardiac output. Balloon inflation is powered by a drive console, which is triggered by the patient's electrical cardiac impulse (electrocardiogram-controlled).
3. *Parallel Assistance:* This approach is aimed at supplanting the heart pumping action by utilizing an implantable mechanical device in parallel that takes over the work of the heart.

Left ventricular assist devices, installed piggyback on the heart, are short-term assists for patients that cannot be weaned from a heart-lung machine, patients with acute left ventricular failure after myocardial infarction, and patients waiting for a heart transplant.

Several long-term electrical left ventricular (heart) assist systems are currently under development in the United States by Abiomed, Gould, Inc., Nimbus, Inc., Novacor Medical, Sarns, Inc., and Thermedics, Inc. (see Figure 5). These devices are either electromechanical or electrohydraulic. The devices contain different types of valves such as clastomer, duramater, bovine pericardium,

FIGURE 6. Schematic diagram of an implantable left ventricular assist device jointly developed by Stanford University and Novacor Medical Research Corporation.

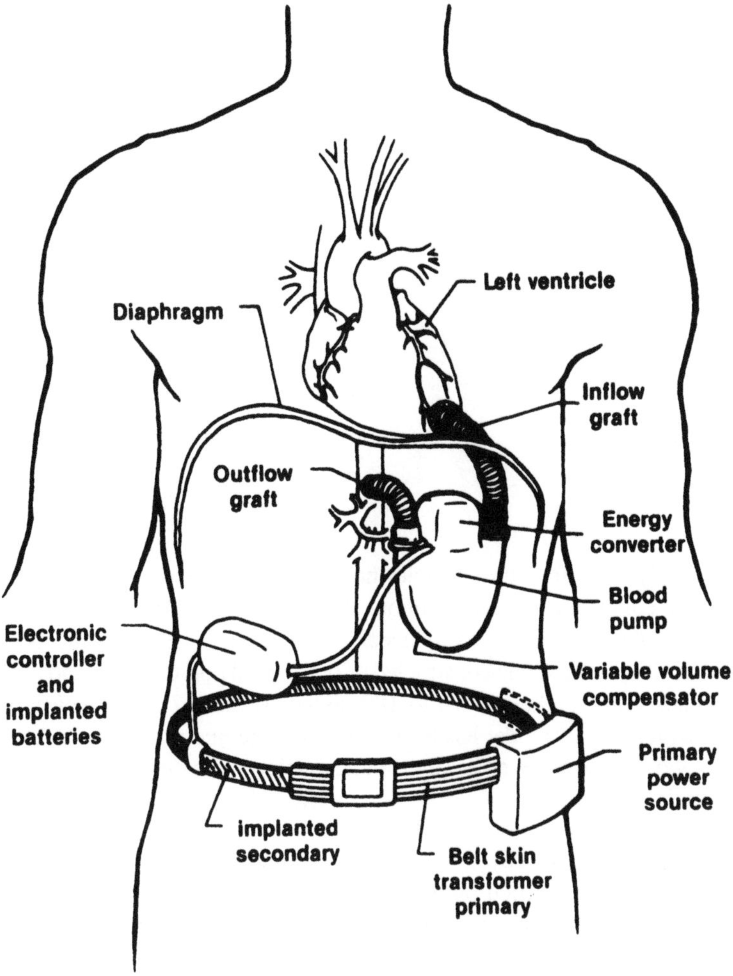

porcine xenograft, and Bjork-Shiley valves. A completely implantable left ventricular assist system is being developed that will eliminate the need for a percutaneous connection to an external power source (Figure 6).

Total Artificial Heart

One of the most dramatic events in this decade was the implantation of the Jarvick-7 artifical heart by Dr. William C. DeVries in Dr. Barney Clark. Although the operation was not a complete success, it must be remembered that Dr. Clark

FIGURE 7. Total artificial electrohydraulic Jarvik-7 heart (courtesy of Ciba).

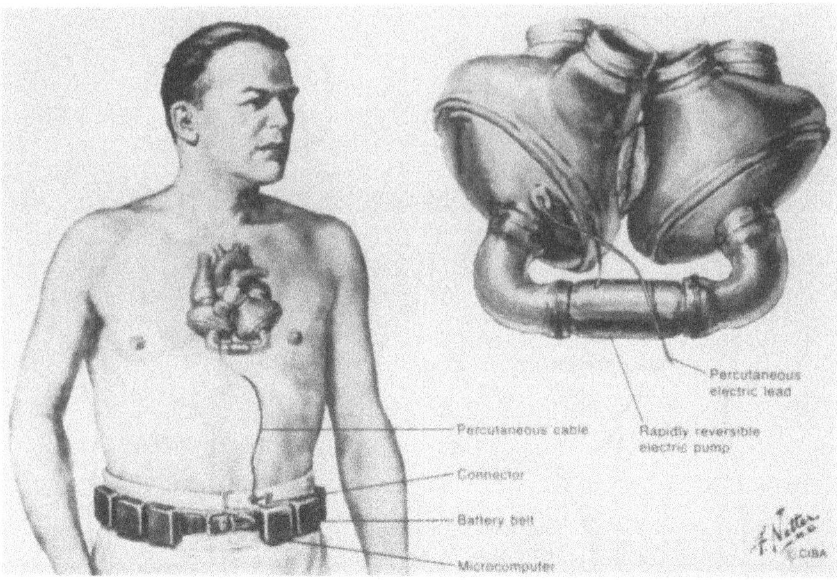

was critically ill before the artificial heart was implanted and that his system was sorely compromised even without the trauma and strain of the operation. Technically the operation was a success. The Jarvick-7 total artificial heart is pneumatically powered and constructed of segmented polyurethane and is suitable for patients with weights of 170 to 180 pounds (Figure 7). The newer Jarvick-8 total artificial heart model has been redesigned geometrically for better fit and will be available in three sizes, the smallest being for patients weighing around 100 pounds.

In addition to Symbion's Jarvick artificial heart, several other artificial hearts are in various stages of development in the United States and abroad. A French artificial heart is being tried by the Artificial Heart System International. It was invented by Dr. D. Lapeyre in the laboratories of the French aerospace firm Aeropastiale, and it is made of plastic and metal.

Artificial Heart Valves

More than 50 artificial heart valve devices have been introduced in the past two decades, but the ideal valve substitute has not been found. An ideally suitable prosthetic heart valve should have adequate hemodynamic performance, resist thrombogenesis, resist degeneration throughout the human life span, be biocompatible, be able to be inserted reliably without requiring unique technical dexterity, and be silent.

FIGURE 8. Prosthetic Cardiac Valve.

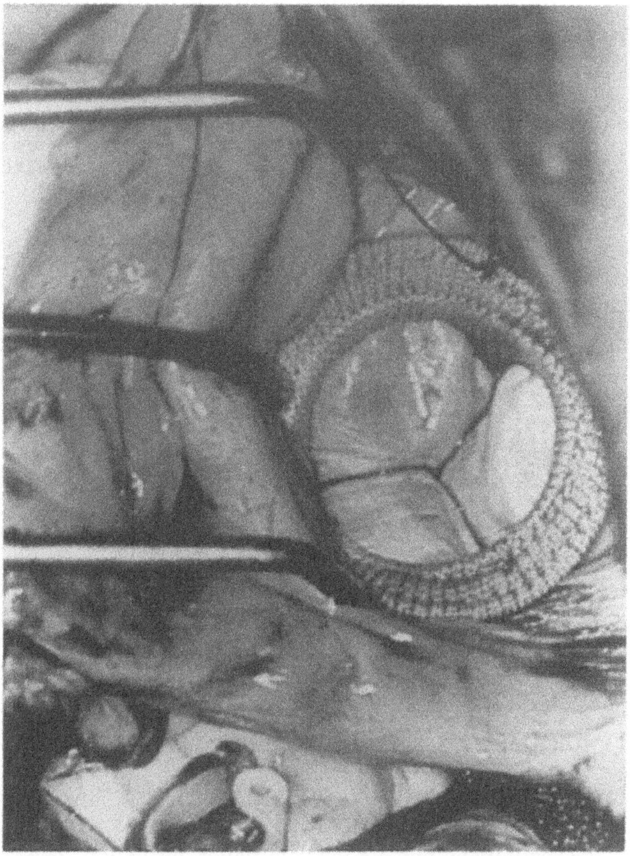

Prosthetic heart valves are available as ball or disk mechanical valves and as tissue valves. The valve device used depends on the patient's life expectancy and on anatomic and hemodynamic factors. Tissue valves are used in patients with absolute medical contraindications against continued use of anticoagulants. Mechanical valves are used in patients with a life expectancy greater than 10–15 years and no contraindications to chronic anticoagulation.

The long-term morbidity and mortality for patients with heart valve replacements may be determined by complications related to the prosthesis itself, which includes mechanical valve failure, thrombosis and thromboembolism, hemolysis, and infection.

Prosthetic heart valve designs in common use include the Starr-Edwards caged-ball valve, the Bjork-Shiley, the Lillehei-Kaster, Medtronic-Hall, Omniscience and the St. Judge tilting-disk valves, the Hancock and the Carpentier-Edwards porcine heterografts, and the Ionescu-Shiley bovine pericardium (Figure 8).

FIGURE 9. Schematic diagram of an automatic implantable cardioverter-defibrillator.

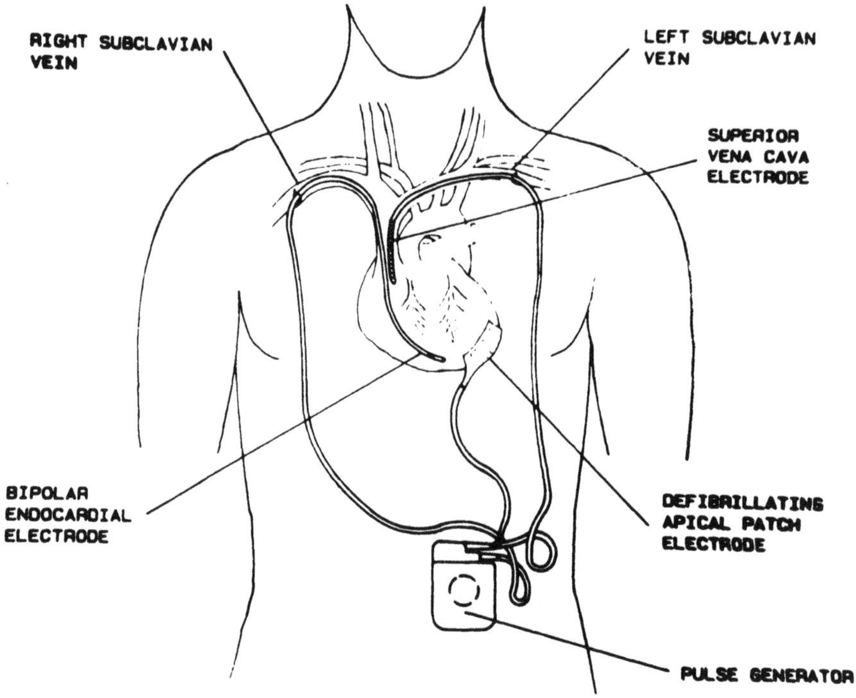

Cardiac Defibrillators and Cardioverters

About 400,000 people die annually in the United States from sudden cardiac death syndrome. This sudden cardiac death usually begins with disturbances in cardiac electrical activity culminating in ventricular fibrillation. The only reliable treatment for ventricular fibrillation is the delivery of a sufficiently strong electrical discharge to the fibrillating heart. This must be done within one or two minutes. Rarely is there enough time to bring proper medical facilities to the patient who develops ventricular fibrillation and consequently sudden death.

Because prompt treatment is required, an electronic device has been developed to continuously monitor the heart, recognize life-threatening arrhythmia, and automatically deliver the needed defibrillatory discharge.

In 1980, a pilot clinical study began at the Johns Hopkins Hospital with the automatic implantable defibrillator (Figure 9). The preliminary clinical data indicates that the device is capable of reliably (1) monitoring cardiac electrical activity for a prolonged time, (2) recognizing ventricular fibrillation and ventricular tachycardias, and (3) delivering effective treatment.

The automatic implantable defibrillator is one development aimed at treating out-of-hospital ventricular fibrillation and other potentially lethal arrhythmias. Presently, a number of important functional and structural improvements have been incorporated into the newer devices, which have such capabilities as cardioverting and extensive noninvasive interrogation.

Clinical experiences to date indicate that the automatic cardioverter-defibrillator can identify and correct ventricular fibrillation and hemodynamically unstable ventricular tachycardias. No undue risks or side effects have been described. Although additional experience and larger studies are needed to reach ultimate conclusions, it is evident that the implanted cardioverter-defibrillator does effectively manage potentially lethal arrhythmias. Results from the first automatic defibrillators have been so impressive that the FDA approved the device for widespread use in 1985.

A new, lightweight cardioverter has been used successfully in patients with sustained ventricular tachycardia. However, the device cannot be used in all patients with sudden-onset tachycardia because it does not have a backup defibrillation capacity.

The most recent development is the combined automatic implantable cardioverter-defibrillator, which prevents sudden arrhythmia death by continuously monitoring the cardiac rhythm. It is an implantable electronic device that identifies ventricular tachycardia and ventricular fibrillation and delivers an effective countershock to restore normal rhythm.

The implantable automatic internal cardioverter-defibrillator offers the potential for a significant reduction in deaths caused by ventricular tachyarrhythmias, but patients must be carefully selected to ensure that the risks do not outweigh the benefits. There must be a detailed preoperative pathophysiological evaluation of the patients. This includes careful documentation of the probable cause of the ventricular tachyarrhythmia, evaluation of other surgical needs of the patient, and evaluation of the interactive effects of pacemakers and concurrent postoperative pharmacologic therapy.

The risks and complications associated with the use of implantable cardioverter-defibrillators are similar to those observed in patients with implanted pacemakers. Because implantation of the device requires extensive surgery and general anesthesia, peri- and postoperative complications can be expected in very sick patients. Complications include infection, postoperative subcutaneous bleeding, and electrode (lead) fractures. Fractures, however, have been virtually eliminated by replacing the silver tinsel material used for fabrication of the leads with drawn braided strands. Lead dislodgment would require repositioning. Spurious electric shocks do occur occasionally and are still a concern, but they have not resulted in known serious arrhythmias or other dangerous effects.

Cardiac Pacemakers

The implantable cardiac pacemakers (Figure 10) have been extensively investigated and successfully utilized. Their medical and legal aspects will be discussed next in some detail.

FIGURE 10. Dual chamber pacemaker with atrial and ventricular leads attached.

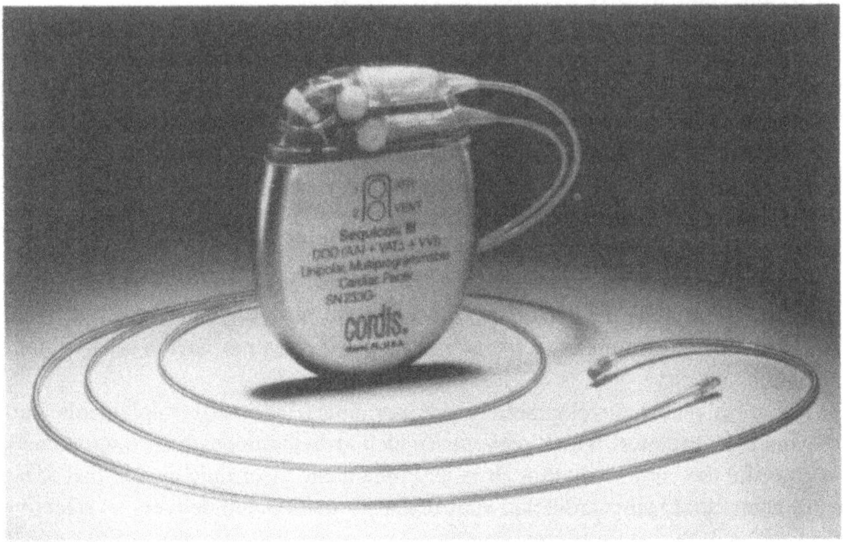

MEDICAL ASPECTS OF IMPLANTABLE CARDIAC PACEMAKERS

Electrical Impulse Generation and Transmission in the Normal Human Heart

The heart has an inherent natural pacemaker rhythm with a highly developed electrical circuitry system that controls the heart rate and the normal sinus rhythm. Electrical impulses are generated in the primary pacemaker, the sinoatrial (SA) node located in the upper portion of the right atrium (a heart chamber). Upon exiting the SA node, the electrical impulse travels first through the walls of the two upper heart chambers, the right and left atria. The electrical impulse travels next through the specialized heart ''wiring''—namely, the atrioventricular (AV) node, the Bundle of His, the right and left bundle branches (or fascicles), and the Purkinje fibers. Finally, the electrical impulse spreads through the muscle cells of the lower heart chambers, the right and left ventricles, causing heart muscular contractions and secondarily pumping blood out of the heart to the body.

Under normal circumstances, every electrical impulse that exits the SA node stimulates the heart muscle of the atrial and ventricular chambers to contract in a timed manner, which leads to optimum heart pump action and blood circulation.

Abnormal and Irregular Heart Rhythms (Cardiac Dysrhythmias or Arrhythmias)

The normal heart beats regularly at a rate of between 60 and 100 beats per minute. Under certain physiologic conditions, as in a conditioned athlete or during sleep, the heart rate may be slow (bradycardia). It may speed up (tachycardia) with exercise, stress, or adrenaline release.

In contrast, abnormal alterations in heart rhythm may result in different types of irregular heart rhythms (arrhythmias) caused by oversensitivity or a system breakdown in one or more components of the native electrical heart circuitry—that is, the nodes, bundles, fibers, and heart muscle cells. When the primary natural pacemaker, the SA node, breaks down, secondary pacemakers generally take over in an attempt to maintain the blood circulation and preserve life. The normally regular heart rhythm may become erratic, ominously fast, or exceedingly slow and may lead to cardiac fibrillation or total electrical cardiac arrest and death.

Cardiac arrhythmias may occur alone. Frequently, however, cardiac disorders are associated with some type of irregular or abnormal heart rhythm. These include congenital heart disorders, acquired valvular disease, coronary arteriosclerosis, cardiomyopathies, pericarditis, and heart trauma, all of which could untowardly affect the normal function of the natural electrical heart circuitry. The heart rate may also be altered by hormones, food metabolites, and pharmaceutical drugs.

Essential Properties of Artificial Cardiac Pacemakers

Certain capabilities of an artificial pacemaker are essential. These include a variety of basic electrical functions. Two of the basic functions of an artificial pacemaker system are, first, its ability to sense and detect very low signals generated by the heart muscle itself, and second, its ability to stimulate the heart muscle to contract.

1. *Pulse Generator:* The pulse generator, or pacemaker power pack, delivers an electrical current pulse to the heart muscle via the pacing lead or electrode. A pulse generator with a capacitor discharge output produces a typical pulse shape of a specific duration and amplitude and a certain pulse energy. The minimum energy required to initiate a stable, repetitive heart muscle stimulation is the threshold energy.
2. *Pacing Lead:* The electrical pulse that is delivered from the pacemaker pulse generator is transmitted to the heart muscle via the pacing lead or electrode. The lead tip surface is in contact with the heart muscle and has an influence on heart muscle stimulation. The higher the current density over the surface and the lower the polarization, the higher are the energy current pulses delivered to the heart muscle.
3. *Impedance and Stimulation Threshold:* Low impedance is of great importance when

checking the pacing lead. The position of the lead tip must be as close as possible to the excitable heart muscle. Heart muscle reacts to the lead tip, which is a foreign body, by building a capsule of connective tissue (fibrosis) around the lead tip. This produces displacement of the lead tip away from the heart muscle, causing an increased stimulation threshold. The heart muscle also reacts to the lead tip with an inflammatory reaction. Both the inflammatory reaction and the formation of connective tissue at the lead tip site may influence the sensing and stimulation of heart muscle by the pacemaker lead.

4. *Refractory Period:* When the pacemaker senses an electrical impulse from the heart, it becomes totally inactivated for a determined period of time. This is called the absolute refractory period. There is a secondary period, which is called the relative refractory period, during which time the detection of a new signal from the heart muscle will initiate a new refractory period. Both the absolute and the relative refractory period are referred to as the refractory period of the pulse generator.
5. *Under- and Oversensing:* Problems can arise with undersensing or oversensing of a pacemaker. A faultless pulse generator may at times be wrongly suspected of malfunctioning when in fact there is a misinterpretation of the clinical situation. In attempting to obtain the best lead tip, one looks for low polarization at the tip surface, high current density by minimizing fibrous tissue growth, low and stable thresholds, low source impedance, and improved electrocardiographic QRS identification at the lead tip-to-tissue interface.
6. *Pacemaker Programmability:* Programmable features of cardiac pacemakers include rate, energy output (voltage, current, and/or pulse duration), refractory period, and other modes of function. Included among their diagnostic and therapeutic capabilities are noninvasive threshold measurement, energy-saving programmability, a battery test phase, and a varothreshold test phase.

Reed Switches

Reed switches are present in most modern pacemakers. They are very well designed, manufactured, and tested. However, the components of the reed switches are relatively fragile and prone to failure. Because they are mechanical switches, the rates at which they open and close are limited compared to electronic or transistor switching rates. Because pacemakers are electronically sophisticated and require high data transfer rates, the reed switches are a significant limiting factor in the communication link.

Reed switches are required in the American Pacemaker, the Cook (ARCO), Cordis/Teletronics, Cardiac Pacemaker, Inc. (CPI), Medtronic, and Pacesetter types of pacemakers. The Daig-Medcor and Intermedics pacemakers do not require a reed switch. Each pacemaker is equipped with a data-encoding scheme and has an actual information transfer rate in the programming systems. Manufacturers have implemented schemes for programming security and verification. Asynchronous spacing during programming is both unnecessary and undesirable. This occurs in systems that have incorporated a magnetic reed switch in the programming system.

The pacemaker operation may be affected by extraneous noise sources and other manufacturers' programmers. The most noticeable effect is aberrant pacemaker rates during programming. This type of programming system results in a temporary inhibition of the pacemaker as long as programming energy pulses are issued by the programmer. Some pacemakers revert to asynchronous pacing, and others develop prolonged pulse-to-pulse intervals.

Pacemaker Codes and Modes of Funtion

Pacemakers are classified by the five-letter code of the Inter-Society Commission for Heart Disease Resources as follows:

1. Position I designates the heart chamber(s) paced:
   A for Atrium;
   V for Ventricle; and
   D for both (Dual) A and V.
2. Position II designates the heart chamber(s) sensed.
   A for Atrium;
   V for Ventricle;
   D for both (Dual) A and V; and
   O for None (zero).
3. Position III describes the mode of pacemaker response(s) to myocardial electrical activity:
   T for triggered;
   I for inhibited;
   D for both (dual) T and I;
   O for neither T or I; or
   R for reversely activated at fast rates only.
4. Position IV describes whether the pacemaker programming functions are:
   O (zero) for not programmable;
   P for programmable as to rates and/or output;
   M for multiprogrammable; or
   C for communicating.
5. Position V refers to special pacemaker antitachyarrhythmic functions:
   B for bursts of pacemaker discharges;
   N for normal rate function;
   S for scanning; and
   E for external.

Thus, as an example, a pacemaker with the designation VVIMN is a commonly used one that:

Position I: paces the ventricle (V);

Position II: senses the ventricle (V);

Position III: responds to myocardial activity by inhibition (I);

Position IV: is multiprogrammable (M); and

Position V: has a rate competition that is normal (N).

Table 1 summarizes the pacemaker types and their modes of function utilizing for simplification the first three letters of the five-letter code.

Pacemaker Power Sources (Batteries)

In 1958, a rechargeable nickle-cadmium battery was used to power the first implanted pacemaker by Senning. That battery proved unsatisfactory, but a later improved model introduced for clinical use in 1973 was remarkably good.

During the 1960s, zinc–mercuric oxide batteries were used to power most pacemakers. Some of those batteries had a small amount of manganese dioxide added to prevent internal self-discharge. Silver was added to amalgamate with the liquid mercury that evolved as the battery cell was discharged.

Plutonium-238–powered nuclear pacemakers were developed and tested in the 1960s and 1970s. Their use has been limited.

Presently, most pacemakers are powered by high-energy lithium anode batteries. The latter have long-lasting lives, and they are reliable, simple, and less costly than nuclear-powered pacemakers. Lithium anode batteries may have a variety of cathodes including iodine, manganese dioxide, bromine, lead iodide, silver chromate, copper sulfide, or thionyl chloride.

Several testing methods are available to accurately predict or determine battery life, such as the accelerated discharge data (ADD) and the capacity achieved from normal discharge data (CANDID), used by Wilson Greatbatch Limited, a major manufacturer of lithium battery cells.

Guidelines for Implanting Permanent Cardiac Pacemakers

Guidelines for implantation of permanent cardiac pacemakers that were developed by the joint American College of Cardiology/American Heart Association (ACC/AHA) Task Force for both single- and dual-chamber pacemakers are noted in Tables 2, 3, and 4.

Follow-up of Pacemaker Recipients (Implantees)

Over half a million individuals in the United States have implanted permanent pacemakers. Follow-up of these patients is accomplished principally by cardiologists in an office setting or via transtelephonic monitoring, the purpose being to detect pacemaker malfunction.

In addition to the history, physical findings, and test results the implantee's office medical records should include the name of the pacemaker manufacturer, generator model number, lead type, and factory-set parameters. The latter may have been altered, and the subsequent program values and the date of the pro-

TABLE 1. Types and Mode(s) of Function of Implantable Pacemakers

Type of Pacemakers	Mode(s) of Function	Position I: Chamber Paced	Position II: Chamber Sensed	Position III: Pacemaker Response
Atrial Asynchronous (fixed rate)	AOO	Atrium(A)	None	None
Ventricular Asynchronous (fixed rate)	VOO	Ventricle(V)	None	None
Atrioventricular Asynchronous (fixed rate)	DOO	Both A & V	None	None
Atrial Demand, Atrial Inhibited	AAT	Atrium	Atrium	Inhibited(I)
Atrial Demand, Atrial Triggered	AAT	Atrium	Atrium	Triggered(T)
Ventricular Demand, Ventricular Inhibited	VVI	Ventricle	Ventricle	Inhibited(I)
Ventricular Demand, Ventricular Triggered	VVT	Ventricle	Ventricle	Triggered(T)
Atrial Synchronous, Ventricular Triggered	VAT	Ventricle	Atrial	Triggered(T)
Atrial Synchronous, Ventricular Inhibited	VDD	Ventricle	A & V	Inhibited(I)
Atrioventricular Sequential	DVI	A & V	Ventricle	Inhibited(I)
Universal Atrioventricular Triggered and/or Inhibited	DDD	A & V	A & V	T and/or I

TABLE 2. Generally Agreed-Upon Guidelines by ACC/AHA Task Force for Permanent Cardiac Pacemaker Implantation

Type of Pacemaker	Indications for Pacemaker Implantation
AAI, Atrial Single Chamber	Symptomatic sinus node dysfunction (sick sinus syndrome), provided AV conduction is shown to be adequate by appropriate tests.
VVI, Ventricular Single Chamber	Any symptomatic bradyarrhythmia, but particularly when there is: 1. no significant atrial hemodynamic contribution (atrial flutter/fibrillation, giant atria) or 2. no evidence of pacemaker syndrome due to loss of atrial contribution or negative atrial kick (a replacement pacemaker)
VVD, Dual Chamber	Requirements for ventricular pacing when adequate atrial rates and adequate intracavitary atrial complexes are present. This includes the presence of complete AV block in patients: 1. requiring atrial contribution for hemodynamic benefit, or 2. with previous or anticipated pacemaker syndrome.
DVI, Dual Chamber	The need for synchronous atrial ventricular contraction with symptomatic bradycardia and a slow atrial rate. Patients with previously documented pacemaker syndrome.
DDD Dual Chamber	Requirement for AV synchrony over a wide range of rates such as: 1. the active or young patient with atrial rates responsive to clinical need, 2. significant hemodynamic need, and 3. pacemaker syndrome during previous pacemaker experience or a reduction in systolic blood pressure of more than 20 mm Hg during ventricular pacing at the time of pacemaker implantation (with or without evidence of VA conduction).

gramming should all be noted and made known to the patient. The patient should carry an identification card that includes most of the above information, together with the telephone number of the patient's cardiologist. The identification card is provided by the manufacturer.

In most instances the diagnosis of pacemaker malfunction is derived from the patient's history, a physical examination, and the twelve-lead electrocardiogram. The latter is the mainstay for evaluating normal and abnormal pacer function.

TABLE 3. Divergence of Opinion Pertaining to Permanent Pacemaker Implantation As Per ACC/AHA Task Force Guidelines

Type of Pacemaker	Not Generally Agreed-Upon Indications for Pacemaker Implantation
AAI, Atrial Single Chamber	Overdrive of supraventricular or ventricular arrhythmias. Hemodynamic enhancement through rate adjustment in patients with bradycardia and symptoms of impaired cardiac output.
VVI, Ventricular Single Chamber	Synotinatuc bradtcarduam where pacing simplicity is a prime concern, in cases of: 1. senility (life-sustaining only), 2. terminal disease, 3. domicile remote from a follow-up center, or 4. intact retrograde VA (ventriculoatrial) conduction.
VVD, Dual Chamber	Normal sinus rhythm and normal AV conduction in patients needing ventricular pacing intermittently.
DVI, Dual Chamber	Overdrive of certain arrhythmias. Frequent supraventricular arrhythmias in which combined pacing and drugs have been shown to be therapeutically effective. Bradycardia-tachycardia syndrome, provided adjustment of atrial rate and AV interval terminates or prevents the emergence of supraventricular arrhythmias with or without concomitant drug administration.
DDD Dual Chamber	Complete heart block or sick sinus syndrome and stable atrial rates. Any patient in whom simultaneous control of atrial and ventricular rates inhibits tachyarrhythmias or in whom the pacemaker can be adjusted to a mode designed to interrupt the arrhythmia.

A hand-held digital analyzer may be used to accurately assess pacemaker rates and intervals such as the automatic interval; the magnet rate; the AV, VA, and hysteresis intervals; the low- and upper-rate limits; and extracorporeal interference rates.

Pacemaker capture, or pacing function, may be evaluated by applying a magnet over the power pack generator. The response to magnet application varies with the pacemaker. When evaluating battery depletion, a decrease in the magnet rate of six pulses per minute, or 10 percent, generally indicates end-of-life of the battery and a need for generator replacement.

TABLE 4. Inappropriate Implantation of Permanent Pacemaker As Per ACC/AHA Task Force Guidelines

Type of Pacemaker	Conditions Where Implanting a Pacemaker Is Inappropriate
AAI, Atrial Single Chamber	Preexisting AV conduction delay or block or if PR interval is inappropriately prolonged by atrial pacing. Inadequate intracavitary atrial complexes.
VVI, Ventricular Single Chamber	Known pacemaker syndrome (a replacement pacemaker) or symptoms produced by temporary ventricular pacing at the time of initial pacemaker implantation. The need for maximal atrial contribution, because of: 1. congestive heart failure, or 2. special need for rate responsiveness.
VVD, Dual Chamber	Frequent or persistent supraventricular tachyarrhythmias, including atrial fibrillation or flutter. Inadequate intracavitary atrial complexes.
DVI, Dual Chamber	Frequent or persistent supraventricular tachyarrhythmias, including atrial fibrillation or flutter.
DDD, Dual Chamber	Frequent or persistent supraventricular tachyarrhythmias, including atrial fibrillation or flutter. Inadequate intracavitary atrial complexes.

Pacemaker Malfunction

The five-letter code system that is used to designate pacemaker modes of function is utilized here to categorize pacemakers malfunctions.

1. Position I mode malfunction indicates failure of the pacemaker electrical discharge to pace (capture or stimulate) nonrefractory myocardial tissue. Causes of position I malfunction include:
   a. Loose lead contact with the generator;
   b. Lead insulation break;
   c. Lead wire fracture;
   d. Electrode (lead tip) displacement due to retraction, dislodgment, or myocardial perforation (penetration);
   e. Higher threshold of myocardial stimulation;
   f. Battery power depletion or end of life; and
   g. Low-threshold energy output programmed inappropriately.
2. Position II mode malfunction indicates undersensing or failure to sense native myocardial rhythm. This may result from:
   a. Poor contact (interface) between the lead tip (electrode) and the endocardium or myocardium;

b. Lead wire fracture;
c. Weak or inadequate intracardiac signal;
d. Component failure of the generator (power pack);
e. Battery power depletion or end of life; and
f. Sensitivity is programmed inappropriately.

3. Position III mode malfunction denotes problems either with inhibition or with triggering of the pacemaker. A generator, not inhibited by native heart rhythm, must produce pacing electrical stimuli; otherwise it is malfunctioning. Causes of position III malfunction include:
   a. Incomplete circuitry, such as loose connection of lead to generator, lead wire fracture, or insulation break;
   b. Component failure of pulse generator; and
   c. Battery power depletion.

   Another important position III malfunction is oversensing by the pacemaker. Causes of pacemaker oversensing include:
   a. Sensing the QRS by a single chamber atrial pacemaker in AAI mode;
   b. Sensing P- or T-waves by a single-chamber ventricular pacemaker in VVI mode;
   c. Sensing nonmyocardial myopotentials, principally pectoral and diaphragm muscles;
   d. Sensing exogenous electromagnetic waves due to microwaves, electrocautery, arc welding, and magnetic resonance imaging; and
   e. Sensing signals emanating from the pacing system itself. These signals include afterpotential sensing of generator output decay; false signals arising from partial lead fracture, magnet application, and electrolysis of dissimilar metals; and cross-talk between electrodes in DVI and DDD systems.
4. Position IV and V malfunctioning modes designated problems with programmability and/or antitachyarrhythmia functions. Examples of such malfunction include pacemaker-induced and pacemaker-mediated tachycardia, as well as failed antitachyarrhythmia functions.

Pacemaker Complications Other Than Malfunction

Like any surgical procedure, the implantation of a pacemaker carries some risk. In addition, there are always those factors which, although carefully controlled for, may go wrong once the device has been successfully implanted (Table 5).

First, there is the possibility of complications from the use of anesthetic agents and the type of surgery. The risk here is a function of whether the implanting physician uses a general or local anesthetic and whether the intrathoracic, transthoracic, or transvenous approaches are used to implant the lead. Such complications may take the form of an adverse drug reaction, perhaps an allergic reaction, which may produce only a mild rash or a serious complication that may be fatal. However, in most cases, this is not a problem.

A second source of problems, from a surgical perspective, would be that of postoperative infection or perhaps hemorrhage. Neither of these is exceptionally common, but they do occur and are surgical risks to be considered. They should be part of the patient's informed consent documentation.

Third, the pacemaker is generally implanted in a subcutaneous skin pocket,

TABLE 5. Complications of Implantable Cardiac Pacemakers

1. Pacemaker (Generator or Power Pack) Malfunction
    a. Microchips (Computer) Portion—Rhythm and Sensing
    b. Battery
    c. Casing
    d. Electrical connection between pacemaker and the electrode lead (wire).
    e. Explosion
2. Electrode Lead Complications
    a. Wire insulation problems (leakage)
    b. Wire (coiled) problems (fracture)
    c. Migration of lead
    d. Thrombosis of veins (or intracardiac chambers)
    e. Attachment problems
        (1) Connection to the pacemaker itself
        (2) Connection to the endocardium (e.g., perforation of heart)
3. Pacemaker Pocket Problems
    a. Infection
    b. Bleeding
    c. Extrusion
    d. Migration (Displacement)
4. Cardiac and Vascular Complications
    a. Thrombosis in the heart and veins
    b. Infection and generalized sepsis
    c. Perforation and cardiac tamponade
    d. Rhythm disturbance: ventricular fibrillation and death, and irregular rhythm
    e. Hypotension and cardiac failure
5. Extracardiovascular Pacemaker Complications
    a. Effects of skeletal muscle on pacemaker
    b. Effects of Pacemaker on skeletal muscle
    c. Necrosis of bowels
    d. Social and psychological problems

where it is held in place. There are times when the pacemaker, perhaps due to pressure necrosis, trauma, or simply gradual mobilization of the units, may extrude, or break out of, its skin pocket. Although this may not cause malfunctioning of the unit, it is quite painful to the patient and, if not treated, may lead to infection and other serious complications. Aside from the pacemaker generator, the impulse transmission or the receiving lead wires may, through slow movement, cause the skin overlying the wires to gradually erode, resulting in tissue death, infection, or perhaps small hemorrhage.

Fourth, the implanting surgeon (or cardiologist) may confront fragmentation, breakage, or knotting of the electrodes while they are being manipulated into place. While moving the electrodes into position, there is the possibility that the surgeon may accidentally puncture the venous walls, or, as the electrode is being moved to its final position, there may be perforation of the atrium or the ventricle of the heart. Consequently, air embolism, hemorrhaging, or thrombophlebitis (inflammation of the vein) may develop.

Pacemaker Leads

There are numerous types of pacemaker leads, some for introduction via the chest wall and others transvenously. One report suggested a seven-letter code for classifying permanent cardiac pacing leads (Table 6) which is similar to the five-letter pacemaker code.

FEDERAL REGULATION OF MEDICAL DEVICES

Medical Device Amendments

The Medical Device Amendments of 1976 (Title 21 U.S.C.S. 360c) give the Food and Drug Administration (FDA) comprehensive regulatory authority over medical devices intended for use and allow the FDA to require that such devices be proven safe prior to entering the marketplace. Medical devices fall into one of the following three classes, representing different categories of risk.

1. *Class I Medical Devices:* These devices involve the least risk to human recipients. Their safety and effectiveness can be assured merely by general regulatory requirements or controls including, for example, prohibitions on misbranding, specific requirements for good manufacturing practices and quality assurance, and record-keeping requirements. These general controls similarly apply to Classes II and III devices as their safety and effectiveness must be assured.
2. *Class II Medical Devices:* In addition to general controls for safety and effectiveness, this class of devices requires "standards" that indeed serve to provide assurances that the devices are both safe and effective.
3. *Class III Medical Devices:* This class of devices must have premarket approval, in addition to general controls and standards, to assure their safety and effective performance. Included in the Class III devices are those that sustain human life and those that prevent disease or injury. Implantable cardiac pacemakers, ventricular assist devices, and artificial hearts fall into this class.

Consumer Product Safety Act

The Consumer Product Safety Act (CPSA) of 1972, which was revised in 1981 (Title 15 U.S.C. §§ 2051 to 2081), has a medical device standard setting that is very similar to the Medical Device Amendments of 1976. The CPSA was created for the purpose of protecting the public against unreasonable risks of injury associated with consumer products. The Consumer Product Safety Com-

TABLE 6. Suggested Nomenclature Code for Cardiac Pacing Leads

Position I Mode	Position II Localization	Position III Fixation Elements	Position IV Material	Position V Tip Form	Position VI Shape	Position VII Polarity
E = endocardial	A = atrial	S = screw-in	C = carbon	C = cylindric	J = J-shaped	U = unipolar
M = myocardial	V = ventricular	Sr = screw-in (retractable)	V = vitreous carbon	R = ring	O = without shape memory	B = bipolar
Ep = epicardial	D = double	Sd = double screw-in	P = platinum	S = spherical		M = multipolar
EM = epimyocardial	Cs = coronary sinus	A = anchored	Pi = platinum-iridium	P = porous		
		H = helicoid	E = Elgiloy	M = multiedge		
		T = tined	A = alloy	V = various		
		F = flanged				
		O = none, without fixation				

Bredikis and Stirbys. 1985. *PACE* 8: 321.

mission was empowered by Congress to make mandatory product safety standards.

Manufacturer liability may be incurred where human injuries result from failure of manufacturers of implantable medical devices to abide by the above-mentioned statutory provisions.

LIABILITY OF PHYSICIANS AND HOSPITALS

The implantation of a pacemaker, defibrillator, or any other cardiac device is burdened with the usual legal problems inherent in any medical or surgical procedure.

Negligence

A physician may be held liable either for negligent failure to implant a pacemaker, defibrillator, and other cardiovascular devices, when such devices are indicated, or for negligently implanting a device that is not medically indicated. Undue delay in implantation of a device may constitute negligence.

A physician may be found negligent for failing to properly advise the patient of the signs of device malfunction. Patients should be warned about the possibility of pacemaker malfunction due to microwave ovens, magnetometers, or radar systems. Patients should be taught how to monitor their own heart rates at home and should know what their own rates should be. They should be advised about which changes in heart rate may signal malfunction. Generator malfunction can lead to sudden death. The physician has a duty to fully inform and educate patients on how to recognize possible warning signs.

A patient who is injured during the implantation procedure may bring a tort action against the attending and consulting physicians, the hospital, and the device manufacturer. The plaintiff may allege any of the following:

1. Negligent failure to reach a decision on whether to implant a device when such is clearly indicated medically;
2. Negligent failure to warn the patient of potential material risks, side effects, and complications;
3. Improper selection of the type of pacing system;
4. Negligent postimplantation care; and
5. Implantation of a particular generator under certain circumstances without appropriate prior electrophysiologic studies.

Negligence could result from the improper placement of a fixed-rate, ventricular pacemaker in a patient who subsequently would develop return of AV conduction, producing symptomatic competition of the pacemaker and the inherent rhythm. Failure to recognize electrophysiologic signs of biological pacemaker function may result in inappropriate surgery with medico-legal implications.

The types of negligence discussed above all involve failure of the physician, hospital, or both to adhere to the appropriate standard of care in treatment of the patient. These types of claims deal with the service aspect of implantation as distinguished from the product aspect. None of the actions discussed so far would include allegations of a defective product.

Prosser sets out four necessary elements for a cause of action sounding in negligence:

1. A duty, or obligation, recognized by the law, requiring the actor to conform to a certain standard of conduct for the protection of others against unreasonable risks;
2. A failure on his part to conform to the standard required. These two elements go to make up what the courts usually have called negligence; but the term quite frequently is applied to the second alone. Thus it may be said that the defendant was negligent but is not liable because he was under no duty to the plaintiff not to be;
3. A reasonable close causal connection between the conduct and the resulting injury. This is what is commonly known as ''legal cause'' or ''proximate cause'';
4. Actual loss or damage resulting to the interests of another.

In pacemaker cases, the treating cardiologist or cardiovascular surgeon is a specialist and is held to a national and more rigid standard of care than the nonspecialist. National standards, set notably by the American Heart Association, the American Colleges of Cardiology and of Cardiac and Thoracic Surgeons, the American Medical Association, and the American Hospital Association, are adopted by the courts.

The standards of care involving negligent pacemaker implantation (surgery) is set by the medical profession. This is an unusual situation in the law because as a general rule common care is not necessarily proper care.

However, the traditional standards of care set by the medical profession itself are being eroded by judicial establishment of legal standards set as a matter of law without a need for expert medical testimony. Presently, negligence as a matter of law has been applied to cases involving physicians' failure to perform simple and safe diagnostic tests and deviation, as well as failure to follow standards set by the Joint Commission on Accreditation of Hospitals and Drug Manufacturers.

Defenses to Negligence

Contributory negligence: to the injury that is caused by the pacemaker recipient. Assumption of the risk by the pacemaker recipient, for example, the ''twiddler syndrome'' where the patient twiddles with the pacemaker leading to erosion of the skin and protrusion of the pacemaker or the wire electrode lead;

Error in Judgment: The physician, in the exercise of due care in making his diagnosis, is under a duty to fully inform himself of the facts in the case. If the physician has exercised due care in informing himself (by ordering appropriate tests, examinations, etc.) as to the patient's condition, an error in the interpretation of these results where medical practitioners could have differed as to the proper interpretation is not negligence.

Running of the Statutes of Limitation: This would be the period during which the law permits the plaintiff to bring an action alleging malpractice, in this case involving pacemakers. This period varies in different states, but it is generally limited to a period of two years. In *Reyes v. Anka Research, Ltd.* (New York, 1981), which dealt with an implantable intrauterine device, the court held that when a foreign object is negligently left in the body, the cause of action will accrue at the time of reasonable discovery of the foreign object and malpractice and not when the object was introduced into the body. The *Reyes* court stated also that the physician who is following the patient-plaintiff with an implanted device has a duty to advise the patient of a manufacturer's recall of the implanted device.

Discovery of Medical Records of Recipients Other Than Patient (Plaintiff)

In *Ziegler v. Superior Court in and for the City of Pima* (Arizona, 1982), the court held that where medical malpractice is claimed for unnecessary implantation of a pacemaker, the plaintiff may be entitled to the medical records of other patients who have undergone similar procedures. In *Ziegler,* the plaintiff, having alleged that the defendant doctors unnecessarily implanted a pacemaker and that the defendant hospital breached its duty to supervise and control the administration of medical services, was allowed on discovery to obtain 24 medical records of other hospital patients who had undergone similar pacemaker implantation surgeries. The court held, however, that the discovery would be limited to the contents of the medical records and that all clues to the identity of the other patients must be deleted.

Lack of Informed Consent or Lack of Informed Refusal

The patient should be fully informed of and involved in each phase of the diagnosis and treatment of cardiac arrhythmias. This legal duty is being imposed by courts in all aspects of medical care. If a patient's differential diagnosis includes cardiac arrhythmia and the physician decides not to confirm the diagnosis by further testing, the patient must be fully advised of this decision and its implications. Also, the physician must fulfill the requirements of informed refusal. If the patient refuses additional testing or implantation of a pacemaker, defibrillator, or other device, the patient must be fully informed and advised of all the material risks of his or her decision to refuse the device. Permanent devices are generally not indicated unless the patient has a potentially life-threatening arrhythmia. Failure to inform the patient as to his or her decision carries potentially serious legal liability.

The initial consent of the patient who is to receive a pacemaker is an absolute necessity. The doctrine of informed consent places a further qualification on the consent, requiring that for the consent to be operative, the patient must have been fully informed of the risks inherent in the pacemaker implantation procedure. Failure to inform the patient vitiates the consent. The cause of action arises if any of the inherent risks occur, regardless of the physician's skill or care.

If a patient undergoes pacemaker implantation without informed consent, the attending or consulting physician may be subjected to allegations of "technical battery" on grounds of lack of informed consent. This is particularly likely to happen if complications occur and the plaintiff proves that a proper warning of the material risks involved in the procedure was not provided by the physician.

Early cases dealing with informed consent tended to emphasize the battery aspect of the theory, while later cases have analyzed it in terms of negligence.

Examples of the requisite disclosures include the hazards of the proposed treatment, the alternative methods of treatment available, and the consequences of forgoing treatment. All disclosures should be readily comprehensible to the layman. Medical terms should be avoided if at all possible and explained lucidly when used.

Therefore, clear explanations and frank disclosures of the risks are essential elements of any consent form prepared for patients.

Breach of Physician-Patient Contract

When treating patients with cardiac rhythm disorders, or for that matter any other ailment, a physician-patient relationship is created that is basically contractual. The physician may vary the standard of care or may even guarantee a cure (when implanting the pacemaker) either by an oral or a written express contract. But when a cardiac patient in whom a cardiovascular device is to be implanted is merely being reassured, the physician should be wary not to inadvertently contract with that patient to effect a cure.

As in any doctor-patient relationship, the cardiologist or thoracic surgeon may be liable for breach of contract if that physician guarantees a specific result or cure. Physicians should avoid making any statements that could be misunderstood as an implied or expressed guarantee of a specific outcome. Generally, the "reasonable man" standard is used to determine whether a contract was made. Would a "reasonable man" in the patient's situation understand the physician's words as a guarantee? If so, legal liability may result for failure to obtain the promised results.

A cause of action based in contract has two major effects. First, the statutes of limitation is longer for a contract action. Second, some elements of damages are lost, including punitive damages.

Abandonment

The patient with a pacemaker must be followed for life. The withdrawal by the physician, for example, by discontinuing necessary follow-up, without the patient's consent, from the existing physician-patient relationship may create liability for abandonment. The physician generally agrees, either verbally, by his actions, or by a preexisting agreement, to treat the patient and to evaluate the function on a continuing basis as well as be on the alert for potential complications resulting from the implanted cardiovascular device.

Abandonment may be characterized as either negligent or intentional. When abandonment results from intentional conduct, punitive damages may be sought be the injured patient (plaintiff).

The characterization of abandonment depends heavily upon the physician's intention and state of mind. Conscious refusal to continue treatment of the patient with an implanted cardiovascular device may have consequences different from mere failure to properly follow up the patient with an implanted device.

"Assault" and Battery

Battery is the touching, intentionally and without consent, of one's person by another. A patient generally consents to a certain amount of contact. This does not mean that the physician is immune from liability for battery. The key is the extent of permitted contact.

The important role played by consent to touching was explained by Justice Cardoza in *Schoendorff v. Society of New York Hospital:* "Every human being of adult years and sound mind has a right to determine what shall be done with his own body; and a surgeon who performs an operation without his patient's consent commits an assault, for which he is liable in damages."

The physician works at the patient's sufferance. The patient may either refuse to give consent initially or may withdraw his consent, thereby precluding treatment.

One caveat is in order when reading decisions dealing with a physician's battery. Although "assault" and "battery" are distinct torts, courts sometimes use the terms interchangeably or refer to a battery as "assault and battery." Since contact is the essence of the tort, a physician may batter an unconscious or anesthetized patient by implanting a nonemergency cardiovascular device.

Patients who require pacemakers may be minors or mentally incompetent due to psychiatric disorders, physical infirmities, and drug misuse or abuse. Here, the physician must obtain a valid consent from a person who is legally capable of rendering such consent, be that person a parent, a relative, or a guardian *ad litem*.

Written consent of the implantee patient should be routinely acquired both in hospitals and in office settings. Written consent forms serve to prevent a cause of action in battery, but they do not prevent a cause of action based upon the patient's lack of informed consent.

In emergency situations, consent is implied by law where a patient requires pacemaker implantation. Here it is presumed that had the patient been conscious or capable of giving consent, he or she would have consented to the cardiovascular implanation procedure.

Res Ipsa Loquitur

Pacemaker surgery is not immune to inadvertently leaving sponges or needles subcutaneously in the subcutaneous pocket housing the pacemaker. Unexplainable pacemaker surgical complications may raise a presumption of negligence.

Res ipsa loquitur is a Latin phrase that means "the thing speaks for itself" and has its origin in early English law. It has become increasingly significant in professional medical malpractice cases. The conditions required for the application of the principle of *res ipsa loquitur* are stated by Prosser as follows:

1. The event must be of a kind that ordinarily does not occur in the absence of someone's negligence;
2. It must be caused by an agency or instrumentality within the exclusive control of the defendant; and
3. It must not have been due to any voluntary action or contribution on the part of the plaintiff.

The primary impact of *res ipsa loquitur* in medical malpractice cases has been to obviate the plaintiff's need to prove negligence by expert medical testimony. Therefore, by introducing circumstantial evidence, *res ipsa loquitur* allows the jury to infer that someone was negligent, without the assistance of expert testimony. The jury acts upon the knowledge of the "common man."

In cases involving multiple defendants, such as a surgical team, *res ipsa loquitur* has been applied to force the defendants to "explain or pay." Here pressure is placed upon multiple defendants to present evidence exculpating themselves. If they do not, the jury is free to assign liability where it sees fit, a chance most defendants would be unwilling to take.

Although the doctrine of *res ipsa loquitur* is generally accepted, its application to medical malpractice cases varies widely in different jurisdictions. Hence, careful research is absolutely essential when *res ipsa* is relied upon in lieu of expert testimony.

Fraud and Misrepresentation

In pacemaker recipients, as in all medical device cases, it is mandatory that honest, complete, and forthright disclosures be given to patients regarding medical facts about the pacemaker, the lead used, and the known complications of surgery, as well as fees for services and prices of the implanted device.

The classic case of fraud involves a physician who has intentionally withheld information vital to the patient. Some jurisdictions, however, have adopted a "negligence" type of rule, imposing liability upon a physician who fails to discover a prior error during a subsequent examination.

Fraud ordinarily requires that the medical device recipient, to his detriment, must have justifiably relied upon a material representation made by the defendant physician that was known by the physician to be false. The disparity in knowledge between the physician and patient, coupled with the natural trust placed in the physician, will satisfy the requirements for fraud in the physician-patient situation.

The statute of limitations in implant cases generally begins to run from the time of the commission of the negligent act, or from the time the act's existence was or should have been discovered, with the exercise of ordinary diligence. It would be manifestly unjust to allow the defendant to profit from his own wrong by concealing his tortious action from the plaintiff until the statute of limitations has expired.

Fraud, therefore, may be an entirely separate cause of action in medical malpractice cases, or it may be used to toll the statute of limitations.

Other causes of action in medical malpractice cases include:

1. Defamation (libel and slander);
2. Invasion of privacy and disclosure of confidential communication;
3. Infliction of mental distress, outrageous conduct by a health care provider, and gross negligence;
4. False imprisonment, wrongful commitment, and abuse of process; and
5. Vicarious, corporate and strict liability.

LIABILITY OF PACEMAKER MANUFACTURERS

Negligence

Manufacturers of defective implantable devices may be held liable under several legal theories. A tort action in negligence may be brought against the manufacturer of a device for defective design or manufacture of the product. Recovery may be based on negligent failure to conform to the appropriate standard requiring due care in design, manufacture, assembly, packaging, inspection, or testing. However, an action in negligence poses difficulty in proving each of the necessary elements.

Strict Product Liability

Difficulties in proving negligence in implanted device cases have led to the development of the doctrine of strict product liability. Under this doctrine, the manufacturer can be held liable for a defect despite the exercise of all possible due care in design and manufacture of the product. No proof of negligence is necessary. Liability is based on the theory that the manufacturer owes a duty of care to the ultimate consumer to protect that consumer from defects. No contractual relationship or privity between the consumer and the manufacturer need exist. Currently, the trend is toward "increased and widespread" application of this doctrine.

Difficulty in applying § 402(a) of the Second Restatement of Torts arises when the defendant is not the manufacturer. The section applies to the "one who sells" the product and is "engaged in the business of selling" the product. Most courts have held that neither physicians nor hospitals fall within the scope of § 402(a). However, hospitals and physicians may incur liability for failure to inspect the device for discoverable defects.

Failing to warn of dangers also may result in a manufacturer's liability regardless of whether a defect exists. The manufacturer may not be subject to strict product liability if adequate warnings of all potential hazards are given to the physician/purchaser. In such cases, the physician's failure to heed and disclose the dangers to the patient is deemed a superseding cause that relieves the manufacturer from liability. However, if the dangers to the patient is deemed a superseding cause that relieves the manufacturer from liability. However, if the dangers and warnings are minimized or downplayed, the manufacturer may be found negligent. Also, if the physician's acts were reasonably foreseeable in light of the warnings, a manufacturer will not be exonerated from liability.

In *Feldman v. Lederle Laboratories* (1984) the plaintiff brought suit against a manufacturer of a drug she had taken that caused her teeth to discolor. The court held that drug manufacturers have a duty to warn of dangers they knew or should have known on the basis of reasonably obtainable knowledge.

A product may be unsafe because of inadequate instructions, and inadequate warning may constitute a design defect. Generally, the manufacturer will be held to a "reasonable man" standard in determinations of whether the warning is inadequate. Five relevant standards concerning the adequacy of warnings have been identified.

1. The warning must adequately indicate the scope of the danger;
2. The warning must reasonably communicate the extent or seriousness of the harm that could result from misuse;
3. The physical aspects of the warning must be adequate to alert a reasonably prudent person to the danger;
4. A simple directive warning may be considered inadequate when it fails to state the consequence that might result from failure to follow it; and

5. The means of conveying the warning must be adequate—the drug manufacturer must bring the warning home to the doctor.

Warranty Cause of Action

Most suits against manufacturers are based on an express or implied warranty. Most pacemakers carry an express warranty for replacement in the event of a defect. Rarely, however, does the patient see this warranty. This, coupled with the fact that the physician selects the brand of implant to be used, makes it very difficult for the patient to prove reliance on an express warranty. To succeed in an action for breach of express warranty, the plaintiff must prove (a) existence of the express warranty, (b) scope of coverage of the warranty, and (c) reliance on the warranty.

Implied warranties include warranty for fitness for purpose and warranty for merchantability. To recover under a theory of implied warranty, the plaintiff must prove (a) that the product was defective when it was sold to him, (b) that because of the defect the pacemaker did not conform to the implied warranty, and (c) that the defect was the proximate cause of the injury.

A New York court held that expert medical testimony would be necessary for plaintiff to succeed on a warranty cause of action. The plaintiff brought an action against Medtronics for breach of express and implied warranty. Evidence at trial showed there were at least three possible reasons why the pacemaker electrode broke, causing the plaintiff's injury. The court held that a finding by the jury as to the cause of the break, *without the aid of medical testimony,* would be highly speculative and presumptuous. Without medical testimony, the jury would have no ground upon which to base a finding of breach of warranty.

Literature supplied with a pacemaker is not an express warranty as a matter of law. In this case, the literature dealt with the "life expectancy" of the power pack. Although there may have been an express warranty as to the power pack, there was none with respect to the electrode. Since there was no allegation that the battery failed, the express warranty was found to be irrelevant.

Problems of Specific Parties

1. *The Plaintiff:* The plaintiff may have difficulty should he desire to bring a class-action suit based on a defective product. In 1977 Medtronics recalled a specific model of pacemaker due to a possible defect. One month later, a class-action suit was instituted by a patient who was required to undergo a second operation to replace his defective pacemaker. Mr. Ross attempted to sue on behalf of himself and 4,000 other patients who were similarly affected by the recall. The court refused to allow the class action because:
   a. the defendant's liability could vary from claim to claim;
   b. damages could range from essentially nonexistent to a suit for wrongful death;
   c. the pleadings did not suggest a preponderance of common questions of law; and

d. issues related to statute of limitations, contributory negligence, and assumption of risk could vary from state to state and would require diverse rulings by the court.

The court concluded that the action was particularly ill suited for prosecution as a class action.

The plaintiff may have a potential problem in obtaining personal jurisdiction over the defendant. The plaintiff must establish that the manufacturer has sufficient "minimum contacts" to allow the court to exercise jurisdiction. Merely placing the pacemaker into the stream of commerce, with no knowledge about where the patient who ultimately receives it will reside, may not be adequate to allow jurisdiction over the defendant in the plaintiff's home state.

2. *Doctors and Hospitals as Defendants:* In general, a warranty cause of action for a defective pacemaker cannot be sustained against a physician or hospital. The courts have generally held that the sale of the device is incidental to the services provided by the hospital and physician and so they are not subject to a warranty cause of action.

Also, at present, courts have generally rejected the application of strict tort liability to the physician or hospital. To come within the doctrine, the defendants must be "in the business of selling" the defective product. The courts have refused to hold that the physician or hospital is engaged in the true "sale" of the pacemaker.

Statute of Limitation

Where a wrongful-death cause of action is brought alleging the death resulted from the placement of a defective pacemaker, the statute of limitations begins to run from the date of death, not from the date of the injury from which death resulted.

Disclosure of Manufacturer's Test Results on a Defective Pacemaker

In a personal injury case caused by a malfunctioning pacemaker, there is no duty on the part of the manufacturer to disclose documents showing test results on the defective pacemaker. Only if the information could no longer be duplicated because of a change in conditions and withholding the information would result in injustice or undue hardship will disclosure be compelled.

In another case, plaintiff brought action for personal injuries caused by a malfunctioning Intermedics, Inc. pacemaker. The defendant requested that plaintiff send the pacemaker back; plaintiff did. Then Intermedics performed tests on the pacemaker, and the plaintiff wanted to discover the manufacturer's testing result.

The court held the documents were entitled to protection from disclosure.

Only if the material could no longer be duplicated because of a change in conditions and withholding would result in injustice or undue hardship would the information be disclosed.

Manufacturer's Duty to Warn

In a 1984 case brought by a pacemaker recipient against the pacemaker manufacturer, the court held that the manufacturer only has the duty to warn the physician of any pacemaker dangers. There is no duty to warn the pacemaker recipient directly.

Duty to Recall

The FDA "Class I recall" may be applied to manufacturers of implantable medical devices, as illustrated by the recent recall of 5,700 Bjork-Shiley heart valves.

Strut fractures were reported for the Bjork-Shiley 60–degree Convexo-Concave prosthetic heart valves in the 29– to 33–mm sizes welded after February 1982. The manufacturer, Shiley, Inc. (Irvine, Calif.), notified all U.S. cardiovascular surgeons and cardiologists on February 18, 1985, asking them to closely monitor patients with these valves and report any failures to the manufacturers. Numerous changes were made in manufacturing and quality control in an effort to eliminate the strut fracture. The Bjork-Shiley heart valve was allowed by the FDA to remain on the market in 1984 because the advantages of reduced clotting overrode the incidence of strut fractures associated with the valve.

In 1978, the California Court of Appeals held in *Tresemer v. Barke* that the physician should have recalled his former patient to advise her of newly discovered dangers that were associated with the use of an intrauterine device, the Dalkon Shield IUD, which had been inserted in the plaintiff's uterus by the doctor in 1972. That was the only contact the patient had with the doctor. Within two years, the Dalkan Shield IUD was removed from the market due to an extremely high incidence of complications associated with its use. Sometime in 1975 the plaintiff discovered an injury that was demonstrated to be due to complications resulting from prolonged use of the Dalkan Shield IUD. The plaintiff sued the physician on the grounds that her injury was caused by the physician's failure to recall her and tell her of the dangers of that IUD which he had learned about after it was inserted. Summary judgment was granted in favor of the physician but was reversed on appeal.

The duty to recall is a unique theory of recovery involving physician malpractice. It emerges out of the physician's continuing duty to inform patients of newly discovered dangers, particularly of implantable devices and, for that matter, pharmaceutical drugs. In 1981, the Supreme Court for Kings County in New York became the second court to recognize the physician's duty to recall. In *Reyes v. Anka Research Ltd.*, the medical facts were similar to those of *Tresemer* except that the IUD was a Majzlin Spring IDU, which was recalled by the Food and Drug Administration in 1973. The plaintiff denied ever having received notification by the physician regarding the danger of continued use of the Majzlin Spring IUD.

The medical-legal implications of the physician's duty to recall, if broadly applied, would encompass virtually any implantable medical device or drug used by health care providers in treating patients. This is apparently the case even though the patient is seen only once or twice over a period of many years and conceivably a lifetime.

The duty to recall is not a medical malpractice theory in the commonly understood sense of medical malpractice. Traditionally, medical malpractice involves an overt act of omission or commission in treating a patient. The duty to recall arises from the continuing status of the physician-patient relationship in cases involving implantable medical devices that imposes a continuing duty to inform the patient of newly discovered hazards resulting from continued use of the device. It is for this reason that the duty to recall may be applied so broadly and may not be limited by the statutes of limitation. Even though actual medical care by the physician may have ceased, the physician-patient relationship may survive or endure and be perpetuated by the implantable medical device introduced into the body of the patient by the doctor.

The duty to recall appears to be more burdensome than the duty of due care imposed upon the physician in the treatment of the patient. It is part of the widely accepted duty to warn doctrine that is imposed on physicians to protect patients when harm is reasonably foreseeable. The question arises as to when if ever, other than a death, the duty to recall would lapse or end. Neither the *Tresemer* nor the *Reyes* court considered this question. From a practical standpoint, the duty to recall requires physicians to maintain detailed cross-referenced medical records that would be readily accessible for the life of every patient. Whenever implanted medical devices are found subsequently to be hazardous, the physician should be able to ascertain from the medical records the vulnerable patients and recall them if necessary.

If product liability litigation where compensation is sought for personal injuries that have allegedly resulted from implantable medical devices, drugs, or chemical agents, the admissibility of epidemiological studies and expert medical testimony based thereon are frequently central issues at trial. It is important to show based on reports of the epidemiological studies that there is or is not a statistical association between the use of a device or exposure to a product and the development of the condition for which compensation is sought. Certain epidemiological studies may contain multiple levels of hearsay so as to make them inadmissible under applicable federal or state law. If the reports of epidemiological studies are inadmissible one must remember that expert opinion testimony should not be based on those epidemiological studies.

Report Implantable Device Problems

Problems with implantable medical devices may be reported to a toll-free number: (800) 638–6725. This program is operated by the U.S. Pharmacopeia under contract with the FDA's Bureau of Drugs and the Bureau of Medical Devices and Diagnostic Products.

Health care providers are encouraged to report:

1. Hazardous or potentially hazardous products;
2. Mislabeling or improper labeling;
3. Incomplete or confusing instructions;
4. Erroneous information;
5. Designs that encourage human error;
6. Performance failure;
7. Nonsterile products;
8. Packaging errors;
9. Defective components;
10. Quality control problems; and
11. Any other situation that could affect the safety and efficacy of a product.

STIMAREC reports on pacemaker malfunction in the journal *PACE*. It is a system of pacemaker vigilance aimed at detecting any malfunction, reporting on follow-up developments, and ensuring that manufacturers of pacemakers do not underestimate the severity of the problem.

In December 1984, Medical Device Report legislation came into effect regarding early detection of dysfunction of pacemakers (pulse generators and pacing catheters) and other prostheses. If a manufacturer learns of a death or a serious complication due to one of their implantation prostheses, the FDA must be informed by telephone within five days and must receive a written report within two weeks. This procedure must also be followed if the dysfunction has not had any serious consequences but might do so in another patient. For example, a case of "no output" detected at routine follow-up must be reported.

Reuse of Implantable Pacemakers and Other Devices

The 1985 report of the policy conference on pacemaker reuse, sponsored by the North American Society of Pacing and Electrophysiology, supported the concept that the reuse of selected cardiac pacemakers is medically safe and efficacious. Over 20 percent of pacemakers are potentially reuseable and cost-effective, but the report urged that legal and technical criteria be developed first.

ETHICAL AND ECONOMIC CONSIDERATIONS

The United States health care system is subject to an ever expanding technologic pace plus an insatiable consumer demand for the most advanced medical care, and yet our health care system faces a system of limited resources and inescapable cost-containment measures. Who shall live? Who shall pay? And who shall decide who will get the next artificial heart implant? Problems include costs of the implants and dilemmas for third-party payers in deciding whether to pay for these procedures. The soaring cost of health care has become a significant factor in determining the zealousness of the physician's search for innovative treatment.

Although it may be distasteful to some, cost considerations vis-à-vis the patient, the community, the state, the payers, and the physician do influence health care delivery. Cost-containment considerations are having an impact on the development of the standard of care. And health care providers have become sensitized to cost containment. They find themselves caught between demand to provide the best possible treatment for patients and the need to keep down the cost of medical care. Fortunately, in many cases the cost-effective use of implantable medical devices and good medicine are one and the same. Physicians and surgeons appreciate that as consumers of health care the patient, the government, and third-party payers demand accountability. Regrettably, however, affordable medical care is by definition selective. When coupled with federal budgetary constraints and resistance by third-party payers to cost shifting by health care providers, the net result may be the rationing of health care. This is indeed the dilemma of the 1980s, and implantation of medical devices is a part of this dilemma.

Thermography: Medical and Legal Implications

Harry Rein, J.D., M.D., F.C.L.M.

INTRODUCTION

Thermography helps diagnose and vividly prove soft tissue injuries, which previously could be proven only subjectively and for which it was frequently said that there was no subjective evidence.[1]

When introduced with proper predicate, thermography can be introduced into evidence even over objection. The author, who has personal experiences in more than fifteen jurisdictions,[2] knows of only one published appellate case keeping thermography out of evidence.[51] In *Crawford v. Shivshankar,* thermography was kept out of evidence because of failure to furnish the photographs pursuant to a pretrial order and because the physician was not properly qualified.

Thermography is heat photography, an imaging technique that accurately distinguishes spinal nerve injuries, peripheral nerve injuries, and soft tissue injuries that have peripheral vasomotor and/or neuropathic direct or reflex changes. It is a totally safe diagnostic test that is noninvasive, uses space-age technology, is done on an outpatient basis and has no side effects.[52] Scientifically sound and economically feasible, thermography is being quickly accepted by the diagnostic communities in this country and Europe. There are two certifying organizations in the United States, the American Academy of Thermology and the International Thermographic Society. Physicians are certified by examination and must have theoretical and practical experience as a prerequisite to take such examinations.

Thermography fits the practice of physicians who concern themselves with the diagnosis and evaluation of injured patients for function loss, impairment, and disability. Lawyers need and use thermography to decide whether certain damages exist, whether there is an important physiologic function loss, whether permanence can be shown, and whether objective evidence of injury exists. The demonstrative value of thermography cannot be overstated. Insurance companies have both used thermography for the same purposes and strongly resisted it, depending on their individual philosophies and internal policies. It must be remembered that a defendant in an adversarial situation is not required to do or prove anything. He often can accomplish his function by criticizing, keeping evidence out, discrediting plaintiff proposals, and creating doubt. For the most part, the burden of proof remains with the plaintiff.

Doctors have the responsibility of determining if and when a patient may return to work and whether any occupational limitations exist. Physicians are asked to make determinations of function loss and impairment. Frequently they are asked to make determinations of disability, but they should not be asked to do so, because disability is considered a social evaluation, while impairment is considered a medical determination.[53] There are many other texts available to provide proper outlines for the determination of the undesirable effects of soft tissue injuries; for example, see *Primer on Soft Tissue Injuries*.[54] Until recently, physicians have depended to a large degree on what the patient describes, the so-called subjective manifestations of an illness. Rarely are social limitations evaluated properly. Laywers are more comfortable with the tangible objective evidence thermography offers. Similarly, doctors prefer to diagnose the objective manifestations of an illness, those things they can see, feel, touch, smell, examine, test, picture, and document. Whenever possible it is helpful to preserve such findings for later reference. Those soft tissue injuries, interferences with nerve function, and neurovasomotor abnormalities that were called subjective were frequently misunderstood. Such patients were not believed and occasionally were accused of exaggerating their complaints or even of malingering.

Thermography opens new vistas of diagnosis to the doctor and allows him to objectively document and justify conditions that he may previously have categorized as "subjective complaints only," "functional overlay," "emotional overreaction," "no objective findings," "I believe my patient but I can't find anything wrong," "if you just wait long enough it will go away" (the illness, the problem, the complaints, or the patient?).

Lawyers may be able to replace such language harmful to a plaintiff's cause with objective documentation. Indeed, defensive objective documentation of a normal thermogram, one that shows symmetry, is even more likely in random studies.[55] Objective documentation of injury—of functional nerve impairment, soft tissue injury, vasomotor abnormality, or substantial nerve damage—should make it easier and more accurate for a physician to say:

"In my opinion there is a permanent injury. . . ."

"These pictures prove a nerve injury of. . . ."

"These symptoms are obviously caused by. . . ."

"These thermograms explain and demonstrate this patient's inability to. . . ."

"This patient has a substantial soft tissue injury of. . . ."

"These findings are consistent with nerve injury of. . . . "

"This kind of thermogram is seen with substantial soft tissue injury, which is likely accompanied by a peripheral reflex neuropathy, probably involving the . . . nerve."

"The asymmetric heat emission seen in this thermogram is most likely due to injury and functional impairment of the . . . spinal nerves. This injury may be anyplace between the intraspinal origin of the nerve, its nerve root, and where it becomes a named nerve."

WHAT IT SHOWS

There are three fundamental questions that are now objectively answered through the use of thermographic techniques. These questions relate to trauma, the soft tissues of the body, and the vertebral column:

Is there a physiologic nerve fiber involvement?

Is there a substantial soft tissue injury?

Is there a reason for the pain in this patient due to either of the above two?

A physiologic nerve injury is one that changes the function of a particular nerve, be it a spinal nerve or a peripheral named nerve from normal to abnormal. It may be temporary or permanent, mild or severe, sensory or motor, mixed, producing few or much symptoms, functionally disabling or not, but it is always objective and out of the patient's control.

Thermography does not care what the patient says, feels, does, wants, requests, complains of, or expects from the test, or whether symptoms are present at the time of the testing or not.

Thermography measures the superficial heat of the skin, comparing right and left in the same patient at the same time under controlled circumstances. Symmetry between the right and left side is considered normal. Asymmetry in a properly done examination requires physician explanation. If asymmetry fits a pattern, appearance, location, and amount and otherwise meets the criteria of a specific recognized functional abnormality, it then proves objectively, to a high degree of reasonable medical probability (over 90 percent), that abnormality exists.[56]

When nerve abnormality, substantial soft tissue injury, or an objective reason for pain is affirmatively shown by thermography, treating physicians will improve their medical management and the quality of the evaluations. Lawyers will better judge how vigorously to proceed, and insurance companies may better be able to tell when to end a claim or litigation. When there are negative answers to all these questions, injuries may be considered less severe.[1, 57]

The primary job of every physician is to be diagnostically accurate and to diagnose physiologically as well as anatomically. A doctor who treates injured patients must consider the social implications as well as the medical ones. A lawyer considers social losses and damages and must relate them to the medical problem. Thermography is a good catalyst merging these goals when substantial injury exists.

The burden of determining whether someone should be compensated for an injury frequently is placed on the physician. Our medical-legal system has established this method, although the physician frequently has insufficient tools, knowledge, history of the patient, or understanding of how that patient functions in the real world. Some doctors have assumed that function and have extended themselves into determining how much such compensation should be. This has happened because lawyers have relinquished the function and have incorrectly assumed that medical evaluations are complete and without bias. Very few physicians are trained to assign impairment ratings.[3] Even fewer physicians understand and can assign true disability ratings, which really should be a jury function. Poorly prepared lawyers have placed this burden on doctors, and properly prepared lawyers must now remove it. Thermography can realign such priorities and definitions by adding objective scientific facts to a case.

HOW IT WORKS

There are two kinds of thermography, electronic and liquid crystal. Electronic thermography is infrared scanning of the skin surface temperature, measuring the superficial 6–8 millimeters (¼ inch) of skin heat accurately, recording and imaging these findings with computerized, high-technology sensing devices that can be made permanent through video recording or still color photography. Infrared thermography, heat photography, measuring the absolute temperature manifested by infrared emission has come to medicine only recently. Infrared has been used in the military, commercial, and scientific communities for more than a century. Barely a day goes by without a newspaper, magazine, news story, TV show, or commercial using infrared photography. It perhaps is best known through old World War I movies demonstrating night vision telescopes and the more recent movie and TV show "Blue Thunder."

Liquid crystal thermography makes the same diagnoses but depends on a skin contact with a chemical that accurately alters its color at specific temperatures. Such chemicals are embedded in plastic materials and are called cholesteric crystals.

Both infrared and liquid crystal thermography compare the right and left sides of a patient and must do so concurrently for the test to have validity. Thermography needs to be done in a temperature-stable, draft-free room. The patient must be equilibrated with the room temperature, wearing only a loose-fitting gown, for 15–20 minutes prior to the test. A series of thermograms, heat pictures, is then taken of the parts of the body to be studied.

Any study of the cervical spine area requires an evaluation of the upper extremities. Similarly, any study of the low back requires an evaluation of both lower extremities. Symmetry is the anatomic and physiologic normal. Certainly there are mild variations, slight differences between right and left, which are also called normal. It is such normalcy that must first be learned by the novice. When significant asymmetric heat emissions exist between comparable surfaces on the right and left sides and when these heat emission differences persist, the thermologist assigns a reason for these differences based on known physiology.

It is possible that certain differences are caused by artifact and even by technical faults by beginners. However, such artifacts can easily be recognized by an experienced reader. A nerve or soft tissue injury abnormality can be diagnosed when a known or recognized pattern appears. Such asymmetric (abnormal) patterns require that the asymmetry be persistent, that an adequate amount of surface area exist in the right number of locations, dermatome patterns and that the asymmetry be of a proper temperature magnitude.

The temperature of the skin, that which is measured by thermography, is directly related to the intradermal blood flow, which is controlled by the autonomic nervous system. This system consists of the sympathetic and parasympathetic nerves. Asymmetric intradermal blood flow changes are an accurate reflection of nervous (neurologic) function or dysfunction.

Before the advent of high technology and computerization, it was extremely difficult to show reproducible laboratory results that substantiated assessments of circulatory disturbances, myofascial pain, trigger points, and spinal nerve root compression syndromes. Now such changes due to neurologic effects on the circulatory system by changes in the physiology of nerves as they supply the dermatomes can be documented and reproduced.

As in any health care procedure, it is important to correlate the results of thermographic imaging with clinical findings. The differential of various physical complaints must determine whether chronic unexplained patterns of pain are psychiatric in nature or represent previously misdiagnosed objective injury. Thermography is of significant value in detecting otherwise overlooked organic disorders, particularly those of sympathetic dysfunction that may be diagnosed as psychogenic in origin, such as reflex sympathetic dystrophy, nerve root irritation, and thoracic outlet syndrome. Thermographic scientific accuracy will increase the number of correct diagnoses. Almost all practitioners who understand thermography will interpret an obvious thermographic abnormality as asymmetry, although a difference might exist in the philosophy of the physician and therefore in how he determines the meaning of the asymmetry. Likewise, symmetric heat emissions will be interpreted as normal.

Thermography has been called a "picture of pain," but it is more than that. It gives a reason for the pain and frequently defines the basis and justifies the existence of what were frequently known as subjective complaints. *Thermography is objective testing.*

BASIC PHYSICS

A few basic concepts of physics are important to thermography.[71] This discussion is limited to infrared radiation, since most clinicians seem comfortable with the concepts associated with direct-contact methods of temperature measurement.

Infrared or telethermography involves the detection of endogenously generated radiation whose energy level and wavelength spectrum are related to the temperature of the point on the body emitting it. Thermography measures these points. Thus, if a certain wavelength band is chosen, as the temperature of an emitting point rises, so will the net energy falling on a detecting sensor. Experiences and concepts of this are familiar. If a person's hand is held laterally near (but not touching) a radiator in a house as it is heating up, the person is able to sense over time that the radiator is getting hotter by the changing sensation of heat in the hand. The person's hand can effectively sense a net increase of infrared radiation falling onto it from the radiator as the radiator's temperature increases. Unlike the eye, which can differentiate certain individual wavelength differences (colors), the hand cannot, although it is quite sensitive to the net radiant energy transmission process.

Infrared radiation is part of the electromagnetic spectrum, with which all human beings are familiar. Through this spectrum there is vision. Infrared waves in the wavelengths used in telethermography are identical to light waves except that they are invisible to the eye and may be thought of as being of a frequency lower *(infra)* than the frequency of red light. Infrared light is also of a longer wavelength. As the frequency of light decreases, its wavelength increases. Frequencies far below that of red light (*infra,* infrared) make up the radio waves. As the frequency of light increases above red, there is a progression through the spectrum of visible light, violet being the highest electromagnetic frequency that can ordinarily be seen as light. Violet is followed by the frequency regions called ultraviolet and then by gamma rays.

A terminology has evolved regarding the infrared spectrum itself. There is near infrared, a wavelength just slightly longer than red light, and then a progression through longer wavelengths called middle, far, and extreme infrared, which have respectively shorter frequencies. Divisions are quite arbitrary except those for visible light, which are determined by the electromagnetic wavelength sensitivities of the human eye.

Electromagnetic wavelengths emitted by a material depend on temperature. As the temperature increases the wavelength of the emitted radiation ("light") shortens. As an example, a metal filament in a bulb will first glow red as it is heated; and as the temperature is raised further, the light given off will be observed to progress through the various wavelengths of light, gradually including more yellows and blues and finally violets. It can be observed that the glowing wire is not a pure producer of wavelengths (colors) but rather produces a band rich in many wavelengths. The particular band produced, however, is a function of the temperature. Increasingly shorter wavelengths and higher temperatures cause a net increase in the spectral emissive power, or energy transmitted. This is the scientific terminology for the phenomenon observed and felt by a hand near a radiator as it becomes hotter.

Since the band of wavelengths produced is a function of the temperature of a point, if one is interested in detecting temperatures in the human body range, the wavelength band given off by a point at that temperature is determined and then a material sensitive in some way to those wavelengths is looked for. Based on the color spectra, it is noted that a black body at 37°C gives off wavelengths of approximately 3 to 50 microns. A material can now be chosen from available known materials having physical properties of sensitivity in this range.

This theory is the basis of thermographic physics.

The materials found most practical in modern telethermography equipment are indium antimonide and mercury cadmium telluride.

The concepts of reflected and emitted light should also be understood. A piece of paper appears white not because the paper itself is several thousand degrees hot but because it is reflecting the light coming from something else that is very hot, such as the filament of a light bulb, the glowing gases in a candle's flame, or the sun. Thus, the room in which thermography is being done should be "dark" with respect to the infrared spectrum around 37°C. This is accomplished by controlling the room temperature, avoiding drafts, and avoiding heating the body being measured by radiant energy.

This theory explains the reasons for the strict protocol and guidelines.

PROTOCOL

Thermography is not in its infancy, but information about it to the general medical, legal, and patient communities is.

The reliability and accuracy of thermography can be maintained if shortcuts are resisted. If the physics and physiology of thermographic techniques are considered, proper cooling equilibration and standardization of procedures will be accepted. All involved in this process should insist on strict criteria.

Thermography must be done in a properly prepared setting, preferably built and designed with an understanding of the temperature needs. The room for testing and equilibration requires temperature stability and should be draft-free. The actual temperature is less important than the absence of change. Any steady temperature in the 66°–75°F range would be adequate.

Equilibration is the process by which the patient is allowed to cool to a skin temperature that will be stable when he is exposed to the ambient room temperature. It has been determined that 15–20 minutes prior to thermographic imaging is sufficient. After being properly prepared, the patient is put into a cooling-dressing room, completely undressed and required to remain free of pressure contact with clothing, belts, bands, furniture, appliances, the wall, or a seat if a lower-body study is to be done.

The patient is then taken into the testing room, which should adjoin the cooling room and be of the same temperature, serviced by the same temperature-control device. The proper views are then taken of the patient. The patient is then asked to return to the cooling room and is reequilibrated for another 15–20 minutes, and the entire process is repeated. The process is then repeated a third time.

To do a proper study, the thermogram must be taken three times, and a

TABLE 1. Color Spectra.

	TEMPERATURE		COLOR	FREQUENCY HZ (CPS)	WAVELENGTH			
								X-Rays
Star	11,000° K =	10,727° C	Black & Bluish-White	High	Short	0.27 0.40	0.3	Ultraviolet
Sun	6,000° K =	5,727° C	Yellow			0.50		Visible*
Red Hot Wire	793° K =	525° C	Red			0.75		Infrared
Hot Wire	773° K =	500° C	Black			0.80	1.2	Near
							3. 6.	Middle
Body Temp.	310° K =	37° C	Black			9.30		
Room Temp.	300° K =	27° C	Black			(3. to 50.) 9.70		Far
							15.	
Liquid Nitrogen	77° K =	-196° C	Black	Low	Long	38.		Extreme
						1000.		Radio Waves

*Infrared Film

significant interpretation depends on consistency of the findings over all three studies. There is an option to do a stress test before the third series. Sometimes the stress of standing for that period of time, particularly if the individual has a significant problem, is enough stress to conduct the test.

Minimally, the standard accepted procedures to be implemented are no smoking for at least an hour prior to testing, proper equilibration and cooling wearing no clothes, a temperature-stable room that is draft-free, and a repeat of the thermographic series as stated above. This time-lapse sequence is important.

As part of the proper technique, the various pictures, studies, and postures should always be done in the same manner, with the same number of views as part of each series. The electronic dials need not be set the same way for each series.

The patient must be under continual observation and monitoring while he is in the examination area. Note that "continual" does not mean continuous but is intended merely to prevent technical errors that will interfere with the interpretation of the thermogram.

If this protocol is followed, a patient cannot create an abnormal thermogram, and certainly cannot convert an abnormal heat imaging to a normal one. Clinically abnormal thermograms will not be created by failure to follow these protocol recommendations. Deviation from them will merely result in a thermogram that cannot be interpreted or one with evident artifacts.

POSITION SEQUENCES

Infrared Imaging

Infrared thermographic imaging requires a strict protocol, as does every other scientific medical technique. The positioning, views, numbers of views, consistency of studies, and development and acceptance of a rational program depend on following a generally accepted, strict protocol. Shortcuts cause problems. None are recommended.

The following is a recommended sequence of pictures to be taken during each of three series, depending on the part of the body being imaged. It is recommended that all the pictures be taken. It should be remembered that infrared heat emission imaging depends entirely on a left-right comparison and relationship. In those pictures where the left and right parts of the body are not on the same view, the time lapse between the two should be minimal, measured in terms of seconds, during which time none of the controls on the electronic unit may be touched. Anything less than this may create artifacts, due to which the thermograms will not be completely interpreted.

The major studies related to thermography in the investigation of trauma, nerve fiber physiologic involvement, and soft tissue injuries consist of the face, upper body, middle body, and lower body. Lesser studies of the extremities and of local portions of the anatomy are included in these, are done for different purposes, and would necessarily follow the same views, except that fewer would be required; one would look for and identify trigger points rather than making a full diagnostic survey.

The upper-body studies are often called a cervical spine series, but the name should be changed because so much more imaging is done and so many more views are taken than the original name defined and described. An upper-body series includes a study of the cervical and high upper thoracic dermatomes and of the soft tissues of the neck, the shoulder, and the entire upper extremities.

Similarly, the middle-body study includes the entire chest and abdominal areas—more than just the thoracic spine. A lower-body study includes the lower abdomen, lower back, buttocks, lower extremities, and feet, and in electronic thermography it should include black-and-white thermography of the lumbosacral area, as well as color infrared imaging of the entire area defined. It is important for the nonexpert to know what is being imaged, how many pictures are taken, and what views and postures are considered. Thermographers have the obligation to be consistent, persistent, and accurate and to provide adequate information and education to those who do not understand these imaging processes and procedures.

Face Series

Frontal: The face is studied head-on, in the anatomic neutral position. The images should nearly fill the screen.

Frontal—Head Extended: As above, but with head extension.

Right Anterior Oblique: The patient, not only the head, is turned slightly to the left, so that more of the right side of the face is imaged. A 30°–45° turn is appropriate.

Left Anterior Oblique: The same in the opposite direction.

Right Lateral: The patient is turned 90° to the left, imaging the entire right side of the face; the ear is included.

Left Lateral: The same in the opposite direction.

Upper-Body Series (Cervical Area and Upper Extremities)

Posterior Neck and Shoulders: The patient faces away from the scanner. The head is slightly flexed to open posterior neck skin folds. The image is to include the neck, the extreme upper thoracic vertebral area, and both shoulders out to the acromial processes on the one view. A closer and/or more distant view may be appropriate.

Right Lateral: The patient and camera remain at the same location while the patient is turned 90° to the right, bringing all of the right side of the neck and deltoid areas into view.

Left Lateral: The opposite. Remember that right/left comparison is the basis for thermographic evaluation.

Right C8 View: The patient faces away from the camera, as in the posterior neck view. The right upper extremity is abducted, raised parallel to the floor. The palm is down, parallel to the floor. The view includes the arm, elbow, forearm, and medial aspect (side) of the small finger. A better alternate is the "prayer position." The view pictures a close-up of the medial aspect of the fifth finger and the medial (ulnar) aspect of the fingers and forearms. The patient faces the scanner, elbows flexed, the fingertips just touching, with the elbows about twelve inches apart. The upper extremities are shielded from the body with cardboard. C8 are clearly studied.

Left C8/Ulnar View: Same. Left upper extremity.

Right C6/C7/C8 View: The patient stands facing the camera. The right upper extremity is abducted parallel to the floor. The palm faces the camera. The view includes the arm, antecubital fossa, forearm, and palm. A better alternate follows the prayer position. With the fingertips still touching, the elbows are fully extended and the lateral edge (C6) of the forearms is visualized.

Left C6/C7/C8 View: The same view of the left upper extremity.

Right Lateral Arm: The patient is turned to the left, the right shoulder facing the camera. It is important that there be proper white cardboard shielding separating the upper extremity from the body. The arm is at the side, the elbow is flexed. This is imaging of the lateral shoulder, lateral arm, and lateral humerus epicondyl areas.

Left Lateral Arm: The other side.

Right Forearm: A continuation of the right lateral arm view. Palm faces shield. Image the elbow, forearm, and dorsum of hand.

Left Forearm: The other side.

Anterior Arms: This view images the anterior shoulders, anterior arms (biceps areas), and the upper thorax and lower neck areas, which images the C3, C4, T1, and T2 dermatomes. The head should be slightly extended. The arms should be shielded from the body with the usual cardboard shields.

Dorsal Forearms: The patient stands facing the camera. The elbows are slightly flexed. A cardboard separates the arms from the body. The palms face the shield; the dorsum of the hands and the dorsal forearms face the camera.

Ventral Forearms: The upper extremity is shielded from the body. The patient faces the camera. The palms are turned to the camera. The elbows are extended.

Dorsum of Hands: The palms are down, touching a fresh cardboard shield, for a close-up view of the back of the hands and all the fingers.

Palms: As above, palms facing the scanner.

Middle-Body Series (For Thoracic Dermatomes)

Posterior: The entire upper back, neck to just below waist, is in focus. Arms are overhead.

Right Posterior Oblique: The arms are elevated over the head, and the body is turned slightly to the right while facing away from the scanner. The same amount of vertical area is included in this view.

Left Posterior Oblique: The patient faces away from the scanner and turns 45° to the left, opposite of above (always comparing right to left).

Right Lateral: The arm remains overhead. Patient turns to right. Right side of chest faces the scanner.

Left Lateral: The other side.

Anterior Thorax: The arms remain above the head and the front of the chest is similarly imaged.

Lower-Body Series (Lumbosacral Area and Lower Extremities)

Low Back: The entire lumbosacral spine including the T11–T12 and the superior inch of the gluteal cleft are included. The waist should be visible. Black-and-white studies with proper cooling (e.g., alcohol spray) as well as color imaging should be done.

Low Back and Buttocks: With greater distance from the patient, a lumbosacral and buttock scan are recorded.

Posterior Buttocks: The patient faces away from the camera. The image should include the posterior superior iliac crest and a small portion of the posterior thighs below the gluteal fold.

Posterior Thighs: The patient faces away from the camera and the lower extremities are separated by 12–18 inches.

Posterior Legs (Calves) and Heels: The popliteal space, legs, posterior ankles, and heels should be included.

Anterior Thighs: The patient faces the camera. The feet are 12–18 inches apart. The areas included are both anterior thighs, the inguinal areas, and the knees.

Anterior Legs and Feet: The scanner focuses lower down, including the knees, pretibial ankle, and dorsum of feet areas.

Right Lateral Thigh (Walking Position): From facing the camera, the patient turns to his left (facing to the right of the technician). The lower extremity closer to the wall away from the scanner is forward. The right leg, the lateral aspect of the right lower extremity, is closer to the camera and becomes the back leg. Both knees are slightly bent. Scanned is the entire right lateral thigh and a significant portion of left medial thigh. Include the entire thigh and bone.

Right Lateral Leg: In the same position scan the knee, legs, and ankles, thereby viewing the right lateral calf and left medial calf and corresponding portions of feet.

Left Lateral Thigh: The opposite position and view of the right, above.

Left Lateral Leg: The opposite position and view of the right, above.

Dorsum of Feet: Both feet, including ankles and toes, fill the screen.

Plantar Surface of Feet: This is a very desirable view. The patient kneels on a soft surface facing away from the camera. The soles of the feet thereby face the scanner. They must be carefully cleaned (alcohol spray is adequate) and blown dry with a cool air dryer, equally for several minutes.

Each full series, or any combination of them depending on parts of the body being studied, should be repeated twice, with proper interval equilibration and cooling time to prevent artifacts and determine organicity of findings.

Liquid Crystal Imaging

Liquid crystal imaging requires the same strict protocol and images the same parts of the body as infrared; but because it is the physical application of a screen to the skin, a slightly different procedure is followed.

Cervical Series

Cervicothoracic spine: Includes neck, trapezius, and upper scapular area bilaterally.

Right Posterior Shoulder: Detector is placed over right trapezius/upper scapular area lateral to cervical spine.

Left Posterior Shoulder: Detector is placed over left trapezius/upper scapular area lateral to cervical spine.

Right Posterior Shoulder and Triceps: From right posterolateral aspect of scapula to upper posterior arm, triceps area.

Left Posterior Shoulder to Triceps: From left posterolateral aspect of scapula to upper posterior arm, triceps area.

Right Lateral Arm: From shoulder to above elbow.

Left Lateral Arm: From shoulder to above elbow.

Right Ulnar/C8 View: View includes medial aspect of patient's right outstretched arm, level with shoulder, from axilla to wrist.

Left Ulnar/C8 View: View includes medial aspect of patient's outstretched left arm, level with shoulder, from axilla to wrist.

Dorsal Forearms: Front view of arms with palms down.

Ventral Forearms: Same as above with palms up.

Dorsal Hands: Extension of ventral forearms above, taken of backs of hands together.

Ventral Hands: Extension of ventral forearms above, taken of both palms together.

Polaroid photo of patient's upper extremities.

Lumbar Series

Lumbosacral Spine: Thermoflex detector applied to LS area above buttocks.

Right Buttock and Left Buttock: Thermoflex detector applied to cover each entire buttock; buttocks may be done together if possible.

Posterior Thigh—Right and Left: Detector applied to area of thigh below buttock and above knee posteriorly.

Posterior Calves Together: From below knee to above ankles.

Anterior Thighs Together: Includes both thighs from below groin to above knee.

Anterior Legs Together: Below knees to above ankles.

Right Lateral Buttock, Right Lateral Thigh, Right Lateral Leg: Patient stands or lies on opposite side and detector is applied in sequential order to obtain three continuous pictures of each anatomical area described.

Left Lateral Buttock, Left Lateral Thigh, Left Lateral Leg: Patient stands or lies on opposite side and detector is applied in sequential order to obtain three continuous pictures of each anatomical area described.

Dorsal Feet Together: Self-explanatory.

Soles of Feet Together: Self-explanatory.

Polaroid photo of subject's lower extremities.

Note: Each liquid crystal detector utilizes a fixed, nonlinear scale that cannot be adjusted and is indicated by a numbered color label that refers to the mid-range temperature in Celsius for that detector. Therefore, until familiarity with temperature sensitivities of different body parts relative to that of the various thermoflex detectors is learned, it may be useful to try several detectors until a good image is obtained.

MEDICAL ASPECTS

Thermography helps establish a diagnosis by demonstrating real reasons beyond those called "functional disturbances." Thermography does not require hospitalization. It helps consultants, who need not examine the patient but can merely review medical records. It gives credibility to certain diagnoses and eliminates others from consideration. Thermography is directly applicable to the following diagnoses, which may result from similar symptom patterns.[4]

Bursitis
Causalgia
Deep Tissue Scarring
Disk Disease
Disk Syndrome
Facet Syndrome
Fasciitis
Herniated Disk
Herniated Nucleus Pulposus
Hypesthesia
Hyperesthesia
Hyperextension Injury
Hyperflexion Injury
Ligament Tear
Lower Motor Neuron Disease
Malingerers
Muscle Tear
Musculoligamentous Spasm
Nerve Entrapment
Nerve Impingement
Nerve Pressure
Nerve Root Abnormality
Nerve Root Irritation
Neuralgia
Neuritis
Neuropathy
Neuropraxia
Paresthesia
Peripheral Axon Disease
Physiologic Nerve Abnormality
Pinched Nerve
Ruptured Disk
Sensory Loss
Sensory Nerve Abnormality
Slipped Disk
Soft Tissue Injury
Somatic Abnormality
Sprain

Strain
Stretched Nerve
Sympathetic Reflex Dystrophy
Tendonitis

Thermography *identifies sensory damage* and helps diagnose, monitor, and predict prognosis accurately. Thermography does not depend on patient participation, nor can a patient reproduce or fake somatosensory dermatome distributions. Electronic thermography is particularly accurate because of its intrinsic technique and because it is independent of patient complaints, attitudes, desires, and symptoms. A negative thermogram will often eliminate the need for myelography and its related hospital care. Thermography can significantly reduce or substitute for independent medical examinations and may be considered a second opinion preceding laminectomy for nerve impingement. In such cases it will accurately suggest and prevent unsuccessful surgery.

Postoperative thermograms establish a baseline. If more symptoms develop later, or if a new injury occurs, the dermatome distributions are a valuable tool differentiating the two events.

Thermography relates extremely well to myelography and EMG. Indeed, thermography and EMG testing combined will yield a 94 percent accuracy rate for spinal nerve involvement.[56]

Accurate objective testing improves diagnostic acumen.

"PICTURE OF PAIN"

Thermography does not provide a *picture of pain* but shows a reason for the pain if there is one, particularly if that cause is physiologic nerve fiber involvement or a substantial soft tissue injury.

Not all authorities agree with this simplified statement.

Three major types of pain can be differentiated and objectively pictured by thermography, as shown by William Hobbins.[72] There are visceral afferent pain, nerve root pain, and spinal cord pain. It is agreed that *symmetry is normal* and that *asymmetric heat emissions require explanation.*

Not only does spinal nerve abnormality, but also skin pathology, local inflammation, tumors, cancers, and acute trauma, cause dermatomal heat emission pattern changes.

Acute inflammation will usually be warm, unless it is severe and accompanied by substantial edema, which causes a decrease in the intradermal vascular flow and a resulting decreased heat emission. For the same reason, dead tissue will be cold, as are most superficial benign tumors. More often than not, skin malignancies will be warm because of increased new vascularity. Hobbins describes trauma in the form of hematoma or fat necrosis as cold.

Referred pain, visceral afferent pain, shows increased heat response in *the segmental dermatome of referral,* according to Hobbins; such a response is called a *thermatome* by Pierre LeRoy. There are commonly known areas of referred pain, and there are many others that are not generally considered in everyday diagnosis.

The common referred regions are below the right shoulder blade, subscapular, in gall bladder pain; McBurney's point in appendicitis; chest pain in pulmonary embolism; and left upper extremity referral with angina. There is dilation of the blood vessels in the local areas of referred pain causing increased heat emission.

It is fairly well established that pain from internal organs, visceral pain, is transmitted over the sympathetic nervous system fibers and not via the parasympathetic fibers. Such pain is due to stretching of the smooth muscles or to spasm in them, as in hollow internal organs, blood vessels, the ureter, or the gall bladder.

Thermographic changes due to nerve root pain, that is, peripheral nerve pain, correspond to the dermatome, rather than to a thermatome. The dermatomal pattern so developed is a major way of distinguishing this type of pain from the one previously discussed. Most of this article concerns itself with peripheral (somatic) pain, rather than visceral pain.

When peripheral nerve pain exists, the sympathetic nervous system responds in a defensive manner. The generalized sympathetic response is one of fright, flight, and fight. The classic sympathetic response occurs in individuals who are in a near accident or acute stress situation, where the event does not occur and spontaneously disappears. Immediately after such an exposure, an individual manifests sympathetic reactions such as dilated pupils, pale cool skin, a dry mouth, and a rapid heartbeat, which gradually disappear. This is the sympathetic reaction. Such a reaction can also occur locally in a dermatomal segment or in parts of such a segment with skip areas. It is this type of reaction mediated through the sympathetic nervous system that is imaged by thermography with spinal nerve physiologic injury or substantial stimulation. Sympathetic dystrophy may be considered a substantial and magnified prolonged extension of this process.

In a full-blown active case of sympathetic dystrophy or reflex sympathetic dystrophy, it might be anticipated that a sympathectomy of the involved area would result in a return of normal temperature from the hypothermia stage, assuming a release of the sympathetic tone. This does not always happen. Whether it does probably depends on the extent of damage and the length of time the dystrophy was present prior to therapy. Thermographic evaluation of a sympathetic block can predict expected surgical relief from sympathectomy.

Cord pain or cord injury also causes a constriction of peripheral skin blood vessels mediated by the same or similar sympathetic reflex or sympathetic direct stimulation pattern.

Hobbins believes (contrary to this author and some other investigators) that in the infrared thermographic evaluation of pain, "the pain must be present at the time of the exam." He states that if it is not, the thermogram must be considered a baseline. Others believe that the thermogram will be abnormal whether the pain is present or not, if it is a result of substantial local soft tissue injury and/or dermatomal nerve fiber involvement. It is perhaps these narrower criteria which may allow both proponents to be correct.

LIBERAL VERSUS CONSERVATIVE

There is bias toward both liberal and conservative medical opinions, and both types should be of equal concern. These may be called overdiagnosis and underdiagnosis. On rare occasions when there is a questionable heat emission difference between the right and left sides in thermography, not satisfying strict criteria, the question arises whether it is better to overdiagnose or to underdiagnose. Doctors face this challenge every day. Is too much diagnosis (the liberal attitude) a danger to the patient? Is too little diagnosis (the conservative approach) an equal or greater danger to the patient? In thermology there are strict standards of interpretation, and the same ones should be used all the time. When strict laboratory tests are performed, this dichotomy will not arise. A treating physician, however, has the added responsibility of telling his patient's story with sympathy.

There is little real risk to the patient with overdiagnosis if it does not lead to surgery, painful procedures, excess expense, danger to life or limb of the patient, fear, or prolonged physical or mental disability. Sometimes, however, the doctor who overdiagnoses, the lawyer who keeps getting additional consultations and referrals, and the patient who is encouraged to undergo more and more treatment by either or both cause a conscious or subconscious belief in the patient that something very significant must be wrong; otherwise there would not be so much concern, treatment, and testing. This is a real danger.

Similarly, there is great risk involved in underdiagnosis because it can result in a person with real pain and symptoms being categorized as "exaggerating" or "malingering." "No one believes me" causes emotional debility. Furthermore, no relief of symptoms is provided. If a surgical condition is present, it will not be corrected when inadequate diagnosis exists. Patients going to many different doctors, and injustice to those patients, can be expected.

TESTIMONY

It is apparent to experienced trial lawyers, but it is often a great surprise to novices, that when doctors are called to testify they suddenly become reticent and will not commit to anything of which they are not "certain." In real life a physician is hardly ever certain of diagnoses that may be life-threatening. A physician is hardly ever certain of what he will find when he recommends surgery. A witness need not be "sure." Doctors routinely treat patients based on presumption, supposition, intuition, and feelings as well as on proven diagnoses. Yet when testifying, the doctor will frequently talk differently than he ordinarily would to a patient or to peers. It is quite common for a physician to tell his patient that a diagnosis is likely, that a thermographic abnormality exists, and that treatment and therapy are directly related to such conditions. When the same doctor is placed under oath, it is not surprising to hear him say that he is not certain about the abnormality and that he does not want to base his treatment on thermographic evidence or on a laboratory result. This doctor has overdiagnosed for treatment purposes and underdiagnosed for testimonial purposes.

It is the borderline cases that present questions of interpretation. However, in thermography there are many fewer borderline interpretations than with other medical procedures. If a choice has to be made and there is a borderline abnormality present on a thermogram, who is to get the benefit of the doubt? If there is litigation, who is to get the benefit of the interpretation? The task becomes easier when the lawyer explains such terms as *medical probability, medical certainty, substantial, substantive, sure, always, never,* or even *more likely than not.* Symmetry in thermography indicates normalcy and health of nerves. The same kind of symmetry is needed in thinking about, talking to, treating, and testifying about a patient's condition.

Perhaps the following chart on causation will help explain how physicians think as compared to what lawyers need in their burden of proof.[58]

Medical Viewpoint	**Legal Viewpoint**
A. *To Cause*	
1. To produce a new condition or pathology;	1. To produce a new condition or pathology;
2. To initiate an underlying disorder.	2. To aggravate an underlying disorder by worsening, hastening, or accelerating its progression.
B. *The Cause*	
1. Etiologic elements, i.e., seeking to assign a cause;	1. Whether a particular event was the proximate, precipitating cause of an injurious result;
2. Various causes of an underlying disorder;	2. One cause that precipitates, triggers, hastens, or worsens some medical condition.
3. The multiplicity of causes and their interrelationships.	3. The one causative element under legal scrutiny, independent of other, coexisting causes.
C. *Preexisting Disorder*	
1. The patient's preexisting condition is important in affecting the end results of degenerative disease processes.	1. The injured party is taken as he is found, not as a normal person but subject to whatever existing medical conditions he had at the time of the event in question.
2. It is important in a particular case that the injurious result would not have occurred in the absense of significant preexisting diseases.	2. Increased vulnerability of the injured party to harm because of preexisting disease does not excuse the one who inflicts harm; it is immaterial that an accident, incident, or trauma would not have resulted in injury or diability had the victim been in good or average health.

3. Because of the preexisting disorder's contributions to the end result, assigning responsibility should involve apportionment based on percentage responsibility for the end result.	3. When death or disability occurs subsequent to a legally significant event, total responsibility is credited to the party effecting the event. Apportionment, in most cases, should not apply.
D. *The Amount of Aggravation*	
1. Responsibility should not be assessed when the degree of aggravation is small in relation to the extent of underlying pathology.	1. The crux of legal causation is the occurrence of aggravation of an underlying disorder, not the degree to which it was aggravated.
2. Responsibility should not be assessed when the degree of hastening of an inevitable end result was minor in relation to the entire clinical picture.	2. The important consideration legally is whether a process and end result was hastened, not how much it was hastened. For example, if death is hastened even by a moment, the result is actionable.
3. Responsibility should not be assessed when an end result is inevitable because of the expected natural progression of the underlying disorder.	3. The inevitability of the end result is unimportant if that result would have occurred had the underlying disorder progressed naturally.
E. *Degree of Proof Required*	
1. Proof means scientific proof.	1. Depending upon the jurisdiction, establishment of legal causation requires "probability," "50.1 percent," "more likely than not," or "reasonable medical certainty," not scientific proof.
2. Equally consistent theories of causation are acceptable as guides in choosing the appropriate medical treatement of the patient.	2. Equally consistent theories of causation do not satisfy standards for legal proof.
3. The alleged causative element must be recognized scientifically as a competent producing cause of the disorder.	3. The alleged causative element must be one recognized scientifically as a competent producing cause of the disorder.

The left column is the way physicians are taught to look at problems. The right column is the way they should think when involved in a medical-legal situation. It is the lawyer's responsibility to set the scene and to teach the doctor the proper language. It is essential that the lawyer always discuss with the physician how he should testify and how he should present his opinions, even though what he will say remains the province of the witness.

EVIDENCE

Thermography appeared to be a major topic of conversation during the early 1980s, but it has since become a diagnostic tool and of more common use as evidence in the courtroom. It is not only an outstanding diagnostic tool but also a potent form of demonstrative evidence that helps *inform and persuade the jury*. Thermography is impressive and believable and graphically shows the presence of an injury and the reason for pain. Its status as scientific proof of physiologic abnormality and its appeal as a form of color "show and tell" make a strong argument for its admissibility at trial.

Thermography is an accepted scientific device like any other medical test. As such, it should not face excessive legal burdens and hurdles, even though it apparently does. Opponents may challenge thermography, just as other scientific techniques were challenged in the past. Other devices have found their way into the courtroom, and so has thermography. Comparable case law exists and is applicable.[5–27]

In *Frye v. U.S.*[7] the "general acceptance" standard became popular. Under that test, something could not be admitted into evidence until it had gained "general acceptance in the particular field in which it belongs." Some courts have adopted that standard; many have changed it and are changing it to a standard that relates more to relevance and whether or not experts depend on it, and even on who the expert is. Some trial courts have decided to, in the words of a judge, "let it in for what it is worth." There are no reported cases at the trial or appellate level that have kept thermography out of evidence based on the *Frye* standard. It should be remembered that the *Frye* standard was originally used in criminal cases, where the standard of proof is substantially different than in civil cases, where thermography is having its legal impact.

It appears that courts will continue to demand that reliability exists and that the thermograms be relevant to the issue. There must be probative value. It is likely that the person offering the testimony will continue to have a burden of proof, the degree varying with the court, greater than that of the opponent.

The Federal Rules of Evidence 401,[28] 403,[29] and 702[30] and *United States v. Williams*[31] are a significant trend. Rule 401 defines logical relevancy, and Rule 403 discusses the balancing of relevancy; both are recognized standards. Rule 702 relates to assisting "the trier of fact to understand . . . to determine" and relates to the qualifications of an expert and to the fact that he "may testify thereto in the form of . . . opinion."

Thermograms have been admitted into evidence in California,[33–34, 60, 61] Delaware,[62] the District of Columbia, Florida,[43, 48] Georgia,[63] Illinois,[44] Louisiana,[32, 47] Michigan,[46, 69] Minnesota,[68] Mississippi,[73] New Jersey,[45] New York,[74] Ohio, and Wisconsin.[70] The author has testified as a physician and expert thermologist several dozen times. Two such cases are of interest.[49, 50] In *Flowers* the judge felt so strongly as to have his opinion published, although from county court. *Palma* is on appeal.

For purposes of payment, before there was an economic pinch, Medicare had determined that thermography was beyond the experimental stage, was to be paid when performed by a physician or under his supervision, and was reasonable and necessary in the diagnosis of peripheral vascular disease, musculoskeletal injury (such as low back injury and herniated disk disease) and inflammatory lesions.[59]

In 1982 the acting director of the Bureau of Medical Devices for the Food and Drug Administration stated that "thermography can be a useful adjunct for diagnosis in many areas, including musculoskeletal injuries."

For years the Department of Agriculture, through federal regulations, has required that certain horses be properly evaluated. Thermography has served an important role in such disputes and has been admitted into evidence in veterinary cases.[60, 61]

PREDICATES

The proper foundations and predicates for thermographic evidence placed before the court will almost surely prevent objections or cause them to be overruled.[35] Each of the following four has its own purposes. The predicates are additive, not repetitious, and are always applicable. Detailing these predicates necessarily depends on the quality and training of the witness.

1. "Thermography is color photography." It pictures the infrared (color) heat emissions from the skin surface. This testimony should invoke the extensive law of photography, recalling its acceptance as evidence provided that the pictures accurately represent the subject matter and are logically and legally relevant.[36]

2. "The thermograms are all identified in a usual and customary way similar to the way (we) identify our X-rays." This recalls the extensive law regarding laboratory tests in general and X rays in particular[39] and overcomes the chain-of-custody argument.[37] The doctor-technician-patient relationship is the same as when X rays are taken. In radiology (as in photography) the technician need not be present[38] for testimony of chain of custody, or technique, if the physician in charge, under whose direction or supervision or control the tests were done, can testify to the usual business routine, custom, and patient identification techniques. Thermograms should be considered in the same manner as X rays, CAT scans, EMGs, EKGs, blood type and Rh, culture/sensitivity studies, and myelography. Hundreds of scientific tests can be named that have never been challenged as to patient identity or chain of custody.

3. Q: "Will it help the jury understand . . . if you show (slides) (the pictures) . . . ?"[40]
   A: "Yes."
4. Q: "Doctor, do you have an opinion . . . regarding . . . ?"
   A: "Yes."
   Q: "What is the basis of your opinion?"
   A: "I base my opinion in this case on thermography and (. . . if anything else . . .)."[41]

All lawyers are thoroughly familiar with these predicates.

QUALIFYING THE EXPERT

Qualifying the thermologist is of the utmost importance. He may be a thermology specialist, and he may also be the treating physician. He must be thoroughly qualified before thermography is offered into evidence. Obviously, the degree and extent of his qualifications and the details presented will vary from case to case with the expected testimony and with the doctor's background, training, and experience.

Like any expert witness, the doctor must be a teacher, so qualified and introduced, and must be given the opportunity to teach the jury. He should relate thermography to his practice and should explain how thermography relates to orthopedics, neurology, neurosurgery, radiology, chiropractics, and problems of injury or trauma. This is an appropriate time for a brief explanation of the science of thermography. If there is a challenge to the scientific efficacy and acceptance of thermography, for example, using the *Frye* standard or something resembling it, the witness must be prepared to give a detailed explanation and to present facts and bases for his statements.

Do not allow qualification of the expert to be waived if he is so credentialed. Prepare and spend time with this phase. He will then be permitted to describe and show pictures of the laboratory, the equipment, and the technique. He should define the physics of infrared radiation and its relationship to skin heat emissions. A brief description of how thermography is used by the military, government, and industry may be of great value.

The patient's thermograms are then identified and described. Differences between right and left are discussed, and areas interpreted as normal are defined. From this point on, the diagnostic skill and acumen of the physican and his thermography interpretation ability are used to build on the teaching that has preceded. All statements related to interpretation should be based on the descriptions given earlier.

The appropriate questions from the following outline will assist in the qualifying process. Naturally, they need to be modified to the witness, depending on how credentialed he is and whether those areas in which he will be qualified are necessary for subsequent substantive testimony.

Introduce yourself to the jury.

Tell us about your medical education.

Do you have any other degrees?

Are you licensed to practice medicine? Where? When?

How long have you been in practice? Where?

Describe your practice.
—(Ask specific questions about the issues in this case as they relate to practice.)

What is board certification?
—What does it mean?

Are you board certified?
—In what?

What is the difference between diagnosis and treatment?

Have you had experience doing both?
—Explain those.

Have you ever done disability evaluations? For whom?
—For lawyers?
—For insurance companies?
—For industry?
—For government agencies?

Is there a difference between impairment and disability?
—Please distinguish the two, impairment and disability, for the jury.

Is there a difference between objective and subjective?
—Please define these for the jury.

With what medical associations have you been associated?

Have you received any unusual awards for your work?

Doctor, do you have any experience teaching physicians?

Have you had experiences teaching people other than doctors?

Have you published any books or articles?

What is your book(s) about?
—Who is it written for?
—Who uses it?

When asking specific questions about thermography, one has reached the stage of going beyond qualifying the witness. Although it is still in that line of questioning, the lawyer can proceed to actually qualify the technique with questions from the following, again depending on the knowledge and expertise of the witness.

Are you in active medical practice now?

What is thermography?

How does it work?

Who uses it and how do they use it?

Describe the equipment.
—(Continue questions until it is understood.)
—How does it work?
—What does it show?
—Are there different kinds of thermography?
—What is the difference between these?
—Which kind do you do?
—How much does the equipment cost?
Is thermography taught or in regular use?
—In medical school?

—In active medical practices?
—In hospitals?
—By government or industry?

Please describe the test and the procedure.

Have you ever been accepted as an expert in thermography in courts? Where?

Do you have any personal knowledge of whether or not thermography is accepted in courts in other states?

Have you written any books or papers or made any presentations about thermography?
—Is this the thermography about which you will be testifying today?

Note: Do not allow voir dire of witness during direct examination. There was the opportunity to do that on discovery. They can cross-examine. Do not offer the witness as an expert. *Assume* he is an expert.

SUBSTANTIVE TESTIMONY

Thermography is ready for the courtroom. It will help the jury understand because it determines whether or not there is something substantially wrong with the patient.

The basic answers given by thermography should be stressed. There is nothing magic about this test or about its scientific validity. The thermogram answers the questions:

Is this thermogram normal or abnormal?

Are these pictures of physiologic nerve fiber abnormality?

Is this a blood supply abnormality to the area depicted?

Is there a substantial soft tissue injury present or not?

Is there a reason for the pain evident?[42]

There must be some specificity about the patient plaintiff to meet the necessary criteria:

Was thermography done under your control, direction, or supervision on . . . ?
—When? Where?

What was done? Describe the procedure.

Do you have the pictures, thermograms, with you?

How are the thermograms identified?

Is that manner of identification usual and customary in your office?

What does each thermogram look like?

How many are there?

Do you know if proper routine and protocol were followed in the performance of the study?
—How do you know?

Do you know of any complaints of Mr./Mrs. ——?
—Were those complaints present at the time of thermography?

In your opinion, based on reasonable medical probability, is there any correlation between the thermographic findings and the complaints?

Thermography is excellent demonstrative evidence. If permanently recorded on videotape, the entire procedure can be shown. It is perhaps better, shorter, and simpler to introduce enlargements of pertinent pictures taken during the thermographic study. Such evidence is then properly described and taken into jury deliberation. The approach to admitting such color thermographic enlargements is:

At my request did you make any enlargements of any of the slides?
—Which ones and why?

Were these marked for identification prior to the deposition?
—How were they marked?

Describe these reprints, these pictures.

Is a thermogram an accurate diagnostic tool?

Is there a difference between objective and subjective, and if so, what is that difference?

Is a thermogram objective?

Did you reach any conclusions in evaluating these thermograms based on reasonable medical probability?

Would it help the jury understand your answers if you showed some of the thermograms?
—(Introduce previously marked thermograms.)

Please describe those to the jury.
—(Slides are "mentioned." Long discussion of "enlargements" to be introduced into evidence. Slides merely mentioned, but not introduced.)
—(Prints are representative of slides.)

Do you have an opinion as to diagnosis, based on reasonable medical probability?

On what do you base your opinion?

What is your opinion?

Note that slides and prints were mentioned above. As a general rule, the thermologist will have produced 35mm color slides or Polaroid-type prints as the basic pictures before enlargement. It is intended that some of these are enlarged for admission into evidence. Three to six would be a proper number to be enlarged to 8 × 10 or even 20 × 30 properly mounted pictures. It is the original slides or prints that are discussed and about which there is introductory testimony. For the purpose of teaching the jury, some slides may be shown. It is the enlargements, typifying the injury and chosen by the physician to best demonstrate the abnormalities about which he has opinions, that are introduced into evidence.

Causation can be simply handled by thermography. For causation there is the requirement that only one injury, the one at issue, and no preceding or intervening trauma to the area exist. That may be stated in a hypothetical question. If more than one injury to the area exists, such as to the neck with arm symptoms, the thermogram will not accurately serve that purpose. Other reliable methods exist.

To establish permanence, what is generally needed is that twelve months must have passed between the last injury and the thermogram for cervical upper-body problems, and that twelve to eighteen months should have passed between the last injury and lower-body, lumbar thermographic studies.

When reaching the testimony regarding pain and suffering, thermology can easily handle the issue, although obviously a great deal depends on the skill and expertise of both the lawyer and the witness relative to this subject matter. Thermographically, the issue of pain is handled simply, quickly, and without a great deal of elaboration after all the preceding testimony has been completed:

Did Mr./Mrs.——complain of pain to you?

What was the complaint?

In your opinion, is that the kind of pain consistent with your diagnosis?

Does a thermogram show pain?

What does it show?

Based on the thermograms, is there a reason for the pain in Mr./Mrs.——?

This should be the end of the direct examination of the expert thermologist.

REFERENCES

1. H. Rein, *Primer on Thermography* (Orlando, Fla., 1983).

2. Orange, Dade, Broward, Duval, Hillsborough, Brevard, Volusia, Alachua, Lee Counties, FL; AK, CA, DE, DC, IL, LA, MI, MS, NJ, NY, OH, WI, and Nassau.

3. *AMA Guides to the Evaluation of Permanent Impairment* (Chicago: American Medical Association, 1971), p. iii.

4. H. Rein, *Primer on Thermography,* 1983.

5. *Chatom v. State,* 348 So.2d 828 (Ala. Crim.App. 1976), rev'd. 348 So.2d 838 (Ala.), acq. 348 So.2d 843 (Ala. Crim.App. 1977).

6. *Commonwealth v. Devlin,* 365 Mass. 149, 310 N.E.2d 353 (1974) (identification of human remains through X-ray comparison).

7. *Frye v. U.S.,* 293 F. 1013 (D.C. Cir. 1923).

8. *Hernandez v. State,* 530 S.W.2d 563 (Tex. Crim.App. 1975) (ultraviolet and infrared spectrographic analysis).

9. *People v. Marx,* 54 Cal. App.3d 100, 126 Cal.Rptr. 350 (1975).

10. *People v. Palmer,* 80 Cal. App.3d 239, 145 Cal.Rptr. 466 (1978) (scanning electronic microscopic analysis).

11. *Reid v. State,* 267 Ind. 555, 327 N.E.2d 1149 (1978) (trace metal detection technique).

12. *State v. Boyington,* 153 N.J. Super. 252, 379 A.2d 486 (App. Div. 1977) (Decatur Ragun).

13. *State v. Coolidge,* 109 N.H. 403, 260 A.2d 547 (1969), rev'd on other grounds, 403 U.S. 443 (1971).

14. *State v. Daniels,* 37 Ohio App.2d 4, 305 N.E.2d 497 (1973) (trace metal detection technique).

15. *State v. Peoples,* 227 Kan. 127, 605 P.2d 135 (1980).

16. *State v. Sharbono,* 174 Mont. 552, 563 P.2d 61 (1977) (gas-chromebiographic analysis).

17. *State v. Smith,* 50 Ohio App.2d 183, 362 N.E.2d 1239 (1976) (modified Harrison-Gilroy test for gunshot residue).

18. *State v. Sparks,* 397 N.C. 314, 255 S.E.2d 373 (1979).

19. *U.S. v. Addison,* 498 F.2d 741 (D.C. Cir. 1974).

20. *U.S. v. Brown,* 557 F.2d 541 (6th Cir. 1977) (ion microprobic analysis).

21. *U.S. v. Bruno,* 333 F.Supp. 570 (E.D. Pa. 1971) (chromatographic analysis of ink).

22. *U.S. v. Debethiam,* 348 F.Supp. 1377 (S.D. Cal.) aff'd *per curiam,* 470 F.2d 1367 (9th Cir. 1972) *cert. denied,* 412 U.S. 907 (1973).

23. *U.S. v. Stifel,* 433 F.2d 431 (6th Cir. 1970), *cert. denied,* 401 U.S. 994 (1971).

24. *U.S. v. Williams,* 583 F.2d 1194 (2d Cir. 1978), *cert. denied,* 439 U.S. 1117 (1979).

25. *U.S. v. Zeiger,* 350 F.Supp. 685 (D.D.C.), rev'd *per curiam,* 472 F.2d 1280 (D.C. Cir. 1972).

26. *United States v. Kilgus,* 571 F.2d 508 (9th Cir. 1978) (forward-looking infrared system).

27. *United States v. Lopez,* 328 F.Supp. 1077 (E.D.N.Y. 1971) (Fluxgate magnetometer).

28. *Federal Rule 401: Definition of "Relevant Evidence."* "Relevant evidence" means evidence having any tendency to make the existence of any fact that is of consequence to the determination of the action more probable or less probable than it would be without the evidence.

29. *Federal Rule 403: Exclusion of Relevant Evidence on Grounds of Prejudice, Confusion, or Waste of Time.* Although relevant, evidence may be excluded if its probative value is substantially outweighed by the danger of unfair prejudice, confusion of the issues, or misleading the jury, or by considerations of undue delay, waste of time, or needless presentation of cumulative evidence.

30. *Federal Rule 702: Testimony by Experts.* If scientific, technical, or other specialized knowledge will assist the trier of fact to understand the evidence or to determine a fact in issue, a witness qualified as an expert by knowledge, skill, experience, training, or education, may testify thereto in the form of an opinion or otherwise.

31. *U.S. v. Williams,* supra.

32. *Brown v. Luguer,* #10, 102 Court of Appeals, 4th Circuit, dec. August 1, 1979 (not designated for publication).

33. *Mayhugh v. Augusteen,* 287434 (Orange County Superior Court, Calif.).

34. *Steid v. Bowen,* 52318 (Los Angeles Superior Court, Calif.).

35. Foundation for admissions. 7 *Am. Jur. Proof of Facts,* Proof 3.

36. Admissibility of photos generally: 9 *ALR* 2d 899; 4 *DePaul Law Review* 95; 3 *Am. Jur. Trial* 1 § 24–39.

37. Weakness of chain of custody evidence went to weight, not its admissibility. *U.S. v. Vasquez,* 476 F.2d 730 (5th Cir. 1973).

38. Photo is [relevant and] a fair and accurate representation of what it depicts. There is no need to use the testimony of the photographer. *Wilkins v. State,* 155 So.2d 129 (Fla. 1963).

39. X-rays: 10 *ALR* 2d 918; 5 *ALR* 3d 303 (proof re: authentication). (Subject to same rule as photographs.)

40. Examination of the relevant thing itself. 4 *Wigmore, Evidence* (2d Ed. 1940 Sec. 1151).

41. Photos admissible if they explain and illustrate a part of some qualified person's testimony. *Evans v. Perry,* 161 So.2d 27 (Fla. 2d DCA 1964).

42. See note 1.

43. *Fay v. Mincey,* 454 So.2d 587 (Fla. App. 2 Dist. 1984).

44. *Wether v. Heckler,* #83–C–9380, 7/23/84.

45. *Procida v. McLaughlin,* 497 A.2d 447, Superior Ct., Camden County 1984.

46. *Argenta v. Shahan,* 354 N.W.2d 796 (Mich. App. 1984).

47. *Garrett v. New Orleans Public Service,* 459 So.2d 746, 11/14/84 (La.)

48. *Bilotta and Blumen v. Department of Labor,* et al., State of Florida, Department of Labor and Employment Security, Case No. 83–3512, Final Order, August 29, 1984.

49. *Flowers v. State Farm,* Case No. 83–2226, Orange County, Florida 1984.

50. *Palma v. State Farm,* Case No. 83–4113, Palm Beach County, Florida 1984.

51. *Crawford v. Shivshankar,* 10 FLW 2019, 1st DCA, August 22, 1985.

52. Food and Drug Administration, 21 CFR.

53. AMA *Guides to the Evaluation of Permanent Impairment.*

54. H. Rein, *Primer on Soft Tissue Injuries* (Winter Park, Fla.: Rolling Press, 1981).

55. Rein, *Random Studies of Thermographing Findings* (unpublished to date.)

56. *Thermology,* Volume 1, 1985, American Academy of Thermology.

57. Wexler, *Thermographic Lumbar Patterns* (Tarzana, Calif.: Thermographic Services, Inc., 1983).

58. Rein, *Primer on Medical Malpractice* (Orlando, Fla., 1983).

59. Medicare Part B, Chapter II, *Medicare and Medicaid Guide,* 1981; *Medicare and Medicaid Guide,* 1983; *Communique* Medical Newsletter, August 1984.

60. *Thornton v. U.S. Dept. of Agriculture,* 715 F.2d 1508 (11th Cir. 1983).

61. *Fleming v. U.S. Dept. of Agriculture,* 713 F.2d 179 (6th Cir. 1983).

62. *Di Giacomo v. Board of Public Education,* Delaware Hearing, 1983.

63. *Howard v. Central of Georgia Railroad Company,* #15095–6, Superior Court of Chatham County (1983).

64. *Blanchard v. A–1 Bit and Tool Co., Inc.,* 406 So.2d 773 (La. App. 1981).

65. *Alexis v. New Orleans Public Service, Inc.,* 449 So.2d 1084 (La. App. 4th Cir. 1984).

66. *Deshotel v. Avondale Shipyards, Inc.* 413 So.2d 208 (La. App. 4th Cir. 1982).

67. *Foreman v. State Farm Mut. Auto Insurance,* 416 So.2d 258 (La. App. 3rd Cir. 1982).

68. *Thorton v. Landis Construction Co., Inc.,* 359 So.2d 719 (La. App. 1978).

69. *Williams v. Payne,* 346 N.W.2d 564 (131 Mich. App. 403, 1984).

70. *Baetutis v. Czerwinski,* #571–463, Milwaukee County.

71. Taken from Eugene Alban, M.D., *The Primer on Thermography* (Orlando, Fla., 1983) Section 6.

72. Alan R. Liss, *Biomedical Thermology,* (New York: Alan R. Liss, Inc., 1982).
73. *Tribou v. Gunn,* 410 S.2d 378 (1982).
74. *Laws v. Empire Realty Co.,* Sup. Ct. of State of New York, Bronx County, Case 16934/82.

Some Legal Aspects of Angiography and Interventative Radiology

Stewart R. Reuter, M.D., J.D.

Angiography has been undergoing a significant evolution in recent years. On one hand, the progressive development of newer, less invasive imaging modalities has caused a significant decrease in the amount of diagnostic angiography being done. The greatest impact has occurred in the neuroradiological procedures, but other diagnostic studies have diminished as well. The remaining stronghold of angiography is in the evaluation of vascular disease. No other technique has been able to duplicate the accuracy of angiography in the evaluation of different types of stenotic lesions of blood vessels all over the body.

On the other hand, angiographers themselves have become more invasive, and a whole new area of radiology known as interventative radiology has emerged. Building on the same techniques used in diagnostic angiography, radiologists have developed successful methods for transhepatic common duct stone removal, internal and external drainage of obstructed bile ducts, and dilatation of biliary ductal stenoses.[1] The same techniques have been applied to drainage procedures in the urinary tract,[2] and the percutaneous insertion of drainage tubes into abscess cavities has rapidly followed the development of the techniques in the biliary and urinary tracts.[3] Similarly, angiographers have begun to dilate arterial stenoses successfully with sausage-shaped balloon catheters (percutaneous angioplasty), achieving long-term results comparable to those achieved by vascular bypass surgery.[4] Recently, balloon angiography techniques have been used to dilate biliary and urinary tract strictures.[5]

Finally, angiographers have become active in both the thrombosis and the thrombolysis of arteries. Bleeding arteries, anywhere in the body, can easily be occluded by injecting emboli or vasoconstrictive drugs through selectively placed catheters.[6, 7] A great deal of experience has now been accumulated with controlling gastrointestinal bleeding. Emboli appear to be preferable for controlling upper GI bleeding, and vasopressin for lower GI bleeding.[8] With this method emergency operations can be converted to elective procedures with an accompanying reduction of mortality; some patients may even avoid an operation entirely. Both traumatic and congenital arteriovenous fistulas and malformations can also be occluded with particulate emboli, and the symptoms caused by massive congenital malformations can be relieved.[9]

Also, vessels occluded by blood clot have been recanalized through the use of selective urokinase infusion.[10] Because the urokinase is injected directly into the clot, much lower doses can be used than with systemic infusion, and the complications can be markedly diminished. However, urokinase remains a very complex drug to use, and a significant, although acceptable, rate of complications still exists, even with selective infusion.

The movement to a prospective, diagnosis related groups (DRG)-based reimbursement formula by governmental and other third-party payers should result in an increased utilization of these types of radiological procedures. They avoid much of the morbidity of comparable operative procedures for the same problems, while at the same time significantly decreasing the length of hospital stay. In a recent article in the *New England Journal,* Dr. Herbert Abrams has pointed out the comparatively greater cost of vascular surgery compared with percutaneous angioplasty.[11]

INCREASING MALPRACTICE LIABILITY EXPOSURE WILL ACCOMPANY THE USE OF INTERVENTATIVE RADIOLOGY

As a general rule, the greater the degree to which a radiologist, or other physician for that matter, practices like a surgeon, the greater the degree to which his or her malpractice liability exposure will approach that of a surgeon. All interventative radiological procedures have a recognized, although generally low and acceptable, rate of complications. The most significant of these involve bleeding, infection, and leakage of bile or urine. As with any other type of interventative procedure, the competence and skill of the operator in performing the procedure will depend on the type of training he has had. Most radiology residency programs now devote a significant amount of time to these procedures, and fellowships in interventative radiology are generally available. However, older radiologists who have been in practice for several years will be tempted to do interventative procedures, and, to a great degree, the skill with which they perform the examination will be related to their previous experience with angiographic procedures and techniques. Also, many nonradiologists who have access to fluoroscopy will be tempted to perform interventative procedures without first having obtained adequate training with the techniques of catheterization. An attorney evaluating a patient who has had a complication of an interventative radiological procedure should carefully evaluate the training and the experience of the physician who did the procedure. In general, a physician is held to the standard of care that he holds himself out to possess. For example, a gastroenterologist who has access to a fluoroscope and who performs percutaneous biliary drainage procedures holds himself out to have the requisite training, experience, and skill to perform the procedures competently. If, in fact, he is inadequately trained or has inadequate experience, this may be brought out in a negligence action if there is a maloccurrence at the time of the procedure, and the gastroenterologist may be faced with a radiologist expert witness who has had adequate training to learn the techniques.

Fortunately, complications related to interventative radiological procedures have, to date, been low and not particularly severe. However, any complication from an interventative procedure may lead to an allegation of negligence, and this will have an impact on the amount of litigation involving radiologists. Since the morbidity and mortality resulting from complications of angiographic and interventative radiological procedures tend to be greater than those occurring in general radiology, the claims will be significantly higher than claims resulting for injuries caused during general radiology. The legal considerations are no different from those applying to any other malpractice litigation in radiology. However, there are a few special problems related to angiography and interventative radiology that require further discussion.

SOME SPECIAL PROBLEMS WITH INFORMED CONSENT

The issue of informed consent is becoming a problem for all physicians, not only radiologists. A recent Rand Corporation study on frequency and severity of malpractice claims found that informed consent was the major cause of the increased number of malpractice claims that led to the malpractice crisis of the mid-1970s.[12] A quick perusal of any index of malpractice cases reaching appellate courts, such as the *Citation,* published by the AMA, reveals that the number of appellate court cases indexed under *informed consent* continues to increase each year. It is certainly an important issue in malpractice cases arising from complications of angiography and interventative procedures.

One problem currently being debated among radiologists is whether the patient needs to be informed of the 1 in 40,000 risk of death associated with the intravenous injection of contrast agents for intravenous pyelogram (IVP), CT, or intravenous angiography.[13] The answer to this question depends on whether the procedure is being done in a ''reasonable physician'' or ''reasonable person'' type of jurisdiction. In the latter, a reasonable person probably would want to know about a chance of death, even though it is only 1 in 40,000. In ''reasonable physician'' jurisdictions, the radiologist needs to inform the patient of the risks and complications about which reasonable physicians in a similar locality inform their patients under similar circumstances. However, the locality rule for radiologists has generally been expanded to a national standard of practice. This obviously includes radiologists from "reasonable person" as well as "reasonable physician" jurisdictions, and the plaintiff could rather easily get expert testimony that the risk of death is revealed by a reasonable physician. Although this problem has not yet arisen, testimony regarding the standard of practice in a "reasonable physician" jurisdiction should probably be given only by experts from other "reasonable physician" jurisdictions.

Other problems radiologists have with informed consent derive from the rather anecdotal, impersonal relationship they have with the patient. Patients frequently feel more comfortable discussing proposed medical procedures with their internist or surgeon than with someone they have never met before. The radiologist may also be uncomfortable informing the patient about alternative procedures, many of which are performed by nonradiologists. Finally, almost all radiologists have had the experience of going to a patient to obtain consent for a radiological procedure, only to find that the patient has not yet been informed of the need for the procedure by the referring physician. All of these problems lead to a situation in which radiologists prefer that the consent be obtained by the patient's physician. However, radiologists must obtain the consent themselves. The reasons are twofold. First, confusion about who is to obtain the consent may result in the radiologist and clinician each thinking that the other has obtained the consent when, in fact, neither has. Second, the time during which the radiologist obtains consent may be the only opportunity he or she has to develop any type of patient-physician relationship prior to the procedure, and even the briefest relationship will be of great value if anything untoward occurs during the performance of the procedure. Moreover, the person doing the procedure should obtain the consent himself rather than sending agents such as nurses, office personnel, or house staff. In two recent appellate court decisions, the court has appropriately held that the responsibility for obtaining the consent lies with the radiologist performing the procedure, not with the referring physician.[14] When a physician sends an agent to the nurse or resident to obtain consent to a procedure, the physician performing the procedure is bound by the inadequate consent, even though he or she does not know what information was given the patient.[15]

Because the issues of informed consent have become an important part of malpractice litigation, radiologists have shown great interest in detailed consent forms, which specify all of the potential complications of a procedure and their relative incidence. Although such forms should certainly not be encouraged for all procedures, they may have value in the many types of angiographic and interventative procedures for which the complications are relatively few and the incidence of complications is well documented.[16]

On the other hand, detailed consent forms are a two-edged sword. Although they are an excellent memorialization of the complications of which the patient has been informed, they equally suggest by implication that the patient has not been informed of the complications that do not appear on the printed form. For this reason, many defense attorneys do not like detailed consent forms, preferring to have the physician make a notation in the chart that the patient has been informed of the risks, complications, and alternative procedures. Juries tend to believe timely notes in patients' charts, and the defendant physician can inform the jury at the time of the trial about those complications of which he usually informs the patient prior to doing various procedures. If the procedure is in any way experimental or unproven, however, detailed consent forms are essential. In one such case, a very well worded consent from was of great benefit to Dr. Denton Cooley when an artificial heart implant failed.[17]

THE INTERVENTATIVE RADIOLOGIST'S PROBLEMS WITH VICARIOUS LIABILITY

Employers are generally liable under the rules of *respondeat superior* (let the master answer) for the torts of their employees that occur within the scope of employment. Thus, hospitals are usually liable for the negligent acts of X-ray technicians and other hospital employees.[18] However, during the early years of this century hospitals were considered to be charitable institutions and were immune to suit under the rules of charitable immunity. Patients injured by a negligent hospital employee, unfortunately, were frequently left to pay their own medical bills because the employee had few resources and the hospital was immune. Under such circumstances, courts did not have a great deal of trouble distorting the normal rules of *respondeat superior* to find that the physician or surgeon had borrowed the employee from the hospital and had assumed liability for acts over which he or she exercised a significant degree of control.[19] The ultimate extension of this distortion became known as the Captain of the Ship Doctrine, under which operating surgeons were liable as a matter of law for the negligent acts of all hospital employees in the operating room during the course of an operation.[20] The only fact to be decided by the jury in the many jurisdictions using this doctrine was whether or not the operation was in progress. Most jurisdictions have now backed away from the arbitrariness of this doctrine and have tried to bring the rules of *respondeat superior* in the hospital back into line with its use in other employment settings.[21] Courts have used the Captain of the Ship reasoning in other settings in the hospital that have characteristics similar to the operating room setting, such as the obstetrical suite.[22]

Although no appellate court has yet held the Captain of the Ship reasoning to apply to special-procedure suites in radiology departments or cardiac cath labs, these settings also resemble in many ways an operating suite. A radiologist or other physician is generally in charge of the procedure, at which a nurse and frequently more than one technician are in attendance, each with separate duties, but always under the control of the radiologist. From a risk-management point of view it is imperative that the radiologist work with the technicians to help train them, to monitor their activities carefully, and to work with the hospital in removing any employees who show signs of carelessness in their work habits.

From a practical point of view, most jurisdictions that have moved away from the Captain of the Ship Doctrine have done so in the context of the negligent sponge count. In doing so they have looked at the hospitals' policies and procedures manuals and have found that, because of a detailed description in the manual of the manner in which the count was to be obtained, the hospital intended to retain control over the sponge count and not to relinquish this control to the surgeon.[23] One of the departments of the hospital that has a detailed policy and procedures manual is the X-ray department. Under the rules of the Joint Commission on Accreditation of Hospitals (JCAH), the radiologist has an active part in the preparation of the policies and procedures manuals for the department. Therefore, the radiologist should work with the hospital to define in as much detail as possible the responsibilities of the technicians and nurses in a special-procedure suite and describe as fully as possible the manner in which such duties as loading the syringe, preparing the trays, hooking up EKGs and pressure transducers, and so on are to be performed. By doing so the radiologist can help to defend an allegation of *respondeat superior* for the technician's or nurse's negligence. Although the rules of *respondeat superior* were originally designed to provide a recovery for an injured patient, it is ironically the hospital, rather than the patient, which today attempts to use the borrowed servant rule and *respondent superior* to transfer a liability to the physician.[24] With the demise of charitable immunity and general liability for hospitals, the patient can recover from the hospital. The hospital or its insurer then names the physician or his or her insurer as a third-party defendant. Also, although almost all states have abandoned the general rule of charitable immunity, many states have included government hospitals in their rules for sovereign immunity and have limited the patient's monetary recovery for injuries occurring in government hospitals. For example, in Texas the limit of liability under the State Tort Claims Act is $100,000.[25] Under these circumstances, the patient still must sue the radiologist or other physician, as well as the hospital, in order to obtain an adequate recovery for the negligently caused injury. Under such circumstances, a detailed policies and procedures manual for the special-procedures suite is of particular importance.

PROBLEMS WITH NEGLIGENT SUPERVISION OF HOUSE STAFF

Most interventative techniques have been developed in university teaching hospitals, and in many instances patients are referred to tertiary care hospitals for the procedures. Many of these tertiary hospitals, even though not university affiliated, have their own residency training programs.

The employment relationships between hospitals, medical schools, and house staff are complex. However, a relatively common pattern exists because of Part A Medicare reimbursement to the hospital for the expenses of house staff. Thus, the hospital usually pays the residents' salaries, but the affiliation agreement between the hospital and a medical school usually delegates the responsibility for supervision of the resident to the medical school. In those states which have retained some sovereign immunity limitations on the liability of state and county hospitals as noted above, (see text accompanying note 25 *supra*), this may cause the plaintiff's attorney to try to find the medical school to be the resident's employer to create an additional source of recovery. However, if the medical school is a state school, the same limitations on liability may apply, and the plaintiffs must become more imaginative. One potential theory of recovery is negligent supervision of the resident by the physician responsible for the case. Although courts have been reluctant to extend liability to a supervising physician not present at the time of the negligent resident act,[26] a physician-teacher, who has accepted responsibility for selecting a resident and supervising his or her training, must exercise that responsibility in a reasonable prudent manner. A breach of the duty to act reasonably under the circumstances, which is the proximate cause of injury to a patient, may result in the teacher-physician being found negligent.[27]

It is important to distinguish between a supervising physician being liable for a resident's negligence under the theory of *respondeat superior* and under the theory of negligence. In the former, the liability for the negligent act of the resident is placed upon the supervising physician because he or she was present and in control of the resident at the time the negligent act occurred, according to the borrowed servant rule and *respondeat superior*. The supervising physician may not have been negligent and in fact may have done everything possible to prevent the negligence. Liability is transferred to him as a matter of public policy. Under the usual operation of the borrowed servant rule, the supervising physician would not be liable unless the supervisor was personally present and in control of the resident at the time the negligence occurred.[28] Under the theory of negligent supervision, on the other hand, liability is not transferred from the resident to the supervising physician. Rather, the supervising physician himself must have been negligent in his supervision to be liable. Generally, the supervising physician acts negligently by allowing the resident to perform an act that he knows or should know that the resident is not capable of performing competently. Under this theory, the supervising physician need not even be present at the time the negligent act occurs. It is therefore essential that all radiologists in teaching hospitals know the terms of the affiliation agreement and their assigned level of supervisory responsibility for house staff.

Physicians with supervisory responsibilities must act in a reasonably prudent manner, and department chairmen should establish reasonably strict criteria for allowing residents to perform medical acts on their own. As plaintiffs' attorneys search for innovative legal theories to spread and increase the liability, negligent supervision will become more of a problem for medical school faculty.

IRRADIATION DURING THE FIRST TRIMESTER OF PREGNANCY

Significant irradiation of a pregnant woman may be the cause of an injury to the fetus, and the physician who administers the radiation may be negligent if he or she fails to determine that the woman is pregnant prior to giving the radiation.[29] Fetal irradiation is part of the complex area of prenatal torts, a broad discussion of which is beyond the scope of this chapter. However, the litigation involving prenatal torts is one of the most rapidly developing areas of medical liability, and lawsuits alleging negligent irradiation of fetuses will certainly increase in number in the near future.

The most dangerous period for fetal radiation occurs during the first month because this is the time that the neurological structures, which are most sensitive to radiation, are developing.[30] Because women are two weeks pregnant before a missed period gives them indication that a pregnancy exists, radiographs should be taken only during the first ten days of the menstrual cycle in women of childbearing years unless an urgent medical situation requires earlier diagnosis.

Cases involving irradiation of a fetus that have reached the appellate courts to date have involved primarily internists and obstetricians. However, as in all matters involving hospital law, the JCAH will have an important impact in this area. JCAH standards have a way of becoming legal standards as well as medical standards. The current standards of the JCAH require that hospital radiology departments establish policies and procedures that assure that women do not receive unwarranted radiation early in pregnancy.[31] Only time will tell, however, whether the duty to avoid fetal irradiation will fall on the hospital or the radiologist who is performing the radiological examination. In the hospital setting, it is probably the hospital that has the best opportunity to appropriately schedule women of childbearing years during the first ten days of their menstrual cycle for radiological examinations by questioning patients arriving at the desk of the X-ray department whether or not they might be pregnant or whether they are using some contraceptive device.

In the office setting, however, the physician or radiologist performing the radiological examination has the best opportunity to prevent negligent radiation of fetuses, and there is little question about where the responsibility will lie. All physicians and hospitals should actively direct their efforts to radiating women of childbearing years only during the first ten days of their menstrual cycle unless they are using some form of contraceptive.

Radiologists performing angiography and interventative procedures should be particularly careful about inadvertently radiating pregnant women because these procedures use a great deal more radiation than simple chest films, skull films, or fluoroscopy. A great deal of fluoroscopy is used, and many films are exposed during an angiographic run. Moreover, angiograms are frequently obtained in the pelvis and abdomen, much closer to the fetus than chest or skull films.

REFERENCES

1. Ring, E. J., and R. K. Kerlan, Jr. 1984. "Interventional Biliary Radiology." *AJR* 142:31.

2. Banner, M. P., and H. M. Pollock. 1984. "Fluoroscopically Guided Percutaneous Extraction of Upper Urinary Tract Calculi." *Radiol. Clin. N. Am.* 22:415.

3. Banner, M. P., and H. M. Pollock. 1984. "Dilatation of Ureteral Stenoses: Techniques and Experience in 44 Patients. *AJR* 143:789.

4. Gruntzig, A. R. 1981. "Percutaneous Transluminal Coronary Angioplasty." *Semin. Roentgenol.* 16:152; Zeitler E., E. I. Richter, F. J. Roth, and W. Schoop. 1983. "Results of Percutaneous Transluminal Angioplasty." *Radiology* 146:57.

5. Salomonowitz, E., W. R. Castaneda-Zuniga, G. Lund, A. H. Cragg, D. W. Hunter, C. C. Coleman, and K. Amplatz. 1984. "Balloon Dilatation of Benign Biliary Strictures." *Radiology* 151:613.

6. Reuter S. R., V. P. Chuang, and R. L. Bree. 1975. "Selective Arterial Embolization for Control of Massive Upper Gastrointestinal Bleeding." *AJR* 125:119.

7. Chuang, V. P., S. R. Reuter J. Walter, W. D. Foley, and J. J. Bookstein. 1975. "Control of Renal Hemorrhage by Selective Arterial Embolization." *AJR* 125:300.

8. Reuter, S. R. 1979. "Embolization of Gastrointestinal Hemorrhage." *AJR* 133:557–558.

9. Palmas J. C., T. H. Newton, S. R. Reuter, and J. J. Bookstein. 1981. "Particulate Intraarterial Embolization in pelvic Arteriovenous Malformations." *AJR* 137:117.

10. Becker, G. J., F. E. Rabe, B. D. Richmond, R. W. Holden, H Y. Yune, R. S. Dilley, N. V. Bang, J. L. Glover, and E. C. Klatte. 1983. "Low Dose Fibrinolytic Therapy: Results and New Concepts." *Radiology* 148:663.

11. Abrams, H. L., and T. M. Doubilet. 1984. "The Cost of Underutilization of Percutaneous Transhepatic Angiography." *New Eng. J. Med.* 310:95.

12. Danzon, P. M. 1982. *The frequency and severity of malpractice claims.* P. 28. Santa Monica: The Rand Corporation.

13. Spring, D. B., J. R. Akins, and A. R. Margulis. 1984. "Informed Consent for Intravenous Contrast-Enhanced Radiography: A National Survey of Practice and Opinion." *Radiology* 152:609.

14. *Patrick v. Nelson,* 293 S.E.2d 829 (N.C. App. 1982); *Halley v. Birbiglia,* 458 N.E.2d 353 (Mass. 1983).

15. *Hill v. Seward,* 470 N.Y.S.2d 971 (N.Y. Supp. 1983).

16. Reuter, S. R. 1982. *Use of detailed consent forms.* Chicago: The American College of Radiology.

17. *Karp v. Cooley,* 493 F.2d 408 (5th Circ. 1974).

18. *Cline v. Lund,* 107 Cal.Rptr. 629 (Ct.App. 1973); *Klema v. St. Elizabeth's Hosp.* 166 N.E.2d 765 (Ohio 1960).

19. Restatement (Second) of Agency § 227 (1957).

20. *McConnell v. Williams,* 65 A.2d 243, 246 (Pa. 1949).

21. *Bing v. Thunig,* 143 N.E.2d 3, 8 (N.Y. 1957); *Sparger v. Worley Hosp.,* 547 S.W.2d 582, 584 (Tex. 1977).

22. *Minogue v. Rutland Hosp.,* 125 A.2d 796 (Vt. 1956).

23. *Sparger v. Worley Hosp.,* 547 S.W.2d 582 (Tex. 1977).

24. *Dessauer v. Memorial Gen. Hosp.,* 628 P.2d 337 (N.M. Ct.App. 1981).

25. Tex. Rev. Civ. Stat. Ann. § 6252–19 (Vernon).

26. *Aubert v. Charity Hosp. of La.,* 363 So.2d 1223 (La. App. 1978).

27. *County of Riverside v. Loma Linda Univ.,* 173 Cal.Rptr. 371 (Cal. App. 1981); *Camp v. Bernalillo County Med. Center,* 633 P.2d 719 (N.M. App. 1981).

28. Reuter, S. R. 1985. "Toward a More Realistic and Consistent Use of Respondeat Superior in the Hospital." 29 *St. Louis U.L.J.* 648–651.

29. *Deutch v. Shein,* 597 S.W.2d 141 (Ky. 1980).

30. Brent, R. I. 1980. "Fetal Teratogenesis: Fetal Risk and Abortion." In *Biological Risks of Medical Irradiations,* New York: ed. Fullerton et al., pp. 224–229. American Association of Physicists in Medicine.

31. Joint Commission on Accreditation of Hospitals. 1984. *Accreditation Manual for* Hospitals. P. 157.

Medical Lasers and the Law

Martin L. Norton, M.D., J.D., and
Edward V. Norton, J.D.

There are many lights in light.

—Talmud, Berachot 52 b

Lasers present legal problems similar to other medical devices in the marketplace. For the physician practitioner there are issues related to negligence law. For the manufacturer and distributor there are the dual problems of product liability and regulatory laws.[1]

This presentation will discuss some of the more pertinent aspects under the three categories of negligence, regulatory laws, and product liability. The physician reader will note that he is touched directly or indirectly by all three considerations. This discussion is intended to inform, but it will not be a primer on all the nuances of the law. We trust it will contribute to understanding and thus ease the way for future developments in laser medicine. While we may discuss these generically, we must always keep in mind our primary concern—the patient treated with a laser.

NEGLIGENCE

The physician has been made painfully aware of the problems of medical practice through the proliferation of malpractice suits brought in recent years. Issues of

---

informed consent, experimentation, criteria of tort actions, damages, the expert witness, and other aspects will be discussed.

Informed Consent

While consent per se would not appear to be a classical tort, most courts currently focus on the materiality of undisclosed information.[2] Here the plaintiff need only show that this information, if disclosed, would have caused the patient (or a reasonable person) to forgo the treatment.[3] Thus, the duty of disclosure is established by judicial interpretation based on the landmark decision of Justice Benjamin Cardozo[4] establishing the right of each individual to determine what shall be done to his or her body.

The laser appears to the practitioner to be a simple medium for his art. The other chapters of this book may disabuse him of some of this simplicity. The area most likely to be the nidus for litigation is that of informed consent. We do not stress that aspect of informed consent relating to the specifics of patient injury, but rather refer to (a) the failure of the practitioner to obtain proper training before using the laser instrument, (b) the failure to become proficient in the use of a specific instrument and modality, and (c) the failure to inform the patient of the level of training and expertise of the laser practitioner.

Appended to this chapter are the criteria for credentialing in the use of medical lasers promulgated at the University of Michigan Hospitals and as formulated in substance for the American National Standards Institute. One notes that they address items (a) and (b) above. Mere observation of laser surgery, or superficial use "under supervision," may be inadequate. Furthermore, each instrument is different; each modality has different characteristics in function, effect, and operational procedures. Expertise with one instrument does not establish competency with another instrument or modality.

The patient is entitled to all information that is material to making an informed judgment upon accepting the laser as the instrument of choice. This is particularly important since in almost all situations there is another surgical alternative, for example, cold knife, cryotherapy, and so on. This concept relates not only to the surgeon but also to the anesthesiologist in his choice of venturi ventilation in contrast to the various types of endotracheal tubes with their respective inherent risks.

Consent also includes a discussion of the ancillary or supporting systems for laser surgery, including the recognition of the risks of anesthesia and the special techniques of ventilation used during anesthesia for laser surgery of the larynx, trachea, or bronchi. A discussion of venturi ventilation, with its potential complications, as commented on in the chapter on anesthesia, is definitely in order. It becomes incumbent upon both the surgeon and the anesthesiologist, therefore, to be alerted to and fully aware of the option of the other practitioner in his management of the specific patient. An example of this situation was the case in Pittsburgh, Pa., where a plastic endotracheal tube was used. The heating of the "protective" foil and underlying tube by the laser caused a fire in the airways to occur. One of the plaintiff's claims was failure of informed consent. While it is incumbent upon the anesthesiologist to fully inform his patient, this does not in itself obviate the responsibility of the surgeon, who is similarly present. He does have joint and several responsibility, at least, to be aware of what is going on and to be sure that his patient is so informed.

Part of the consent issue is recognition of the extent to which consent must be obtained. The patient must be advised of the plan for the procedure, of the alternatives that are available, and of the potential problems of both or either situation as well as the reasons why there is a choice on the part of the physician for a specific mode of treatment. In a rather unusual decision one court has gone so far as to say that even totally unacceptable alternatives must be discussed.[5] While this decision does not reflect the general trend, the fact remains that this court did come down with its decision on the basis that "if there is only one choice there is no choice at all." This extreme approach fails to take into account that there was, in fact, an alternative for the patient—namely, not to have the procedure done at all.

On the issue of duty or responsibility, it becomes readily evident that there is an interaction between the surgeon and the patient and the anesthesiologist, that is, teamwork. Thus, it is conceivable that the legal principle of joint and several liability would be invoked in this context. *Joint and several liability* refers to the liability of joint tortfeasors for the same injury to persons or property. It includes those who act together in committing wrongs or whose acts, if independent of each other, unite in causing a single injury.[6] Here the plaintiff can institute legal action against either or both of these parties or execute judgment against both.

Human Experimentation versus Innovative Management

Lasers have caught the imagination of the public and the profession. New applications, however, have not quite kept pace with marketing by the manufacturers. We are, therefore, faced with the question of when an experimental procedure or application becomes first an innovative and ultimately an accepted modality. This author (M.L.N.) addressed the question from the philosophic and sociologic context, coming to the conclusion that the integrity of the physician and the profession is sorely tested.[7] Investigational review boards, human study committees, ethics committees, and the like provide some restraint. However, enthusiasm, ego, and/or the desire to help the patient can work adversely to the patient's interest. Animal experience and practice under supervision are urged before exposing patients to risks that may be, as yet, incompletely understood. Irving Ladimer eloquently expressed the situation as follows:

> the term "experimentation" must be considered objectively so that it is recognizable as a legitimate scientific endeavor which can be advanced by the recognized research sci-

entist. The legal issue would then become not experimentation versus accepted practice of the art of medicine but an evaluation of the plan and conduct of research in relation to specific fact situations and whether the research was conducted with due regard to the interests of the subject. The law has a duty to comprehend the scope and element of diverse human activity and their places in society if it is to assist in making individual judgment and setting or recognizing general values.[8]

The professionals of the Food and Drug Administration and their advisory panels have assisted with solution of the dilemma for instrumentation entering the marketplace. This will be discussed below.

Criteria of Tort Actions

A tort action in negligence (malpractice) requires the plaintiff to demonstrate the defendant's (a) duty or responsibility, (b) failure of that duty or responsibility, (c) injury to the patient, and (d) proximate relationship between the failure of duty and that injury.

At this point, we must point out that most legal actions (lawsuits) take place in the lower judicial courts. In fact, many cases are settled out of court. Thus, the predominance of cases will not be found in the literature. Information from the lower courts is primarily anecdotal. Furthermore, because of the relatively short period of time in which lasers have been in medical use, very few cases to date have reached the appellate courts, where case reports are documented. Consequently, we discuss legal principles herein on the basis of legal analogy. This is no different from using established principles of physics or chemistry to solve problems or equations in different situations.

Damages and Negligence Actions

The laser surgeon may expose the patient to great risk. This is most manifest in intraluminal surgery, such as surgery of the aerodigestive tracts. This is because of proximity to vital structures such as the innominate and pulmonary artery (carinal and primary division bronchial surgery). The physician understands the immediate injury to the patient. However, two areas cause great consternation to physicians. First, there is the claim for damages such as emotional stress, loss of parental or a child's comfort and guidance, loss of consortium, and the like. This concerns the physician because he is usually focused solely on the patient's direct needs. At law and in practice, we must recognize that the patient's disease and therapy do not exist in a vacuum. The patient as a whole, the interaction of family response and environmental (sociologic) factors, all determine the functional response of the ill to their disease; and response to therapy, while difficult to quantify in sociologic studies, similarly must be considered.

The second point of contention is the "collateral source rule." This concept asserts that compensation received by the injured party "from a source initially independent of the tortfeasor . . . should not be deducted from the damages which the plaintiff would otherwise collect'' from the negligent party.[9] In other words, a tortfeasor may not benefit from the fact that the plaintiff has received money from other sources as a result of the defendant's tort, such as sickness and health insurance. This would appear by some to be an unjust rule in that there is really a calculated compounding of cost and a dual recovery. The first recovery is by the payment of medical bills by the insurance companies or other sources, and the second payment is the punitive damages awarded by the court.

Some argue that the phrase *punitive damages* is an unfair statement and that it is really a recompense for what has been paid for, that is, suffering, time from loss of work, and so on. It is painfully evident, however, that the nature and extent of damages include emotional distress, pain and suffering, and other parameters that are very difficult to quantify. The response has been to quantify them primarily on an emotional basis. In reality, one soon recognizes that the basic motivation is not only to obtain recompense for actual expenditures incurred but also to impose retribution.

While one ordinarily thinks of punitive measures in relation to criminal law, there is no doubt that there are sufficient criteria to call this a punitive measure even in civil or equity law. An example of this is a situation where double or triple the award is given to a party because of an alleged malice or misrepresentation. Treble damages are often awarded by statute for antitrust violations. Yet another example of such punitive measure is situations wherein the landlord of a leased property retains a security deposit. In some areas failure to properly return that security deposit results in double or triple payment back to the lessee. This borderline area, mainly the area of the landlord-tenant law, is more frequently considered a civil law action, with the addition of punitive damages. In response to this, advocacy of the ''structured settlement'' has met with initial success. It permits a long-term payment source based on purchase of annuities and other investment plans, thus diminishing the immediate financial impact on insurance companies, and hopefully, insurance premiums.

Some states also distribute judgments based on comparative negligence.[10] Comparative negligence is a damage apportionment system that assesses liability in proportion to fault. This approach is an alternative or replacement for the traditional doctrine of contributory negligence; it abridges but does not eliminate contributory negligence as a defense.[11]

The classical form of contributory negligence originated with Lord Ellenborough's opinion.[12] This defense was available only in situations where the plaintiff's negligence was a cause of the plaintiff's injuries at least in part. Traditionally, the party who was at least 51 percent contributorily negligent bore the full responsibility.

The Expert Witness

In medical negligence cases the expert witness is almost indispensable. Currently, in areas of laser complications, however, we are seeing a spate of ''laser experts'' whose appearance for plaintiffs' cases raises real questions as to expertise. The acceptance of an expert as such falls within the discretion of the presiding judge. The burden is even greater due to the relatively short time we have been using this modality and the constantly changing instrumentation and applications in the struggle against disease. Caution is urged to avoid career witnesses or organizations composed of panels of professional witnesses with only minimal understanding of the physics and tissue responses related to various laser instruments and modalities and little real clinical experience.

In fact, the issue of "standard of care" still is in flux. New lasers are constantly being introduced such as the dimer often called Encimer, exemplified by the neodymium-YAG combination with krypton, and neodymium-YAG combination with potassium titanite phosphate (KTP), as well as laser-activated dyes.

Standard of care usually refers to that "degree of skill, care and diligence exercised by members of the same profession, . . . in light of the present state of medical and surgical science."[13] Where technology and applications sciences advance as rapidly as with lasers, however, we must be sure that criteria of care are, in fact, established and generally accepted. Individual prejudices must not be substituted for scientific principles and controlled clinical observation. We can be helped, if only peripherally, by organizations such as the American National Standards Institute and the American Society for Testing Materials, which have, on a multidisciplinary basis, addressed this issue, as well as by the Food and Drug Administration.

REGULATORY INTERACTION

The physician involves himself in regulatory considerations in three ways. First, he may be involved as an investigator primarily concerned with scientific research objectives and with funding from manufacturers for those projects. Then there is the more pervasive consideration of the impact on medical malpractice cases of Food and Drug Administration regulation (e.g., labeling). Similarly, those duties and responsibilities of the physician include participation on institutional review boards (IRBs), FDA review panels, and so on.[14] We discuss these interactions and how the physician is involved.

The Investigator

As new lasers come to the fore they must be developed under investigational device exemption parameters.[15] New instrumentation cannot move in interstate commerce unless approved by the FDA. To gain this approval, the manufacturers must submit "substantial evidence" that the device is safe and effective. This requires adequate and well-controlled investigations, which ultimately involves both animal and human subjects.

The investigator first obtains approval (for human studies) from the IRB.[16] Informed consent, however burdensome, is an ethical, moral, and legal obligation. The predesigned protocol must be followed. If there is any deviation from the protocol, the entire process must be initiated anew. Adequate case histories must be documented, and the records should be retained for inspection until the entire process (study under investigational device exemption, Food and Drug Administration premarket approval, marketing, and statute of limitation for negligence action) is completed. The research sponsor, the IRB, and the FDA are all entitled to adverse effects reporting. The sponsor in turn must inform the investigator about all available preclinical studies, potential side effects, hazards, and contraindications.

The investigator *is* subject to malpractice action on the issue of "reasonableness." Keep in mind that all such suits must demonstrate that the physician investigator did not exercise a reasonable level of skill and care (standard of care). This applies even more so to investigative procedures, since presumably there are other approaches to therapy for the patient (including doing nothing). FDA approval merely signifies that the expected benefit, if any, sufficiently exceeds the expected risk to render the instrument therapeutically reasonable. The *practicing* physician (clinician) is entitled to a *presumption* that a specific product can be safely and effectively used for the specific purpose studied and as approved by the FDA panel.

Investigation status is a major factor in these malpractice suits, and clinicians usually argue the need for discretion in selecting therapy for their patients. Clinical investigators, however, have their discretion significantly curtailed and are specifically limited to the approved protocol.

In summary, investigational devices are limited by FDA regulations to approved investigators and for approved uses. Despite this, some individuals have been known to use investigational devices without approval or for indications outside the scope of the protocol. A prime example is the Thomas Creighton case at the University of Arizona Medical Center (March 1985), where no attempt was made to obtain investigational device exemption (IDE) approval from the FDA for the use of an artificial heart device. This recent mechanical heart transplant situation demonstrates an unnecessary apparent confrontation between the medical community and the FDA. If the developers of that particular device had initiated the IDE process, even in a less than complete manner, it is doubtful that the situation would have been as it appeared. First, section 21 C.F.R. 812.10, entitled "Waivers," allows the agency to grant a waiver from[16] any requirement the FDA finds . . . is unnecessary to protect the rights, safety, or welfare of human subjects." In addition, an approved IDE can be supplemented at any time to include such changes as a new procedure involving the device or different considerations for use. There *are* instances where the agency has rapidly approved the one-time or individual use of a device that had not yet received formal IDE status when it was demonstrated to be a case of dire emergency or represented the only hope for a patient. Whatever the reason, it is illegal, and such practices would seem to leave the practitioner(s) and their sponsor(s) open to the full spectrum of regulatory and civil legal actions.

The initial decision as to whether a device constitutes a "significant risk" (defined in 21 C.F.R. 812.3(m)) is made by the institutional review board, not the FDA. The agency can come in after the fact and disagree with the IRB, and where abuse or noncompliance occurs, the agency can require formal IDE submission even for devices that meet the conditions of the definition. Of possible concern would be the implications for practitioners and IRB panel members who are involved in the decision to utilize the abbreviated requirements allowed when it is decided a device meets the definition and the agency subsequently disagrees and requires formal submission of an IDE application. Such situations would seem to put the parties involved in a weakened malpractice position.

Physician Participation on IRBs and FDA Panels

The Food and Drug Administration has the responsibility, as a division of the Department of Health and Human Services, of reviewing medical devices for safety and efficacy under the Medical Device Amendments of 1976 and the Radiation Control for Health and Safety Act of 1968. In order to fulfill this responsibility advisory panels have been established on which sit prominent knowledgeable physicians and other individuals. Similarly, institutional review boards are required for investigational uses.[17] For this work to have a salutary impact on patient care, physicians and other professionals must be willing to spend the time and effort required. Because of the implications for manufacturers, issues of conflict of interest must be avoided.[18] Therefore, FDA advisory panel members undergo a long process of selection involving extensive disclosure of assets, activities, affiliations, and so on.

Disclosure of Financial Interests

Upon completion of the clearance process you will receive an SF–50 (Notification of Personnel Action) and an HEW–410 (Supplemental Information—Expert or Consultant). It is important that you note any exclusions that may be shown on the HEW–410 in order to avoid actual, potential or appearance of conflict of interest derived from financial interests which include, but are not limited to, investments, employment, grants or contracts which you, your spouse, minor child, blood-relative residing in your household, partner, etc., may have or are negotiating.

The President, May 8, 1965, issued Executive Order 11222 which requires that certain information regarding financial interest be obtained for each year of service. To facilitate updating the information each year, it is suggested you keep one copy of the FD–2637 (Confidential Statement of Employment and Financial Interests) in your files for reference purposes. If you accept new employment or obtain new financial interests prior to the annual renewal, the HHS Standards of Conduct require that you submit this information immediately. I must stress the importance of keeping your statement current. (Proprietary communication from manufacturer to the F.D.A.)

It is further mandated by statute that the FDA be advised of any contracts, grants, or other monetary involvements. The obvious purpose is to assure fair and impartial expert participation. Many physicians either object to such disclosures, the confidentiality of which is protected by 21 U.S.C. 331(j) and 18 U.S.C. 207, or are unwilling to spend the time and effort to comply. Next, there are meetings, which must be open to the concerned public under the Freedom of Information Act.[19] This means travel to Washington, D.C., for meetings. While the U.S. government does pay for travel and a small stipend for meetings, these payments are minimal. Unless the physician is willing to accept the burden as a duty to country, his profession, and ultimately the patient or investigational subject, the public interest cannot be served. Thus, the authors recommend this "obligation" as a privilege of the profession.

Institutional review boards place less of a time and "red tape" burden on the physician. The review committee must recognize, accept, and conduct itself with due gravity in considering the implications of its function. Mere automatic approval of projects submitted or inaction in follow-up monitoring of projects can be disastrous for the patient or investigational subject. Political approval of projects (you approve my proposals today so that I will approve yours tomorrow) cannot be accepted as a matter of integrity, professionalism, and the public welfare. In addition, this risks legal action in event of injury to the subject/patient. We must keep in mind that these committee members, the institution, and the investigational team are all liable for injuries produced. These committees are not usually legally protected by peer review statutes. (Peer review statutes usually protect *post hoc* review committees from legal liability to reviewed individuals. The public-interest aspect is to provide a mechanism for quality control of patient care and investigational practices.)

In summary, we do need topnotch physicians cognizant of their moral, ethical, and legal obligations for investigational premarket approval and medical device peer review committees.

PRODUCT LIABILITY

Product liability is another area of tort law to be considered briefly. It is usually described as the responsibility of the manufacturer to those individuals who can reasonably be expected to use the products so manufactured. It encompasses not only those whom the manufacturer intended to purchase the instrumentation, but also those who, while not the intended buyers, might ultimately come into possession of the product or be injured by it.[20] The physician *is* a peripheral participant.

The manufacturer may be liable for mistakes in design, manufacture, or testing; for failure to warn; in contract for breach of statutory or common law warranties (of merchantability or fitness for purpose intended); or in strict liability for marketing a defective product.[21] The courts will impose liability upon a doctor or hospital where there is proof of misuse of the device *or continued use* of the device in the face of known or reasonably discoverable defects[22] or negligent selection of the particular device for the task at hand.[23] Additionally, the courts will impose a duty to inspect devices before use. The application of these principles should be self-evident in the case of laser instrumentation.

The question of whether physicians and hospitals should be held liable under the theory of *strict liability* (no fault) in tort has been addressed by some commentators.[24] The rationale for this has been the *deep pocket theory*. The party who is injured as a result of a defective product usually is unable to bear the financial consequences. The source of financial retribution (physicians and hospitals with financial resources including impersonal insurance coverage) therefore becomes the target. Fortunately, most state courts have rejected this extension, so far.[25]

A concept closely related to that of "strict liability" is *res ipsa loquitur*. Under this evidentiary doctrine a presumption of negligence on the part of a defendant may be raised where it can be shown that the instrument that caused the harm was under the control and management of the defendant and that the accident would not have occurred in the ordinary course of affairs if the defendant had used proper care. In some cases courts have applied this doctrine against the physician and hospital even where it was *possible* that the manufacturer was the culpable party.[26] A different approach was taken by the Supreme Court of New Jersey[27] stating that (338 A.2d 7) "the *burden of proof* [emphasis added by author] in fact does shift to defendants. All those in custody of that patient or who owed him a duty, . . . should be called forward and should be made to prove their freedom from liability."

In fact, a doctor or hospital may be liable for:

a. negligent misuse of a device;
b. negligent selection of a device;
* c. failure to inspect or test the device;
* d. using the device with knowledge of its being defective.

These four theories of failure of duty particularly items (c) and (d), are clearly applicable to practitioners of the laser art. A practical example is the situation wherein the surgeon assumes the laser to be in focus without testing it *before each case* or at least each day. Liability for failure to make reasonable testing of inspection for latent defects may be the prime basis for legal action.[28] Similarly, though perhaps worthy of greater condemnation, is the circumstance where there is foreknowledge of a dissimilarity between the focusing He/Ne indicator beam and the actual CO_2 burn site. The use of this latter instrument thus is rampant with risk to the patient and liability for the physician, hospital, and their agents. An analogous situation, yet to be tested, is proceeding with administration of an anesthetic by the anesthesiologist with full knowledge that the surgeon has not yet tested the laser for focus and function (including sufficient gas). In the event the machine malfunctions, and an alternate approach is not immediately available (e.g., in the case of stenosis of the trachea) and the patient is shown to have thereby been injured by either the malfunction or an "unnecessary" anesthetic, legal risk may accrue to all parties concerned.

Another option available to the plaintiff is the legal concept of joinder. Here the physician is charged with negligence in use of an instrument, but this time the physician is joined by another alleged culprit—the manufacturer of the laser. This joinder of the laser manufacturer is an example of how, until recently, the applicability of product liability concepts to medical malpractice has been largely ignored.[29]

The most interesting defense for the manufacturer is product misuse. If the product liability defendant establishes misuse by the physician, a case of malpractice will also be convincingly established. If the plaintiff does not prevail on his product liability concepts theory due to the product misuse defense, his negligence theory against a defendant physician has been enhanced. Thus the plaintiff patient is in a "can't lose" situation, and the surgeon "can't win." A prototype of this scenario was *Ethicon, Inc. v. Parten,* where the product misuse defense was raised.[30] The court granted a directed verdict for the doctor and the hospital in all negligence actions and cross-actions for misuse against the physician and the hospital by the manufacturer seeking contribution and indemnity. The court indicated that the burden of proof required to establish a right to contribution or indemnity would be the same as in a case for medical malpractice.[31] Thus, while the physician, who stands in a position of special trust and responsibility, may endanger the welfare of his patient because of misuse of a medical instrument, he may also place the manufacturer in a position of liability. In so doing, he may expect the manufacturer (in self-interest) to proceed and act against him legally.

There is a trend developing in this era of DRGs and TEFRA[32] that potentially increases risk-management problems for hospitals and some physician managers. This relates to service contracts provided by manufacturers. The manufacturers' or distributors' service contracts are quite expensive. Therefore, some maintenance departments and individuals do in-house maintenance and servicing equipment. What now appears as a less expensive alternative to service contracts may turn out to be a costly choice, perhaps a pyrrhic victory. The automobile industry is the classic example of this legal defense argumentation by manufacturers' counsel. In the medical instrument context the issue would be whether the hospital assigned as its agent a maintenance or repair man who was properly trained and skilled to handle the specific device (i.e., laser). Of course, "where an act of negligence is a substantial factor in bringing about an injury, it does not cease to be a legal and proximate cause thereof because of the intervention of a subsequent act of negligence of another which contributed to the injury, if the prior act of negligence is still operating, and the injury inflicted is not different in kind from that which would have resulted from the prior act."[33] Manufacturers of equipment tend to shift the blame on the theory that the appropriate care in utilizing, maintaining, and repair was not taken.[34] The plaintiff need only show that defendant hospital had care, control, or custody of the laser at the time the negligent risk was created by utilizing the services of its inadequately trained maintenance personnel.[35] The key to this approach is that while "intervening negligence" may not insulate the manufacturer entirely, it expands the defendant pool to include the hospital, physicians, or other personnel who were involved in assigning the inadequately trained maintenance man and with the additional theory of breach of "implied warranty to fitness for use intended."[36]

The complexity of the above argumentation reflects the many interrelationships in medical practice between patient, manufacturer and practitioner of medicine.

We have presented herein some of the highlights of the manifold relationships in the medical device field. Physicians, hospitals, and manufacturers interact in bringing their respective products to the service of the patient. The introduction of lasers in patient care is a prime example of these relationships and associated responsibilities.

APPENDIX: LASER SAFETY

Charge

A process to credential physicians at University of Michigan hospitals.

Recommendation

Ref: 1. Minutes of the Credentials Committee of September 28, 1983.
2. American National Standard for the safe use of lasers (ANSI Z 136.1—1980, pp. 60–63).
3. Current and/or revised policy for delineation of clinical privileges by each service (Bylaws, Rules and Regulations of the Medical Staff at the University of Michigan as amended February 25, 1983, Article VII, Section I).

A. Delineation of clinical privileges by each service will be initiated by the individual desiring such privileges who will certify to the respective chairman or chief of the department, section, and/or division that he/she fulfills the recommended guidelines. The chairman or chief or designee, reviews the application and provides prior authorization and approval of credentials, certifying same to the Credentials Committee. The Credentials Committee will then review the chairman's/chief's certification and notify appropriate offices (including the certification and notify appropriate offices (including the LSO). The committee will keep a file of approved individuals with credentials in laser application.

B. Recommended guidelines for laser credential approval:
1. Demonstrated understanding of laser physics, power density, and laser tissue interaction.
2. Experience in animal laboratory as preparation for patient experience.
3. Demonstrated formal course "hands-on" training.

and/or

4. Experience and approval in patient application under direct and immediate supervision of trained operator of the laser.

5. The requisite experience must be related to the specific class of instrument to be used. (Note: It is dangerous to assume that all instruments are alike or that all media—CO_2, Nd:YAG, Argon, Ruby, Erbium, etc.—are the same in effect.)

C. Recommended: (a) General training to be provided by each department, section and/or division to employees working with or around lasers stressing safety and operational hazards. (b) Development of institutional laser safety training program to include:
1. Fundamentals of laser operation (physical principles, construction, etc.).
2. Bioeffects of laser radiation.
3. Relations of specular and diffuse reflections.
4. Nonradiation hazards (electrical, chemical, reaction by-products, etc.)
5. Control methods.
6. Overall management and responsibilities.
7. Medical surveillance practices.
8. Ancillary problems in laser usage (airway management, etc.)

REFERENCES

1. Federal Food, Drug and Cosmetic Act of 1938; Medical Device Amendments of 1976; H.R. Rep. No. 94–853, 94th Cong., 2d Sess. (1976) as amended; 21 C.F.R.; Laws Enforced by the U.S. Food and Drug Administration (1981); Radiation Control for Health and Safety Act, 1968; 42 U.S.C.; 18 U.S.C. and FOIA 5 U.S.C., as well as pertinent Office of Management and Budget and U.S. Customs Provisions and Occupational Safety and Health Act of 1970, P.L. 91–596 (1970), 29 U.S.C.A. SS 651 *et seq*.

2. *Lipscomb v. Memorial Hospital,* 733 F.2d 232, 336 (4th Cir. 1984); *Canterbury v. Spence,* U.S. Ct.App. for the D.C. Cir., 1972, 150 U.S. App. D.C. 263, 464 F.2d 772 (1972); *cert. denied,* 409 U.S. 1064, 93 S.Ct. 560, 34 L.Ed. 2d 518.

3. *Hartke v. McKelway,* 707 F.2d 1544, 1549–50 (D.C. Cir.) *cert. denied,* 104 S.Ct. 425 (1983).

4. *Schloendorf v. Society of N.Y. Hospital,* 211 N.Y. 125, 105 N.E. 92 (1914).

5. *Martha Logan v. Greenwich Hospital Association et al.,* Conn. Sup.Ct., No. 10969, Sept. 6, 1983.

6. *Bowen v. Iowa Nat. Mut. Ins. Co.,* 270 N.C. 486, 155 S.E.2d 238, 242 (1967).

7. Norton, M. L. 1973. "When Does an Experimental/Innovative Procedure Become an Accepted Procedure?" *The Pharos of Alpha Omega Alpha* 38(4):161–165.

8. Ladimer, I. 1954. "Ethical and Legal Aspects of Medical Research in Human Beings." *J. Pub. Law* 3 (Fall):467; Ladimer, I. 1957. "Human Experimentation: Medicolegal Aspects." *N. Eng. J. Med.* 256:18.

9. *Kirtland & Packard v. Superior Court for County of Los Angeles,* 59 Cal.App. 3d 140, 131 Cal.Rptr. 418, 421; *Helfend v. Southern Cal. Rapid Transit Disc.,* 84 Cal.Rptr. 73, 2 Cal.3d 1, 465 P.2d 61, 73 (1970).

10. *Placek v. City of Sterling Heights,* 405 Mich. 638, 275 N.W.2d 511, 527–528 (1979).

11. *West v. Caterpillar Tractor Co.,* 336 So.2d 80, 90 (Fla. 1976); see also *Butand v. Suburban Marine and Sporting Goods, Inc.,* 555 P.2d 42 (Alaska 1976).

12. *Butterfield v. Forrester,* 103 Eng. Rep. 926 (1809).

13. *Gillette v. Tucker,* 67 Ohio St. 106, 65 N.E. 865, (1902); see also *Bruni v. Tatsumi,* 46 Ohio St.2d 127, 129, 346 N.E.2d 673, 676 (1976).

14. Federal Advisory Committee Act; Publ. No. 92–463, 86 Stat. 770 (1972); (Kahan, J. S. 1984. "Medical Lasers and the Law." *Medical Device and Diagnostic Injury* 6:11, 83–85, 118–119 (November); Kahan, J. S., and J. N. Gibbs. 1985. "The Impact on Medical Malpractice Cases of Food and Drug Administration Regulation. "Submitted for publication; Kahan, J. S. "Laser and Electronic Medical Devices: An Overview of Food and Drug Administration Regulation." 38 *Food and Drug Cosmetic L. J.* 220 (1983).

15. 21 C.F.R. 812.140–812.150.

16. E. Schwartz, 1983. "Institutional Review of Medical Research." 4 *J. Legal Med.* 143; see also 21 C.F.R. Part 56, 1984.

17. Schwartz, "Institutional Review."

18. Standards of Conduct, 45 C.F.R. Part 73; Fed. Reg. 46:15, 7368–7385.

19. Freedom of Information Act, 5 U.S.C. S 552; see also Fed. Advisory Committee 5 U.S.C. S 901 *et seq.*

20. Restatement (Second) of Torts, Sect. 402A, subsect. 2a and b; *Bowles v. Zimmer Mfg. Co.,* 277 F.2d 868 (7th Cir. 1960) applying Michigan law; *Ribando v. Amer. Cyanamid Co.,* 37 Misc.2d 603, 235 N.Y.S.2D 110 (Sup.Ct. 1962).

21. Rubin. 1974. "Manufacturer and Professional Users Liability for Defective Medical Equipment." 8 *Akron L. Rev.* 1, 99, 110.

22. *Shepard v. McGinnis,* 257 Iowa 35, 131 N.W.2d 475 (1964).

23. *Phillips v. Powell,* 290 P. 441 (Cal. 1930).

24. Russell. 1972. "Product and the Professional: Strict Liability in the Sales-Service Hybrid Transaction." 24 *Hastings L.J.* 111; *see also* "The Medical Profession and Strict Liability for Defective Products—A Limited Extension." 17 *Hastings L.J.* 350 (1965).

25. *Silverhart v. Mount Zion Hospital,* 20 Cal. App. 3d 1022, 98 Cal.Rptr. 187 (1971); *Magrine v. Krasnica* 94 N.J. Super. 228, 227 A.2d 539 (1967), aff'd. sub nom.; *Magrine v. Spector,* 100 N.J. Super. 223, 241 A.2d 637 (App. Div. 1968), aff'd. 53 N.J. 259, 250 A.2d 129 (1969).

26. *Dierman v. Providence Hospital,* 31 Cal.2d 290, 188 P.2d 12 (1947).

27. *Anderson v. Somberg,* 67 N.J. 291, 338 A.2d 1, *cert. denied,* 423 U.S. 929 (1975).

28. *Tenant v. Barton,* 164 Wash. 279, 2 P.2d 735 (1931); *Stafford v. St. Clair's Hospital* 19 Misc.2d 710, 187 N.Y.S.2d 351 (Sup.Ct. 1959).

29. 3 Frumer and Friedman, Products Liability S 34A (1978).

30. *Ethicon, Inc. v. Parten,* 520 S.W.2d 527 (Tex. Civ. App.—Houston [14th Dist.] 1975).

31. *Bowles v. Bourden,* 219 S.W.2d 779 (Tex. 1949).

32. Tax Equity and Fiscal Responsibility Act of 1982; P.L. 97–248.

33. 2 Restatement, Torts, SS 440–442, 447.

34. 18 Def. L.J. 196 (1969) summarizing defendants' arguments in *O'Brien v. Yoder Co.,* (W.D. Wis. 1968).

35. *Hanberry v. Hearst Corp.,* 81 Cal.Rptr. 519, Ct. App. 4th Dist., 1 Cal. App. 3d 149 (1969).

36. *Connoly v. Hagi,* 24 Conn. Sup.Ct. 198, 188 A.2d 884 (1963).

Chronometric Causes for Obstetrical Malpractice

Bernard J. Ficarra, M.D., Sc.D., LL.D.

> God dealt well with the midwives: and the people multiplied, and waxed very mighty.
>
> —Exodus 1:20

Law has utilized ad infinitum the sentence "Time is of the essence." It has been evoked in courtrooms to the point of echolalia. Scientific usage of time has been less dramatic. Researchers do not watch the clock. Surgeons in the operating room observe the time for the benefit of the patient and not for personal reasons. Obstetricians know that every room in the obstetrical suite has a clock, but all too often they forget to look at it.

Another term for a clock, usually one that is extremely accurate, is chronometer. An instrument that also records time is called a chronograph. As used in medicine, a chronograph records small intervals of time in physiologic and psychophysiologic experiments. The measurement of time by intervals or periods is called chronometry, and in medicine, chronometry is the study of mental processes in relation to time. This mental chronometry attention is the basis upon which chronometric causes for obstetrical malpractice are alleged. Therefore, delays in performing certain medico-surgical acts to safeguard the mother and/or her baby are the subject matter for this propositum.

Before these topics are presented, certain terms used in the practice of obstetrics must be defined. These words and phrases are listed alphabetically for simplification.[1]

1. *Amniocentesis:* aspiration of the amniotic sac to obtain fluid for laboratory study.
2. *Amnion:* the innermost of the fetal membranes forming a fluid-filled sac for the protection of the embryo.

3. *Breech presentation:* in obstetrics *presentation* means that part of the fetus which is palpated through the cervix of the uterus at the beginning of labor; when the buttocks or feet of the baby are palpated the word *breech* is used.
4. *Cesarean section:* delivery of a baby through an abdominal incision.
5. *Cerebral palsy:* paralysis due to a lesion of the brain; also used as a synonym for spastic diplegia.
6. *Chorioamnionitis:* specific infections of the membranes, amniotic fluid, and fetus are included under this general term.
7. *Chorion:* the outermost enveloping tissue (sac) of the growing zygote, or fertilized ovum, that serves as a protective and nutritive covering.
8. *Dystocia:* abnormal labor or childbirth.
9. *Gestation:* period of development of the young in viviparous animals from the time of the fertilization of the ovum, i.e., pregnancy.
10. *Gestosis:* any toxemic manifestation of pregnancy.
11. *Hypoxia:* low oxygen content or tension, a deficiency or diminished oxygen in the inspired air.
12. *Obstetrics:* that branch of surgery which deals with the management of pregnancy, labor, and the puerperium (the period or state of confinement after labor).
13. *Oxytocic drugs:* medications that pertain to, are characterized by, or promote oxytocia (rapid parturition); an agent that hastens evacuation of the uterus by stimulating contraction of the myometrium (musculature of the uterus).
14. *Oxytocin:* one of two hormones formed by the neuronal cells of the hypothalamic nuclei (brain) and stored in the posterior lobe of the hypophysis (pituitary gland), the other hormone being vasopressin; it stimulates uterine muscle contractions; used to induce active labor or to cause uterine contraction after delivery of the placenta.
15. *Parturition:* the act or process of giving birth to a child.
16. *Pelvimetry:* the measurement of the dimensions and capacity of the pelvis.
17. *Perinatal:* pertaining to or occurring in the period shortly before and after birth, in medical statistics generally considered to begin with completion of 28 weeks of gestation and variously defined as ending 1–4 weeks after birth.
18. *Pitocin:* a sterile aqueous solution of synthetic oxytocic hormone; indicated for the initiation or improvement of uterine contractions.
19. *Pitressin:* a synthetic vasopressin of the posterior pituitary gland in a sterile aqueous solution.
20. *Placenta:* the cakelike organ within the uterus that establishes physiological communication between the mother and child by means of the umbilical cord.
21. *Prematurity:* an underdevelopment of an infant born before the proper time.
22. *Toxemia:* a condition in which the blood contains poisonous products; a general infection in which the blood contains toxins but not bacteria.
23. *Toxemia eclamptogenica:* a pathologic condition associated with gestation characterized by a disturbance of metabolism with fever, albuminuria, water retention, capillary injury, acute hypertension, and convulsions/cerua in severe cases.

24. *Uteroplacental insufficiency:* failure of the placenta to supply adequate nutritional and respiratory life support systems to the unborn infant.[2, 3]
25. *Vasa praevia:* presentation of the velamentous vessels across the internal os of the uterus, seen with a low implantation of the placenta.

ANTENATAL CARE

The obstetrical management of a pregnant woman from the time of pregnancy confirmation to the onset of labor is recognized as the antepartum, prenatal, or antenatal period. It is an essential time for the future mother, whose hopeful aim is to have a child free of all anatomicophysiologic deficiencies.

The delivery of a normal, healthy baby must not be left to chance or serendipity. A pregnant patient and her unborn child must be observed attentively with an established, programmed routine. All treatments and instructions must be administered with scientific rigidity. If a strict protocol is not adopted and adhered to, legal culpability will fall upon all those involved, including ancillary personnel such as medical or nursing attendants in obstetrics.

The responsibility for proper medical care commences from the moment of conception and continues through the antenatal period, during labor, the in-hospital postpartum days, and the time thereafter at home. This medico-legal obligation ceases when the attending obstetrician discharges the mother and the baby's care is assumed by a competent pediatrician who becomes responsible for his/her own professional acts.

Every person who assists a gravid woman to pass through parturition must be prudent. In its fullest sense, prudence includes skill plus good judgment in the use of all known resources, both human and mechanical. Responsible prenatal management is the first step in fulfilling the lofty ideals of obstetrical excellence.

The quintessence of knowledgeable antenatal care is to be alert to all that is new and important in prenatal diagnosis. Among the best of these new medical techniques is transabdominal amniocentesis. It is recommended when there is suspicion of a genetic disorder. Such techniques have enabled intrauterine detection of genetic disorders to expand geometrically over the past two decades. The indications for transabdominal amniocentesis include the following:

1. Pregnancy in women over 35 years of age to detect any chromosomal abnormality in the fetus;
2. History of prior children with chromosomal abnormalities as trisomies and translocations;
3. Serious X-linked disorders overtly known or in women carriers of X-linked recessive disorders;
4. Suspected carriers of some 80 known inborn errors of metabolism which can be detected;
5. Previous Down's syndrome in a family; and
6. Neural tube defects.

According to H. L. Nadler:

Transabdominal amniocentesis is recommended at 15–16 weeks gestation. It is advised that ultrasonography be done prior to the test in order to determine the presence of twins, to possibly aid in the location of the placenta, and to estimate gestational age based on fetal head circumference. Tests recommended as routine study on all amniotic fluid samples assayed during the second trimester of pregnancy include determination of α-fetoprotein and cytogenetic analysis of the cultivated cells. The precise tests to be carried out depend on the disorder to be monitored. The α-fetoprotein determination for detection of neural tube defects and chromosome analysis should be done in all cases as a screening technique.[4]

In antenatal diagnosis via transabdominal amniocentesis the time of performance is to be remembered. This same thought was emphasized by task force members and others at a National Institutes of Health conference on early delivery and fetal maturity. This group of experts reported:

Indications for early delivery are fairly clear-cut, encompassing a previous low-birth-weight infant; maternal ill-health, such as renal disease; or newly arising obstetric problems, for example, toxemia. When repeat cesarean section is planned, determination of fetal maturity is useful since in 15% of these deliveries the infant weighs less than 2,500 gms.[5]

"For handling 'the pregnancy of uncertain duration requiring early intervention,' " the task force recommended the following steps:

1. If possible, measurement of biparietal diameter by ultrasonography before 26 weeks of gestation should be done. If the result agrees with other indicators of gestational age, the duration of pregnancy may be considered established. If there is disagreement, a second measurement of biparietal diameter should be done four to six weeks later.
2. Pregnancy complications often arise after the 26th week of gestation which is a time when ultrasound is less accurate. In these cases it is recommended that amniocentesis be performed and pulmonary maturity measured by estimating surfactant composition in a sample of amniotic fluid. The most dangerous complication of premature delivery is respiratory distress syndrome (RDS). Detection of a 'mature' composition of surfactant in amniotic fluid is a strong indicator that delivery is safe."[5]

For clarity of medical purpose, as well as for legal protection, the antepartum written clinical record must cover any obstetrical problem, an assessment thereof, and the management of it with or without success. There must be no attempt to camouflage any imperfect therapy. As to the timing of doctor visits, it is a standard for the normal pregnant patient to be examined every four weeks until the 36th week of pregnancy. Thereafter, weekly visits to the obstetrician are mandatory. Diligent reasonableness requires that any pregnant patient with active medical problems be examined and treated more frequently.[6] In all matters obstetrical, time is of the essence to fulfill the objective of prenatal care, which is the delivery of a healthy baby without impairing the health of the mother.

DELAYS IN OBSTETRICAL MANAGEMENT

Unlike any other patient, the pregnant woman is a duality. The attending physician must not only examine and treat the future mother but must give equal attention to the unborn child. Physicians must realize that fetal monitoring does not always save babies. Obstetricians cannot base their entire faith, comfort, and judgmental decisions on fetal monitoring alone. The element of human judgment in obstetrical practice cannot be diminished. As the human factor lessens, there is an anticipated increase in fetal disorders, injuries, and abnormalities.

In order to eliminate fetal distress, as far as it is possible to do so, obstetricians employ electronic fetal monitoring and study the fetal blood. Internal electronic monitoring identifies the fetal heart rate beat by beat via the attachment of an electrode to the fetus and another to the mother. External electronic monitoring avoids invasion of the uterus but does not provide the precision of measurement afforded by internal monitoring.[7]

The normal fetal heart rate between contractions will average 140 beats per minute ranging from no less than 120 to no more than 160 beats per minute. Usually the fetal heart rate falls slightly during and after the acme of the uterine contraction, returning quickly to normal with the cessation of the contraction.[8]

Changes in the fetal heart rate that persist or recur are warning signals that alert medical/nursing attendants to a danger. Delay in recognition of these warning signs may invite disaster, whereas prompt delivery of the baby may save its life. Therefore, the medical observer must be aware of and recognize each of these changes in fetal heart rate:

1. A pattern of early deceleration, which suggests a transient increase in the baby's intracranial pressure from head compression;
2. A pattern of late deceleration, which is an advisory alert of a slowing down of the heart rate in the contraction phase and is most often the consequence of hypoxia and associated metabolic derangement from uteroplacental insufficiency; and
3. A pattern of variable deceleration, an ominous sign in which the slowing of the fetal heart rate does not correlate precisely with any phase of the contraction cycle. It is attributed to blood inadequacy from compression of the umbilical cord.[8, 9]

When these three categories of deceleration in the fetal heart rate persist, prompt delivery of the baby is urgent for its salvation. Without deceleration or acceleration, persistent bradycardia, or slow heart rate, is not ipso facto indicative of fetal distress. It is more likely to be associated with congenital heart disease.[8]

According to R. Beard and P. Eddington:

> Fetal blood sampling may demonstrate that the severely hypoxic fetus becomes acidotic which is reflected in the low blood pH. The most reliable method of determining fetal asphyxia is continuous fetal heart rate monitoring with selective fetal pH scalp blood

determinations. Clinically significant fetal acidosis may be identified by demonstrating the value for the fetus to be at least 0.20 pH units less than that of maternal blood.[10]

Infant care and fetal life support have become poignant medico-legal topics for active governmental concern. These topics exemplified in the American Medical Association's decision to file a friend-of-the-court brief in a lawsuit challenging new regulations on the treatment of severely handicapped newborns:

> The AMA's amicus curiae brief is in support of a lawsuit filed by the American Academy of Pediatrics and the National Association of Childrens' Hospitals seeking to block enforcement of the rules. These regulations require all hospital maternity wards, obstetrical departments, and nurseries to post notices warning that failure to feed and care for handicapped infants is prohibited by law.[11]

The concern with infant morbidity and mortality is reflected further by the aroused investigation in Texas of certain infant deaths:

> The United States Center for Disease Control (CDC) plans to investigate reports of mysterious infant deaths at a hospital in San Antonio to determine if they are homicides. CDC experts were called to determine what factors may have led to an apparent high rate of mortality among infants and small children in a pediatric intensive care unit at the county's hospital over the past five years. The deaths have been termed suspicious as a special grand jury has been impaneled.[12]

With this increasing attention given to infant health matters, it behooves the medical profession to be attuned to the legal hazards of medical delay, delinquence, or failure to fulfill the professional obligation to the patient, who is entitled to the best available obstetrical surveillance and treatment. Not only must these requisites be satisfied, but they must be rendered within the time limits to safeguard the health of the mother and her offspring.

Improper timing may be the basis upon which a breach in the duty owed to a patient may incur liability. When medical knowledge affirms that with each uterine contraction there is a variable temporary reduction in the flow of oxygenated maternal blood through the placenta to the infant, any delay in proper oxygen supply can have deleterious effects on the unborn child. "Labor has been referred to as a stress test for the fetus which may be handicapped by intrinsic fetal disease, placental disease, cord compression, maternal disease, drugs administered for analgesia or anesthesia, maternal hypotension from the supine position (or from fright, anxiety, shock), conduction anesthesia, or any combination thereof."[9]

Emphasis is placed upon those obstetrical areas wherein medical malpractice may be alleged when there is delay in performing certain acts and procedures or in recognizing disorders that should be identified. Culpability can be attributed to medical attendants who cause harm to the pregnant patient or her child when there is a delay in:

1. Amniocentesis performance;
2. Administration of proper anesthetic agents;
3. Recognition of breech presentation;
4. Cesarean section procedure;[13]
5. Counting and timing uterine contractions;
6. Diagnosing chorioamnionitis, hypoxia, placental disruption, or uteral placental insufficiency;
7. Detection of a fall in fetal heart rate, with or without an imperfection in or inadequacy in fetal monitoring;
8. Dystocia identification;
9. Forceps application;
10. Genetic disease discovery;
11. Newborn distress or illness evaluation by obstetrician or pediatrician;
12. Oxygen use (or cessation of misuse);
13. Oxytocic drug administration (these drugs may be improperly or hastily given, also);
14. Taking pregnant patient to delivery room;
15. Treating premature infant; and
16. Giving drugs for analgesia, anesthesia, bleeding, shock, etc. (includes misuse of or wrong dosage of drug).

The fundamental error in the above sixteen categories is failure to act with celerity and dexterity. If an injury occurs to the mother or her child because of this failure then obstetrical malpractice has occurred. The three essential elements to any medical malpractice action are:

1. That a professional relationship between the physician and the patient actually existed;
2. That the physician departed from some duty that he/she owed to the patient; and
3. That the departure was the proximate cause of an injury (imputed, sustained, or proven).

By *proximate cause* is meant "that cause which as a natural and continuous sequence, unbroken by an intervening cause, produces the injury without which it would not have occurred."[14] Thus, the law demands that any physician who renders professional services must meet these three requirements:

1. He/she must possess the same degree of learning, skill, and ability that other physicians similarly situated possess;
2. He/she must use reasonable care in applying his/her knowledge to the patient; and
3. He/she must exercise his/her best judgment in rendering treatment.[15]

It is well to remember that to institute a medical malpractice cause of action, it is not necessary to set forth in detail the evidence upon which the claim is based. It is sufficient to allege adequate facts to imply a duty owed to the patient with a negligent failure to discharge that duty.[16]

To avoid the allegation of obstetrical malpractice, the sixteen time delays enumerated must serve as a tocsin against falling into the morass of professional liability. Among the time delays are those that have to do with drugs, which should be given paramount consideration. The great danger in prescribing many drugs to pregnant women because of their ill effects on the fetus has been documented. For the obstetrician the administration of oxytocic medication is not without hazards.

The oxytocic drugs are those which pertain to, are characterized by, or promote oxytocia (rapid parturition). They are chemical compounds that hasten the evacuation of the uterus by stimulating contractions of the myometrium (musculature of the uterus). Oxytocic activity is founded upon the pharmacodynamic physiology of oxytocin. This is one of two hormones that are formed by the neuronal cells of the hypothalamic nuclei in the brain and are stored in the posterior lobe of the hypophysis, also known as the pituitary gland or body. (The other hormone formed by these cells is vasopressin.) Because it stimulates contraction of the uterine musculature, oxytocin is used to induce active labor or to cause contraction of the uterus after the delivery of the placenta.[1, 2, 3]

The oxytocic drugs used most frequently in obstetrical practice have attached to them a caveat which lists their side effects, untoward reactions, and the proper indication for their use, as well as the contraindications to their usage. The acceptable known oxytocic drugs are listed in the *Physicians' Desk Reference*.[17] They are:

1. Ergotrate maleate solution supplied in ampoules;
2. Ergotrate maleate tablets;
3. Methergine tablets, also in solution;
4. Oxytocin solution;
5. Pitocin solution; and
6. Syntocinon solution.

Ergotrate maleate in solution or tablet form is ergonovine, which is the hydroxyisopropylamide of lysergic acid. It is obtained from ergot and has been shown to possess all of the oxytocic activity of ergot itself. Indications for its use are the prevention and treatment of postpartum or postabortal hemorrhage and of puerperal morbidity. It is contraindicated for the induction of labor and in cases of threatened spontaneous abortion. Allergy to the drug is another contraindication to its use.[17]

Methergine in either solution or tablet form contains methylergonovine maleate. This drug includes a rapid and sustained tetanic uterotonic effect, which shortens the third stage of labor and reduces blood loss. As to time, it must be remembered that after intravenous administration the onset of its action is immediate. After intramuscular injection it takes effect in 2 to 5 minutes; after oral administration, 5 to 10 minutes. The elapsed time is necessary information if one is considering an additional dose. This drug is indicated as routine postpartum management after the delivery of the placenta, for postpartum atony or hemorrhage, and subinvolution of the uterus. It should not be administered intravenously as a routine because of the possibility of inducing sudden hypertension and/or cerebrovascular accidents. When intravenous administration is considered as a lifesaving measure, it must be given slowly over a period of no less than 60 seconds with careful monitoring of the blood pressure. Reported adverse reactions to methergine have been nausea, vomiting, transient hypertension, dizziness, headache, tinnitus, diaphoresis, palpitation, temporary chest pain, and dyspnea.[17]

Oxytocin is an aqueous solution containing in each milliliter an oxytocic activity equivalent to 10 USP posterior pituitary units. It acts on the smooth muscle of the uterus to stimulate contractions. In addition, it has a stimulant effect on the mammary glands. Oxytocin is indicated for the initiation or improvement of uterine contractions, where this is desirable and considered suitable, in order to achieve early vaginal delivery for fetal or maternal reasons. Oxytocin is contraindicated with an unfavorable position of the fetus, cephalopelvic disproportion, fetal distress, severe toxemia, cord presentation (or prolapse), total placenta praevia, and vasa praevia. When this drug is given for induction or stimulation of labor, it may be administered only by intravenous infusion (drip method) and with adequate medical supervision in a hospital. All patients receiving intravenous oxytocin must be under continuous observation by trained personnel with a thorough knowledge of the drug who are qualified to identify complications. A physician competent to manage any complication should be available immediately.[17] The following adverse reactions to this drug have been reported:

1. Fetal bradycardia;
2. Neonatal jaundice;
3. Anaphylactic reaction;
4. Postpartum hemorrhage;
5. Cardiac arrhythmia;
6. Fatal afibrinogenemia;
7. Nausea/vomiting;
8. Premature ventricular contractions; and
9. Pelvic hematoma.[17]

Pitocin is an aqueous solution of synthetic oxytocic hormone. The drug is prepared synthetically to avoid possible contamination with vasopressin or its antidiuretic and cardiovascular effects. The physician should be cognizant of the fact that even highly purified synthetic oxytocin contains inherent pressor-antidiuretic properties that may become manifest following administration of large doses. Pitocin is indicated for the initiation or improvement of uterine contractions, when this is desirable and considered suitable. Warnings and precautions with pitocin are the same for all oxytocic drugs. Severe water intoxication with convulsions and coma has occurred, associated with a slow oxytocic infusion over a 24–hour period. Maternal death due to oxytocin-induced water intoxication has been reported.[17]

Syntocinon (oxytocin) is a synthetic polypeptide (consisting of eight amino acids) that has been synthesized commercially for intravenous or intramuscular injection. When given in appropriate doses during pregnancy, it is capable of eliciting graded increases in uterine motility from a moderate increase in the rate and force of spontaneous motor activity to sustained tetanic contraction. The pharmacologic and clinical properties of syntocinon are identical with the naturally occurring oxytocic principle of the posterior lobe of the pituitary gland. Its use is indicated for the medical rather than the elective induction of labor. Elective induction of labor is defined as the initiation of labor for convenience in an individual with a term pregnancy who is free of medical indications.[17] The contraindications for using this drug are similar to those for other oxytocic medications.

"Oxytocic drugs stimulate the motility of the uterus. Their principal uses are to induce labor at term, to augment uterine contractions during desultory labor, to control postpartum and postabortal hemorrhage, and to induce therapeutic abortion."[9] The most commonly used oxytocic agents are pitocin and syntocinon.[18]

Timing in the administration of these drugs is as important as are the exact indications for their use. Giving these medications too late or too early may prevent the anticipated pharmacodynamic results. When the drugs are not used as indicated or an improper dosage is given, complications may arise. This can occur when the obstetrician of record is not in attendance and the supervision of the patient is entrusted to another person lacking in oxytocic supervisory competency.

According to the *Physicians' Desk Reference:*

> All oxytocic agents are potentially dangerous. Mothers and infants have been injured, and some have died because of their injudicious use. Hyperstimulation of the uterus during labor may lead to uterine tetany (with a marked impairment to the uteroplacental blood flow), uterine rupture, cervical or perineal lacerations, amniotic fluid embolism, and trauma to the infant (e.g., hypoxia or intracranial hemorrhage). Because of these hazards which result from overdosage, oxytocic agents must be administered under conditions of meticulous observation. (P. 1131)

Any delay in recognizing a complication (from whatever source) that leads to hypoxia can result in cerebral damage. Fetal hypoxia may eventuate secondarily from multiple pathologic disturbances of the umbilical cord or the placenta or from other complications of pregnancy, difficult labor, or delivery. The end result is brain damage. Meconium may be present in the amniotic fluid of anoxic fetuses. The major limelights in obstetrical practice are the time-honored principles that emphasize excellent antenatal and intrapartum care of the gravid patient so that hypoxia will be avoided, if possible. When it does occur, it must be detected immediately and treated aggressively, to avoid irreversible brain damage.[19] Brain cells are highly sensitive to lack of oxygen. They do not possess the physiologic capacity to regenerate when prolonged hypoxia/anoxia causes damage beyond the biological point of no return.

Severe hypoxia and cerebral concussion or hemorrhage are the most important causes of cerebral palsy.[9] The relationship between cerebral palsy and prematurity, birth injury, and asphyxia has been known for many decades.[9] Past medical research "has related long-term sequelae like cerebral palsy, mental deficiency, epilepsy, and speech disorders to complications of pregnancy."[9] A linkage has been found between the above mentioned neurological disorders and prematurity (low birth weight), prenatal hemorrhage, third trimester bleeding, toxemia of pregnancy, placenta praevia, abruptio placenta, cord prolapse, and breech delivery.[20] In view of the deleterious effects of these pathophysiologic disturbances the imperative necessity of identifying them quickly if hypoxia/anoxia is to be avoided is self-evident. Failure to correct any oxygen deficiency can lead to various neurologic impediments.[21, 22]

CITATIONS ON OBSTETRICAL MALPRACTICE

The print media seem to rejoice journalistically when a lawsuit concerns a baby. An example is the story of a million-dollar award to a brain-damaged child. A janitor at a medical center in Flint, Michigan, found a newborn infant, abandoned as dead, gasping for breath in a doctor's scrub room. Three and a half years later a court battle terminated in a legal settlement that could amount to $13 million for the brain-damaged child.

This sad event commenced when the infant was deprived of oxygen for several hours after her birth. The infant was born as a diagnosed 20–week fetus and determined to be nonviable by the obstetrician in attendance. Three hours after her birth, the janitor found the baby in a doctor's scrub area. The plaintiff's attorney maintained in his bill of particulars that the infant might have developed normally if she had been treated in the hospital's neonatal unit. No one explained how the infant got into the scrub room. When the baby was found, she was taken to a nursery for normal babies instead of the neonatal unit. Nurses administered oxygen and warmed the infant's body, which had become so cold that no temperature reading was obtained on the thermometer.[23]

In what has been labeled a record-breaking settlement, a severely retarded child in California has been awarded an annuity in a structural settlement that could add up to $122 million. The child, who was born at a university hospital in 1980, sustained brain damage when she was deprived of oxygen for several minutes after birth. The end result is that she has spastic quadriplegia.[24]

A highly publicized benchmark case centers on a decision in which a New York appeals court upheld the righting of an ancient wrong. It concerned increasing the oxygen administration for a prolonged period of time to a premature infant, even though it was common practice to do so at the time of occurrence.

CASE REPORT ON OXYGEN

On July 3, 1953, a male infant weighing only three pounds was delivered five to six weeks prematurely. More than two decades later, he began malpractice proceedings against the hospital that had given him premature nursery care and against two of its physicians, charging that their treatment had blinded him through overexposure to oxygen. The court entered a judgment for the man, awarding him $2,887,000 in damages, and the defendants appealed.

At the time of his birth, more than half of all the premature babies of the plaintiff's size died in infancy. Many who survived either sustained brain damage or were blinded by retrolental fibroplasia (RLF). First identified in 1942, the disease reached epidemic proportions in the U.S. in the late 1940s and early 1950s. Ironically, the surge in RLF cases coincided with widespread advances in lifesaving techniques used on premature infants. All the techniques involved liberal use of oxygen. In the summer in which the plaintiff was born, many physicians still believed liberal administration of oxygen to prematures helped prevent death or brain damage. Yet doubts were spreading. A significant segment of the medical community had begun to link oxygen with RLF. Just weeks before the plaintiff's birth, a major hospital released a study on prematures that concluded "prolonged oxygen therapy may be related to the production of RLF." Upon his arrival in the hospital that gave him premature nursery care, the plaintiff was examined by one of the defendant physicians, a pediatric resident, who described his condition as "good, his color pink, cry vigorous and clear lungs throughout." He was, the resident wrote, "a vigorous premature infant, in good condition with no abnormalities or anomalies." The resident directed that the infant be placed in an incubator with oxygen at three to four liters. Later that evening, aware of its links with RLF, the resident ordered the oxygen "reduced . . . as tolerated." Next day, he said the infant appeared 'to be doing well.'

Nurses subsequently reduced the oxygen flow from three to two-and-one-half liters, and the concentration in the incubator from 35 percent to 30 percent. Hospital records show the infant's condition remained good; nothing necessitated increased oxygen. Nevertheless, another staff physician, Dr. E, countermanded the resident's order, on instructions from the chairman of the hospital's department of pediatrics. Without examining the infant or consulting his parents, Dr. E sharply boosted the infant's oxygen. According to the appeals court, "the concentrations of oxygen went from two-and-one-half to five liters in one day, and over a span of 28 days in increased dosages up to a high of nine liters, and from an environment of 30 percent oxygen to a high of 82 percent." The change in treatment was part of the hospital's participation in a study on prematures. One out of three prematures was to be given increased oxygen, two out of three reduced oxygen. "This method of distribution was designed to subject the least number of babies to the risk of blindness that statistics would permit," the appeals court explained. On three occasions while the infant was in the high oxygen environment, eye examinations showed haziness. On removal from the high-oxygen environment, the infant was found to have severe hemorrhages in both eyes, plus scarring of the retina. The plaintiff became totally blind aside from faint light perception in the left eye. Except for a brief stint in his family's business answering phones [and a part-time job as an interviewer with the Blind Guild, he has been unable to find employment.]

The defendants' position was that they had followed medical practice accepted in 1953. The appeals court disagreed. The hospital (and Dr. E) cannot avail themselves of the shield of acceptable medical practice when a number of studies including their own had already indicated that increased oxygen was both unnecessary and dangerous, particularly for an otherwise healthy baby, and especially when the attending physician . . . had recommended a decrease. Furthermore, the hospital permitted a healthy infant to remain in a precarious position after symptoms of a disease of which it was aware, and indeed, was studying, had been detected.[26]

The appeals court found the doctor who had ordered the oxygen reduced innocent of any wrongdoing but upheld the malpractice charges against Dr. E and the hospital. It gave the plaintiff 20 days to accept a reduction of damages to $1,500,000 or go through a new trial on the issue of damages only.[25, 27]

CASE REPORT ON ABSENTEE OBSTETRICIAN

When a 21–year-old woman began having labor pains, she tried to contact her obstetrician, only to learn from his answering service that he was on vacation. She was told that another obstetrician, Dr. X, was taking her doctor's calls, and she was instructed to go to a hospital—not the hospital where her own obstetrician had told her the baby would be delivered. The woman arrived at the hospital at 5:30 P.M. and a licensed practical nurse took a brief history, recorded her blood pressure, pulse, respiration, and temperature. She was prepped, fetal heart tones were taken, and her pains were assessed. But she was not examined to determine dilation of the cervix. At 6:15 P.M. the information was given to Dr. X's answering service, and at 6:30 P.M. Dr. X called for the first time to inquire about the patient. On the basis of the information given, he prescribed 100 mg of Demerol and 20 mg of Largon. At 7 P.M. the woman's contractions subsided from moderate to mild, and she fell asleep. At 7:30 P.M., Dr. X phoned and was told her condition. At 10:15 P.M. Dr. X phoned again and ordered another round of the same dosages of Demerol and Largon. At 11 P.M. the woman had a "bloody show" and moderately high pains at regular intervals. An hour later her "water bag" ruptured spontaneously, and a large amount of meconium was found in the fluid. Dr. X was notified at once. Fifteen minutes later, and with only a nurse in attendance, the woman gave birth to a six-pound, 10–ounce viable baby girl.

The baby did not cry at birth; the coloring was pink, with blue extremities. The nurse suctioned fluid and blood from the infant's nose and mouth. She noted poor breathing, with deep retractions, and administered oxygen by mask. Fifteen minutes after the baby was born, Dr. X arrived and ordered the baby to be placed in the nursery incubator at 12:45 A.M. The baby gave a weak cry at this time, and its color and breathing improved. At 1 A.M. the baby was still retracting. Dr. X left the hospital between half an hour and 45 minutes later. Before leaving, he did not request any tests or consult a pediatrician. At 2 A.M. the infant's respiration was "poor," and oxygen was administered by mask. Ten minutes later the emergency room physician found the baby's breathing shallow. It was pronounced dead at 2:22 A.M.

In a subsequent medical malpractice suit, the woman alleged the following negligent acts of omission: the unavailability of her own obstetrician; Dr. X's absence at her baby's birth and his ordering medication without personally examining her; the baby's death due to improper care and treatment; no hospital staff doctor on duty at the time of birth. The trial judge dismissed her suit because she failed to prove that either physician or the hospital did anything contrary to the standard care in the community. When she appealed, the appeals court termed her own obstetrician "remiss" for not telling her his vacation intentions. But it agreed with the trial court judge that neither he nor the hospital had been guilty of omission or negligence. Dr. X's culpability was another matter. Testimony of his expert witnesses, both obstetricians, conflicted sharply with that of the woman's expert, a pediatrician. But on one point they were in accord: "that meconium in the amniotic fluid is a definite danger warning. Had [Dr. X] tended to his patient at delivery, he should have recognized this warning sign and acted accordingly." The appeals court said evidence showed that Dr. X left the hospital when the infant was in obvious critical condition and minutes before death. The court noted Dr. X's absence at birth, his failure to request an examination for dilation of the cervix—information which would have indicated time of delivery. Furthermore, crucial diagnostic tests were not made despite noted cyanosis and ever worsening breathing retractions. Supplemental breathing techniques were omitted. (Dr. X) performed minimal services and did not recognize the crisis, which accounts for [his having had] no consultation with a specialist.[26]

Dr. X, the appeals court concluded, failed to use reasonable care, diligence, or his best judgment, and his negligence is causally connected to the outcome. His treatment was below acceptable medical standards in the community and the lower court opinion to the contrary is clearly wrong. The appeals court awarded the mother of the dead child $40,000 in damages and assessed all court costs against Dr. X.[26]

CASE REPORT ON CARELESS USE OF PITOCIN

After a normal first stage of labor, an obstetrician ordered the administration of pitocin to his patient when effacement and dilation of the cervix were complete and the fetal head was not yet engaged. The patient, a 42–year-old woman delivering her second child, received pitocin for over an hour, but only four fetal heart readings were noted on the chart. The child was born with severe respiratory distress. An anesthesiologist attempted to resuscitate the infant with an Ambu-bag but was unsuccessful. Later the child was found to be suffering from athetoid cerebral palsy. He is unable to walk, stand, sit, or speak normally. The child sued the obstetrician, the anesthesiologist, and the hospital. He alleged that the pitocin was improperly administered and that there was inadequate monitoring of the fetal effects of the drug and an inadequate attempt at resuscitation. A jury awarded the child $7.5 million.[26, 29]

CASE REPORT ON CESAREAN SECTION DELAY

An 18–year-old unmarried woman became pregnant in January 1978. During her first visit to her obstetrician, he noted that her pelvic area was below normal in size. He intimated that a cesarean procedure was a possibility. A pelvimetry examination indicated that it would be very risky for a baby to pass through the birth canal in a normal fashion. Neither the glucose tolerance test nor an ultrasound test was used.

On November 21, 1978, almost four weeks past the expected delivery date, the mother admitted herself to the hospital. The baby was above average in size. The physician determined that a normal delivery would put both mother and baby at high risk. Nevertheless, the physician did not order fetal monitoring or alert hospital personnel to schedule a cesarean section.

By noon fetal heart tones had dropped alarmingly. The baby was in distress, and the mother was moved to the delivery room. No cesarean section was ordered because the physician said that there was insufficient time for the procedure. A few minutes later, a prolapsed cord was noted. The baby was stuck in the birth canal, and the physician could not remove the baby. The last fetal heartbeat was noted at 12:35 P.M. In order to remove the dead baby, the baby's shoulders had to be broken.

During the malpractice action, experts testified that if a cesarean section had been performed at noon, a healthy, normal child would have been born. They testified that the physician had failed to evaluate the child adequately and had failed to perform a cesarean section. A jury returned a verdict against the physician for $125,000.

On appeal, the decision was affirmed. The question of whether the father of the illegitimate child was entitled to share in the wrongful death award was not before the court. The trial court properly rejected efforts by the physician to admit evidence on the fact that the mother was not married during her pregnancy.

The evidence supported a finding that the physician had been negligent. The amount of the award was not excessive, even though there was no evidence of the child's potential earnings, the court concluded. Thus the verdict of $125,000 for the wrongful death of the infant during delivery was affirmed by the Illinois Court of Appeals.[30]

CONCLUSIONS

The synergistic cynosure of medical practice appears to be fading. This thought has been verified by the multiple medico-surgical, esoteric professional demerits which in former decades were alien to the practitioners of medicine. Among these is the malpractice ogre, examples of which have been recorded in this discussion on obstetrical pitfalls that may trap into malpractice the attending physician who supervises and advises pregnant patients. Imparted faulty knowledge erroneous information or medico-surgical incompetency gives rise to a breach in patient confidence. This lack of trust is the first spark that ignites the flame of medical malpractice.

All that has been written or spoken on professional liability leads to one conclusion: with malpractice, as with any communicable disease, prevention is preferable to treatment. There is no permanent cure for medico-surgical malpractice in any specialty. However, prophylactic measures diminish the frequency of its recurrence.

The best protection against all malpractice is prevention. A quotation taken from the *New York Law Journal* emphasizes this concept: "Diligent preventative measures taken by each of us will do more to alleviate our professional liability problems than all those tort changes suggested by our proponents within and without our profession."

Because of the potential, realistic, devastating effects of medico-surgical malpractice on the availability, quality, and cost of all medical care in the United States of America, the problem must be resolved before it becomes an unmanageable Frankenstein's monster. A solution through prevention must be approached pragmatically and maturely.

Often persons in medico-surgical practice have been indicted for legal immaturity. This opinion is not applied solely to the medical profession. Many other professional people in our nation have been accused of a similar deficiency. For their responses to the malpractice morass, many physicians have been censured for acting with the impulsiveness of adolescents. Perhaps the medical profession has contributed to this uncomplimentary reaction, because there are some of our colleagues who have lost the touch of professionalism. Many have discarded the gold tasseled cap and the verdant striped academic gown of medicine to become medical technicians or medical shopkeepers.[33]

To counteract this declining image, a resurrection of the primeval faith in the medical profession is needed. As members of a learned, distinctive profession, people of medicine must "pursue this scholarly discipline in a way that inspires confidence and trust . . . [and] prizes expert performance of a skill above financial gain."[34]

The grave obligation of maintaining high standards of professionalism does not permit erosion around the edges of knowledge. It does not allow a lowering of the strict code of moral behavior. Neither does it sanction tolerance of the ethical transgressions that are the hallmarks of unprofessionalism or eliminate necessary patient care. Succinctly, unstinting professionalism will eliminate the accusation of negligence. Success will be assured because professional dignity is the cornerstone that supports the mutually respectful physician-patient relationship, which is the intrinsic, essential matter that coalesces medico-surgical sanity, sanctity, sincerity, and salvation.

REFERENCES

1. *Dorland's Illustrated Medical Dictionary,* 25th ed. Philadelphia: W. B. Saunders Co., 1974.

2. *Blakiston's New Gould Medical Dictionary,* 1st ed. Philadelphia: The Blakiston Co., 1949.

3. *Stedman's Practical Medical Dictionary,* 12th rev. ed. Baltimore: William Wood Co., 1935.

4. Nadler, H. L. 1978. "What's New and Important in Prenatal Diagnosis?" *Medical Tribune,* New York, April 26, 1978.

5. Medical News, *JAMA* 241 (16, April 20, 1979): 1666–69.

6. *Standard for Obstetric-Gynecological Services* by American College of Obstetricians and Gynecologists (One East Wacker Drive, Chicago, Ill., 60601), 1983.

7. "Electronic Fetal Monitoring: How Necessary?" Medical News, *JAMA* 241, (17, April 27, 1979): 1772.

8. Pritchard, W., and K. MacDonald. 1976. *Williams Obstetrics,* 15th ed. New York: Appelton-Century-Crofts.

9. Pegalis, S. E., and H. F. Wacksman. 1980. *American Law of Medical Malpractice.* Vol. 1, sections 1:1–5:18. Rochester, N.Y.: The Lawyers Co-Operative Publishing Co.

10. Beard, R., and P. Eddington. "Should Fetal pH be Used in the Diagnosis of Fetal Asphyxia?" In *Preventability of Perinatal Injury*, edited by K. Adamson and Howard A. Fox (Lawyer's Co-op, 1980). Quoted by Pegalis and Wacksman on p. 369 of vol. 1.

11. No author. "AMA to File Amicus Brief in AAP Suit." *American Medical News*, April 8, 1983, p. 1.

12. No author. "Infant Deaths Investigated in Texas". *American Medical News*, April 8, 1983, p. 26.

13. Hobbins, J. Review of 245 scheduled cesarean sections. Report from Dept. Obstetrics and Gynecology at Yale University School of Medicine. Quoted in *JAMA* 241 (16, April 20, 1979): 1675.

14. *Reder v. Hanson*, 338 F.2d 244 California Court of Appeals 8, 1964.

15. *Prestegord v. Glenn*, 451 S.W.2d 791 Texas Court of Appeals, 1970.

16. *Vitelli v. Wilmington Medical Center, Inc.*, 276 A.2d 744 Delaware Superior Court, April 5, 1971.

17. *Physicians' Desk Reference*, 38th ed. Oradell, N.J.: Medical Economics Co., 1984.

18. *AMA Drug Evaluation*, 3rd ed., (Chicago: AMA Publications, 1977).

19. Greenhill, A., and B. Friedman. 1974. *Biological Principles and Modern Practice of Obstetrics*. Philadelphia: W. B. Saunders Co.

20. Cavanagh, D., and M. Comasi. 1977. "Fetal Hypoxia and Birth Injuries." In *Obstetrics and Gynecology*, 3rd ed., edited by David N. Danforth. New York: Harper and Row.

21. McManus, F., M. Rang, G. Chance, and J. Whittaker. 1977. "Is Cerebral Palsy a Preventable Disease?" *Obstetrics and Gynecology Journal* 50 (1, July):71–77.

22. Adamson, K., and H. Fox, eds. 1975. *Preventability of Perinatal Injury*. New York: Alan R. Liss.

23. *R. and M. Densteadt v. Hurley Medical Center*, Flint, Michigan. Reported in Sunday *New York Times*, January 3, 1982, page 47.

24. *American Medical News*, October 1, 1982. Quoted in *Medical Liability Advisory Service* 7 (10, October 1982).

25. *Burton v. Brooklyn Doctors Hospital*, 452 N.Y.S.2d 875 New York Supreme Court, Appellate Division, First Department, July 22, 1982.

26. *Medical Liability Advisory Service* 17 (10, October 1982).

27. No author. 1983. "Medicolegal Decisions: Liability Found in Giving Infant Increased Oxygen." *American Medical News* (March 18), page 19.

28. *Moran v. Dean*, No. 12986, Louisiana Court of Appeals, 4th Circuit, 416 So.2d 351, June 8, 1982.

29. *Mertsaris v. Physicians Hospital*, New York Supreme Court, Kings County, Index no. 20562/79, May 28, 1982. Reported in ATLA Law Reporter, vol. 25, no. 8, October 1982.

30. *Jones v. Karraker*, 440 N.E.2d 420, Illinois Supreme Court, Appellate Division, September 21, 1982. Rehearing denied October 21, 1982.

31. No author. 1983. "MD Liable for Wrongful Death Due to Negligence in Delivery." *American Medical News* (April 22/29), page 18.

32. Kramer, C. 1957. "Medical Malpractice." *New York Law Journal*, November 13. Quoted in editorial, *New York State Journal of Medicine*, July 1975.

33. Ficarra, B. J. 1978. "Prophylaxis against Medical Negligence." In *Legal Medicine 1978*, ed. Cyril H. Wecht. New York: Appleton-Century-Crofts.

34. Ingelfinger, F. 1976. Editorial. *New England Journal of Medicine* 294: 334.

Surrogate Motherhood: A Womb in Livery

Harold L. Hirsh, M.D., J.D., F.C.L.M.

INTRODUCTION

The situation of surrogate motherhood, where one woman bears a child for another, is not a new or uncommon one. Historical writings as early as the Old Testament illustrate this: "So Sarah said to Abraham, 'Listen now! Since Yahweh has kept me from having children, go to my handmaiden. Perhaps I shall get children through her.' " So did Rachel and Leah with Jacob when it appeared that Rachel was barren, and Leah was fearful of being outproduced.[1] But modern technology has provided us with advances in medicine, particularly genetics, that have taken procreation out of the cohabital bed and into the laboratory. Although reproductive technology can be used to compensate for infirmities in human reproductive systems, it may also threaten society by disrupting normal human relationships.[2]

Progress in family planning technology has enabled women to conceive and bear healthy children by artificial insemination. This procedure involves injecting the sperm of the donor into the woman carrier to impregnate her without the parties engaging in sexual intercourse. This capability is useful in several situations. It enables couples who would otherwise be incapable of having biological offspring to have children who are biologically related to at least one partner or even to both. For example, where physiological impediments, other than sterility, prevent conception through normal means, artificial insemination may be used to circumvent these problems by introducing the male partner's semen directly into the location or sphere or the ovum (AIH). These situations might arise, for example, when the male's sperm count or sperm motility is low, when the female has blockages or scar tissue in the vagina or tubes, or when there is chemical or immunological incompatibility between the male sperm and the female secretion. If the artificial insemination is successful, the child will be the biological offspring of both members of the couple.

Artificial insemination is also useful where the male partner is sterile or impotent. In this case, the woman may be artificially inseminated with the semen of an anonymous donor (AID) and bear a child that is her biological offspring.

There is still another situation where the wife is either infertile or sterile or for some reason unable to carry a pregnancy to full term. A woman's reproductive abilities may be impaired by previous miscarriages, abortions, or damaged fallopian tubes. This can make it physically impossible or dangerous for her to give birth. In such a case the couple may seek a woman to carry the child with the male as the biological father. This woman acts as a surrogate mother for what will ultimately legally be the infertile couple's child. The woman carrier will be artificially inseminated with the male partner's sperm, bear his child, and then relinquish all rights after the birth to the biological father and his mate.

Surrogate motherhood, the converse of artificial insemination of the wife by a donor, has the potential for becoming an attractive alternative to an infertile couple when the wife is sterile rather than the husband. To that end, all the parties who may be involved directly or indirectly are best advised to understand the legal aspects at this time.

ARTIFICIAL INSEMINATION

What is artificial insemination (AI)? It has become a widely accepted and useful form of therapy in infertility and sterility, although not considered socially acceptable until relatively recently. Surrogate motherhood by AI is a new wrinkle. In the United States there are at least ten thousand infants born each year as a result of donor artificial insemination (AID) and an unknown but probably lesser number following artificial insemination with husband's semen (AIH).

There are three types of artificial insemination, distinguished by the semen donor:

- *AIH—Homologous:* this is an insemination of a wife with her husband's sperm because of the physical difficulties of conception. The child is considered that of the couple.
- AIC—combined: the sperm of the husband and an unidentified donor are combined for physiological reasons. There may later be a paternity test to tell if the husband is the father. Here the legal status is less certain, but probably the child is considered that of the couple.
- AID—heterologous: the wife is inseminated with the sperm of an unidentified, unrelated donor. This is used where the husband is sterile, where there may be a risk of hereditary diseases or an Rh incompatibility. Here the legal rights vary with jurisdiction.

It is important to note that although relatively successful, the option of artificial insemination is open only to couples where the infertility problem lies with the husband—only 30 percent of all sterile couples.

Male donors of sperm for artificial insemination are paid for each ejaculation, and the risks they incur are negligible compared to those of a surrogate mother. This has been considered a form of discrimination since women have so far been forbidden to participate in artificial insemination situations for money compensation.[3, 4] While most would agree that the manner of participation of a woman in a surrogate mother arrangement is not the same as that of a man in an artificial donor situation, the social and legal obstacles are similar and should be examined.

The medico-legal problems[5–7] inherent in artificial insemination may very well be applicable in surrogate motherhood. Although artificial insemination statutes were not drafted with surrogate motherhood in mind, and it is unlikely that courts would hold these statutes absolutely controlling, state legislatures and courts are likely to give great weight to the statutory and case law of artificial insemination because of its loose analogy to surrogate motherhood.

In a case with an interesting twist, a husband who consented to artificial insemination of his wife failed to prove that he had withdrawn his consent after the initial procedures resulted in a miscarriage, a New Jersey trial court ruled.[8] The husband and wife separated after the wife became pregnant, and the wife filed for divorce, seeking support for the child. The husband contended that he had withdrawn his consent to the insemination before conception occurred. The court found that the consent of the husband, once given, was presumed to be effective when pregnancy occurred unless he established by clear and convincing evidence that it had been revoked. The court found that he had not met that burden and as the lawful father of the child bore at least partial responsibility for the child's support.

THE ARTIFICIAL INSEMINATION PROCESS

The standard of care for the physician includes a careful history and physical examination of the surrogate mother candidate and the biological father as well as a culture for cervical or semen gonorrhea, serum tests for syphilis, AIDS, hepatitis, RH typing, rubella titer, and a month of basal body temperatures (BBT) demonstrating a biphasic pattern of the potential surrogate mother.

The physician should genetically and hereditarily screen both the surrogate and the potential biologic father (semen donor) to eliminate any potential present or future medical problems. Although there has been little legislation in this regard with respect to artificial insemination at least two jurisdictions do mandate genetic screening.[8] Family, social, and occupation histories are critical for both parties.

The placement of the semen is important. The most common method of insemination is to place either fresh or frozen semen on the cervix and allow excess volume to flow into the posterior vaginal pool. The use of cervical caps or vaginal packs has been advocated, but without significant evidence of improvement in conception rates. The intrauterine deposition of small (less than

0.2 mL) amounts of semen has also been advocated and may have certain theoretic advantages under some restricted conditions.

The timing of artificial insemination is crucial. Once ovulation has occurred, fertilization must take place within 24 hours. Therefore, sperm should be available during this time either by a new insemination or the release of sperm from the cervical crypts. Since the time of ovulation is usually established retrospectively, an estimation of the expected time is made from evaluation of previous months' temperature charts, and inseminations planned accordingly. This means that for optimal results inseminations will have to be carried out several times over a three- to six-day period. When patients have irregular variable cycle lengths, clomiphene citrate may be used to standardize the time of ovulation.

The frequency of the inseminations bears a relationship to the incidence of success (pregnancy). Most practitioners have chosen to inseminate at two-day intervals because of the demsonstrated capacity of the cervical crypts to maintain and feed sperm into the upper Mullerian system for at least 48 hours after insemination. However, evidence indicates that frozen sperm are not maintained in the cervix for as long as fresh sperm, and thus a daily schedule of inseminations with frozen sperm has been recommended. The avoidance of intercourse during periods of insemination has been advocated for reasons analogous to those against mixing husband and donor sperm.

The matching of the surrogate mother and biologic father candidates also involves physical characteristics such as body build, skin, and hair coloring. Some practitioners have elected to match for other characteristics, but most do not control for A, B, O blood type. Rh-negative women should, however, receive Rh-negative donor semen whenever practicable. Race-specific testing (sickle cell disease, Tay-Sachs disease) should be done when applicable. Care must also be taken in isolated populations to ensure against consanguinity between donor and recipient. The emotional background of the participants is very important.

Psychological screening of the surrogate to ensure that she is able to cope with pregnancy, willing to undergo medical testing during pregnancy, agreeable to amniocentesis and an abortion if the need arises, and capable of relinquishing her parental rights after birth is a difficult but critical aspect of surrogate motherhood selection.

Some have questioned whether verifying the infertility of the wife of the biologic father should become the standard of care.

Placing this duty on the physician results in the physician's potential liability for negligence in screening, the physician faces the same potential liability in screening married couples.[9] Following the tradition established in the context of artificial insemination by donor, the selection of the surrogate should be left to a consulting physician who can best determine the physical compatibility of the surrogate and the benefiting couple. Hand in hand, with responsibility comes potential liability for the physician.

RESULTS OF ARTIFICIAL INSEMINATION

As to the success of artificial insemination, the large number of children born by artificial insemination shows no greater incidence of congenital defects than do children in the general population. Nor is there a greater rate of spontaneous abortion among artificial insemination conceptions.

In general one can expect that 60 to 70 percent of healthy recipients will conceive during six cycles of insemination, with over 60 percent of conceptions occuring in the first three cycles. Only about 10 percent of pregnancies resulting from artificial insemination can be expected after the first six cycles. It therefore seems prudent to bring a more extensive evaluation of the artificial insemination recipient after six well-timed cycles. Such a protocol will prevent unnecessary evaluations of most artificial insemination patients and result in the discovery of other contributing factors in well over 50 percent of the failure group.

Is there a medical preference for fresh as contrasted to frozen semen? The use of frozen semen has become increasingly widespread because of the convenience it allow in scheduling; the wide range of characteristics that may be potentially available for selection; the ability to screen every specimen in advance for gonorrheal infection; and the availability of semen from a commercial supplier. When a practitioner considers using frozen semen he must weigh its advantages against the lower rate of success inherent in its use, 50 percent versus 70 percent for fresh. There have been questions raised concerning the possibility of congenital defects in children conceived with the use of frozen semen.

Artificial insemination (AID) is being used with a new twist. A eugenics high-intelligence sperm bank laboratory in Escondido, California, was founded two years ago. About twenty scientists, including Nobel Prize winners, have donated sperm. The laboratory recently announced the first birth to result from this program of providing sperm donations from eminent scientists to women who are selected on the basis of their intelligence. Through the medium of artificial insemination, a mathematician in his thirties has become the father of a healthy, nine-pound baby girl, a spokesman for the Repository for Germinal Choice has reported.

The baby was born on April 21 in Chicago to an unidentified married woman who lives in a rather small town in a sparsely populated state, the sperm bank spokesman said. The sperm were delivered by Greyhound bus and applied by her husband at home.

Three other women also have been inseminated through the sperm bank's auspices, but there have been no other births.

THE CONTRACT

A contract is an agreement between two or more persons that creates an obligation to do or not to do a particular thing. Its essentials are competent parties, subject matter, a legal consideration, mutuality of agreement, and mutuality of obligation. The concept of freedom to contract generally permits the exercise of great latitude between the parties to structure the terms of their agreement and to specify the expectations and liabilities of all parties.

Generally, a surrogate mother arrangement occurs when a married couple, of which the wife is infertile or physicially unable to carry a pregnancy to term, contract with another woman who agrees to be artificially inseminated with the husband's sperm, carry and bear the baby, and then give up all custodial rights to the natural father. Subsequently, a ''fee'' is paid to the surrogate mother for medical expenses and the burden of pregnancy. The wife of the natural father then adopts the child and assumes parental rights. While this appears to be a straightforward procedure, it is fraught with legal and social difficulties.

The need for such arrangements arises, basically, from the increasing scarcity of babies.[10] Because of the wide availability of contraception and abortions,[2] there are fewer babies to adopt, and, as a result, the adoption procedure has become more stringent and selective. A working couple may postpone childbearing until after their peak fertility years,[11] and if an infertility problem does surface, it may not be recognized until it is too late to adopt.[12]

In 17 percent of the couples in the United States one of the partners is infertile, more often the wife.[13] In some cases, there are medical solutions for an infertility problem,[3] but for many there are not. Surrogate mothering offers what adoption doesn't: a biological tie of the child with one of the parents.[10] This is especially important to those couples who don't consider adoption an alternative: ''Adoption doesn't cure infertility.''[3]

In a surrogate mother agreement the parties are the man (husband) and woman (wife) who seek to have a child and the surrogate who agrees to carry that child fathered by the husband. Generally, under the terms of the basic agreement the surrogate agrees to (1) undergo artificial insemination, (2) carry the baby to full term, and (3) relinquish all material rights after the child's birth. The male agrees to (1) have his sperm used to artificially inseminate the carrier, (2) be identified as the biological father at the time of the child's birth, (3) accept financial responsibility for the child, and (4) take custody of the baby. He may be obliged to legally adopt the child. The noncarrier woman agrees to (1) treat the child as her own and (2) adopt it in accordance with state law if necessary.

Beyond this basic agreement, additional terms may be agreed upon and included in the contract. For example, the surrogate mother could agree to make a conscious effort to ensure her health and safety and that of the baby, visit a doctor regularly, check into the hospital at the time labor commences and delivery is imminent, and undergo various necessary tests, such as amniocentesis, to determine the health of the child, if indicated. The couple may agree to pay medical and legal expenses and to take out insurance for the surrogate and the child. The parties may also include provisions to compensate the surrogate financially for lost wages and for undertaking the risks associated with pregnancy.

LEGAL CLIMATE (ENVIRONMENT)

Surrogate parenting contracts are most likely unenforceable in every state in the United States. The unenforceability is based on two separate grounds, the existence of penal code sections that may be violated, and the general public policy against contracts for adoption.

At the outset, the contracting parties need to know whether a surrogate motherhood contract is legal. If courts recognize its validity, then freedom-of-contract principles would grant wide latitude in the terms used in the contract. A contract that is determined to be illegal, however, will be unenforceable. Additionally, a surrogate motherhood contract may subject the parties, including the physician, to potential criminal sanctions for baby selling.

The mere fact that the parties have signed an agreement outlining their respective obligations does not mean that their agreement will be judicially enforced.[14] An agreement may be struck down here, inter alia, if it is violative of state law, or where it offends public policy.[12] Surrogate mother contracts that provide for payment to the natural mother may be struck down because they violate state adoption laws and/or because they are in violation of the public policy prohibiting the sale of children.[15] The rule under which public policy determinations are construed is whether or not the agreement is injurious to the public.[16] Public policy requires the law to protect the interests of the surrogate and her child, the parents-to-be, and the public. State regulation of the specific contract provisions is permissible where a fundamental right is not involved, provided such regulation is neither arbitrary nor oppressive and bears a real and substantial relationship to the public health, safety, or morals, or some other phase of the general welfare.[17]

Participants should be aware that, today, those who participate in surrogate motherhood do so without being certain of the legal climate and consequences.[18–21] Our present legal system simply has not yet adequately addressed the problems represented by a surrogate mother contract.[22] Legislation to regulate the practice is in the early stages of development, and few cases have been decided thus far.[23–25]

When courts and state officials have considered the legality of the surrogate motherhood contract, they have questioned its acceptance in accord with and its effects on public policy. Some have rejected the concept. Surrogate motherhood is yet another example of medicine racing ahead of the ethical and legal establishment.

On the surface, the surrogate mother alternative to childbearing appears to be a reasonable and readily workable solution for the childless couple. Closer scrutiny, however, reveals a myriad of problems, which the law must address.[3] To some extent it has been approximated, but in a different context, probably never anticipating the surrogate mother situation. Some of the areas which must be addressed either by the legislatures or by the courts concern adultery, illegitimacy of the child, intestate succession, the relationship between the couple and the surrogate mother, the obligation to the child, adoption, the responsibility for the child after the birth, payment of costs, freedom to contract, enforceability of the contract, child support, and remedies for breach of the contract.

Contracts that require the doing of an illegal act for performance by one or both of the parties are essentially void and unenforceable. While a statute will rarely interfere with a couple's right to have children,[12] even a well-worded surrogate mother contract may offend public policy.

There is an argument that if the state feels it can and should exercise control over some births, what is to stop it from seeking to regulate all births?[6] In contrast, the state does have the power to make laws to cover family life when they feel it is in the public interests and there is no "unlimited right to do with one's body as one pleases."[26] The courts have shown they will uphold this power of the state when there is an issue of public policy like the payment of consideration to the mother in *Doe v. A.G.*[27]

There has already been proposed legislation to deal with surrogate mother arrangements in several states, and there is a well-organized network of surrogate mother/natural parent arrangements through a proposed, workable surrogate mother contract in use in Kentucky.[28] There is a surrogate mother newsletter operating out of Ann Arbor, Michigan, apparently not as a personal column to match parents with prospective surrogates, but for education and information of current legal and medical status. The governments and the courts will not be able to ignore the situation much longer without making legislation or jurisprudence that recognizes the changes that are necessary to protect the parties involved.

The surrogate motherhood procedure may implicate third parties who are intricately involved in the process—the physician who performs the insemination and the attorney who drafts the contract. Because of this and the uncertainty of the law at present the involved physician is best advised to keep abreast of legal developments and have legal counsel.

As to the attorney who drafts the contract, he must define the duties of the parties involved. Since the surrogate's rights and interests are not identical and may actually be contrary to those of the contracting couple, she should retain her own attorney. Because of this legally uncertain area attorneys may have fears about their potential liability. However, while the attorney must competently advise his client and properly structure the contract, it is very unlikely that he will be held responsible if one of the parties fails to perform or if other difficulties ensue. One of the problems is that the contract may be held to be illegal; this may give rise to professional ethical concerns as well as civil liability and criminal sanctions.

CONSTITUTIONAL ISSUES

Although family interests per se are not mentioned in the Constitution, the decision of whether or not to bear children has been characterized as a highly personal one and has been given the status of fundamental right. If the right to privacy means anything, it is the right of the individual, married or single, to be free from unwarranted governmental intrusion into matters so fundamentally affecting a person as the decision whether to bear or beget a child.[26, 29–31]

On the basis of these and other cases related to marital and familial relationships, the Michigan Court of Appeals recently upheld the decision of a couple to have a child by a surrogate mother. The plaintiffs, Jane and John Doe, a married couple, filed a request for a declaratory judgment stating that their surrogate motherhood arrangement was legally permissible.[26] The Does were joined in their complaint by Mary Roe, the prospective surrogate mother. The Does proposed to have Mary Roe conceive a child with John Doe through artificial insemination. After birth, the Does would take custody of the child once he or she left the hospital, and Mary Roe would consent to the couple's adoption of the child. Mary Roe would receive at least $5,000 plus medical expenses and health insurance and disability insurance coverage.

This suit actually arose as a class action by a group of prospective adoptive parents and prospective surrogate mothers, challenging the constitutionality of the Michigan statute that prohibited the offering, giving, or receiving of any money or other consideration or thing of value in connection with adoptions. In addition, the plaintiffs sought to enjoin the state from prosecuting them for proceeding with their adoption plans. The plaintiffs based their case on the following three arguments: (1) that the Michigan adoption statute[32] was void for vagueness, (2) that the constitutional right of privacy protected the plaintiffs' proposed arrangements from state interference, and (3) that the state lacked an interest in prohibiting payment of surrogate mothers compelling enough to outweigh the plaintiffs' right to privacy.

The trial court considered whether or not this arrangement violated the Michigan statute,[13] which prohibited offering giving or receiving "any money or other consideration or thing of value" in connection with the placing of a child for adoption. In dismissing their complaint, the court held that the right of privacy is not absolute, and that the state's interest, as expressed in the statute, is to prevent commercialism from affecting a mother's decision to execute a consent to the adoption of her child. The court declared "baby bartering" to be against the state's adoption laws and public policy and opined that it is a fundamental principle that children should not and cannot be bought and sold under any circumstances.

PUBLIC POLICY IMPEDIMENTS TO THE SURROGATE MOTHERHOOD CONTRACT

The recent onslaught of media publicity in the United States regarding the surrogate mother situations that have come to public attention seems to indicate that the state is prepared to follow us into our bedrooms, but the present legislatures are not prepared, and were never intended, to encompass the legal status of a contract for a surrogate mother. Consequently, at the present such contracts are basically illegal and worse, perhaps, they have been labeled immoral and contrary to public policy by groups in society and the courts. Women who enter into surrogate mother contracts for financial necessity have been dubbed "second-class concubines."

Why would a woman enter into a surrogate mother arrangement? A Michigan psychiatrist who has handled the psychological counseling of over 151 women who have applied to be surrogate mothers has found that most women have had a prior live birth and are primarily motivated by money. Others have a desire to be pregnant and see real advantages to giving over the baby to make another couple happy. Some women have offered to provide the service free,[33] but these are rare altruists; most surrogate mother contracts have involved a fee of about $10,000.

The physician found in his counseling of surrogate mothers who have actually given up custody to the natural father and his wife that most had no verifiable symptoms of guilt. Some have experienced grief symptoms—crying, sleeplessness, and so on—while others have shown no sense of loss.[3]

These findings may help to uphold the theory that the "maternal instinct" venerated by our society has no medical basis and exists only from sociological influences.[33] The practice of surrogate mothering is seen as trying to redefine the mother/child relationship and the genetic base of the family and, because of this, is perceived as a danger. It is seen as extending to further alienate individuals by giving people a chance to be single parents and selfishly choose not to be a part of a family unit.[34] Following from this is the fear that society will suffer from the breakdown of the formal family structure. They talk in terms of premeditated abandonment by the surrogate mother.

However, people who have actually been involved in the surrogate mother arrangement seem to think otherwise. The phrase "premeditated abandonment angers them; they believe that the child has more love and concern than probably the majority of the children that are conceived. The argument that surrogate mother arrangements will detract from the sanctity of the marriage relationship is not as strong today because having children no longer appears to be the primary reason for getting married.

Since other practices such as abortion and artificial insemination have been implemented and regulated despite societal disapproval, it is argued that "the legal system should begin to anticipate and answer the legal problems that may result from new expanding technologies and ways of creating human life."[6, 10]

It may be that contract is not the appropriate area in which to litigate surrogate mother arrangements.[6] As aforementioned, the contracts have been found by the courts to be illegal and void as against public policy. More importantly, there are limits within the permissible scope of contract law for remedies for breaches of the contract's terms by one or both of the parties,[11] and the surrogate mother contract is one full of possible breaches and no real means by which the contracting parties can protect themselves.

A PROMISE MADE MAY NOT BE A DEBT UNPAID

While the principles of freedom to contract would suggest that the state should not interfere with the power of the parties to create rights and duties between themselves,[2] the problems that could arise in a surrogate mother contract should a breach occur indicate that some legal guidelines must be set up.

If the surrogate mother refused to be inseminated, the process would stop there, and the natural parents would receive restitution for any money they had paid up to this point of repudiation. But what if the surrogate mother procured an abortion or the child was born defective because she breached the contract provisions of taking proper care of herself by not smoking, drinking, or taking drugs? Here the natural parents would suffer both money damages and emotional harm—a tort based on negligence. There may be the likelihood of equitable relief, but in a tort action the natural parents would have to show a duty of the surrogate, express or implied, to maintain an adequate level of care of herself during pregnancy that a reasonable pregnant woman would. As well as a breach of duty, the natural parents would have to show that the surrogate's negligence was the proximate cause of the injury—this could be a problem in birth defect situations because there can be a latency in the genes of either of the parents undetectable in a medical exam that resulted in the defect.[15]

In the case of breach by abortion, the couple may get damages for the money they have already advanced, but it is unlikely that any court would enforce specific performance on a contract for personal services.[10, 35] There is no constitutional right in the natural father to prevent the surrogate from having an abortion.[20] "If neither a husband nor the state has an interest sufficient to compel an individual to make particular choices relating to conception and abortion, it is unlikely that parties to a contract have a right to affect such choices."[11]

If after the birth of the child the surrogate and her husband refuse to relinquish custody, there is little the natural father and his wife can do to exercise their contractual rights, except that the rights of the natural father may be taken into account at a custody hearing if paternity is proved. Then, even if he is denied custody, he may still be required to pay support.[36]

An American case that has been adjudicated, not on compensation but on custody, *In re James Noyes* (Cal. Sup. Ct., filed 1 February 1981), involved a Californian surrogate mother who was having a child for a single man from New York. When she changed her mind and refused to relinquish the child, the father filed suit for custody, paternity rights, and visitation. The Los Angeles Superior Court ruled that the mother could name the child, and she was awarded temporary custody pending a final hearing. She was then granted exclusive custody when the father dropped the suit,[37] presumably because he realized the illegality of the contract, but he was granted the right to have his name placed on the child's birth certificate as father.

These decisions exemplify the attitude of our society that there is something inherently wrong with a woman who would conceive and carry a child to term, only to give it away for money. "The sovereign has an interest in a minor child held superior even to that of the parent; hence, there is a public policy against the custody of such a child becoming a subject of barter."[38]

A recent case[39] has only complicated rather than clarified the legal status of surrogate motherhood. A 29–year-old widowed mother of three children agreed to act as a mother surrogate for a childless couple after she read an article in a newspaper that described a lawyer who made such arrangements. She consented but did not sign a written contract with the couple agreeing to turn the baby over to them after the child was born. She was not paid a fee for acting as a surrogate, but her medical expenses were paid. She did not have a written contract with the physician who performed the artificial insemination process. The male's semen was frozen and flown in from New York, and she was inseminated in the doctor's office located in California. The first attempt was unsuccessful. A second attempt two months later succeeded.

After the child was born, the mother surrogate refused to give up the child. The biologic father sued. The issue never came to trial because a settlement was worked out between the attorneys in the chambers of a California Superior Court judge. The woman was to keep the child and the father would have no custody, no visitation rights, and no obligations for support. California law holds that the donor of semen to a person other than his wife is not considered the natural father. In California unmarried fathers have rights and obligations, while semen donors do not. The male was named on the birth certificate as the father.

The decision in *Doe v. A. G.*[27] viewed the constitutionality of the protected decision to have the child through a surrogate mother separately from the contractual agreement between the parties. The court sustained the actual decision to have a child by this procedure but did not give the same deference to the terms of the contractual agreement. Specifically, the court refused to uphold that part of the agreement calling for financial compensation of the surrogate in excess of medical expenses actually incurred.

In upholding the statute, the court determined (1) that it was not unconstitutionally vague, since it gave specific and fair notice to those it applied to; and (2) that although the right of privacy encompasses such marriage-related activities as procreation and contraception, it does not give plaintiffs the right to use the statutory authority of the probate court to affect the adoption of a child wherein such contract provides for valuable compensation.

This conclusion was reached by the Michigan Court of Appeals, which stated:

> The statute in question does not directly prohibit John Doe and Mary Roe from having the child as planned. It acts instead to preclude plaintiffs from paying consideration in conjunction with the use of the state's adoption procedures. In effect, the plaintiff's contractual agreement discloses a desire to use the adoption code to change the legal status of this child. We do not perceive the goal as within the realm of fundamental interests protected by the right of privacy from reasonable governmental regulation.

The Michigan Court of Appeals determined that the decision whether and how to bear a child constituted a fundamental interest "protected by the right to privacy." It held, however, that the state's interest, as expressed in the statute, is to prevent commercialism from affecting a mother's decision to execute a consent to the adoption of her child. It established a dichotomy between the right to use the surrogate mother procedure and the right to pay the surrogate. The court found that the freedom to have a child through surrogate motherhood is not denied but also found that the law prohibits payment to the surrogate. The court declared "baby bartering" to be against the state's public policy and stated: "it is a fundamental principle that children should not and cannot be bought and sold. . . . The evils attendant to the mix of lucre and the adoption process are self-evident and the temptations of dealing in 'money market babies' exist whether the party be stranger or friends."

It also upheld the constitutionality of the provision that prohibited the exchange of money or other consideration in connection with adoption proceeding. The statute was attacked as an invasion of privacy by a married couple who intended to pay an artificially inseminated surrogate mother a sum of money plus medical expenses in exchange for the right to adopt the child at birth. The court held that the contract manifested a desire to change the child's legal status, and that such a contract did not fall within the fundamental right to bear or beget a child.

Furthermore, the court concluded that the state has a compelling interest in prohibiting the use of mercenary considerations to create parent-child relationships, stating that the resulting impact upon the family unit would strike at the very foundation of human society. It noted that the wife's infertility, not the state's prohibition against payment to the surrogate, prevents the couple's exercise of their rights to bear and beget children. Neither the U.S. nor the Michigan Supreme Court would accept the case for review. It appears that an unpaid volunteer surrogate mother, if found, would pass legal muster.

The question raised in this case—whether couples who cannot bear their own children can pay surrogate mothers to do so—is currently being much debated in courts and state legislatures. Courts frequently have held that such financial arrangements negate the voluntariness of a natural mother's consent to relinquish her child; since most statutes require unconstrained consent as a prerequisite to a valid adoption, such holdings effectively preclude the compensation of surrogate mothers. Consequently, advocates of this method of adoption are seeking changes in present law through judicial or legislative action.

State regulation of the specific contract provisions is permissible where a fundamental right is not involved, provided such regulation is neither arbitrary nor oppressive and bears a real and substantial relationship to the public health, safety, or morals, or some other phase of the general welfare.[13] Several legislatures are considering outlawing surrogate motherhood as against public policy.

In a related Michigan case,[22] the Michigan Court of Appeals again upheld the constitutionality of the state statute that prohibits the exchange of money or other considerations in connection with adoption proceedings. The statute was attacked as an invasion of privacy by a married couple who intended to pay an artificially inseminated surrogate mother $5,000 plus medical expenses in exchange for the right to adopt the child at birth. The court held that the contract manifested a desire to change the child's legal status, and that such a contract did not fall within the fundamental right to bear or beget a child.

CUSTODY

Because the issue in custody hearings is always the best interest of the child, the court will usually not take away a child from the surrogate mother unless there is some grave misconduct by her, leaving the natural parents only the possibility of recovering the money they paid. The arrangement can proceed, so to speak, illegally if all parties do what they have agreed to do, but no matter what they put on paper all they really have is a "gentleman's agreement" unenforceable in a court of law.[13]

Although the question of unconscionability arises from the perceived unfair bargaining power of the surrogate mother who needs the money and the natural father who can afford to pay, within the agreement the surrogate mother really has the legal advantage.[37] The funds are almost always placed in trust for her from the confirmation of conception and the couple accepts all responsibility for the child born regardless of any physical or mental handicap. The surrogate mother is further indemnified by the adopting couple should the state demand support from the "parents" in the event a severely handicapped child is born and placed in the state's care.

The remedies of the natural parent are few; he can only wait and hope the surrogate acts in good faith. Once the child is born the surrogate mother is also in a better position to claim custody should there be a dispute. The surrogate mother, then, is in control of the pregnancy and the parents must be satisfied with the doctor's screening and the surrogate's word.[40]

The only obvious protection the adopting couple has under present law against the possibility of a custody battle or an action for intentional infliction of emotional distress is the practitioner's choice in selecting a surrogate mother who will fulfill her responsibility under the contract voluntarily.

Two authors have noted that it seems clear that for the better protection of all parties involved, as well as for the best interests of the child, "the surrogate parent arrangement calls not only for a new outlook on the tradition of contract law. It also demands an instrument which must encompass and overcome a strong public policy against its very existence as well as provide broad protection for all parties concerned."[34]

ADOPTION

In this country, adoption is entirely a creature of statute; it was unknown at common law. Thus adoption statutes traditionally are and always have been strictly construed. In most states, statutes impose criminal penalties for paying or receiving money in connection with the surrender of children for adoption. Most states do allow payment of medical and hospital expenses associated with the birth of the child who is to be adopted. These provisions have serious implications for the involved physician. There are some states in which it is not against public policy to pay other provable necessary expenses, such as food and rent, incurred by the mother during pregnancy. In other jurisdictions, however, even payment of the natural mother's medical expenses to the physician and hospital expenses is considered akin to the ''sale'' of the baby. In any case, the sale of children is illegal. The physician recipient of fees for the medical service can be considered a party to the criminality, particularly if he was also involved in the arranging especially the adoption.

A surrogate motherhood contract may be found invalid if it violates public policy or state adoption laws. Two kinds of adoption statutes, both of which attempt to end the black market trade in babies, may affect a surrogate motherhood contract. Almost half of the states bar or restrict the independent placement of children for adoption. These states do so by requiring the use of a state adoption agency as an intermediary for the adoption to be legal.[42] However, such statutes usually do not restrict adoptions by blood relatives.[43] In a situation involving an unmarried surrogate mother, these restrictions are not an impediment, since the natural father is one of the adopting parents.

A case in point involves a trial court decision in Kentucky in March 1983.[44] The judge held that a surrogate mother may note relinquish her parental rights under existing Kentucky laws even though she may want to. The court held that Kentucky law allowing a woman to relinquish her parental rights was designed to transfer custody to a ''licensed child placement agency'' rather than to an individual. The judge further held that paternity must be determined by blood tests, not just by an affidavit by the father acknowledging paternity. In this particular case the ruling was moot since the biological father already had the newborn child with him in another state.

Another major problem with the surrogate mother contract, some claim, is that it contravenes all adoption legislation that forbids payment to the parent to procure an adoption. As has been noted, courts have held that such arrangements negate the voluntariness of the natural mother's consent to relinquish her child, since most statutes require unconstrained consent as a prerequisite for adoption, such holdings effectively preclude the compensation of surrogate mothers.''[40]

The hooker in the adoption laws that may affect a surrogate motherhood contract is the classic baby barter provision found in all state adoption laws.[42] This type of statute explicitly prohibits any person from offering, giving, or receiving any money or other consideration in connection with the placing for a child for adoption.[32] On its face, this type of statute would seem to apply to any surrogate mother arrangement where the surrogate receives a fee in return for her services. In fact, this was the finding in a Michigan case[27] in which the issue of payment to the surrogate mother arose. It may also involve the physician who receives a fee, albeit for his medical services. This is particularly true if he is involved in the adoption aspect. There are many viewpoints as to what the fee entails and why it should not be considered consideration for "baby selling."

The anti-baby-barter provisions derive from a public policy inherent in the fabric of American law which holds that children should not be treated as chattel subject to barter. The parent's right of control or custody of a child is not a property right that may be bargained away. Financial gain should not be the primary or even a secondary motivation for encouraging a natural parent to relinquish parental rights, and intermediaries such as the physician should not be given the opportunity to profit from the adoption transaction. The legal implications for the physician are serious from a criminal point of view and also administratively, i.e., loss of license,

In *Doe v. A. G.*,[27] the only reported case to date involving surrogate mother arrangements to be adjudicated on the point of money compensation, the court held that:

> Mercenary considerations used to create a parent-child relationship and its impact on the family unit strikes at the very foundation of human society and is patently injurious to the community.

The payment is seen to taint the arrangement and vitiate the surrogate mother's consent to the adoption.

The payment is also seen as going against the idea that children are not the property of their parents and cannot be treated as the subject of barter.[55] In *Wiley v. Lawton,* 132 N.E.2d 34 (1956), the former husband of a remarried woman was in arrears of paying child support to her. The wife and her new husband contracted with him to forgo the arrears and pay him $5,000 for his consent to the new husband's adoption of the child of the former marriage. The court held that the contract was void as against public policy in an action brought by the state adoption authorities.

The British High Court made a similar decision[45] in a custody hearing where a couple had paid a prostitute £3,000 for her agreement to be artificially inseminated with the husband's semen and then relinquish the baby after its birth. Once pregnant, the girl changed her mind, and after the baby was born she refused to give it up, even after the couple offered her their car and their house. Three days later, the couple took possession of the child and the girl reported it kidnapped. The court granted care and control to the natural mother, holding the contract was pernicious for the sale of a child and subsequently void. They further ordered the father to pay child support and granted him visitation rights.

Because of the public controversy created by the surrogate motherhood arrangement, the attorney general of Kentucky issued an opinion[46] declaring surrogate parenthood to violate at least the Kentucky state laws as well as a strong public policy against the buying and selling of children. Since the attorney general's opinion is not binding law, he filed a civil suit that the surrogate parenting process be declared illegal in Kentucky and that surrogate parenting contracts be declared invalid and unlawful in the state. Consistent with the opinion the attorney general filed a complain with the court seeking to revoke the corporate charter of Surrogate Parenting Associates, which had been organized to arrange surrogate mother contracts, on the grounds that it was guilty of an abuse and misuse of corporate powers, privilege and franchise "detrimental to the interest and welfare of the commonwealth." In the alternative the attorney general asked for a permanent injunction against Surrogate Parenting Associates "to prohibit it from engaging in any business in connection with the surrogate parenting process." The attorney general challenged the group's right to do business on the basis of statutes relating to procedures for adoption and for termination of parental rights.

The court said that the process by which a surrogate mother's rights were terminated was in accordance with state law.[24] Because a legal relationship existed between the father and the child, the court said, any dealings between the father and the surrogate mother with regard to the child could not properly be characterized as an adoption.

According to the applicable law, no petition for a termination of parental rights could be filed earlier than five days after the child's birth, thus giving the natural mother a minimum amount of time for deciding whether or not to keep her baby. The court said that even if the signing of a surrogate parenting agreement constituted a petition for termination, the surrogate could only relinquish rights according to the law.

The attorney general also challenged the surrogate parenting procedure under the statute prohibiting payment or collection of fees in order to procure a child for adoption purposes. The court said that the father was not paying to gain rights to the child because he already had a legal as well as a natural relationship. The father was paying the surrogate for her services of carrying the child and her relinquishment of parental rights, leaving him as the only person with a legal relationship to the child and making the child available for adoption by the wife of the biological father. Because there was no statutory prohibition against payment for termination of parental rights, the court said that it could not create one. The court pointed out that courts may interpret policy but that policy must be established by the legislature. The surrogate parenthood group's activities were not in violation of state law, the Kentucky trial court ruled.

The Ohio attorney general issued a similar opinion in early 1965.[47] The question presented to the attorney general was whether or not a person or group not licensed as a private placement agency violated the adoption laws of Ohio if the person engaged in activities that might be characterized as brokering for the services for surrogate mothers. The attorney general determined that these arrangements would, in fact, violate state adoption laws.

In like fashion the Oklahoma attorney general has opined[48] that surrogate parenthood contracts are illegal because they violate the Oklahoma Trafficking in Children statute. A member of the statute legislature requested an official opinion on the legality of surrogate gestation contracts. The attorney general stated that state law did not permit an unmarried woman to be artificially inseminated. Contracts in which parents unable to parent or conceive children contract with a third party to bear a child through artificial insemination in return for compensation and then adopt the child are unenforceable. Those contracts violate the Trafficking in Children statute. However, that statute does not apply except in cases where compensation above medical expenses is paid and adoption is planned or taken place, the attorney general said.

Several legislatures are considering outlawing surrogate motherhood as against public policy.[49, 50]

Lawyers who have dealt with and support the legislation legalizing surrogate mother contracts argue that the payment is not for the adoption or the relinquishing of custody, but for the service she performs and the possible risks it entails.[13] They contend that these statutes do not purport to make it a crime to pay someone for becoming pregnant or having a baby, and this omission confirms that surrogate motherhood was never intended as a target of the anti-black market statutes.[10]

They argue further that in these cases the spirit of the law, not the letter, should prevail.[10] But unfortunately, there are very few surrogate mothers who are altruistic and will participate without some payment,[15] and the money compensation brings the arrangement right under the statute's provisions. What is clear, however, is that the stigma associated with so-called baby selling persists even where the father is biologically related, and that such clauses in the contract are a likely target for the court to strike it down.[38]

However, the surrogate mother status differs in many ways from the "black market" situation that the statutes were drafted to prevent, and this makes the broad interpretation of the "exchange of consideration" in adoption laws questionable in its application in this area. In the black market situation, the pregnancy is usually unplanned and the mother is acting under duress because of financial need and emotional upheaval.[11] The surrogate mother agreement does not have these characteristics: The mother's natural will to act in the best interests of the child is not overborne by the money consideration.[34] It is better than a private adoption because of the biological tie and because the child is specifically planned and wanted by the natural parents. And because the agreement is made prior to conception, there isn't the financial/emotional pressure of the unwanted child on the mother. It would appear that this could only strengthen the resulting family unit, which opponents of the arrangements see as being threatened by the "womb external to the marital union."[2]

Surrogate mother arrangements present a unique situation. The donor whose semen impregnates the woman will, along with his wife, rear the child and thereby remain involved long after the surrogate mother's role is terminated. The surrogate mother who will carry and bear the child remains involved in the relationship for a definitive period of time—nine months, the period of gestation.

Public policy requires the law to protect the interests of the surrogate and her child, the parents-to-be, and the public.

The interests of the child are of paramount concern because the child is obviously unable to protect itself. Children are not chattel, and bartering them is outlawed by common law and as a matter of public policy in all states and expressly by legislative enactment in many states.[2]

It is unclear whether the prohibition against financial compensation exceeding the actual expenses associated with the pregnancy should apply to the surrogate mother arrangement. One court has outlawed such a contractual arrangement. Will other states? What is clear, however, is that the stigma associated with "baby selling" persists even where the father is biologically related and that such clauses in the contract are a likely target for the court to strike down.[19, 27]

Proponents of surrogate mother agreements highlight the several distinguishing factors between this arrangement and "baby selling."[12, 15] The key distinction between the surrogate mother arrangement and the baby-selling agreement relates to the timing of the contract by the involved parties.

Black-market sales of babies are moneymaking ventures that typically involve an unplanned pregnancy of an unwanted child. The mother is frequently unwed with limited financial resources.[19] It is easy to envision the woman in these circumstances caving in to the pressure of an avaricious opportunist intermediary who has convinced her that relinquishing her child is in the best interest of both mother and child. Furthermore, the adoptive parents will not have undergone the screening procedures required in agency adoptions, and may not have the emotional ties associated with being biologically related to the infant as in the surrogate mother situation.

In contrast to the "baby-selling" arrangement, the children born in the surrogate relationship are biologically related to the father and conceived as part of a premeditated plan to which the legal mother has consented. The surrogate mother willingly agreed to the arrangement before she ever became pregnant. She subjects herself to the procedure with full knowledge that she would relinquish all rights to the infant once it was born.[19, 51] Under this view, the payment is not for the infant, but rather for the service performed, that is, for carrying the child to full term. The surrogate mother makes emotional, physical, and financial sacrifices. In truth, she rents her body for a period of nine months with ensuing physicial and emotional wear and tear. She places her health and life on the line. Should she be entitled to compensation, or may she do it only as a "good Samaritan"?

The view from the opposite extreme does not permit any financial compensation to the surrogate mother under any circumstances. The rationale for this view is that it permits only women who are exclusively altruistic to become surrogate mothers and provide children to otherwise childless couples while preventing the degradation of childbearing into a mercenary profession that exploits financially needy women.[50] It is consistent with our Judeo-Christian ethic and public policy of encouraging childbearing and the virtues, pleasures, and bliss of parenthood to an otherwise barren couple.

It is clear, however, that prohibiting financial compensation of any sort would diminish the number of women willing to participate in surrogate mother arrangements.[19, 50] Few women are financially able to forgo gainful employment to engage in such a completely altruistic pursuit as bearing a child without payment of expenses and the concomitant loss of wages, plus compensation for the wear and tear and potential hazards of pregnancy and delivery. On the other hand, it is of course possible that a woman could be lured into the agreement seeking financial gain, but such an agreement would be both exploitative of the woman and contrary to public policy in the same manner as black-market baby sales.

This type of abuse can be avoided by legislative enactment and judicial oversight. Legislation establishing a ceiling on the amount of remuneration (comparable to the concept of compensatory special damages) a surrogate mother may receive has been proposed in Michigan. If the surrogate changes her mind, or suspects overreaching in the agreement, she may seek protection for herself and her child by applying to the courts for a determination of the validity and enforceability of the contract. The possibility that the couple may not get their child where the contract is procured by financial coercion should serve to curb any overzealous drafting of the contract. On the other hand, as to the surrogate mother, the law may (or should) consider that a promise made is a debt imposed. The same would be true for a reneging couple; they would be required to at least pay the cost of rearing the child.

ADULTERY

Can the artificial insemination of a surrogate mother be considered adulterous for the purposes of divorce? The early American cases have followed the Canadian decision of *Orford v. Orford* (1921), 58 D.L.R. 251 (S.C.C.), where the estranged wife was denied alimony on the grounds that she employed artificial insemination without her husband's consent and that this amounted to adultery. While this is the ratio, there are examples in the judgments which indicate that the bench may have suspected that the child was not, as purported, a result of artificial insemination but of an indiscretion on Mrs. Orford's part, which is probably the real reason for the decision. The court noted, "[M]y conclusion upon the facts . . . is that her story as to the artificial insemination is not to be believed. . . . I find as a fact that the plaintiff was guilty of adultery in that she had sexual intercourse in the ordinary way with Hodgkinson."

The more modern decisions[52–54] have held that adultery implies an act of physical sexual intercourse which neither artificial insemination or surrogate motherhood involve and go further to find that if the husband of the surrogate mother condones the artificial insemination, the ground of adultery can be defeated. There is an unwillingness to extend the decision *Orford* which indicates that the question is not whether there was an act of sexual intercourse, but the "surrender of one's reproductive facilities or powers to a married person" and most of the criticisms of the decision are based on its application to nonsexual acts.[55]

LEGAL STATUS OF CHILDREN

Paternity/Legitimacy

Problems of an equitable nature are encountered because legislatures have not anticipated surrogate parenting involving artificial insemination. Every state, in one form or other, has dealt with the issue of parentage; only eight states have passed the Uniform Parentage Act (UPA).

Actually, the legal status of artificial insemination children or offspring is not well defined in the legal codes of most states. At least twenty states have now passed legislation on some aspect of artificial insemination.[56, 57] Typical state legislation provides that the husband is deemed the father of the child if the has consented in the insemination.[58] Some states also sever the parental relationship which the man donor might otherwise have as the biological father of the child.[59]

Implicit within the various statutory language is the clear understanding that a child created by the articial insemination of an unmarried woman by an anonymous donor has no natural father. Since the woman is unmarried, there is no presumption of paternity on the part of any man. On the other hand, a second clear statement of intent is that a child created by means of AIH is a legitimate child.

The key bioethical question created by the artificial insemination statutes is presented in the situation of AID with the consent of the husband. The husband is treated in law as if he was the natural father of the child thereby conceived. The parentage of the child and the fatherhood of the husband is absolutely established and apparently is based on one of two factors: either the consent of the husband to the artificial insemination of his wife, or the familial relationship of the husband to the recipient of the insemination at the time the insemination is performed.

The donor of semen provided to a licensed physician for use in artificial insemination of a woman other than the donor's wife is treated in law as if he were not the natural father of a child thereby conceived. The language of the various statutes makes clear that the consent or lack of the consent of the donor is irrelevant to the parentage of the child and that the donor in this situation has no standing to claim parentage. Therefore, it seems clear that the parentage of the child, as well as standing to claim paternity, is based on the family relationship between the husband and his wife, the recipient of an artificial insemination, while a husband must consent to the AID insemination of his wife in order to be treated in law as the father of the child created.[60–62] While there may be legitimate state interests in maintaining the unity of the family, the failure to allow standing to an unmarried donor to adjudicate paternity where standing is allowed on the part of a husband may run afoul of the United States Supreme Court decisions that have held that reproductive autonomy belongs to the individual and not to the family as a unit.[26, 29–31]

The child born of a surrogate mother arrangement creates many problems of legitimacy. Most often, the question of testate succession arises when a child is born out of wedlock of his natural parents, but in most states, this may be resolved by formal adoption.[2]

In early decisions in the United States,[63] children born through artificial insemination were considered legally illegitimate because they were conceived by the mother with a man who was not her husband. The trend today seems to be toward finding that the child is legitimate if the husband of a valid marriage accepts that the child was born within that marriage. Nineteen American states have accepted children born through artificial insemination as legitimate. In *People v. Sorenson,*[53] the majority said "no valid public purpose is served by stigmatizing an artificially conceived child as illegitimate." But there is a quesiton whether a child born of a surrogate mother arrangement would be found illegitimate based on this same reasoning; it is not born within the marriage unit into which it is to be permanently placed.[6]

A step-parent adoption by the biological father's wife may remove the stigma of illegitimacy because then both of the legal parents would be married, but even prior to becoming the legal mother, the natural father's wife may be held accountable as the legal parent if she "actively participates and consents to the conception of a child by the surrogate mother."[50]

Paternity of the child may not arise as an issue unless there is a dispute that the child is not that of the natural father, or if there is a custody battle between the natural father and the surrogate mother. This may be countered in the original contract between the parties by having the surrogate mother's husband agree to relinquish all paternity rights to the child.[35] But, notwithstanding the contractual difficulties, there is a strong legal presumption that a married woman's husband is the father of her child.[6]

In California, childbirths by artificial insemination where the donor is anonymous, are covered by the California Civil Code, § 7005(b), The Uniform Parentage Act: "[T]he donor of semen provided . . . for use in the artificial insemination of a woman other than the donor's wife is treated in law as if he were not the father of the child thereby conceived." This is primarily to relieve the anonymous donor of any legal responsibility but would make it difficult for the natural father to assert his paternity rights to a child born to the surrogate mother inseminated with his semen.[1] However, the presumption could possibly be rebutted by the clear evidence of blood tests, the inseminating doctor's testimony, and the relinquishing of paternity rights by the surrogate mother's husband; the acknowledgment of paternity by the natural father may give him legal responsibility as well.[4]

In the case of *C.M. v. C.C.*,[8] the court recognized the paternity of a man who had donated sperm to a friend for artificial insemination expecting a relationship with the child. When the mother refused, the man brought action for declaration of paternity, which the court found was a reasonable belief on his part, and it subsequently awarded him visitation rights and ordered him to contribute to support and maintenance. This was based on the fact that the donor was known at the time of the insemination and that he had expressly manifested his intention to be the father of the child created in the same manner as most fathers act toward their children.

The court, in essence, held that parentage in the case of AID is a matter of the intention of the donor and that standing must be granted to the donor in order to protect his fundamental constitutional rights. The facts are completely analogous to the situation presented in the surrogate parenting arrangement. When the courts are presented with a case of a married surrogate (and her husband) who wishes to keep a child created in a surrogate parenting arrangement, they will have to reconcile the fundamental right to procreation held by the natural father and the surrogate mother as well as the possible detrimental effects on the family unit.

In *Synkowsky v. Appleyard,*[22] both the plaintiff and the defendant were married but not to one another. The plaintiff's marriage was barren of children while the defendant's marriage produced two children. The plaintiff and the defendant agreed that the defendant would submit to artificial insemination by the plaintiff's semen and the plaintiff would pay the defendant $10,000 plus medical expenses for her surrogate parenting. Subsequently, the defendant was successfully artificially inseminated and the plaintiff filed suit, five months before the child was born, for an order of filiation declaring his paternity of the child, according to Michigan's Paternity Act. The state's attorney general intervened and moved for dismissal of the suit on the grounds that the Paternity Act was intended to deal with a child born out of wedlock. The child in this case, he argued, was not born out of wedlock because two state statutes establish the presumption that a child born to an artificially inseminated married woman is treated for all purposes as her husband's child. Both statutes make the husband's consent to the artificial insemination a prerequisite to application of the presumption. The defendant's husband signed a nonconsent form.

The trial court dismissed plaintiff's claim not on the grounds that the attorney general argued, but because the court interpreted the Paternity Act as having the limited purpose of securing financial support for children born out of wedlock. The court declined to interpret the act more broadly because to do so would sanction surrogate parenting arrangements, which it viewed as being contrary to public policy. The court of appeals affirmed.

Finding that the question in this case involved a child born out of wedlock, according to the new definition of "out of wedlock" in the Paternity Act (i.e., "a child which the court has determined to be a child born during the marriage but not the issue of that marriage"), reversed the lower courts and sent the case back to trial court, where the order of filiation will probably be granted.

When artificial insemination is undertaken for the purpose of enabling the wife of a sterile husband to give birth to a child, a state statute presuming the legitimacy of that child poses no particular problem. However, where the wife is to function as a surrogate parent, the state's position on the legitimacy of the child controls the rights and responsibilities of the biologic father.

Physicians involved in artificial insemination should be aware of the controlling law in their state and should be prepared to counsel their patients on the potential problems that could result from the birth of a child conceived by artificial insemination.

CRIMINAL LAW

Surrogate parenting may be a crime in many states. Most states have enacted penal code sections which proscribe the payment or offers to pay a parent for consenting to adoption or to pay or offer to pay for the custody of another human being, the latter may also be, in effect, an antislavery statute. Further, while most practitioners find it necessary to advertise for surrogate mothers, many states prohibit such advertising when in connection with an adoption. Many of the obstacles presented by the penal codes could, as has been noted, be overcome if the surrogate mother were not paid for her services.

The parties entering into a surrogate mother contract face criminal sanctions in some states. For example, the California Penal Code, § 273(a) (West Supp. 1977) makes it a misdemeanor to pay anything of value for the consent or cooperation of a parent to the adoption of his or her child. This also forbids the payment of living and maternity benefits to the mother. The contract itself would fall under § 181, which creates a felony punishable by two to four years imprisonment to pay ". . . money or deliver . . . anything of value to another, in consideration for having a person placed in his custody". The latter provision is strictly to prohibit a "slavery" situation but may as well be applied in a broad interpretation to the surrogate mother situation.

As well, in most states it is illegal to consent to an adoption prior to five to ten days after the birth, so in a surrogate mother agreement where consent is given even prior to insemination, "the mother's consent could be held void."[11]

There is a real possibility that the penal code sections are susceptible to constitutional attack. In the event of indictments against any of the parties including the physician or against their representatives, there is a strong likelihood that the penal statutes will trip over their own vague language and fall before state and federal constitutional guarantees of privacy as expounded in the numerous Supreme Court decisions[25, 26, 29–31, 56] dealing with the subject when it comes to surrogate motherhood arrangement.

It should be noted that these penal code sections are not inherently defective; rather they have become defective by reason of the advances in medical science which allow a biological nexus between the natural father who is the "payor" and the child produced by the surrogate mother. This biological nexus creates a situation unforeseen by the drafters so that the penal code provisions could call into question violations of fundamental rights.

The available legal literature reveals the situation as one that will continue with or without legislation and supports the initiation of corrective measures to avoid unjust results. It has become a question of the law falling behind medical reality. As one author has noted, "these penal code sections are not inherently defective; rather they have become defective by reason of the advances in medical science which allow a biological nexus between the natural father who is the "payor" and the child produced by the surrogate mother. This biological nexus creates a situation unforeseen by the drafters . . . and calls into question violation of fundamental constitutional rights, first defined after the passage of the statutes.[64] Since fundamental rights are involved. regulations imposing a burden on the exercise of those fundamental rights may be justified only by compelling state interest, and narrowly drawn to express only those interests.

Another potential criminal issue arises as the result of the existence of statutes in many states poviding that any adoption release executed by the natural mother before the birth of the baby is invalid. The courts have always required, even if such release are not forbidden by statute, that the burden of proving the validity of a parental surrender falls on the party wishing to uphold it. The mother does not have to provide evidence of actual coercion or intimadation, fraud, decist or subterfuge to have a parental surrender declared invalid. The crux of the issue in these cases, when a woman is promised the necessities of life in return for the surrender of her child, is obvious. Problems may ensue for the physician if he undertakes to arrange a private adoption and makes the mother's consent to surrender of the child a precondition of his attendance during childbirth. Normally, such a surrender would be invalid under the principles of fraud and duress. It is reasonably forseeable that the physician could not only have civil but criminal legal problems.

Another basis for declaring the surrogate motherhood contract invalid and subjecting the parties, including the involved physician, is the Thirteenth Amendment of the United States Constitution, which prohibits slavery and the sale of one person by another. Children, like other people, cannot be bought and sold. Whether payment was made before the woman is inseminated or after the baby is born seems irrelevent; the intention of the arrangement is to fulfill a contract for the payment of money in exchange for a human being.

This has serious implications for the physician. Would this be a violation of the child's civil rights? Failure to treat a deformed newborn was, however erroneously, considered a potential civil rights violation by the federal government in the Baby Doe case.[65]

RIGHT TO PRIVACY AND CONFIDENTIALITY

In the United States, the right to privacy has been upheld in decisions to keep the state out of the couple's right to procreate. If the right to privacy means anything, it is the right of the individual, married or single, to be free from unwarranted governmental intrusion into matters so fundamentally affecting a person such as the decision whether to bear or beget a child.[11, 15] On the basis of these and other cases related to marital and familiar relationships, the Michigan Court of Appeals recently upheld the decision of a couple to have a child by a surrogate mother.[27]

In *Griswold v. Connecticut,* 381 U.S. 479 (1965), the Supreme Court reversed a conviction under a statute which made the use of contraceptives a criminal offence. It was held that the statute was invalid as invading the couple's right to privacy.

The Supreme Court went further in *Eisenstadt v. Baird:*[31]

> [I]f the right to privacy means anything, it is the right of the *individual* married or single, to be free from unwanted governmental intrusion into matters so fundamentally affecting a person as the decision whether to bear or beget a child.

The court recognized procreative autonomy and attendant restriction on state regulation of such matters. But, would the courts extend this reasoning to the surrogate mother arrangement, or is it restricted to the questions of contraception and abortion?[32]

MEDICAL RECORDS

Some additional problems are foreseeable. One of the problems confronting physicians involved in surrogate motherhood situations is the problem of records. Under artificial insemination by a donor, the exact identity of the biologic father is not known because more than one donor is used at the insemination. Furthermore, the husband agrees to be the father and is listed on the birth certificate.

In surrogate motherhood arangements, on the other hand, the mother and biologic father are known. Since adopted children now have access to their records in many jurisdictions[63, 64] will they be able to discover their surrogate mother, and one day go looking for Mama? This becomes even more critical now that paternity blood testing and identification is essentially 100 percent accurate and may be required by the courts.[19] Will the supply of surrogate mothers advised of these medicolegal facts shrival up when this information is divulged; and it should be conveyed before the parties become involved. Otherwise the physician may be at peril based on lack of complete informed consent by the surrogate mother.

The issue of whether the identity of the surrogate mother should or should not be kept from the child is unresolved under current law. The issue is analogous to the adoption and artificial insemination issues of confidentiality with strong arguments on both sides. In many children, the strong psychological need to know one's biological parents favors disclosure. From a purely medical point of view, medical records may be needed later in life to determine the history of a previously undetected disease. The arguments against disclosure recognize that the surrogate mother may want her identity kept confidential. Moreover, this may even be a provision of the contract, without which the surrogate mother might be wary of participating.[52]

An unresolved case that has some bearing on this problem involves a women in her early thirties who is presently publicly looking for her natural father after recently learning that she was conceived by artificial insemination (AID). She has identified the inseminating physician who knows only that her father is one of 55 Jewish medical students (who purveyed his ejaculum for $25). Geneticists have given her a list of possible characteristics after studying her and her mother. Blood type can point the fickle finger of fate at the putative father.

She contemplates several legal actions: recognition of her paternity by the biologic father, paternal support and a "wrongful life" action against the physician because of a claimed unhappy childhood characterized by physical and mental abuse brought about by an emotionally unstable mother, resulting from inadequate physician screening and no genetic counseling. Furthermore, records of the mother as well as the family were poorly kept and the birth certificate was fradulent because a nonbiologic father was indicated. Incest is a potential problem. Psychological repercussions could develop after the child discovers the identity of the surrogate mother leading to family disruptions.

Since no laws directly control whether the surrogate mother's identity may be revealed, parties must analogize from other areas to determine the law's most likely course. The laws in a given jurisdiction governing the identity of the natural parents of an adopted child probably will be applied to the surrogate mother arrangement, given the similarity between the two situations. Whether the parties can agree to a result other than that dictated by statute will depend upon whether the statute is meant to fill the interetics of an agreement, or is intended to prohibit private agreement. This will vary from jurisdiction to jurisdiction.[54]

Obviously, this uncertainty applies even more forcefully to the surrogate mother situation. This legal limbo should reinforce the practitioner's desire to adequately explain the procedure to the involved couple and to obtain a clearly worded consent from them. It is the obligation of the inseminating physician to maintain adequate records so that, should inheritable disease result, an indentification of the donor is possible. What happens to the records of the physicion who retires dies or who sells his practice is unsettled.

Many couples involved in artificial insemination conceptions will want to know whether the child should be informed of his origins. While the psychologic implications of this information on the child have not been thoroughly studied, it is believed that such information should be imparted some time before maturity is attained.

In a related case, the Oregon Supreme Court ruled that a mother had a cause of action for breach of confidential relationship against a physician who revealed her identity to the daughter she had given up for adoption.[66]

The 21–year-old daughter sought out the physician when she wanted to establish contact with her biological mother. The physician gave the daughter a letter stating that it was important for her to find her biological mother because he remembered giving her diethylstilbestrol (DES). This statement was untrue and was made only to help the daughter breach the confidentiality of the records of her birth and adoption. Hospital personnel, relying on the letter, permitted the daughter to make copies of her mother's medical records, which enabled her to locate her mother.

The mother brought an action against the estate of the physician, who had died. The trial court entered judgment for the estate. An appellate court reversed on counts of breach of a confidential relationship and invasion of privacy.

On review, the Oregon Supreme Court said that if the mother had claim, it arose from a breach of a professional duty to keep her secret rather than from a violation of her privacy. The court said that the claim was not that the physician had pried into a confidence but that he had failed to keep one.

The court pointed out that in a number of decisions it had been held that unauthorized and uprivileged disclosure of confidential information obtained in a confidential relationship could give rise to damages. The court agreed with the appellate court that the mother could proceed under her claim of breach of confidentiality in a confidential relationship. The court reversed the appellate court's decision with respect to the claim of invasion of privacy and affirmed as to the claim of breach of confidence and sent the case back for further proceedings.

This case could serve as a precedent in a case involving the revelation of the indentity of a surrogate mother. In the unlikely event that the physician is indiscreet in protecting the privacy and confidentiality of the parties, they could conceivably be sued for invasion of privacy and/or breach of confidentiality.

CIVIL LIABILITY FOR THE INVOLVED PHYSICIAN

We have already indicated the potential civil liability of the physician involved in surrogate motherhood arrangements. The doctor who is involved in the screening and/or selection of the surrogate mother may be liable in negligence to the biologic father for failing to properly select and monitor as well as for failing to actively and affirmatively intervene if the mother reneges on her promise to be inseminated, take care of herself during the pregnancy, failing to submit to necessary diagnositic and threapeutic measures and ultimately not willing to surrender the child. Conversely, it seems unreasonable to expect that the physician would be liable to the mother if the biologic father and his wife failed to live up to their end of the bargain legally.

It goes without saying that a physician charged with performing the artificial insemination negligently may be held liable under the doctrines of negligence,[67] negligent genetic counseling wrongful birth or life,[72] a even outrage or the negligent inflication of emotional injury.[64]

As to wrongful life,[68-72] when a child is born with defects as a result of negligence of the physician prenatally and/or during the pregnancy seven states now allow the child to sue for "wrongful life." This cause of action is undoubtedly available to a child regardless of the nature of their conception-artificial insemination and surrogate motherhood.

In addition to being liable in negligence, the possibility that the parties could sue for the tort of outrage or intentional infliction of emotional damages.

What can a physician do to avoid civil and criminal liability as well? He should keep in mind the following considerations:

- Appropriate selection of the surrogate mother and matching with the biologic father;
- Problems inherent in the artificial insemination procedure;
- Continuing care during the pregnancy;
- Use of amniocentesis;
- Problems incident to abortion;
- Completion of the birth certificate;
- Privacy and confidentiality;
- The legitimacy and enforceability of payment of expenses, including costs and lost wages;
- The nature and extent of the state's interest in these agreements will also be addressed insofar as it is a necessary adjunct because of its role as *parens patria,* and as legislators of public policy;
- The situation where a single male wishes to father a child using the surrogate procedure.

Most of the arrangements to date have involved the husbands of married couples who were to be the biologic father. However, should the arrangements become legal they could be extended to include single parents.

POSITION OF ORGANIZED MEDICINE

The Judicial Council of the American Medical Association considered and reported that problems may arise when a woman agrees to become pregnant through artificial insemination for the purpose of relinquishing the newborn to the sperm donor and, usually, his infertile wife. The report pointed out that physicians who participate in surrogate motherhood arrangements may be placing themselves in legal and ethical jeopardy. The report opined that the welfare of the child should be a foremost consideration. In ordinary adoption proceedings, an appropriate agency usually investigates prospective adoptive parents to determine their fitness. This precuation is not always present in surrogate motherhood arrangement.

The council noted press accounts of a surrogate mother who gave birth to a microcephalic child who was not the offspring of the semen donor. If the child is defective, both the prospective adoptive parents and the woman who gave birth to the child may be unwilling to assume the responsibilities of parenthood.

A woman who has contracted to bear the child may decide to have an abortion or refuse to give the child up for adoption, the council noted.

Another consideration is the psychological impairment that may occur in a woman who deliberately conceives with the intention of bearing a child that she will give up. Grief, which may last a lifetime, has been reported following the mother's giving up her child for adoption.

The AMA report also envisioned other difficult situations in surrogate motherhood, such as a decision by the mother to abort or her refusal to release the child after birth.

As a consequence of the report, surrogate motherhood was opposed by the AMA. Delegates to the interim meeting adopted the Judicial Council report enumerating the grave ethical, legal, and psychological risks of a woman's being paid to bear a child for another. These arrangements they noted, do not appear to serve societal interest and do not provide a satifactory reproductive alternative was the philisosphy enunciated.

Surrogate motherhood does not represent a satisfactory reproductive alternative for people who wish to become parents. The report suggests that physicians not become involved in the financial or legal aspects of a surrogate motherhood arrangement.

The report also expressed considerable concern about the potential legal and ethical jeopardy that physicians who participate in such arrangements face. When all considerations are brought together, these arrangements do not appear to serve societal interests.

On the other hand, the Council spokesman emphasized that the report does not declare it unethical for an obstetrician or other physician to perform the usual services required in caring for a pregnant surrogate mother. But it does say that other alternatives are better, and it also warns physicians not to become involved in contractual agreement.

The report is similar to the policy statement made by the American College of Obstetricians (ACOG) and Gynecologists. "While the decision to participate or not in the surrogate motherhood alternative is an individual one for each physician to make, ACOG has significiant reservations about this approach to parenthood."

Though generally in agreement with the AMA's position, a spokesman for the American College of Obstetricians and Gynecologists, testified before the AMA reference committee examining the report that the wording might be too strong. He indicated that ACOG did not think surrogate motherhood should be used very often, but there could be a situation in which this might be the best way to handle the problem.

Nevertheless, there is concern that the AMA report might convey the impression that the arrangement is never an acceptable alternative. In one out of 100 infertile couples, surrogate motherhood might be considered the only alternative, and some would have liked to have seen the report's wording softened in this regard.

The report, as adopted by the House of Delegates, raised concerns about the possibility of double scenarios. In length, there are a lot of potential problems that could complicate this kind of arrangement. There are legal risks involved, and the physician should be aware of them.

EPILOGUE

What are the legal aspects, implications and consequences for those who get involved in surrogate motherhood arrangements? It is not possible to know for certain at this time. The physician has the potential for being a hero, a fallen hero or a villain. To some degree it depends on the extent of his involvement. It basically revolves on how the "law" ultimately appreciates surrogate motherhood. It will probably be a mixed bag. For the present the perils and pitfalls are formidable, even foreboding. At present, you pays your money and take your chances.

REFERENCES

1. Genesis 16.6; Genesis 30:1–5.

2. Vieth, P.: "Surrogate Motherhood: Medical Reality in a Legal Vacuum", 8 *J. Leg.* 140 (1980).

3. Erlenbusch, P.: "Planned Parenthood: The Surrogate Alternative", 29 *R.L.F.* 2d 51 (1982).

4. Epstein, P.: "Surrogate Mothers", Canadian Bar Association Conference, p. 18 (April, 1983).

5. Harris, L.: "Artificial Insemination and Surrogate Motherhood—A Nursery Full of Unresolved Questions", 17 *Williamette L. Rev.* 913 (1981).

6. Patterson, S.: "Parenthood by Proxy: Legal Implications of Surrogate Birth, 67 *Iowa L. Rev.* 385 (1982).

7. Cuisine, D. J.: "Womb Leasing—Some Legal Implications", 128 *New L.J.* 824 (1978).

8. N.Y. Health Care, Art. 21 (1959); or Rev. Statute 677.370 (1979).

9. Fogany Brabender, D.: "Wrongful Birth: Should Liability Be Imposed Upon a Physician Who Fails to Warn Parents of the Risks of Defects in Their Unborn Children?", *Gonzag L. Rev.* 14(4) 891 (1979).

10. Black, P.: "Legal Problems of Surrogate Motherhood", 16 *New England L. Rev.* 611 (1981–82).

11. Townsend, M. D.: "Surrogate Mother Agreements: Contemporary Legal Aspects of a Biblical Notion", 16 *U. of Richmond L. Rev.* 467 (1982).

12. Erickson, E. A.: "Contracts to Bear a Child", 66 *Calif. L. Rev.* 611 (1978).

13. Bird, K.: "Surrogate Motherhood Agreements: Hers? Yours? Ours?", 2 *California Lawyer* 21 (1982).

14. Jabro, J.: ''Surrogate Motherhood: The Outer Limits of Protected Conduct'', 1981 *Det. Col. L. Rev.* 1131 (1981).

15. Mady, T.: ''Surrogate Mothers: The Legal Issues'', 7 *Am. J.L. & Md.* 323 (1981).

16. *Custer Public Power District v. Loup River Public Power District,* 162 Neb. 300, 75 N.W.2d 619 (1956).

17. Korechny, N.: ''Surrogate Mothers, The Current Legal Issues'', *Medical Trial Technique Quarterly,* (in press).

18. ''Notre Surrogate Mother: The Legal Issues'', *American Journal of Law & Medicine* 7(3): 323, 342–344 (Fall 1981).

19. Keane, N.: ''Legal Problems of Surrogate Motherhood'', *Southern Ill. U. Law J.* 2:147, 149–152 (1980).

20. Brophy, A.: ''A Surrogate Mother Contract to Bear a Child'', *J. Family L.* 201–263 (1982).

21. Note: ''Surrogate Mother Agreements: Legal Aspects of a Biblical Nation'', *U. of Richmond L. Rev.* 16(2), 467 (1982).

22. *Syrkowski v. Appleyard,* 362 N.W.2d 211 (Mich. App. 1985).

23. Note: ''Surrogate Motherhood: Medical Reality in a Legal Vacuum'', *J. of Legislation* 18:140 (1981).

24. *In re Baby Girl,* 9 Fam. L. Rep. 231 (Ky. 1983).

25. *Kentucky v. Surrogate Parenting Associates,* 10 FLR, 105 Ky. Cir. Ct., Franklin Cir. (1983).

26. *Roe v. Wade,* 410 U.S. 113 (1973).

27. *Doe v. Attorney General,* 307 N.W.2d 438 (Mich. App. 1981), IV. denied; 414 N.W.2d 875 (1982), cert. denied, 103 S.Ct. 834 (1983).

28. Brophy, K.: ''Surrogate Mother: Contract to Bear a Child'', 20 *J. Family L.* 263 (1982).

29. *Griswold v. Connecticut,* 381 U.S. 479, 14 L.Ed.2d 510, 85 S.Ct. 1678 (1965).

30. *Carey v. Population Services International,* 431 U.S. 678, 52 L.Ed.2d 675, 97 S.Ct. 2010 (1977).

31. *Eisenstadt v. Baird,* 405 U.S. 428, 453, 31 L.Ed.2d 349, 92 S.Ct. 1029 (1972).

32. Mich. Comp. Laws Ann. § 710.54(1) (West Supp. 1983–1984).

33. *Boston Globe,* p. 29 (May 30, 1980).

34. Handel and Sherwyn: ''Surrogate Parenting'', 18 *Trial* 57 (1982).

35. *Dockery v. Hamner,* 202 So.2d 550 (Ala. 1967).

36. *C.M. v. C.C.,* 152 N.J. Super 160, 377 A.2d 821 (1977).

37. Rushevsky: ''Legal Recognition of Surrogate Gestation'', 7 *Woman's Rights L. Rep.* 107 (1982).

38. *Williston on Contracts* § 1744 at 88 (Lawyer's Cooperative Publishing Co., New York, 1972).

39. Feldman, W.: ''Wombs for Rent, Surrogate Mothers and Semen Donors'', *Legal Aspects of Medical Practice,* Vol. 10, No. 5, p. 8 (May, 1983).

40. Greenburg, L. J., and Hirsh, H. L.: ''Surrogate Motherhood and Artificial Insemination: Contractual Implications'', 29 *Med. Tr. Tech. Q.* 149 (1983).

41. Note: ''Surrogate Motherhood: Medical Reality in a Legal Vacuum'', *Journal of Legislation* 8, 140 (1981).

42. Note: ''Surrogate Mothers: The Legal Issues'', *American Journal of Law & Medicine* 7(3), 323, 342–44 (Fall 1981).

43. N.J. Stat. Ann. § 9:3:39 (West 1977).

44. Unpublished case. Reported in *Washington Post,* p. Cl, col.6 (March 10, 1983).

45. *London Times,* p. 1, col. 8 (June 21, 1978).

46. Opinion, Attorney General of Kentucky, No. 81–18 (January 26, 1981), "Surrogate Mother Contracts Declared Illegal by Kentucky Attorney General", *Family Law Reporter* 7, 2247 (February 17, 1981).

47. Opinion, Attorney General of Ohio, No. 83–001 (January 3, 1983).

48. Opinion, Attorney General of Oklahoma, No. 83–162 (September 29, 1983).

49. Comment, "Surrogate Motherhood in California: Legislative Proposals", *San Diego L. Rev.* 18(2), 341, 379 (March 1981).

50. Hoften, W. Van: "Surrogate Motherhood in California: Legislative Proposals", *San Diego L. Rev.* 18, 341 (1981).

51. Andrews, J.: "Should Our Laws Be Changed to Reflect The New Moral and Medical Realities?", 4 *Fam. Advocate* 20 (1981).

52. *Beckwith v. Beckwith,* 379 A.2d 955 (D.C. App. 1977).

53. *People v. Sorenson,* 437 P.2d 495 (Cal. 1968).

54. *Benson v. Benson,* 102 So.2d 748 (Fla. Dist. C.A. 1958).

55. Finegold, W.: "Artificial Insemination" (Thomas Bros. Press, Springfield, 1976).

56. Flannery, et al.: "Test Tube Babies Legal Issues Raised by In Vitro Fertilization, *Georgetown Law Journal* 67(6), 1295, 1305 n. 68 (August, 1979).

57. "Law and Ethics of A.I.D. and Embryo Transfer", CIBA Foundation Symposium (1973).

58. Cal. Civ. Code § 7005(a) (1983); La. Civ. Code Ann. Art. 188 (West Supp. 1984).

59. Conn. Gen. Stat. Ann. § 45.69 (Rev. 1958); N.C. Gen. Stat. § 49 A. 1 91976).

60. *In re Lisa R.,* 13 Cal.3d 636, 119 Cal.Rptr. 475, 532 P.2d 123 (1975).

61. *R. McG. v. J.W.,* 615 P.2d 666 (Colo. 1980).

62. U.S. 645, 31 L.Ed.2d 551, 92 S.Ct. 1208 (1972).

63. *Gursky v. Gursky,* 242 N.Y. Supp.2d 406 (1936).

64. Flickinger, R. N.: "Surrogate Motherhood: The Attorney's Legal and Ethical Dilemma", 11 *Capital U.L. Rev.* 593 (1982).

65. *American Academy of Pediatrics v. Heckler,* 561 F.Supp. 395 (DDC 1983); *U.S. v. University Hospital of the State of New York at Stoney Brook,* U.S. D.C. E.D. N.Y., No. CV 83–4–818; November 17, 1983, C.A. 2, No. 83–6343, February 23, 1984, Motion for rehearing derived May 7, 1984; *Weber v. Stoney Beach Hospital, et al.,* U.S. Supreme Court, Dkt. to 83–583, February 23, 1984; *American Hospital Association v. Heckler,* No. 83 Cir. 2638—CLB, S.D. N.Y. 1983, Memorandum and Order, May 31, 1984.

66. *Humphers v. First Interstate Bank of Oregon,* 696 P.2d 527 (Ore. Sup. Ct. 1985).

67. Hirsh, H. L.: "The Legal Noose Gets Tighter", *Legal Medicine 1982* (W. B. Saunders Co., Philadelphia).

68. *Becker v. Schwartz* and *Park v. Chessen,* 386 N.E.2d 867, 46 N.Y.2d 401, 1415 N.Y.S.2d 895 (1978).

69. *Berman v. Allen,* 400 A.2d 8 (N.J. 1979).

70. *Gildner v. Thomas Jefferson University Hospital,* 451 F.Supp. 692 (E.D. Pa. 1978).

71. *Procanek by Procanik v. Cell,* 478 A.2d 755 (N.J. Sup. Ct. 1984).

72. Lehr, C. M., and Hirsh, H. L.: "Wrongful Conception, Birth and Life—A Question of Viability", *Medicine and Law,* 2:199–208 (1983).

73. "Surrogate Motherhood Opposed", *American Medical News,* p. 3 (April 23, 1984);

''AMA Raps Surrogate Motherhood An Ethical and Legal Quagmire'', *Medical World News*, p. 24 (January 9, 1984).

ADDITIONAL REFERENCES

Curie-Cohen, et al.: ''Current Practice of Artificial Insemination by Donor in the United States'', *New England Journal of Medicine*, 300(11) 585, 588 (March 15, 1979); Shaman: ''Legal Aspects of Artificial Insemination'', *Journal of Family Law*, 18:331, 332 (1980); Oakley: ''Test Tube Babies Proposals for Legal Regulation of New Motherhoods of Human Conception and Parental Development'', *Family Law Quarterly*, 8:385 (1974); Reich, W.: *Encyclopedia of Bioethics*, 1448–51 (Gale Research Co., Detroit, 1978).

Massey v. Parker, 369 So.2d 1310 (La. 1978).

ADDENDUM

A unique surrogate mother situation was reported from Cleveland in the November 21, 1985, issue of the New York Times. It reported a case in which a 37–year-old woman underwent a hysterectomy after her uterus ruptured in pregnancy. Three of her eggs were later removed, and one of them was fertilized with her husband's sperm. Then it was placed into the uterus of a 22–year-old friend who had already had two normal pregnancies. The fetus appears to be normal, and the pregnancy is completely uncomplicated. When the child is born, it will be turned over to its genetic parents.

The embryo transfer is a whole new horizon. It offers the infertile couple the opportunity to have a child that biologically belongs to both of them. The host mother is truly, in every respect, an incubator.

Malicious Deprivation of Hospital Staff Privileges

Marvin H. Firestone, M.D., J.D., F.C.L.M., and
Robert Schur, J.D.

INTRODUCTION

This chapter, devoted to the discussion of the litigation of disputes over medical staff privileges, is intended to address the various theories underlying recovery in tort and contract by a physician against a hospital, medical staff, or individuals who wrongfully deny, limit, or interfere with hospital staff privileges, as well as the possible issues of denial of due process of law and antitrust violations that may be involved. Although a variety of actions may be available in such cases, it is convenient to use the general term *malicious deprivation* for purposes of this discussion.

The physician may face any number of discriminatory practices, which may be based upon social, professional, racial, personal, or economic biases. Once deprived of staff privileges, the physician is likely to find it difficult to obtain privileges elsewhere.[1] Thus, the process tends to become self-perpetuating and may result in the physician's complete inability to earn a living in his chosen profession, causing major upheaval in the physician's life.

The incidence of malicious deprivation of staff privileges is on the rise. With the increase in the number of medical school graduates, pressure in the job market has increased and competition for the limited number of hospital staff positions has become more intense, thus increasing the likelihood that hospital staff privileges will be denied or limited on an unfair basis.

Discrimination Based on Professional Factors

Cases in this category include both systematic exclusions of certain types of professionals, such as osteopaths, and exclusions of individuals because of differing medical methods or philosophies, as, for example, where conservative staff members disapprove of the use of relatively new techniques by the "loner" or "newcomer" general physician or specialist.

In the systematic type of exclusionary practice, the basis for discrimination may be the physician's particular school of treatment. In the early case of *Hayman v. Galveston,*[2] the Supreme Court refused to enjoin the enforcement of hospital rules that excluded osteopaths from practice in a teaching hospital operated jointly by the city and the state university. The case was followed in a number of states on the basis that the usefulness of a hospital would be impaired if there were found to be a "right" to practice in public hospitals for practitioners of all the different schools of medicine. Thus, in the Colorado case of *Newton v. Board of Commissioners,*[3] the court held that an osteopath licensed to practice in the state had no constitutional right to practice in a county hospital, stating:

> [A] regulation excluding . . . devotees of some of the numerous systems or methods of treating diseases . . . is neither unreasonable nor arbitrary. . . . [I]f the right to practice medicine in the county hospitals is open to all the different schools of medicine, there would be constant jealousies and dissatisfaction between the rival schools . . . which probably might or would greatly lessen the usefulness of the public hospital.[4]

Although no longer used to exclude osteopaths in most communities, such an approach is still widely seen as a basis for denial of staff privileges to certain factions of the health care professional community.

Discrimination Based on Race

The courts have historically had little problem in finding that exclusion of a physician from the medical staff of a hospital on the basis of race is improper and subject to injunction. The main dispute in these civil rights cases, as in others, has been the public-private distinction and the plaintiff's capability of proving some connection between the hospital governing board and the state, such that "state action" may be found for purposes of the Fourteenth Amendment and 42 U.S.C. § 1983. Further discussion of these issues appears below. An illustrative case is *Eaton v. Grubbs,*[5] a case in which the Fourth Circuit held that the state of North Carolina had become so involved in the conduct of a "private" hospital as to render the hospital an "instrument of the state."[6] The facts supporting the finding included the construction of the hospital on city and county land donated for the purpose, local government construction and operating funds, and state tax exemptions. The result of the finding was that the hospital was prohibited under the Fourteenth Amendment from practicing discrimination against and segregation of black physicians and patients.[7]

Economic Discrimination

Often there are economic factors that lead hospital governing board members and ''well-entrenched'' physicians to deny privileges to potential competitors or exclude them from the medical staff. One example may be where a ''closed-staff'' system for one department, such as radiology, is adopted in order that a specific radiologists' partnership may receive all the hospital's business. Such closed-staff arrangements have generally been held proper, as, for example, in the California case of *Blank v. Palo Alto–Stanford Hospital Center*.[8] In that case, a physician who was a member of the hospital staff and fully entitled to all privileges of such membership was nevertheless denied the use of the hospital's X-ray facilities. The reason for the exclusion was the hospital's contract with a radiology partnership, which provided the operation of the department on an exclusive basis. The court held that such an arrangement was not unreasonable or arbitrary, did not violate hospital rules giving staff members access to the facilities needed for treatment of their patients, and was ''justifiable in view of the ends to be accomplished.''[9]

A more troublesome case in this area arises when an influential member of the medical staff feels threatened by the plaintiff's competitive presence. In such a case, the exclusion of the physician from the staff is likely to be ostensibly for other, perhaps seemingly legitimate reasons when the basis, in fact, is economic. This type of case has been more and more prevalent and is the most insidious problem confronting us in this area of litigation—especially in the subspecialty surgical fields.

Discrimination Based on Social or Personal Factors

Perhaps the most common basis upon which discrimination is practiced against physicians is the ''personality conflict.'' To the extent that a physician is excluded from or deprived of staff privileges simply because he is disliked by board members or other staff physicians, he has suffered a malicious deprivation. Usually, however, other reasons will be fabricated for such actions.

THE PHYSICIAN'S LEGAL CLAIMS

Physicians who have been denied or deprived of staff privileges in a discriminatory manner may have a number of legal theories upon which to base a claim. The major portion of that body of law which has developed in this area is concerned with the availability of judicial review of the decisions of hospital governing boards.[10] An area that also has received considerable attention concerns the antitrust laws, where physicians have attempted to prove unlawful restraints on trade or monopolization by the hospital board and staff. Many of the same obstacles faced by plaintiffs in these actions, including statutorily created immunities for medical peer reviewers, must be overcome in pursuit of claims sounding in tort or contract.

Bad Faith

The importance of the allegations of bad faith or malice cannot be overemphasized in any action for denial or deprivation of staff privileges. For lack of such allegations, a physician's libel suit was dismissed in the Texas case of *Mayfield v. Gleichert.*[11] In light of certain incidents involving conflicting views between the plaintiff and other staff physicians on proper treatment provided to patients, the chief of the hospital's department of obstetrics and gynecology had issued a report to the medical staff recommending that the plaintiff physician be suspended. The plaintiff was unable to prevail in her claim because she could not overcome the defendant's qualified privilege without an allegation of malice.[12] In *Nashville Memorial Hospital v. Binkley, Inc.*,[13] the Tennessee Supreme Court dismissed the plaintiff's claim against the hospital for unreasonable denial of staff privileges, finding the hospital to be private and not an instrument of the state. Nevertheless, the court went on to hold that a cause of action would lie against those defendants against whom the plaintiff had pleaded a conspiracy to injure him in the practice of his profession. The court stressed that malice was a necessary element[14] but was willing to infer it:

> It is . . . an actionable wrong for two or more persons to conspire maliciously and without justification or excuse to injure or damage another in the conduct of a lawful business or profession. Furthermore, it is not necessary to expressly allege malice so long as it is alleged that the damage was done by the defendants intentionally and without legal justification, for malice is inferred from such allegations.[15]

Once past this threshold defense, the plaintiff may pursue theories for the "malicious deprivation" claims, including (1) breach of contract, (2) defamation, (3) tortious interference with contract or with the practice of the profession, (4) antitrust, (5) unlawful discrimination under 42 U.S.C. 1983, and (6) conspiracy to commit any of these.

Contract

The contract theory is based on the hospital's bylaws, which may contain terms and provisions that define the physician-hospital relationship. These bylaws constitute, in whole or in part, an enforceable contract between the hospital and the physician, and courts have so held. In *Berberian v. Lancaster Osteopathic Hospital Ass'n,*[16] the plaintiff physician sought an injunction against the hospital and its medical director to restrain them from discharging him from the medical staff. The hospital bylaws provided for a hearing, notice of charges, and a right to appeal before any discharge. Dr. Berberian had received none of these protections. In issuing the injunction, the court held that "the hospital had, in legal contemplation, entered into a contract whereof the provisions of the staff bylaws, as approved by the hospital's board of directors, constitute the legally binding terms."[17] Of course, the terms of the contract are always written and adopted unilaterally and may contain provisions more favorable to the hospital than to the physician.[18]

Defamation

Defamation actions may be among the most promising where the physician has been subjected to revocation of existing hospital staff privileges, ostensibly for incompetence or the like. The common-law elements of defamation are well known to any attorney. The major obstacle, beyond the statutorily granted immunity, is common-law immunity or privilege. It is the proof of bad faith or malice that will obviate such defenses.[19]

Interference

Interference with contract involves showing that the defendant(s) intentionally and maliciously induced one party, the hospital, to refuse to perform its duty under the bylaws.[20] Like breach of contract, interference of contract is available only to physicians who have lost their privileges, not to those initially denied. The conspiracy element may figure prominently in a case alleging this type of tort. In the *Nashville* case,[21] the plaintiff physician charged that the hospital and the individual defendants had conspired to unlawfully deprive him of his hospital staff privileges. The court said in part:

> Everyone has the right to establish and conduct a lawful business or engage in a lawful profession, and is entitled to the protection of organized society, through its courts, whenever that right is unlawfully invaded. An actionable wrong is established against anyone who is shown to have intentionally interfered with that right, without justifiable cause or excuse. It is, therefore, an actionable wrong for two or more persons to conspire maliciously and without justification or excuse to injure or damage another in the conduct of a lawful business or profession.[22]

The theory of interference with plaintiff's practice of the profession, which may incorporate interference with contract, presents several interesting aspects. It would seem an appropriate claim where the physician has been subjected to privilege deprivation as well as defamatory statements made by peers, suspension by state licensing officials, damaged reputation, inability to attract patients, or general inability to continue with medical practice. A number of jurisdictions have recognized this cause of action in such cases.[23] In *Ascherman v. San Francisco Medical Society,*[24] a California appellate court reversed the trial court's dismissal of a physician's action against eighteen defendants seeking, in part, to enjoin them from conspiring to interfere with the practice of his profession. The complaint alleged that several defendants, had "arbitrarily, capriciously, and maliciously injured plaintiff in his profession by making false charges in securing the dismissal of the plaintiff from the hospital."[25]

Defenses to action for interference with practice of the profession include good faith. Therefore, malice must be pleaded and proved in other to prevail.

Another defense that will defeat an interference claim is proof that the physician-hospital contract was terminable at will.[26] Contracts terminable at will create no property interest in the physician, so that constitutional claims for their breach are likewise ill fated.[27]

It should also be noted that a cause of action for interference with contract or business relationship cannot be brought against any person or entity who is also a party to the contract, for example, the hospital. This raises the specter of the "corporate shield" defense, discussed below in connection with antitrust liability.

Such actions, if successful, open the door to compensation for injuries usually not compensable in contract actions, including emotional distress and pain and suffering.

Antitrust

Actions in the nature of antitrust may be brought under federal or state laws or may be brought as tort actions for civil conspiracy. Since civil conspiracy depends on the proof of some other tort, and since possible tort actions have already been discussed above, this section will focus on violations of federal and state antitrust statutes, specifically the Sherman Act, 15 U.S.C. § 1 (Suppl. IV 1980).

The Sherman Act provides in pertinent part:

> Every contract, combination in the form of trust or otherwise, or conspiracy in the form of trust or otherwise, or conspiracy in restraint of trade or commerce among the several states, or with foreign nations, is declared to be illegal. . . . Every person who shall monopolize, or combine or conspire . . . to monopolize any part of the trade or commerce among the several states . . . shall be deemed guilty of a felony.[28]

An action by a physician against a hospital under the antitrust laws is unavoidably fraught with problems. Proof of each element involved may be difficult, and various defenses have often proved successful. Initially, the elements of proof will be:

1. An action complained of that affects interstate commerce;
2. An agreement;
3. Two or more parties to that agreement;
4. An unreasonable restraint of trade;
5. A causal connection between plaintiff's injuries and the act.[29]

There must be a combination or conspiracy to unreasonably restrain interstate commerce, or to monopolize a part of interstate commerce, proven.[30] Furthermore, there must be proof of commercial motivation of the defendant individuals.[31]

An antitrust action may lie where a physician can produce evidence to the effect that review committee members have, as a group, "boycotted" that physician, either at the outset by denying the initial application for privileges or by later suspending those privileges for the purpose of reducing competition and protecting patient-physician ties.

However, a lawsuit against the boycotting physicians may be stymied by either of two defenses. First, many states protect the actions of peer review committee members by statute.[32] Second, peer review committee members have, on occasion, successfully hidden behind the shield of the hospital corporation. As agents of such a corporation, committee members may be viewed collectively from a legal standpoint and their actions viewed as acts of the corporation. Thus, in *Sokol v. University Hospital, Inc.*,[33] the court held that "where the act complained of is the act of a corporation, the fact that the concurrence of a number of the personnel of the corporation is required to generate the corporate act does not satisfy the Sherman Act requirement of an agreement, combination or conspiracy." Therefore, to be successful in an antitrust action in jurisdictions following the *Sokol* rule, a physician plaintiff must be prepared to show that peer-reviewing physicians acted beyond the scope of their corporate duties or authority or that the combination or conspiracy included persons not agents of the hospital corporation.

In the case of *Weiss v. York Hospital,*[34] the district court held that the hospital had violated Section 2 of the Sherman Act by engaging in willful behavior calculated to establish a monopoly. The court further found that the medical staff itself, as a separate entity, violated Section 1 of the act by engaging in a conspiracy to exclude osteopaths from its membership. On appeal, the Third Circuit reversed as to antitrust liability of the hospital but affirmed as to the medical staff, stating that the entity could be liable under the Sherman Act because it was comprised of a group of physicians, each of whom was "an independent economic entity" competing for medical business in the community.[35] Each physician on the staff, the court said, "has an economic interest separate from and in many cases in competition with the interests of other medical staff members. Under these circumstances, the medical staff cannot be considered a single economic entity for purposes of antitrust analysis."[36]

Two other defenses to antitrust actions should be noted. One such defense, that of "good faith," has already been discussed in connection with other causes of action and is equally effective in antitrust cases, as recognized by a federal district court in Florida in *Feminist Women's Health Center, Inc. v. Mohammed.*[37] This case held that an objective, good-faith standard would be applied to determine whether physicians acted in order to protect recognizable medical or ethical standards; if so, the antitrust action would be denied.

Another possible defense is based on the 1943 case of *Parker v. Braun*.[38] This defense necessitates showing that the defendants' actions were legally mandated by the state. If state law required peer review members to conduct an investigation upon the information they had available, and furthermore to take disciplinary action in light of the results of that investigation, the argument goes, their anticompetitive conduct is exempt under *Parker*. This argument has, to date, proved unsuccessful in the peer review context, most notably in the *Feminist Health Center* case,[39] *supra*, where the court refused to find a coercive effect in Florida's immunity statute. An interesting twist to the argument, and one that has perhaps prevented its vigorous use, is that it is inconsistent with the position defendants must take on the issue of state action for the purposes of the Fourteenth Amendment in a civil rights claim.

In order to invoke jurisdiction under the Sherman Act, proof of the hospital's involvement in interstate commerce is necessary. According to one commentator, "[P]rior to 1976, courts usually held that physician plaintiffs did not establish sufficient interstate commerce nexus *[sic]* for coverage under the Sherman Act."[40] In 1976, the United States Supreme Court decided *Hospital Building Co. v. Trustees of Rex Hospital*.[41] Since *Rex*, the commentator notes,

> [C]ourts have recognized a defendant hospital's activities as having a substantial effect on interstate commerce if virtually all of the supplies, drugs and equipment were purchased outside of the state; if a substantial portion of the hospital's revenue was generated from federal funds such as Medicare and Medicaid or third party payors located outside the state; if the hospital attracted a significant number of out-of-state patients; or if the construction of a major portion of the hospital's facilities had been financed by federal or out-of-state funds [citations omitted].[42]

Some courts still view hospitals as not engaged in interstate commerce, however.

Violation of Section 1 of the Sherman Act is analyzed by the courts under two standards. The first is the "per se" rule, the second the "rule of reason." Both apply to the charge of defendants' "concerted refusal to deal."

A "concerted refusal to deal" may involve parties conspiring to make it difficult or impossible for others to compete in the same market at the same level (the "horizontal boycott"); or it may refer to an attempt by conspirators to achieve some other goal than the exclusion of competitors.

Under "the rule of reason" analysis, courts examine the reasonableness of the restraint in terms of its nature and effect, its purpose, and the condition of the industry in its absence. Under the "per se" rule, the court invalidates a "price fixing" or "plainly anti-competitive" practice without examining any arguments of redeeming social or economic value of the scheme.[43]

These differing judicial approaches have received considerable recent attention in the staff privileges area due to the recent case of *Jefferson Parish Hospital District No. 2 v. Hyde*,[44] decided in 1984. In *Hyde*, the U.S. Supreme Court considered an anesthesiologist's antitrust challenge to an exclusive contract between a hospital and an anesthesiology firm, Roux and Associates. The contract effectively prevented the plaintiff physician from admission to the medical staff of the hospital. After years of litigation, the physician had obtained a judgment in the Fifth Circuit Court of Appeals to the effect that the contract was illegal "per se" as an unlawful "tying arrangement" between the hospital's surgical patients (the "consumer") and the anesthesiology services of the particular firm (the "product").

The Supreme Court unanimously reversed, holding that the contract did not violate Section 1 of the Sherman Act under a "rule of reason" analysis, which standard was properly applicable to such contracts rather than the "per se" standard. The "per se" standard, the Supreme Court said, is to be applied only where a "tying arrangement" is shown to "restrain competition on the merits by forcing purchases that would not otherwise be made."[45] "A lack of price or quality competition," the Court stated, "does not create this type of forcing."[46]

What does the *Hyde* decision mean, in practical terms, for the physician who finds that an exclusive contract between one medical firm and a hospital effectively prevents his admission to the medical staff ? At the very least, it means that the physician *must* prove anticompetitive effects so severe that all or nearly all of the patient population in the hospital's geographic market area will be forced to purchase necessary medical services from the contracting firm in order to receive the desired treatment. When will a physician be able to prove this? In a large metropolitan area, probably never. In a smaller, perhaps rural area, where patients have little choice of medical care facilities, the challenge may stand a fair chance.[47]

Due Process and Civil Rights Claims

Due process and civil rights claims rest on the fundamental principle, derived from the Fifth and Fourteenth amendments to the United States Constitution, that no person shall be "deprived of life, liberty, or property without due process of law." Because these provisions apply only to governments and not to private persons, there is a requirement that some "state action" be shown to have caused a deprivation of a protected "property" or "liberty" interest. The prohibition is extended to private persons by legislative enactment, 42 U.S.C. § 1983, in cases where the nongovernmental defendant acts "under color of" state law; thus the state-action requirement is preserved. Because medical staff privileges can often be shown to constitute a protected property interest, these federal protections are the source of numerous actions against hospitals, doctors, and other defendants for deprivation of those privileges. Most commonly, these "due process" claims arise where the ousted physician claims that the hospital governing board has not afforded him what amounts to "a fair trial" before taking disciplinary action against him.

Judicial Review

The courts, in considering the right of a physician to due process before a hospital tribunal, were at one time overwhelmingly in agreement. The basic premise was that the threshold question in any action by a physician against a hospital for a civil rights violation was the "public" or "private" status of the institution. Where the hospital was owned by a state or municipality, erected and operated with public funds, and run by persons publicly elected to their positions (or appointed by governmental bodies), it was a "public" hospital such that its acts were acts of the state subject to judicial review and subject to attack under the Fifth and Fourteenth amendments to the Constitution and under 42 U.S.C. § 1983.

If, on the other hand, the hospital was a "private" institution, constitutional guarantees of due process were not applicable and its acts were not subject to judicial review. A private hospital was defined as one "that is owned, maintained and operated by a corporation or an individual without any participation of any governmental agency in its control."[48] In addition, the use of government funds in construction or the fact that a hospital was operated for the benefit of the public did not make it a "public" institution.[49]

The movement toward liberalization of the application of due process standards began in California and New Jersey courts and can now be seen in the decisions of the courts of a large minority of the states. There is, however, no one formula or principle that may be said to be the "minority rule." In nearly all states, the threshold question remains the public or private character of the hospital. In addition, many courts recognize a third class, the "quasi-public" institution, whose activities are often said to be subject to judicial review, albeit with varying degrees of limitation.

The initial inroads on the "private hospital" defense were made by plaintiffs relying upon the doctrine of the "quasi-public" entity. The private hospital had to be shown to be on the receiving end of a substantial amount of government money, such as Hill-Burton funds. In time, some courts came to require no specific showing of a governmental financial link where other factors clothed the hospital with a "public" character. Where a private hospital is the only facility of its kind available to a significant local population, it may be held to perform "quasi-public" functions making it amenable to suit and to judicial review of its procedures. For example, the Hawaii Supreme Court accepted the "quasi-public" argument in *Silver v. Castle Memorial Hospital,*[50] saying: "The 'quasi-public' status is achieved if what would otherwise be a truly private hospital was constructed with public funds, is presently receiving public benefits, or has been sufficiently incorporated into a governmental plan for providing hospital facilities to the public."[51] The court stopped short of holding that in the absence of funding, the "governmental plan" would be enough, saying that it need not reach that question. The clear hint was that if faced with the question, it would so hold. The court stated that hospital officials "must never lose sight of the fact that the hospitals are operated not for private ends, but for the benefit of the public.''[52]

In California, several landmark cases have paved the way for due process actions against ''private'' institutions. The most important of these is the 1974 case of *Ascherman v. San Francisco Medical Society.*[53] In *Ascherman,* the court of appeals built upon the theory previously developed in the California courts that a ''private entity does not have absolute discretion to deprive a person of a substantial right.''[54] The court concluded that an existing staff member of a hospital is entitled to due process by a hospital board including a hearing, even if hospital bylaws do not so provide. The court said in pertinent part:

> The unmistakeable trend of the judicial decisions and legislative enactments in this state supports the principle that a private hospital may not deprive a physician of staff privileges without granting him minimal due process of law protection.[55]

The court also examined a large array of cases from other jurisdictions, a few of which will be discussed below. The California approach can also be seen in *Ezekial v. Winkley,*[56] decided in 1977. In *Ezekial,* a surgical resident in a private hospital sought damages and injunctive relief, alleging he was not accorded ''fair procedure'' in his dismissal from the hospital's residency program. The California Supreme Court held, on the basis of the plaintiff's valuable property interest in his membership in the program and his ''common law right'' of fair procedure, that the hospital was obliged ''to afford him rudimentary procedural and substantive fairness.''[57]

Another 1977 case, *Anton v. San Antonio Community Hospital,*[58] reaffirmed California's stance on the public-private dichotomy. A commentator has summarized:

> In *Anton,* a physician was not reappointed to the staff of the hospital. He alleged a denial of fair procedure in his hearing by the hospital's judicial review committee, whose decision was sustained by the hospital board of directors. One issue before the California Supreme Court was whether the trial court could employ the broader review under the administrative mandate, § 1094.5 of the California Code of Civil Procedure, rather than under the traditional mandate. In holding that California Code of Civil Procedure § 1094.5 was applicable, the Court noted that minimal common law procedures are required for physician staff privileges determinations. The *Anton* decision reaffirms the requirement that fair procedure must accompany a hospital staff privileges determination for both public and private hospitals, and it greatly expands the judicial review of such determinations.[59]

A brief look at several other jurisdictions is in order. In New Jersey, the landmark case of *Greisman v. Newcomb Hospital*[60] early on paved the way for the state courts' scrutiny of private hospitals' admissions decisions and procedures by proving that a ''private'' hospital that had a virtual monopoly on hospital services in its area was ''in no position to claim immunity from public supervision and control.''[61]

Alaska courts have also given the "quasi-public" classification a broad application. In the case of *Storrs v. Lutheran Hospitals and Homes Society of America*,[62] a physician's hospital staff privileges were suspended after one of his patients died of postoperative complications. Upon the plaintiff's request for a restraining order against the hospital, the court ordered that the hospital judicial review committee conduct a hearing, which followed. The Plaintiff had counsel, cross-examined witnesses, and presented his own testimony. The final decision by the review committee approved the summary suspension of privileges and restored the plaintiff's privileges in part (restricted privileges). The plaintiff's appeal to the appellate review committee ended in total suspension of privileges. The plaintiff then sought injunctive relief and compensatory and punitive damages in the trial court, which granted the hospital summary judgment. On appeal, the Supreme Court of Alaska held:

> [A]lthough Fairbanks Memorial Hospital is not a public hospital . . . it is a quasi-public hospital because it is the only hospital serving the community, the construction of the hospital was funded in significant part by state and federal grants, and over 25% of the funds received for hospital services come from governmental sources. Consequently, we hold that the hospital cannot violate due process standards in denying staff privileges for the reasons explicated in the following cases: *Peterson v. Tucson General Hospital, Inc.* 114 Ariz. 66, 559 P.2d 186 (Ariz.App. 1976); *Anton v. San Antonio Community Hospital,* 19 Cal.3d 802, 140 Cal.Rptr. 442, 567 P.2d 1162 (1977); *[Silver],* 497 P.2d 564, and *[Greisman],* 192 A.2d 817.[63]

Peterson, cited by the Alaska court, is an Arizona case that arose out of the denial of staff membership to an osteopathic physician. Although affirming the court of appeals' ruling that the hospital's refusal to grant plaintiff's reapplication was proper, the Arizona Supreme Court held that:

> (1) Judicial review depends on public/private/quasi-public classification; (2) "Quasi-public" status is achieved if what otherwise would be a truly private hospital was constructed with public funds, is presently receiving public benefits or has been sufficiently incorporated into a governmental plan for providing hospital facilities to the public.[64]

The court went on to examine the implications of the fact that Tucson General was the only osteopathic hospital in Tucson: "[it] thus constitutes a virtual monopoly since it is the only hospital in which [an osteopath] may have staff privileges. We conclude that judicial review is proper." The court then cited a line of cases following the *Greisman* rationale, for the proposition that monopolistic character is a factor in determining whether a hospital is "quasi-public," and went on to find no deficiency in the process used by Tucson General in its denial. The court emphasized that these concepts were part of its holding and necessary to its decision.[65]

Other states have refused to move away from the "private hospital—no review" position. An Illinois court,[66] insisting that it adhered to the view of "the vast majority of the federal circuits'' and ''state courts which have decided the issue,'' rejected ''another possible basis for review . . . in the power of the courts to regulate private businesses or industries impressed with a public interest and to see that their discretionary powers are exercised reasonably and for the public good, and in accord with minimal common law requisites of fair procedure.'' The court cited *Greisman,* among other cases, and concluded that Illinois law had not yet accepted judicial review, stating:

> While we agree that it is no longer true to state . . . that the doctrine of non-review is ''supported by 'the overwhelming weight of authority, almost approaching unanimity' '' [citation omitted], . . . we do not feel justified in departing from the rule laid down in [an earlier Illinois case rejecting judicial review].[67]

Some courts continue to justify the judicial review of hospital board actions by finding ''state action'' whether the claim is one of lack of due process or of racial or other discrimination. In each of the following federal court cases, ''state action'' was found to exist for purposes of 42 U.S.C. § 1983:

1. *Eaton v. Grubbs,* 329 F.2d 710 (4th Cir. 1964): In absence of Hill-Burton funds, regulations prescribed under Hill-Burton Act applied to hospital by state were enough to establish ''state action.''
2. *Holmes v. Silver Cross Hospital,* 340 F.Supp. 125 (D.Ill. 1972): License by state, plus pervasive state regulation of hospital business, sufficient to establish ''state action.''
3. *Doe v. Charleston Area Medical Center, Inc.*, 529 F.2d 638 (4th Cir. 1975): Hospital policy of refusing nontherapeutic abortions based on state prohibitory statute; therefore, ''state action.''
4. *Sokol v. University Hospital, Inc., supra,* n.33 (D.Mass. 1975): Accreditation licensing, Medicare and Medicaid programs enough.
5. *Meredith v. Allen County War Memorial Hospital,* 397 F.2d 33 (6th Cir. 1968): Only hospital in area financed in part by public funds, commission members appointed by county government; therefore, tied to state.
6. *Ruffler v. Phelps Memorial Hospital,* 453 F.Supp. 1062 (S.D.N.Y. 1978): Civil commitment of plaintiff to mental home; private hospital's action of confinement was state action where state expressly depended on use of private facilities to effectuate public policy of providing psychiatric treatment to those who needed it.[68]

Requirements of Due Process

Once a court has determined that it will intervene in a private or public hospital's disciplinary proceeding, it faces the question of the level or scope of its inquiry and the nature of the ''fairness'' it will impose. Formulations vary from the specific mandates of procedure (notice, time to prepare defense, written statement of charges, right to counsel, right to call witnesses) to a general requirement of fundamental fairness.[69] The quasi-judicial body must ''act fairly and its decision must be based on sufficient evidence."[70] Some courts would also impose the requirement that the tribunal be impartial.[71]

Generally, there is no requirement that hearings be formal or follow courtroom procedure. Participants need not follow formal rules of evidence.[72] Some courts have upheld the practice of allowing the physician to be represented by counsel only when the hospital's counsel is to be present.[73] In other states, including New Jersey, the physician has a right to counsel at all hospital hearings.[74]

Courts agree that the physician is entitled to notice of the charges. Notice must be written[75] and reasonably specific[76] and must be presented such that the physician has adequate time to prepare a defense.[77]

Finally, there is some question as to the precision that is required in the articulation of standards which are to be applied. In a Fifth Circuit case, *Sosa v. Board of Managers of Val Verde Hospital,*[78] the court said:

> Admittedly, standards such as "character, qualifications, and standing [in the community]" are very general, but the court recognizes that in the area of personal fitness for medical staff privileges precise standards are difficult if not impossible to articulate. The subjectives of selection simply cannot be minutely codified. . . . On the other hand, it is clear that in exercising its broad discretion the board must refuse staff applicants only for those matters which are reasonably related to the operation of the hospital. Arbitrariness and false standards are to be eschewed.[79]

According to a commentator, "*Sosa* has been cited with approval not only in the federal courts under a constitutional due process analysis, but also in state courts where its reasoning has been applicable to the determination of common-law fair procedure."[80]

REMEDIES TO REINSTATE PRIVILEGES

In addition to damages based on contract and tort theories, mandamus may lie to compel a public hospital to admit a physician to its staff or to grant him a hearing. In cases against private hospitals, the equivalent remedy of injunction may be had.

In *State ex. rel. Bronaugh v. City of Parkersburg,*[81] the West Virginia Supreme Court found that mandamus was the proper remedy in an action by a licensed physician against the governing board of a public hospital that had refused him reinstatement as a medical staff member following a three-month suspension. The hospital had based its refusal upon the fact that another private hospital had revoked the plaintiff's privileges "for good and sufficient cause."[82] The court, finding that Bronaugh had a right to practice in the public hospital, rejected the defendant's argument that mandamus was improper where another remedy was available and held that mandamus was the only proper remedy for restoring the status quo.[83]

In a California case, *Volpicelli v. Jared Sydney Torrance Memorial Hospital,*[84] a physician had brought a due process denial claim based on the revocation of staff privileges for refusal to pay a fifteen-dollar increase in annual membership dues. The court there issued an injunction against the hospital, preventing the physician's discharge until proper proceedings for disciplinary action could be had.[85]

SUMMARY

The growing problem of discrimination against physicians seeking hospital staff privileges may be met by various tort and contract actions against hospitals and medical staff members. In many jurisdictions, the obstacles presented by common-law and statutory immunities and the unavailability of judicial review for actions involving private hospitals pose formidable obstacles. However, the current trend in the courts would seem to be toward actionability.

NOTES

1. A private hospital usually may deny privileges based on another hospital's denial. *See State v. City of Parkersburg,* 148 W.Va. 568, 136 S.E.2d 783 (1964).

2. 273 U.S. 414, 71 L.Ed. 714, 47 S.Ct. 363 (1927).

3. 86 Colo. 446, 282 P. 1068 (1929).

4. 282 P. at 1071.

5. 329 F.2d 710 (4th Cir. 1964).

6. *Id.* at 715.

7. *Id.* For more on the public/private distinction, *see Annot.,* Action of Private Hospital as State Action under 42 U.S.C. § 1983 or Fourteenth Amendment, 42 A.L.R.3d 463; *Annot.,* Exclusion of or Discrimination against Physician or Surgeon by Hospital, 37 A.L.R.3d 645.

8. 234 Cal.App.2d 377, 44 Cal.Rptr. 572 (1965).

9. 44 Cal.Rptr. at 583.

10. *See* Annotations cited *supra* n. 7; Drexel, *The Antitrust Implications of the Denial of Hospital Staff Privileges,* 36 U. Miami L.Rev. 207 (1982); Note, *Denial of Open Staff Hospital Privileges: An Antitrust Scrutiny,* 26 St. Louis U.L.J. 751 (1982).

11. 484 S.W.2d 619 (Tex. Ct. Civ. App. 1972).

12. *Id.* at 627.

13. 534 S.W.2d 318 (Tenn. 1976).

14. *Id.* at 321–322.

15. *Id.* at 322.

16. 395 Pa. 257, 149 A.2d 456 (1959).

17. 149 A.2d at 459. *See also,* e.g., *St. John's Hosp. Medical Staff v. St. John Regional Medical Center, Inc.,* 245 N.W.2d 472 (S.D. 1976).

18. *See* Groseclose, *Hospital Staff Privilege Cases: Braving the Dismal Swamp,* 26 S.D.L. Rev. 1 (1981).

19. *See* Note, *The Legal Liability of Medical Staff Peer Review Participants for Revocation of Hospital Staff Privileges,* 28 Drake L. Rev. 692 (1979).

20. Restatement (Second) of Torts §§ 766, 766A, 766B.

21. *Supra* n.13.
22. 534 S.W.2d 318 at 321. *See also Willis v. Santa Ana Community Hospital Ass'n.*, 26 Cal.Rptr. 640, 376 P.2d 568 (1962); *Feminist Women's Health Center, Inc. v. Mohammed*, 586 F.2d 530 (5th Cir. 1978); *cert. denied* 444 U.S. 924 (1979).
23. *See*, e.g., *Cowan v. Gibson*, 392 S.W.2d 307 (Mo. 1965); *Nashville Memorial Hospital, Inc. v. Binkley, supra* n.13; *Raymond v. Cregar*, 38 N.J. 472, 185 A.2d 856 (1962).
24. 39 Cal.App.3d 655, 114 Cal.Rptr. 681 (1974).
25. 114 Cal.Rptr. at 686.
26. *See*, e.g., *Claus v. Gyorkey*, 674 F.2d 427, 33 Fed.R.Serv.2d 1542 (5th Cir. 1982)
27. *See Board of Regents of State Colleges v. Roth*, 408 U.S. 564, 92 S.Ct. 2701, 33 L.Ed.2d 548 (1972).
28. 15 U.S.C. § 1–2.
29. *See Unibrand Tire and Product Co. v. Armstrong Rubber Co.*, 429 F.Supp. 470 (W.D.N.Y. 1977), and Note, *supra* n.19, 28 Drake L.Rev. at 703.
30. 15 U.S.C. § 2 (1976) and Note, *supra* n.19, 28 Drake L.Rev. at 703.
31. *Id.*
32. *See*, e.g., Colo. Rev. Stat. § 12–43.5–103 (1975), immunizing committee members and witnesses before review committees from "any civil action brought by a physician who is the subject of review by such committee if such member or witness acts in good faith within the scope of the function of such committee."
33. 402 F.Supp. 1029 (D. Mass. 1975).
34. 745 F.2d 790 (1984).
35. *Id.* at 815.
36. *Id. See also Arizona v. Maricopa County Medical Society*, 457 U.S. 332 (1982).
37. 415 F.Supp. 1258 (N.D. Fla. 1970).
38. 317 U.S. 341.
39. *Supra*, n.22. *See also Goldfarb v. Virginia State Bar*, 421 U.S. 773, 790–91 (1975).
40. Note, *Denial of Open Staff Privileges: An Antitrust Scrutiny*, 26 St. Louis U.L.J. 751, 755 n.25 (1982).
41. 425 U.S. 738, 96 S.Ct. 1848, 48 L.Ed.2d 338 (1976).
42. 26 St. Louis L.J. at 760.
43. *See* Drexel, *The Antitrust Implications of the Denial of Hospital Staff Privileges*, 36 U. Miami L.Rev. 207, 214–215 (1982).
44. 466 U.S. 2,104 S.Ct. 1551, 80 L.Ed.2d 2 (1984).
45. 104 S.Ct. at 1566.
46. *Id.*
47. For further discussion of "tying arrangements" and the *Hyde* decision, *see* Wilson, *Exclusive Arrangements between Hospitals and Physicians: Making the Successful Challenge after Jefferson Parish*, 6 J. Legal Medicine 373 (1985).
48. *Shulman v. Washington Hospital Center*, 222 F.Supp. 59 (D.D.C. 1963).
49. *See Shulman*, 222 F.Supp. at 61.
50. 53 Hawaii 475, 497 P.2d 564 (1972), U.S. *cert. denied*, 409 U.S. 1048 (1972), U.S. *reh. denied*, 409 U.S. 1131 (1973).
51. 497 P.2d at 569.
52. *Id. See also Peterson v. Tucson General Hospital, Inc.*, 114 Ariz. 66, 559 P.2d

186 (Ariz. Ct. App. 1976); *Shulman, supra,* n.48; *Greisman v. Newcomb Hospital,* 40 N.J. 389, 192 A.2d 817 (1963).

53. 39 Cal.App.3d 623, 114 Cal.Rptr. 681 (1974).

54. *See* 114 Cal.Rptr. at 696 and authorities cited therein.

55. 114 Cal.Rptr. at 696.

56. 20 Cal.3d 267, 142 Cal.Rptr. 418, 572 P.2d 32.

57. 572 P.2d at 39.

58. 19 Cal.3d 802, 140 Cal.Rptr. 442 (1977), 567 P.2d 1162.

59. Cray, *Due Process Determinations in Hospital Staff Privilege Cases,* 7 Hastings Const. L.Q. 217, 243 (1979).

60. 40 N.J. 389, 192 A.2d 817 (1963).

61. *Id.* at 821.

62. 609 P.2d 24 (Alaska 1980).

63. *Id.* at 28.

64. 559 P.2d 186, 189.

65. *See id.* at 191.

66. *Jain v. Northwest Community Hospital,* 67 Ill.App.3d 420, 385 N.E.2d 108 (1978).

67. 385 N.E.2d at 113.

68. For the above-cited and other cases, *see* Annot., 42 A.L.R. Fed. 463 (1979) and 42 A.L.R. Fed. S. 17 (1983).

69. *See, e.g., Park Hospital District v. District Court,* 192 Colo. 69, 555 P.2d 984.

70. *Wyatt v. Tahoe Forest Hospital District,* 174 Cal.App.2d 709, 345 P.2d 93 (1959).

71. *See, e.g., Storrs, supra,* n.62, 609 P.2d at 28 n.12.

72. *See Gilbert v. Johnson,* 419 F.Supp. 859 (N.D.Ga. 1976), *aff'd in part, rev'd in part,* 601 P.2d 761 (5th Cir. 1979).

73. *Silver, supra* n.50.

74. *Garrow v. Elizabeth General Hospital,* 79 N.J. 549, 401 A.2d 533 (1979).

75. *Silver, supra* n.50.

76. *Moore v. Board of Trustees of Carson-Tahoe Hospital,* 88 Nev. 207, 495 P.2d 605, U.S. *cert. denied,* 409 U.S. 879 (1972).

77. *Klinge v. Lutheran Charities Association,* 523 F.2d 56 (8th Cir. 1975).

78. 437 F.2d 173 (5th Cir. 1971).

79. *Id.* at 176–177.

80. Hein, *Hospital Staff Privileges and the Courts: Practice and Prognosis,* 34 Fed'n Ins. Counsel Q. 157, 171 (1984) (citations omitted).

81. 148 W.Va. 568, 136 S.E.2d 783 (1964).

82. 136 S.E.2d at 785.

83. *Id.* at 787.

84. 109 Cal.App.3d 242, 167 Cal.Rptr. 610 (1980).

85. *See also Gotsis v. Lorain Community Hospital,* 46 Ohio App.2d 8, 345 N.E.2d 641 (1974).

Sustaining Quality of Life for Patients with Terminal Illnesses

John T. Rago and Stephen Poljak

INTRODUCTION

Developments in medical science have made us incredibly adept at saving and prolonging life. But like most forms of progress, our ability to artificially sustain life has given rise to a series of perplexing questions. Specifically, we are called upon to decide when it becomes morally and legally defensible to discontinue or not to initiate treatment for the incompetent, terminally ill patient.

The scenario is no longer novel. While the lives of thousands are artificially sustained in intensive care units and hospices across the country, families, doctors, lawyers, and the courts find themselves faced with conflicting imperatives. It is the business of saving lives that often causes us to subject our loved ones to often futile and dehumanizing treatment.

A clear understanding of the legal aspects of dying will be essential if we are to deal humanely with this crisis in the lives of the patient and the patient's family and friends. But first we must consider some of the questions that necessarily accompany this area of medical progress. At what point is a life no longer worth living? When is a person to be allowed to die with dignity? Who may speak for the incompetent patient? Whose wishes and desires control this situation: those of the patient, the medical community, or the public at large? What if there is a disagreement among the three? Is our judiciary capable of deciding such personal and far-reaching issues? Is its involvement appropriate?

Clearly, such questions on whether to sustain quality of life embrace a variety of issues beyond the scope of this paper. It will focus on the case law regarding the rights of those involved in the decision-making process and the contributions and dimunitions resulting from judicial intervention.

CHANGING ATTITUTES TOWARD SUSTAINING QUALITY OF LIFE

As medical science develops measures by which we can postpone or prolong the process of dying, certain fundamental values of human life are thrust into the tenuous realm of choice. Most people continue to regard life as something sacred, something that no one may dispose of at will. But medical science enables us to take an alternative view of suffering and death. It forces us to decide whether we have a right to choose to die, and the choice appears no longer to be in conflict with our sense of human dignity. Today it seems apparent that a competent patient has the right to decide about his or her medical care—even if it means ending treatment and accepting a death that could be postponed. But how does modern society exercise its influence on behalf of the patient unable to choose for himself ? Does the family of the patient whose death is inevitable have similar certainty of their right to choice? While this question has been with us for decades, there is surprisingly little uniformity on the issue of whether to sustain quality of life.[1]

This chapter will first consider how our attitudes have been shaped on this matter of vast social challenge and will then undertake a review and criticism of judicial authority.

In June 1984, a *New York Times*/CBS News poll asked 1,593 Americans the following question: "Medical technology now enables doctors to prolong the lives of many people who are terminally ill. Do you believe doctors should stop using these techniques if the patient asks, even if that means the patient will die?"[2] Seventy-seven percent answered yes, only 15 percent said no, and 8 percent had no opinion. We might, therefore, ask what has occurred to alter our moral and ethical insistence upon the sanctity and preservation of human life.

During the first three decades of this century, there was relatively little activity in what we would today refer to as a right-to-die movement.[3] While isolated incidents of human suffering generated some notice of the impending dilemma, the physicians and others who affirmed the right to die were said to be suffering from curious delusions and ignorant follies. In many minds, such advocacy was thought to warrant criminal sanctions. However, despite this hostile climate, many physicians and scholars at the turn of the century persisted in their support of the fundamental right of self-determination for the terminally ill. Among them was Dr. Charles Eliot Norton, a distinguished Harvard scholar and humanitarian, who openly endorsed the concept of euthanasia.[4] His position, not surprisingly, brought condemnation and ridicule from *The New York Times:*

> Now it is Dr. Charles Eliot Norton whom an unfortunate impulse has moved to express belief in the "right" of one person to decide that these, those, or the other circumstances not only justify, but in reason oblige him to confer the boon of death upon a suffering fellow mortal. This curious delusion has fastened on many people before, but few of them indeed have been euthanasiasts as bold as Dr. Norton.[5]

In that same year, the Ohio state legislature unsuccessfully introduced what many believe to be the first bill *Introduced in an English-Speaking* Country in support of euthanasia. In an editorial titled ''Euthanasia Bobs Up Again,'' *The New York Times* said:

> Something considerably worse than ignorant folly—something that verges upon the immoral if not into the criminal must have possessed the Ohio legislature when it consented, as it did this week, to receive, consider and order a second reading of a euthanasia bill. . . . The mitigating feature of this bill is its utter impracticability, for of course no doctors above the grade of common hangmen would undertake such an atrocious and always completely unjustifiable task.[6]

Understandably, these and other equally vehement attacks did much to discourage those who philosophically advocated death as a public good. Their impact was felt for nearly four decades as a shroud of relative silence overcame *the movernent* to consider the personal rights and values of those affected by the dying process.

After only minimal success on behalf of the rights of the terminally ill, Dr. Charles Francis Potter founded the Euthanasia Society of America (ESA) in 1938. Its purpose was to educate the public on sensitive matters affecting the terminally ill. This international coalition of medical doctors, theologians, and others advanced the belief that, with adequate safeguards, the choice of immediate death rather than prolonged agony should be available to the dying. It was this society which forced into the open a series of moral, ethical, and legal considerations surrounding the human initiative in death and dying. But their efforts had only a limited impact on the growing debate.

Evidence of their inability to alter public opinion is found in the failed attempts to establish right-to-die legislation in Nebraska, New Jersey, Connecticut, Ohio, and New York. It was apparent that in this period prior to 1960, there could be no movement on the right-to-die issue until support for it came from beyond those traditionally concerned.

At this point it is fitting to recall the position of the Catholic church, specifically a declaration by Pope Pius XII that retains its full force according to Christian teaching. In an address to a group of anesthesiologists, the pope was asked to consider the following question: ''Is the suppression of pain and consciousness by the use of narcotics permitted by religion and morality to the doctor and the patient (even at the approach of death and if one foresees that the use of narcotics will shorten life)?''

The pope said: ''If no other means exist, and if, in the given circumstances, this does not prevent the carrying out of other religious and moral duties: Yes.'' In this case, of course, death is in no way intended or sought, even if the risk of it is reasonably taken; the intention is simply to relieve pain effectively, using for this purpose painkillers available to medicine.

However, painkillers that cause unconsciousness need special consideration.

For a person not only has to be able to satisfy his or her moral duties and family obligations; he or she also has to prepare himself or herself with full consciousness for meeting Christ. Thus Pius XII warns: "It is not right to deprive the dying person of consciousness without a serious reason."[7]

Implicit in his remarks and entirely consistent with the church's present position is the belief that when life is irrevocably on the decline, physicians may abandon extraordinary or heroic efforts to postpone death when recovery is no longer possible.[8] A further expression of this principle was offered by the Catholic church through the United States Catholic Conference in 1974. Here the church defined *extraordinary* as "all medicines, treatments and operations which if used, would not offer reasonable hope of benefit."[9] It was yet another demonstration of the Catholic church's desire to contribute to the cause of self-determination in the dying process.

Theologians have since recognized the distinction between ordinary and extraordinary care. They have maintained that humans have a moral and ethical responsibility to seek and accept ordinary care to save their lives. A precise definition of these varying levels of care is difficult to articulate. But one of the most often quoted definitions is proffered by a Roman Catholic ethicist, Gerald Kelly:

> Ordinary means are all medicine, treatments and operations which offer reasonable hope of benefit and which can be obtained and used without excessive pain, or other inconvenience. Extraordinary means are all medicines, treatments and operations which cannot be attained or used without excessive expense, pain or other inconvenience, or if used would not offer a reasonable hope or benefit.[10]

The authors do not suggest that the attitudes of modern society toward this sensitive health care issue have been shaped solely through the efforts of the Catholic church. But it can be said with some certainty that ecumenical religious support, more than any other single factor, has helped remove many of the moral obstacles that have precluded any progress in this area. It is to the credit of our religious leaders that the dying and those concerned with the question whether to sustain quality of life can find peace and comfort in the teachings of their faith. The next section will consider whether our courts have produced a similar harmony.

ROLE OF THE COURTS

It has been suggested by some that the courts should exercise their discretion when dealing with issues of withholding or withdrawing treatment from terminally ill patients. Others strongly argue that our courts are not the forum for such highly personal matters, citing many serious personal and religious reasons that often render it advisable for the courts to respect the autonomy of all parties involved. Some of the cases we will consider demonstrate this awareness by the courts, but too often, as we shall see, the courts go beyond their appropriate scope, thus invading the traditional physician-patient-family decision-making process. The authors will discuss the problems resulting from judicial intervention but will first undertake an analysis of specific precedents in a number of jurisdictions in order to understand the variety of legal rights affecting the concerned parties.

Beginning in 1975, the courts considered a number of right-to-die cases: the *Quinlan* case in New Jersey, the *Saikewicz* and *Spring* cases in Massachusetts, the Brother Fox (*Eichner*) case in New York, and the *Severns* case in Delaware, to mention only a few. In these and other decisions, which will be discussed, the courts have been far from unanimous in their suggestions of possible candidates to make health care decisions on behalf of the incompetent, terminal patient.

In 1975, the Karen Ann Quinlan case was the first judicial decision to interpret the constitutional right of privacy as a basis for withholding or withdrawing life support from a terminal patient. Karen Ann Quinlan, a New Jersey resident, was in a persistent vegetative state as a result of respiratory arrest in 1975. Her father sought court appointment as her guardian as well as the express power to authorize the discontinuance of all extraordinary procedures for sustaining his daughter's vital life processes. While the lower court refused the requested relief, the New Jersey Supreme Court reversed. In its widely acclaimed ruling, the court said:

> The termination of treatment pursuant to the right of privacy is within the limitation of this case, ipso facto lawful. . . . We think the state's interest contra weakens the individual's right to privacy as the degree of bodily invasion increases and the prognosis dims. Ultimately there comes a point at which the individual rights of the patient overcome the state's interest.[11]

The court added that decision making regarding health care is the responsibility of the guardian, family, and physician with review by a hospital ethics committee but *without the need for judicial review*. The court declared that "decision-making within health care . . . should be controlled primarily within the patient-doctor-family relationship."[12]

Proponents of the right-to-die movement endorsed the *Quinlan* decision while many others remained undetermined as to its impact. It is interesting to note that the New Jersey Catholic Conference applied the teachings of the Catholic church in an amicus curiae brief in the *Quinlan* case, requesting the discontinuance of the extraordinary means that were being used to sustain her.[13] (Despite the time lapse since the April 1976 decision to remove Quinlan from the respirator, interest in her case, has not faded. In 1985, Karen Ann Quinlan died at the age of 31, ten years after the respirator was disconnected.)

The constitutional right to privacy was affirmed as the basis for a dying patient's right to refuse treatment in *Superintendent of Belchertown State School v. Saikewicz,* 373 Mass. 728, 370 N.E.2d 417 (1977). However, this court detracted from the reasoning in *Quinlan* by calling on the courts to be *actively engaged* in resolving life-decision questions.

Joseph Saikewicz was a sixty-seven-year-old patient in a state mental facility. With an IO of 10, Saikewicz was diagnosed as suffering from an irreversible form of leukemia. An official from the state hospital asked the court to appoint a guardian to authorize the use of chemotherapy. However, the guardian, joined by two physicians, protested such treatment because of the inescapable fear and pain Saikewicz would endure compounded by his inability to understand the procedure. The lower court decided the patient's interests outweighed those advanced by the state, and on appeal the Supreme Court of Massachusetts affirmed, saying:

> [A] right to privacy against unwanted infringements of bodily integrity is an expression of the sanctity of individual free choice and self-determination as fundamental constituents of life. The value of life as so perceived is lessened not by a decision to refuse treatment, but by the failure to allow a competent human being the right of choice.[14]

The court further ruled that future cases involving an incompetent patient should be brought to probate because, the justices said:

> We take a dim view of any attempt to shift from the duly established Courts of proper jurisdiction. . . . There we *reject* the approach adopted by the New Jersey Supreme Court in the *Quinlan* case of entrusting decision of whether to continue artificial life support to the patient's guardian, family, attending doctors and hospital ethics committees.[15]

The *Saikewicz* decision was greeted with mixed emotions in medical circles. Physicians felt the requirement of applying to the courts to confirm such decisions was inappropriate. Subsequently, the Massachusetts case *In re Dinnerstein* offered some clarification to physicians who feared liability for withholding or withdrawing treatment from incompetent patients without judicial approval. In its opinion, the court narrowed the need for court intervention when it said:

> It presents a question peculiarly within the competence of the medical profession of what measures are appropriate to ease the imminent passing of an irreversibly terminally ill patient in light of the patient's history and conditions and wishes of the family. That question is not one for judicial decision.[16]

This language specifically removed the potential burden of liability for failing to give resuscitation orders even in the most irreversibly ill patients. (It is noteworthy that *Dinnerstein* was the first case to uphold the validity of Do Not Resuscitate [DNR] orders.)

Still unsatisfied (or unclear) by its first two right-to-die cases, the state of Massachusetts sought to expand upon its position taken in *Saikewicz* through *In re Spring*, 405 N.E.2d at 115 (1980). Earl Spring, 77, suffered from advanced senility and "end stage" kidney disease. He received five-hour dialysis treatments three times a week. Heavy sedation was often required to overcome his resistance to the treatment. Proceedings began in 1978 when Spring's family petitioned the probate court for an order to terminate the treatments. But the case lasted nearly fifteen months on hearings, appeals, reversals, and stays from January 1979 until the Massachusetts High Court issued its opinion in May 1980. The court made it clear that it did not hold that judicial approval is always a prerequisite to withholding or withdrawing treatment from an incompetent patient. But it did indicate a list of ten factors in deciding whether or not the court's presence *might* be needed. The court further said: "Whenever a physician in good faith decides that a particular treatment is not called for, there is a risk that in some subsequent litigation the omission will be found to have been negligent."[17] (It should be noted that this position created a great deal of concern throughout the medical profession. The authors will discuss the consequences of this judge-made liability later in this paper.) The court was aware of the strain on Mr. Spring's family imposed by the lengthy judicial process, and it stressed the need to expedite such cases. However, the justices reaffirmed *Saikewicz,* stating: "Again we disapprove shifting of the ultimate decision-making responsibility away from the duly established court of proper jurisdiction" (405 N.E.2d at 123).[18]

The state of New York was first faced with a right-to-die case in what has become popularly known as the Brother Fox case. Brother Fox was an 83–year-old member of the Catholic Order of Marionists. During an operation in 1979, some difficulties occurred, causing Brother Fox to lapse into a permanent vegetative state. The Reverend Phillip Eichner, his superior, requested that he be taken off the respirator, but hospital officials and physicians refused. Father Eichner petitioned the trial court for relief, which was granted upon evidence that Brother Fox was opposed to extraordinary measures to sustain life within the context of the case of Karen Ann Quinlan. Prior to his incapacitation Brother Fox had made his feelings known at a meeting of his religious community.

The district attorney appealed the trial court's decision, and Brother Fox's treatment was continued pending review. Brother Fox died before the final disposition of his case, but the appellate level was called upon to reach a resolution, owing to the substantial public-policy issues at stake. In 1980, the Appellate Division of New York ruled that Father Eichner was entitled to the relief sought, but, in so finding, the court established a complicated set of procedures to be followed before life-sustaining measures could be withdrawn. The opinion was widely criticized as too cumbersome and intrusive. In 1981, the court of appeals affirmed Father Eichner's relief but refused to promulgate elaborate procedures to be used for future cases. The opinion identified the courts' role as follows: "unlike the legislature, the Courts are neither equipped nor empowered to prescribe substantive or procedural rules. . . . Our role especially in matters as sensitive as these, is limited to resolving the issues raised by the facts presented in particular cases" (52 N.Y. 2d at 370, 438 N.Y.S.2d at 269).[19]

Perhaps the most notable departure from previous decisions on this issue was New York's refusal to affirm a withdrawal of treatment based on the "right to privacy" analysis. The court sidestepped the argument, saying it was a disputed constitutional question that the United States Supreme Court had repeatedly declined to consider.

The rationale chosen by New York for these cases is grounded, instead, in the common-law principle that a patient has the right to decline treatment. The court added to this principle the standard of "clear and convincing" evidence of a prior expression of intent on the part of the incompetent patient before an order to terminate treatment could issue.

The court applied the Eichner standard in the companion case of *In re Storar,* 52 N.Y.2d 363 (1981). However, *Storar* is distinguished from *Eichner* by the fact that the patient had never been competent and thus was incapable of expressing his views on life-sustaining measures for the terminally ill.

John Storar, 52, was profoundly retarded and suffered from an incurable cancer of the bladder. His mother, who was also his legally appointed guardian, refused to continue his frequently required blood transfusions, claiming they were causing her son pain. The hospital sought a court order to continue treatment, and the trial court ruled that Storar's mother was the appropriate person to make a "substitute judgment" on behalf of her son. However, on appeal, the Appellate Division rejected the trial court's approval of decision by proxy for the incompetent patient. Unlike *Quinlan* and *Saikewicz,* where a "substitute judgment" standard permitted a guardian to make judgments on behalf of incompetent patients afflicted by terminal illnesses, New York held firmly to the notion that in the absence of "clear and convincing evidence" of a prior expression of intent, no parent or guardian can act to terminate life-sustaining treatment. The state, said the court, as *parens patriae* may inject its concerns for keeping a patient alive if the wishes of the patient are unknown. As a result, *Storar* is the only decision of the highest state court to order continuance of a disputed treatment.

To this point, we have seen how five jurisdictions have considered the issue of whether and under what circumstances life-support systems may be withheld or withdrawn for patients. On this question the courts are in general agreement (although the foundations for their decisions rest on different grounds). They have differed, however, in one important regard, and that is on the question of who should make the determination to discontinue or not initiate treatment. The Massachusetts Supreme Judicial Court in *Saikewicz* concluded that only the court could make the judgment. The New Jersey Supreme Court, in the *Quinlan* case, concluded the physician and family could make the judgment in conjunction with the hospital ethics committee. New York, on the other hand, accepts only a prior statement. In the following case, we will see how the state of Washington creates a hybrid of these approaches.

The Washington Supreme Court decision in *Matter of Welfare of Colyer,* 660 P.2d 738 (Wash. 1983), adopted another approach by mandating the appointment of a guardian for the patient. Bertha Colyer, 69, suffered a cardiopulmonary arrest. She was resuscitated but sustained massive brain damage in the process owing to a lack of oxygen for ten minutes. She was kept alive by a respirator but remained comatose in a permanent vegetative state. Mrs. Colyer's husband was appointed guardian, and he petitioned the court to authorize removal of the life-support system. The court appointed a guardian *ad litem* and after a hearing concluded the life-support system should be withdrawn. The court noted that other states that recognized the patient's right to refuse life-sustaining treatment did so on one of two theories: (1) a constitutional right of privacy and (2) the common-law right to be free from an invasion of one's bodily integrity.

Perhaps the most novel aspect of the decision was that once a guardian is appointed, the court determined it did not need to be involved in the actual decision of whether or not to withhold life-sustaining treatment. The court said that termination of life-sustaining support, if made in good-faith compliance with the procedure set forth by the courts, would not be criminal.

The following guidelines were provided by the court for the right to refuse treatment by an incompetent person:

1. The unanimous concurrence of a prognosis board, consisting of two disinterested physicians qualified to make determination on the patient's particular condition plus the attending physician, that the patient's condition is incurable and there is no reasonable medical probability of returning to a cognitive, sapient state. If no agreement can be reached, a court may be petitioned to make such findings on a standard of "clear and convincing" evidence.
2. Court appointment of a guardian, including the appointment of a guardian *ad litem* for purposes of the guardianship proceeding, to report on the appropriateness of the proposed guardian.
3. Exercise of the patient's right to refuse treatment by the guardian if, in the guardian's best judgment, that is what the patient would have chosen had he or she been competent.
4. As an alternative, a court determination of the rights and wishes of the incompetent made by the guardian *ad litem* appointed to represent the incompetent patient.[20]

In short, while the court recognized the cumbersome nature of the legal process, it mandated these safeguards to ensure that the decision to end life-sustaining treatment is made by someone with the best interests of the patient solely in mind.

One of the most recent cases on the issue of sustaining quality of life involved an 83–year-old New Jersey woman being kept alive by a nasogastric feeding device. She was suffering from advanced organic brain syndrome and other serious ailments when her nephew and guardian sought to have the nasogastric tube removed. The court-appointed guardian *ad litem* disagreed, but the trial court held in favor of the nephew. The Superior Court of New Jersey reversed the trial court, stating that the decision to remove the patient's feeding tube was tantamount to active euthanasia. During the judicial process, Clair Conroy died, but the appellate and, ultimately, the New Jersey Supreme Court had decided to take up the issue despite Conroy's death since the matter was of substantial importance.

Ruling for the guardian *ad litem,* the Superior Court noted that none of the diseases that had put Conroy in her physical state were fatal—although she would never recover from them, it was not possible to determine when or from what cause she would die. The appellate court held:

> [T]he right to terminate life-sustaining treatment based on a guardian substitute judgment should be limited to incurable and terminally ill patients who are brain dead, irreversibly comatose, or vegetative, and who would gain no medical benefit from continued medical treatment. . . . Thus there can be no justification for withholding nourishment which is not really "treatment" at all, from a patient who does not meet these criteria.[21]

This set the stage for the New Jersey Supreme Court's most important decision in this area since *Quinlan.* Three justices voted to hear the case at the Supreme Court level (the minimum number that can cause a case to be heard in front of the seven-member panel). Federal interests crept into the case when members of the President's Commission for the Study of Ethical Problems in Medicine were granted a request to file an amicus curiae brief. In all, at least seven organizations joined in filing amicus briefs.[22]

In a well-considered opinion, the Superior Court's ruling was reversed, but not before the Supreme Court had exhorted the legislature to "frame a comprehensive plan for resolving these problems." In the interum, the court established limiting standards under which life-sustaining treatment might be withdrawn. (It should be noted that these standards apply to the court's narrow holding that treatment can be withheld from elderly nursing home residents suffering from serious and permanent mental and physical impairments who will *probably* die within a year even with the treatment, and who, though formerly competent, are now incompetent and incapable of making decisions on the question of treatment.)

The court articulated the following procedures for withdrawing or withholding treatment from patients like Conroy:

1. *Limited Objective Test:* This test requires an examination of medical evidence and trustworthy evidence of the patient's wishes. In the absence of trustworthy evidence the following test may be applied.
2. *Pure Objective Test:* This test requires a balancing of the net burdens of the patient's life with the treatment against the benefits the patient derives from life.
3. *Subjective Test:* This test, says the court, is consistent with the notion that the right a petitioner seeks to effectuate is a very personal right to control one's own life—so the question is not what a reasonable person would do under these circumstances but what the patient would do if she were able to choose for herself.[23]

Once these three tests are satisfied, the only role of the courts is the legal determination that the patient is incompetent and the designation of a guardian if the patient does not already have one. (The court concluded that in the case of Clair Conroy, the three tests had not been adequately addressed.)

Despite judicial attention, confusion remains over the rights and liabilities of those faced with the decision to end a life. For example, is it legally or morally wrong to withhold treatment from defective infants? And what, if any, liability, civil or criminal, should these individuals endure? The authors will briefly discuss these problems in the pages that follow.

CRIMINAL LIABILITY: A "JUDGE-MADE" PROBLEM

Some decisions involving the terminally ill have discussed the potential criminal liability of physicians for withholding or withdrawing life-sustaining medical treatment. As the court observed in *In re Spring:* "little need be said about criminal liability: there is precious little precedent, and what there is suggests that a doctor will be protected if he acts in good faith judgment that is not grievously unreasonable by medical standards."[24]

Apparently California did not heed the wisdom of this opinion when the state decided to bring criminal charges of murder and conspiracy to commit murder against two physicians in *Barber/Nejdl v. Superior Court and People of California,* 147 Cal.App.3d 1006, 195 Cal.Rptr. 484 (1983).

Clarence L. Herbert suffered severe brain damage following elective abdominal surgery. After Herbert lapsed into an irreversible coma, his family authorized the removal of his respirator. When the patient continued to breath, his doctor ordered the removal of the intravenous tube, depriving the patient of nourishment and hydration.

After Herbert's death the state brought charges against the two physicians under California Penal Code § 187 for the unlawful killing of a human being without malice.

The trial court dismissed the charges on the basis that there was no evidence of either unlawful conduct or malice aforethought. The charges were reinstated by the Superior Court only to be rejected once again by the California Court of Appeals. A final disposition of the case was made by the Court of Appeals, which found that the doctors' failure to continue treatment, although intentional and done with the knowledge that Herbert would die as a result, was not an unlawful failure to perform a legal duty since their actions were not a deviation from normal medical practice.

While many have praised the *Barber* decision as laying to rest the potential question of criminal liability, others have argued that it adds to the climate of apprehension and conservatism in the treatment of the dying.

ANALYSIS OF COURT INTERVENTION: DIMINISHING PATIENTS' RIGHTS

Until the *Quinlan* case in 1975, judicial review was not thought to be necessary except in cases of conflict among family members or between the family and physicians with regard to a choice of treatment. Numerous jurisdictions have since addressed the issue.

Prior to *Quinlan,* most hospitals, physicians, and families were reluctant to authorize the termination of life-sustaining treatment for fear of bringing about civil or criminal liability. As a result, physicians resuscitated nearly everyone, causing many families to suffer both emotional and financial ruin. To the courts' credit, *Quinlan* brought national attention to the right-to-die issue. It generated a decade of increasing openness of discussion on death and ushered in an era of judicial awareness. Various courts called upon the states to address this sensitive issue, and justices in three such cases stressed the need for clear legislative action to establish adequate legal guidelines:

The Florida Supreme Court
[T]he issue . . . is not one which is well suited for resolution in an adversary judicial proceeding. It is the type of issue which is more suitably addressed in the legislative forum.[25]

The New York Supreme Court, Appellate Division
[A]n act of the New York Legislature would . . . be most welcome and appropriate. No one seriously doubts the legislature has far greater capabilities to gather relevant data and to elicit expressions of pertinent opinion to the issues at hand.[26]

The Delaware Supreme Court
We earnestly invite prompt attention of the general assembly . . . governing these matters which are, in the words of *Quinlan,* of transcendent importance.[27]

Although our courts have recognized the need for the legislatures to speak on these issues, they continue to impose their own remedy for discontinuing or not initiating treatment of the incompetent patient. If left to the authors, the best form of review would be no review at all. But as students we realize the law often takes the more difficult path.

It was the *Quinlan* court that offered the best process of review when it concluded that decision making regarding the terminally ill should remain within the family-patient-physician relationship. Unfortunately, subsequent decisions have strayed from this rationale and either directly or through interpretation caused considerable erosion to the *Quinlan* concept of review. For example, in *Storar,* the New York court refused to permit a proxy decision, choosing instead to rely upon the common-law principle that a person can determine what will be done with his own body. Since John Storar had been profoundly retarded since birth and, consequently, unable to speak on the subject, the court refused to explore what he might have wished in such a situation. It ordered, instead, continued treatment, which did nothing but postpone dying and add to Storar's discomfort.

Perhaps the best examples of judicial meddling can be found in the case of *New Mexico ex rel. James Robert Smith v. The Honorable Harvey W. Foat*, No. 14768 (N.M. 1983). In the New Mexico case, a patient receiving hemodialysis for severe kidney-related ailments lapsed into an irreversible coma. The best medical advice offered no hope of recovery, adding that no treatment could save his life or benefit his health. The court appointed a religious visitor who together with the hospital, physician, family, and a legal guardian called upon the court to permit a cessation of life-sustaining treatment. In a one-page opinion the Supreme Court reversed the lower court, stating there was no statute in New Mexico that would grant the authority of a guardian to discontinue treatment. The immediate result of the ruling was that a patient unable to speak for himself may be subjected to a broad range of medical care that will only postpone death.

Several of the more intrusive court cases have come out of New York and Massachusetts, where it has been determined that decisions to terminate the life of an incompetent, terminally ill patient must reside within the judicial process. Without too much imagination, one can easily appreciate the amount of time court procedures consume and the unnecessary hardship that necessarily follows.

These decisions exemplify what the authors consider unnecessary and bothersome interventions by our courts. They highlight the unpredictability of court intervention on this issue, which serves to undermine the judicial principles of consensus and reliability. They create an image of the judiciary as intrusive and overbearing, and most importantly, the cases demonstrate the courts' tendency to bureaucratize the issue. If courts continue to interfere in the traditional decision-making process of patient, physician, and family the situation will continue to worsen. Because the patient may be forced to undergo any form of treatment that may sustain life, the point may soon be at hand where a patient with a terminal illness will elect to be treated in a state where his rights to terminate life support are respected. Parents and family members may attempt to move incompetent, terminally ill patients to states where they will be granted the ability to compel termination. Courts will become further involved by trying to stop such moves solely for the purpose of ending another life, by perhaps taking the terminally ill patient into judicial custody for his own protection.

We must be careful not to overlook the fact that many of these decisions have been reached without the benefit of legislation. With regard to this issue, the authors are certain that most courts have been uncomfortable with their role in shaping policy on the right of the dying.

So what recourse do we have? The Supreme Court of Georgia made an argument to disenfranchise the courts when it said: "While courts are always available to protect the rights of the individual, the condition of this individual is such that the decision is one to be made by the family and the medical community."[28] The language may not be substantial, but the message is quite clear. There is, in the absence of extraordinary circumstances, only a limited role for our courts in matters so highly personal.

As the court suggests, the judicial process is always available to people whose interests are in conflict. But in the case of a patient who has the support of his family and physician to terminate or not to initiate health care, the courts should defer to their judgment. In cases such as these we suggest the best process of review is that made by the family and physician with an eye toward the religious beliefs of the patient. If the decision can be reached at this level, the matter should be closed.

APPENDIXES

An essential principle of life is our fundamental right of self-determination. As we enter an age in which we can do almost anything, how do we decide what choices to make? Should we defer to the courts and allow them or the legislatures (or both) to impose their policy preferences on society? Or can we deal with some of these questions on our own? Cardinal Joseph Bernardin, archbishop of Chicago, has asked the question: "In a time when we can do anything technologically, how do we decide morally what we never should do?

There are a great many factors to be considered when making these determinations which the authors have not been able to address, such as health care costs, DNR orders, medical school instructions/policies, hospices, durable powers of attorney, and living wills, to mention only a few. The appendixes are intended to highlight some of these areas in an attempt to provide a more complete review of this subject.

Appendix 1: Withholding Treatment from Defective Infants

This may be the one area under the topic of sustaining quality of life that has been given the most attention in recent years. It is an issue on which public opinion is strongly divided.

Many feel that the defective newborn has individual constitutional rights to medical treatment, while others are strongly convinced that the decision of withholding medical treatment is a personal one in the hands of the parents and the medical staff. This issue is not as easily rationalized as when the patient is an 80–year-old man who has previously made known his desire not to be kept alive by life-sustaining procedures. This patient may be only a few hours or minutes old when the need for immediate life-sustaining techniques is most critical. A delay of only minutes is often fatal to the child. In this instance, there is no time to call on a court of law to sort out the legal questions or to ponder the constitutional issue involved in the case.

The proper place for the determination of whether a child should or should not receive medical treatment is with the parents. However, the parents should not be allowed to make such a decision unless counseled by competent medical professionals. It therefore becomes necessary for the doctors to share increasing responsibility in the making of such decisions. Because we are seeing an increased survival rate among infants from defects that previously would have been fatal, doctors must use caution when advising parents as to the possible chances of survival and quality of life. Since the doctor is the parent's ultimate source of expertise in this matter, it is up to the doctor to balance the rights of the child with the chances of survival. Acceptable quality of life as opposed to preferred quality of life must always be in the doctor's mind when advising parents. It is important to consider that a child has nothing to use in comparison when determining what is acceptable quality of life. Parents and doctors must refrain from putting themselves in the place of the child. Knowing what a normal person knows about how life is lived would inevitably condemn a severely impaired child. It is up to the doctor, therefore, to advise the parents as competently as possible, for it is on his advice and often his advice alone that a parent makes his or her decision.

Many of these children survive to live lives of reduced capacity and ability. If society chooses total and consistent treatment of impaired newborns, then it must also be willing to assist such people in leading their lives as productively as possible. Many parents are financially unable to maintain a child with a severe physical defect. Society must therefore make a commitment to the handicapped to step in where a parent cannot provide the adequate support. Without such a commitment, we will be condemning a child and its family to a life of increased suffering, hardship, and misery. This fact is obvious in light of some of the present Baby Doe cases. (It should be noted that the preceding does not implicitly suggest the authors' belief in abortion. Such matters encompass many legal and moral issues that go beyond the scope of this paper.)

Governmental Response

The federal government has attempted to provide some regulation in the area of critically ill newborns. Responding primarily to public concern over the death of Baby Doe in Indiana in 1982, the Department of Health and Human Services (DHHS) issued a "Notice to Health Care Providers" otherwise known as the "Baby Doe Rule."[29] The regulation required health care facilities receiving federal financial assistance to post throughout the hospital a notice stating, "Discriminatory failure to feed and care for handicapped infants in this facility is prohibited by federal law." The notice further provided that anyone knowing of an infant being denied customary medical care should contact a 24–hour hotline for handicapped infants. Nowhere in the regulation was customary medical care defined. On April 14, 1983, Judge Gerhard Gesell of the United States District Court for the District of Columbia struck down the rule as being unconstitutionally vague.[30]

In February 1984, the DHHS issued a second Baby Doe Rule virtually identical to the previous one. This rule focused on infant care review committees, recommended by the American Academy of Pediatrics. Although the new rule did not mandate the creation of such committees, their formation was strongly recommended. In addition, the rule did not refer to the previously indefinable phrase "customary medical care." However, on December 27, 1984, the United States Court of Appeals for the Second Circuit affirmed the district court's decision that this rule was also invalid.[31]

Legislation concerning the issue of critically ill infants recently passed both houses of Congress and was signed into law by the president. This Amendment to the Child Abuse Prevention and Treatment Act, passed in 1984, requires states to have in place procedures for health care facilities to notify the state authorities of suspected instances of withholding medically indicated treatment from disabled infants.[32] The phrase "medically indicated treatment" is defined as:

> the failure to respond to the infant's life-threatening conditions by providing treatment (including appropriate nutrition, hydration, and medication) which, in the treating physician's or physicians' reasonable medical judgment, will be most likely to be effective in ameliorating or correcting all such conditions, except that the term does not include the failure to provide treatment (*other* than appropriate nutrition, hydration, or medication) to an infant when, in the treating physician's or physicians' reasonable medical judgment, (A) the infant is chronically and irreversibly comatose; (B) the provisions of such treatment would (i) merely prolong dying, (ii) not be effective in ameliorating or correcting all of the infant's life-threatening conditions, or (iii) otherwise be futile in terms of the survival of the infant; or (C) the provision of such treatment would be virtually futile in terms of the survival of the infant and the treatment itself under such circumstances would be inhumane.[33]

The DHHS is required to publish regulations implementing the new requirements and to provide technical assistance to the states. However, the DHHS is not authorized to investigate individual Baby Doe cases, as was the intention under the previous Baby Doe rules.

Appendix 2: Political and Legislative Action and Related Developments

Influenced by judicial activity and growing policy concerns, "death with dignity" has gained considerable political and legislative support since *Quinlan* in 1975.

Through 1980, the highest courts of only four states took up the issue of whether to allow the termination or withholding of treatment from an incompetent, terminally ill patient. A vast majority of states were silent on the question, and those individuals responsible for such decisions remained unclear as legislative initiative and judicial precedents lagged. However, since 1980, interest in the problem has increased.

Living Wills

In 1967, the concept of living wills was introduced by Luis Kutner, a Chicago attorney and president of the World Habeas Corpus Organization.[34] At a meeting of the Euthanasia Society, Kutner offered his suggestion of a living will as a morally and legally defensible act by which an individual could make his wishes known concerning his own death. In support of his proposal, Kutner cited the common-law principle that an individual has the right to make decisions regarding his or her own body. Since this conference, living will legislation has been enacted in 23 states with legislation pending in 17 more.[35]

Appendix 3: President's Commission for the Study of Ethical Problems in Medicine and Biomedical and Behavioral Research

The subject of a terminal patient's right to die received federal attention in 1983. In its report *Deciding to Forgo Life-Sustaining Treatment* the President's Commission did the following:

1. Criticized hospitals for limiting the terminal patient's ability to choose death.
2. Called for efforts by health care professionals to enhance a patient's decision-making powers.
3. Suggested the use of surrogate decisions on behalf of the incapacitated patient.
4. Encouraged legislative and judicial clarity on the matter.
5. Suggested durable powers of attorney as a device for decision making.[36]

NOTES

1. For the purposes of this chapter it is important to define what the authors mean when using the phrase "quality of life." The authors have been greatly influenced in their understanding of this phrase as a result of an article written by Vincent J. Collins, M.D., entitled "Considerations in Prolonging Life: A Dying and Recovery Score" appearing in the book *Death, Dying and Euthanasia* (New York: Alphein Books, University Publications of American, 1980).

Implicit in the phrase "sustaining quality of life" is the idea of a physician actively or passively treating a terminally ill patient coupled with a patient's right to die. Active treatment includes all resuscitations once a heart has stopped, all intravenous therapies, chemical therapies, radiations, and so on. Active treatment has the connotation of a physician performing some therapeutic act to prolong life, thereby delaying the moment of clinical death. Passive treatment is what we perceive as the other end of the medical therapy spectrum. Instead of actively treating a terminal patient, the physician omits performing any heroic acts of resuscitation; there is no active intravenous therapy of any kind, including feeding and hydration. In simplest terms, passive treatment means that a physician provides a terminally ill patient with the most comfort possible to alleviate any pain and lets nature take its course. Death is allowed to occur as a result of the illness and there is no attempt to postpone its arrival.

These two types of treatment are in no way to be construed as including euthanasia. Euthanasia is seen as the active intervention in the ending of a life. It is an overt act that should carry with it all civil and criminal liabilities associated with murder, manslaughter, or negligence. Euthanasia does not have associated with it the dilemma of prolonging life or not prolonging life, as the other two treatments implicitly do. Euthanasia is a decision to actively take another's life. The authors do not in any way see the topic of euthanasia as an aspect in sustaining the "quality of life."

2. *New York Times*/CBS News Poll, June, 1985.

3. The expression "right to die" has taken on a variety of meanings over the years. While it is more popularly known as the movement that succeeded the efforts of the Euthanasia Society of America (ESA), the authors wish to limit its meaning to the specific rights and responsibilities of those affected by the dying process.

4. Euthanasia. Before proceeding further the authors feel compelled to distinguish the range of meanings given to the term *euthanasia*. The Vatican Congregation for the Doctrine of the Faith, June 26, 1980, set forth the following position in its *Declaration on Euthanasia:* "The word euthanasia is used in a more particular sense to mean mercy killing, for the purpose of putting an end to extreme suffering or saving abnormal babies, the mentally ill or the incurably sick from the prolongation, perhaps for many years, of a miserable life, which could impose too heavy a burden on their families or on society."

5. Norton, C. E. As reported in *New York Times* (editorial). January 5, 1906, p. 8.

6. "Euthanasia Bobs Up Again." As reported in *New York Times* (editorial). January 25, 1906, p. 8.

7. Pius XII, address of February 24, 1957, *AAS* 49 (1957):147.

8. Recent popes have explained these principles, which retain full force. See Pius XII, address to those attending the Congress of the International Union of Catholic Women's Leagues, September 11, 1947, *AAS* 39 (1947):2483; address to midwives, October 29, 1951, *AAS* 43 (1951):835–854; speech to the International Office for Documentation, October 19, 1953, *AAS* 45 (1953):744–754; address to those taking part in the ninth Congress of the Italian Anesthesiological Society, February 24, 1957, *AAS* 49 (1957):146; Paul VI, address to the members of the United Nations Special Committee on Apartheid, May 22, 1974, *AAS* 66 (1974):346; John Paul II, address to the Bishops of the United States, October 5, 1979, *AAS* 71 (1979):1225.

9. John Paul II, address to the Bishops of the United States, October 5, 1979.

10. Kelly, G., *The Duty to Preserve Life, 12 Theological Studies*, pp. 550–556 (1951), as quoted in *Eichner v. Dillon*, 73 App. Div. 2d 431, 426 N.Y.S.2d 517, 527 (1980).

11. *In re Quinlan*, 70 N.J. 10, 355 A.2d 647 (1976).

12. *Id.*

13. *Id.*

14. *Superintendent of Belchertown State School v. Saikewicz*, 373 Mass. 728, 370 N.E.2d 417 (1977).

15. *Id.*

16. *In re Dinnerstein*, 380 N.E.2d 134 (1978).

17. *In re Spring*, 405 N.E.2d 115 (1980).

18. *Id.*

19. *In re Eichner*, 52 N.Y.2d 363, 420 A.2d 64, 438 N.Y.S.2d 266 (1981).

20. *In re Colyer*, 99 Wa.2d 144, 660 P.2d 738 (1983).

21. *In re Conroy,* 446 A.2d 303 (1983).

22. *Id.*

23. *Id.*

24. *Spring,* at 118.

25. *Satz v. Perlmutter,* 362 So.2d 160, aff'd 379 So.2d 359 (1980).

26. *Eichner,* at N.Y.2d 363, N.E.2d 438 (1981).

27. *Severns v. Wilmington Medical Center, Inc., et al.,* 421 A.2d 1334 (1980).

28. *In re L.H.R.,* No. 41065 (Ga. Sup. Ct., October 16, 1984).

29. Lawton, S., E., Carder, and A. Weisman. 1985. "Recent Governmental Actions regarding the Treatment of Seriously Ill Newborns." *The Journal of College and University Law* 1:166–201.

30. *Id.*

31. *Id.*

32. *Id.*

33. *Id.*

34. Kutner, L. 1970. *The Human Right to Individual Freedom: A Symposium on World Habeas Corpus.* Miami, Fla.: University of Miami Press.

35. Alabama Natural Death Act, ALA. CODE §§ 22–8A–10 (1981); Arkansas Death with Dignity, ARK. STAT. ANN. §§ 82–3801–3804 (1977); California Natural Death Act, CAL. HEALTH & SAFETY CODE §§ 7185–7195 (1976); Delaware Death with Dignity, DEL. CODE ANN., Tit. 16. §§ 2501–2509 (1982); District of Columbia Natural Death Act of 1981, D.C. CODE ANN. §§ 6–2421–2430 (1982); Florida Life Prolonging Procedure Act, FLA. STAT., Chap. 84–58 §§ 765.01–15 (1984); Georgia Living Wills Act, GA. CODE ANN. §§ 31–32–1–12 (1984); Idaho Natural Death Act, IDAHO CODE §§ 39–4501–4508 (1977); Illinois Living Will Act, ILL. ANN. STAT., Chap. 110 §§ 701–710 (1984); Kansas Natural Death Act, KAN. STAT. ANN. §§ 65–28, 101–109 (1979); Louisiana Life-Sustaining Procedures, LA. REV. STAT., 40:1299.58–.10 (1984); Mississippi Act Senate Bill No. 2364, Chap. 365, Laws of 1984; Nevada Withholding or Withdrawal of Life Sustaining Procedures, NEV. REV. STAT. §§ 449.540–690 (1977); New Mexico Right to Die Act, N.M. STAT. ANN. §§ 24–7–1–11 (1977); North Carolina Right to Natural Death Act, N.C. GEN. STAT. §§ 90–320–322 (1977); Oregon Rights with Respect to Terminal Illness, OR. REV. STAT. §§ 97.050–.090 (1977); Texas Natural Death Act, TEX. STAT. ANN., Art. 4590h (1977); Vermont Terminal Care Document, VT. STAT. ANN., Tit. 18 §§ 5251–5262 and Tit. 13 §§ 1801 (1982); Virginia Natural Death Act, VA. CODE §§ 54–325.8:1–13 (1983); Washington Natural Death Act, WASH. REV. CODE ANN. §§ 70.122.010–70.122.905 (1979); West Virginia Natural Death Act, W.VA. CODE, Chap. 16, Art. 30 §§ 1–10 (1984); Wisconsin Natural Death Act, WISC. STAT. §§ 154.01 et seq. as created by 1983 Wisconsin Act 202 (1984); Wyoming Act, WY. STAT. 33–26–§§ 144–152 (1984);

36. President's Commission for the Study of Ethical Problems in Medicine and Biomedical and Behavioral Research. 1983. *Deciding to Forgo Life-Sustaining Treatment.* Washington, D.C.: U.S. Government Printing Office.

Alternative Health Care Delivery Systems: Health Maintenance Organizations and Preferred Provider Organizations

Dale H. Cowan, M.D., J.D.

Public and private purchasers of health care services are focusing considerable attention on the rapidly escalating increases in the costs of these services. In an effort to reduce the rate of increase in these costs, both government and private groups—corporations, insurance companies, and entrepreneurs—are exploring a variety of alternative payment schemes.

The major activity undertaken by government has been the institution under Medicare of the prospective payment system (PPS) according to diagnostically related groups (DRGs). Activities being pursued by private groups include the sponsorship and organization of alternative delivery systems (ADSs), including health maintenance organizations (HMOs) and preferred provider organizations (PPOs).

This chapter reviews the key characteristics of HMOs and PPOs and discusses the salient business considerations and major legal issues that affect their organization and operation.

CHARACTERIZATION OF HMOS AND PPOS

Health Maintenance Organizations

HMOs are medical care organizations, either for profit or not for profit, that "accept responsibility for the provision and delivery of a predetermined set of comprehensive health maintenance and treatment services to a voluntarily enrolled group for a prenegotiated and fixed periodic capitation payment."[1] A comprehensive review and discussion of HMOs was written by Dustin L. Mackie and Douglas K. Decker and published by Aspen Systems Corporation in 1981.[2]

The reader is referred to that publication and others referenced therein for detailed information regarding the development, structure, organization, and management of HMOs.

HMOs represent an alternative health care delivery system that creates financial incentives for providers to control the financial costs of the health care they provide. The basis for these incentives is that, in contrast to the fee-for-service system in which providers are reimbursed per unit of service provided or cost incurred, HMOs must operate within fixed budgets. HMOs are at risk financially because they must provide the health care required by their members within their fixed budgets.

Regardless of the organizational structure (to be discussed below), HMOs share five common characteristics. These are:

1. A defined population of enrolled members;
2. Payments by the members, which are determined in advance for a specific period of time and are made periodically;
3. Medical services that are provided on a direct service basis rather than on an indemnity basis;
4. Services that are provided to patients by HMO physicians for essentially all medical needs with referral to outside physicians being controlled by HMO physicians;
5. Voluntary enrollment by each family or member.

These characteristics help distinguish HMOs from the traditional fee-for-service system. For example, in contrast to the fee-for-service system, HMOs are highly organized systems for providing health care. In the usual fee-for-service system patients may seek care from any practitioner, generalist or specialist. In HMOs, a primary care physician, such as a family physician, general practitioner, or general internist, is responsible for providing or requesting all health care services. All referrals to specialists must be approved by the primary care physician. This requirement has two effects. First, it restricts patients to using physicians who are participating practitioners in the HMO unless the services needed are not provided by one of the HMO's practitioners. Second, it helps integrate the services that are provided, minimizes duplication of services, and helps assure that services are provided in a logical sequence that is appropriate to the condition being managed.

Another distinction between HMOs and the fee-for-service system is the payment mechanism. Payment in the fee-for-service system is based on utilization and is rendered after the service has been provided. Payment in HMO plans is prospective and for fixed amounts. Payments by subscribers to HMOs are therefore analogous to insurance premiums. Because payments are prospective, they are independent of the services that are provided.

The size of the capitation payments is based on the size and characteristics of the population served by the HMO. Actuarial assumptions contributing to the size of the capitation include age, sex, racial characteristics, and other identifiable demographic and risk factors. From these assumptions, estimates are made of the number of hospital days per thousand enrollees per year, the total number of days that will be required in a given period of time, the total number of physicians needed, and the number of physicians in various specialties.

HMOs meeting designated criteria may achieve federal qualification in accordance with the Health Maintenance Organization Act of 1973, 42 U.S.C. §§ 300e to 300e–17 (1976 & Supp. III 1979). Requirements for federal qualification include:

1. A basic benefit package;
2. An open enrollment annually;
3. Defined consumer representation on the board of directors;
4. Coverage based on community rating rather than on experience rating.

Federally qualified HMOs may adopt one of three organizational structures: staff, group, or individual practice associations (IPAs). Staff model and group model HMOs are the two forms of HMOs that antedated federal interest in alternative delivery systems in the early 1970s and the passage of the HMO Act of 1973. Staff model HMOs arose from cooperative health care movements in which consumers contributed funds to form nonprofit corporations designed to provide health care at reasonable costs for predetermined, prepaid rates. The physicians in staff model HMOs are salaried employees of the HMOs. As an incentive to contain costs, the physicians may receive a portion of any surplus remaining at the end of each fiscal year if premiums exceed expenses. The physicians are ordinarily prohibited by their contracts from providing health care to persons other than members of the HMOs. Examples of staff model HMOs are the Group Health Association of Washington, D.C., and the Group Health Cooperative of Puget Sound.

Group model HMOs are prepaid group practice plans (PPGPs). The physicians in group model HMOs may be organized as partnerships or as corporations. The professional group is commonly a multispecialty group. It contracts with the HMOs to provide health care to the HMO members. In this model, the physicians are not employees. The group receives a capitation payment for each subscriber plus a share of the program's net income, if any, as a group. In turn, it pays participating physicians on a salaried or fee-for-service basis. Individual physicians may see non-HMO patients on a fee-for-service basis. In order to meet standards for federal qualification, prepaid care must constitute 35 percent or more of the group's activity. Examples of group model HMOs are the Ross Loos Medical Group in Los Angeles, the Kaiser-Permanente Medical Care Program, and the Euclid Clinic in Euclid, Ohio.

Staff or group model HMOs can reduce health care costs 10 to 40 percent.[3] This reduction is mainly attributable to reduced rates of hospitalization and to greater efficiencies of operation. Alain C. Enthoven lists several advantages that HMOs have for economy and quality.[4] These include:

1. The method of payment gives the organization a prospective budget.
2. Practice in a multispecialty group offers advantages apart from the method of payment including ease of consultation and reassurance of mutual professional support.
3. There is a strong financial incentive to match carefully the facilities to the needs of the population being served.
4. There are economic and professional incentives to match the specialty mix to the needs of the population.
5. Group practice enhances opportunities for quality control.

Offsetting these advantages are several potential disadvantages or impediments to the development of HMOs. These include the time and costs needed to organize and establish them on a financially sound basis and the need for patients to change physicians in order to become members. Additionally, there is a perception (never documented to my knowledge) that the care provided to patients is impersonal. Finally, there is some reluctance on the part of physicians to accept what they view as limitations on their professional independence.[5]

The newest type of HMO organizational structure that satisfies federal requirements is the individual practice association (IPA). IPAs are organizations of physicians often working as solo practitioners who join together voluntarily and enter into agreements with other organizations to provide medical services to a defined population. The individual physicians may continue practicing in their own offices and may be paid on a fee-for-service basis. There are no limits on the number of non-HMO private patients IPA physicians may see on a fee-for-service basis. Comprehensive health benefits are provided to the enrolled population for a fixed prospective periodic payment.[6]

To reconcile the prospective capitation payment by subscribers with the fee-for-service reimbursement of physicians, an arrangement is created whereby subscribers pay fees to the IPA. The IPA reimburses the physicians according to a formula that is agreed upon in advance. The physicians thus agree on a fee schedule and bill the IPA rather than the subscriber when they render a service.

The reimbursement agreement often calls for the IPA to pay a percentage of the agreed-upon fee, usually 80–90 percent. The remainder is held back and provides a financial reserve for the IPA. If there is a surplus at the end of the fiscal year, all or a portion of the amount held back is paid to the physicians. By causing the physicians in the IPA to share in the risk, the agreement creates a financial incentive for the physicians to control costs.

Some agreements between physicians and IPAs call for the physicians to receive a predetermined prospective capitation payment for each subscriber who signs up with each physician. The payment is made monthly. The physicians are responsible for paying all costs for ancillary services they order. Additionally, they pay the professional fees for specialty consultations they request. The physicians may retain any funds remaining after paying for outside services. However, they are responsible for paying from their own pockets for costs that exceed the prospectively paid amounts up to a limit of, say, 5 percent over the amounts initially received. This approach, like the one described in the previous paragraph, creates a financial incentive to control costs.

Additional features of IPAs may include peer review of the appropriateness of service and payment of hospital costs of subscribers or cooperation with insurance carriers that offer hospital insurance policies.

Like staff and group model HMOs, IPAs have advantages and weaknesses. Advantages of IPAs include the following:

1. They can be established relatively easily and inexpensively.
2. They require only minimal changes in the practice style of established physicians.
3. Patients who enroll may continue receiving care from their own physicians (provided the latter join the IPA).
4. The fee-for-service system rewards productivity and provides incentives for physicians to be attractive to patients.

Weaknesses of IPAs include the fact that:

1. There may be little matching of numbers of participating physicians or specialty mix to the needs of the enrolled population.
2. There may be little opportunity to limit physician participants to those whose practices do not generate high costs.
3. There may be little motivation for a reduction in costs generated by the majority of physicians whose practices are near the norms.[7]

Since IPAs are relatively new forms of HMOs, data regarding their performance are as yet incomplete. However, Enthoven wrote, "[IPAs] or similar fee-for-service organizations can control cost if they must. Competitive necessity is the key factor."[8] Support for this observation is provided in the report prepared by the staff of the Physicians Health Plan of Minnesota and published by the Department of Health and Human Services.[9]

Until the 1980s, the growth of HMOs in terms of numbers of plans and numbers of subscribers was relatively slow. In 1980, HMOs provided health care to approximately 5 percent of the population in the United States. Since 1980, the growth in the number and the population served by HMOs has been dramatic. In June 1981, there were 243 operational HMOs serving an enrolled population of 10.3 million members. By early 1984, 323 HMOs were operating throughout the United States with a membership totaling 13.6 million.[10]

In the 1970s, annual increases in enrollment ranged from 10 to 15 percent. In 1983, different HMOs were reporting enrollment increases ranging from 25 to 49 percent, although nationally, HMO enrollment increased by 15.3 percent over the previous year.[11]

The most active region for HMO activity is the area of Minneapolis–St. Paul,

Minnesota. By mid-June 1984, six nonprofit HMOs reported a market penetration of 36 percent.[12]

Increasingly, new HMOs are being established by national chains such as Kaiser Foundation Health Plan, Inc., Blue Cross and Blue Shield Association (operated by local Blue plans), CIGNA Healthplan, Health America Corp., and Prudential Health Care Plan, Inc. In 1983, fourteen such HMO firms owned or managed more than one plan in more than one state and together held 68.8 percent of the market.

Preferred Provider Organizations

PPOs are the newest alternative health care delivery system designed to control the rising costs of health care.[13] Numerous definitions of PPOs have been suggested by different writers, speakers, and observers of health care delivery systems. The following definition is one of many that could be set forth.

PPOs may be defined as associations or organizations of physicians and hospitals that contract with employers or insurers to provide comprehensive health care services to subscribers on a fee-for-service basis.

The definition encompasses several key features of PPOs. One feature is that PPOs constitute a health care delivery system or plan. It provides a degree of organization that does not exist in the traditional fee-for-service system. A second feature is that it is a mechanism for facilitating contracts between purchasers and providers of health care services. This also represents a departure from the traditional fee-for-service system. In that system, there is no direct agreement between health care providers and those who purchase health care services. Rather, a third party, either a private insurer or a governmental program, serves as a fiscal intermediary between the purchasers and the providers. In contrast, PPOs involve direct contracting between these parties.

A third feature is that the providers are reimbursed on a fee-for-service basis for a comprehensive range of services provided to the subscribers. The system does not change the basis for reimbursement but allows for reimbursement for a range of services that may be broader than those covered by standard indemnity policies.

PPOs share most or all of the following characteristics:

1. A panel of providers, including physicians and hospitals, whose numbers may or may not be limited;
2. Negotiated fee schedules, which may, but need not, include discounts from existing fees;
3. Review of utilization or claims including some form of control mechanism;
4. Flexibility in the choice of provider—no "lock-in" of consumers;
5. A financial incentive for inducing consumers to select the preferred option;
6. Rapid turnaround on providers' claims;

7. No assumption by the providers of financial risk;
8. Use of primary care physicians as the entry point or "gatekeeper" in the system.

The chief means by which PPOs seek to achieve their goal of controlling the rate of increase in health care costs are the negotiated fee schedules and the programs for monitoring the utilization of services rendered or ordered by the participating practitioners.

PPOs differ in several significant respects from HMOs:

1. There is no prepayment to the providers in PPOs of capitation payments.
2. PPO providers are not at financial risk for losses resulting from the costs of services they provide or order.
3. Subscribers to PPO plans are not restricted or "locked in" to using the PPO hospitals or physicians.
4. PPOs are not subject to the same regulatory requirements as HMOs.

The preservation of fee-for-service reimbursement, the absence of prepayment of fees, and the absence of financial risk are three key features of PPOs that enable them to attract physicians to their panels of providers. It is apparent, however, that the very features that attract physicians to PPOs (and dissuade them from joining HMOs) represent the key ingredients that underlie the success of HMOs in containing health care costs. Whether groups seeking to perform effectively in slowing the rate of increase of health costs can do so without these key ingredients remains to be seen. Preliminary data from several PPOs having widely different structures and operational schemes suggest PPOs can maintain quality medical care and be cost-effective.

ORGANIZATIONAL ISSUES OF HMOS AND PPOS

A number of organizational issues arise in the process of developing HMOs and PPOs. These directly affect their operation. They include:

1. The organizing or sponsoring entity;
2. The organizational structure;
3. The composition of the governing board;
4. The selection of professional and institutional providers;
5. The fee structure.

HMOs and PPOs may be organized or sponsored by an entity or group in one of three different classes: providers, purchasers, and third parties. Provider sponsors may be practitioners, hospitals, or joint ventures between practitioners and hospitals. Purchaser sponsors include employers, business coalitions, union trust funds, and insurers. Third-party organizers or sponsors include third-party administrators (TPAs), brokers, and entrepreneurs.

The nature of the sponsors affects all other aspects of the organizing effort, the major operational issues, and the legal considerations (described below).

A variety of organizational structures have been adopted for the organization of HMOs and PPOs. The most common organizational forms are corporations, either for profit or not for profit, and limited partnerships. Other forms may be adopted but are generally felt to be administratively cumbersome or to entail unacceptable liability risks.

Regardless of the organizational form adopted, considerations arise with respect to the legal obligations of the organizers and participants, professional liability, the effect of state statutes and regulations, tax consequences, and exposure to antitrust liability.

The composition of the governing board has major consequences for the issue of control over the policies of the HMO or PPO. The board composition is mainly dependent upon the nature of the organizing or sponsoring entity. For example, physician-sponsored PPOs tend to have boards composed mainly of physicians. By contrast PPOs sponsored by insurers may have few or no physician members. The composition of the board may be expected to influence key organizational and operational decisions such as the number and type of practitioners on the provider panel, the choice of hospital providers, the fee structure, and the utilization review process.

Regardless of sponsorship, HMOs and PPOs need to determine whether and on what basis practitioners should be selected for membership in the provider panel. Factors affecting whether or not participants should be selected to the provider panel include the consequence of selection for coherence and preservation of relationships within a medical staff, the potential for antitrust liability if interested practitioners are excluded (boycott), and the ease with which procedures for discharging poor performers can be developed and implemented.

Criteria that might be used to select practitioners include the specialty, membership on a particular medical staff, geography, quality or efficiency according to some standard, and willingness to accept specified restrictions on fees or utilization.

In general, HMOs and PPOs sponsored by providers open the provider panel to all members of the involved medical staff who wish to join. By contrast, nonprovider-sponsored groups tend to select providers according to specified criteria.

The fee structure is critical to the marketability and performance of HMOs and PPOs. Several considerations affect the fee structure. Key questions are:

1. Will reimbursement be on a capitated or a fee-for-service basis?
2. How and by whom are fees determined?
3. What control do individual practitioners have over their fees?
4. Is a relative value scale used? If so, how are the conversion factors established?
5. How often and on what basis are fee schedules revised?
6. How are disputes over fees resolved?

A major issue affecting the fee structure of provider-sponsored HMOs and PPOs is their potential antitrust liability in attempting to establish a uniform fee schedule.

OPERATIONAL ISSUES AFFECTING HMOS AND PPOS

The key issue affecting the operation of HMOs and PPOs is the program for utilization review. Since reduced utilization of resources, particularly of hospitals, is the single greatest potential source for reducing costs, the design and management of the utilization review program are critical for HMO and PPO management.

Components of utilization review include:

1. Preadmission certification of selected (or all) elective admissions;
2. Concurrent review of all hospital admissions including analysis of the appropriateness of use of services, surgery, and length of stay;
3. Retrospective review of activities in the office and the hospitals.

A number of considerations affect utilization review programs. These relate to who does the review, the source of standards according to which utilization of resources is analyzed, monitoring the review program, access to the data, protecting confidentiality, the liability attaching to the review program, and the availability of insurance programs to protect the HMO or PPO and those conducting the review program. Each of these considerations must be addressed in order for the utilization review program to be effective and credible.

Other operational issues are those relating to claims administration and to marketing. The mechanics for administering claims can have a major impact on the acceptability of the HMO or PPO for both providers and patients.

Effective marketing is essential if HMOs and PPOs are to achieve their goals. Marketing efforts must be addressed to both employers and employee/subscribers. Numerous factors affect the marketing activity. Ultimately, however, the performance of the HMO or PPO, that is, its ability to control costs while providing quality medical care, will be the most significant factor in the marketing effort.

LEGAL CONSIDERATIONS

Establishing HMOs and PPOs requires that attention be paid to a multiplicity of legal issues. The major areas of law that apply to these organizations are:

1. Federal and state antitrust laws;
2. Federal and state laws pertaining to HMOs;
3. State insurance laws;

4. State laws pertaining to corporations and partnerships;
5. Federal and state tax laws;
6. Federal and state securities laws;
7. State laws pertaining to professional and corporate liability.

The effects of these laws will vary according to specific characteristics of HMOs and PPOs, including sponsorship, organizational form, board composition, manner of selecting practitioners, method of financing, manner of establishing the fee structure, and the scope and method for monitoring utilization.

ANTITRUST ISSUES

The most important legal issues raised by HMOs and PPOs, particularly those sponsored and established by providers, arise from federal and state antitrust laws. The key areas of concern from the standpoint of antitrust are pricefixing and boycott.

Although HMOs and PPOs may be formed and controlled by insurers, third-party administrators, and entrepreneurs, the major risks for antitrust violations lie with HMOs and PPOs formed by provider groups. In view of the tendency for practitioners and institutions to develop HMOs and PPOs as joint ventures, the antitrust considerations for HMOs and PPOs will be reviewed using the perspective of joint ventures.

Critical antitrust issues arise with respect to price determination, membership, utilization and peer review, and monopolization.

Price agreements by individuals or entities that are otherwise competitors constitute the classic type of horizontal restraints. They are subject to scrutiny using the per se standard, and thus any arguably procompetitive benefits are insufficient to justify their anticompetitive effects.[14]

Price determinations by bona fide joint ventures of physicians and hospitals may be analyzed under the rule-of-reason standard, provided the two parties combine capital, assets, or knowhow and the combination either facilitates entry into new markets or creates efficiencies or new productive capacity unachievable by either party alone.[15]

Horizontal price agreements by joint ventures should not be treated as "naked" restraints and be per se unlawful if they are necessary consequences of or ancillary to the functions and activities of the joint ventures. To assist in the analysis, specific issues respecting the product and geographic market are relevant. These include:

1. The nature of the product being offered:
   —whether it is the same as or different from that presently available,
   —The area in which the product will be offered,
   —The intended consumers of the product;

2. The likelihood the product or services would be made available without the joint activities of the co-venturers;
3. Whether the activities of the joint venture increase the choices available to consumers and/or payors with respect to the specific products or services offered;
4. The market share of the joint venture.[16]

The antitrust issues affecting membership relate to the parties that comprise the joint venture and the selection and exclusion of physician providers.

In discussing participation in joint ventures, C. Weller cites William Baxter of the Antitrust Division:

> There is a popular notion about that the real problem with a joint venture between a set of companies is that someone will get left out, that somehow it is unfair to the companies that aren't permitted to join and [that] the . . . solution to these problems is to write in a clause that anybody else can get in the club if they want to get in the club.
>
> That is a very serious misperception. . . . The real problem with joint ventures is not that they are insufficiently inclusive. The real problem with joint ventures, if there is a problem with a joint venture, is that they are too inclusive.[17]

To determine whether a joint venture is too inclusive, it is necessary to consider the size of the physician group in relation to the physician market and the size of the hospital or hospital group in relation to the hospital market. Each of these considerations requires a determination of what constitutes the relevant product market (e.g., types of physicians or hospital services provided) and the relevant geographic market.

No agreement exists as to the share of the market joint ventures can control before their market power raises antitrust concerns. Market shares varying from 15 to 40 percent have been mentioned, although most commentators focus on market shares of 15 to 20 percent as not being presumptively unlawful.[18]

If membership either through equity participation or as a participating provider becomes necessary for a provider to compete, then denial of membership or expulsion raises antitrust concern. Such exclusion or expulsion must have a reasonable basis, preferably on noneconomic grounds.[19] To be acceptable, membership rules must be shown to be justified by the legitimate competitive needs of the entity and "the requirements of the rules themselves must be reasonably necessary to the accomplishment of the legitimate goals and narrowly tailored to that end."[20]

Examples of membership selection standards that are reasonably related to a joint venture's business success include requiring physicians to have privileges at the co-venturing hospital and requiring cost-effective performance by physicians as determined by neutral, nondiscriminatory criteria.

An example of a selection criterion subject to challenge as not being dictated by demonstrable business necessity is one that excludes a class of providers on the basis of training, such as podiatrists or psychologists.[21] On the other hand, exclusive arrangements such as between a group of specialists (e.g., anesthesiologists, pathologists, radiologists) and the entity may not be per se unlawful.[22]

Discriminatory treatment may be considered a boycott or concerted refusal to deal.[23] Further to reduce risks of litigation or increase the likelihood of withstanding antitrust attack, due process procedures should be available to enable excluded or terminated providers to challenge adverse decisions, similar to those used by hospitals on privilege issues.

Utilization review and peer review are essential activities of alternative delivery systems. Utilization review commonly includes preadmission certification of elective procedures, concurrent review of all hospitalized patients to determine the appropriateness of diagnostic and therapeutic maneuvers, retrospective review of hospital care provided, and retrospective review of the use of ambulatory services.

Such review requires the setting of standards of care and a determination that the actions of individual providers conform with these standards. Additionally, the review requires that some one person on a panel of individuals, commonly physicians, perform the evaluation. From an antitrust standpoint, the major concern is joint action by competitors.

Utilization and peer review programs are proper under the antitrust laws. However, they should be conducted so as to avoid joint actions for anticompetitive purposes or effect, that is, to avoid appearing as boycotts.[24]

Whether or not alternative delivery systems become certified by state insurance laws is immaterial to the antitrust analysis of peer review activities since the Supreme Court has ruled that such activities do not fall within the "business of insurance" exemption to the antitrust laws set out in the McCarran-Ferguson Act.[25]

Provided utilization and peer review programs are undertaken as a necessary consequence of the joint venture and not for anticompetitive purposes, they should pass muster as not violative of the antitrust laws.

The establishment of services such as an HMO or PPO by a joint venture composed of a hospital and its staff physicians raises the possibility that the entity will monopolize or attempt to monopolize the delivery of such services within the service area. To minimize the likelihood that an antitrust challenge to such activities could be successfully brought, there should be no restrictions on the source from which providers or patients can obtain the services. Additionally, there should be no requirement that providers refer all or a specified percentage of their patients to the entity established by the joint venture.

To the extent that providing home or extended care services requires entry of personnel into the hospital to interview the patient or review the chart, outside entities should be entitled to the same rights of entry as the entity created by the joint venture.

The establishment of different rates of reimbursement (discriminatory reimbursement) of other entities may be viewed as a boycott.[26] Possible defenses against allegations of boycott include the relevant market and legitimate business goals.[27]

REGULATORY AND LIABILITY ISSUES

The regulatory and liability issues arise in the process of organizing HMOs and PPOs and during their operation. The major legal considerations that affect the organizational phase of HMOs and PPOs relate to state insurance laws, federal and state HMO laws, state corporation laws, federal and state securities, and federal and state tax laws. The manner and degree to which state laws may affect the organization of HMOs and PPOs varies considerably in different jurisdictions. Federal and state laws exist that regulate the formation, structure, and operations of HMOs. By contrast, no specific enabling or regulatory legislation for PPOs exists at the federal or state level, although drafting of applicable laws is presently underway.

The applicability of state insurance laws differs for HMOs and PPOs. As noted earlier, HMOs operate under an insurance concept. They combine risk spreading and delivery of health care services. Consequently, HMOs are generally subject to state insurance laws except in those jurisdictions having HMO laws.

PPOs do not function under an insurance concept and are generally not considered subject to the insurance laws. Insurance laws would, however, affect PPOs sponsored by insurance companies. Additionally, the adoption by any PPO of a fee structure based on capitation could cause their activities to be subject to state insurance laws.

Provisions in state insurance laws that may be potentially inhibitory to PPOs include:

- Free choice of provider;
- Antidiscrimination;
- Minimum benefit;
- All payor rate setting.

Since the applicability of both HMO laws and insurance laws to PPOs is being actively reviewed in many states, sponsors of PPOs and their counsel must be aware of the situation that exists in their respective areas.

HMOs and PPOs must comply with applicable state laws that pertain to business associations whether they be partnerships, corporations, or professional corporations. These laws may specify requirements for registration, filing, capitalization, and ownership. Corporation laws specify corporate formalities, and laws affecting professional corporations commonly restrict corporate purposes and the nature of the shareholders.

Federal and state securities regulations affect the capitalization of proprietary corporations. Exemptions exist under the Federal Securities Act for offerings that are intrastate or are private or limited. State securities laws vary. For example, there is no registration requirement in Ohio for issues offered solely by a corporate issuer and purchased by no more than ten persons.

An issue for HMOs and PPOs established as not-for-profit corporations is whether membership fees might be considered a security and therefore invoke securities laws. The answer will depend on the language and interpretation of the relevant state statute.

Tax issues affecting HMOs and PPOs fall into two categories. One is the tax status of the organization. The other is the effect of the organization on the tax status of hospitals that are nonprofit organizations exempt from federal income taxation under Section 501(c)(3) of the Internal Revenue Code. The issue relating to HMOs and PPOs is the possibility of attaining tax-exempt status under §§ 501(c)(3) or 501(c)(4) of the I.R.C. Some HMOs qualify for 501(c)(3) tax-exempt status. It is unlikely, however, that PPOs will qualify for tax-exempt status.

The issues affecting hospitals arises in the context of provider-sponsored HMOs and PPOs. The specific issues are loss of tax-exempt status and liability for unrelated business taxable income (UBTI). The resolution of the issues relates in part to the sponsorship of the HMO or PPO: hospital, physician, or hospital-physician joint venture. Activities of hospitals that might jeopardize their tax-exempt status include providing capital or operating funds, rent-free space, or services. The question is whether such contributions inure to the benefit of private individuals. The question regarding UBTI is whether revenues received by hospitals for services other than patient care might be considered UBTI.

The major legal issues that arise during the operational phase of the HMO and PPO relate to the responsibility health care providers have for providing proper medical care, preventing avoidable injury, contracting with providers and purchasers, and monitoring utilization.

The liability of PPOs may be viewed as analogous to that of hospitals. Two legal theories therefore appear applicable: *respondeat superior* and corporate liability. The activities of PPOs most likely to trigger these are the selection of providers and the supervision of the actions of the providers.

HMOs and PPOs are basically contracting entities. The agreements set out the rights and responsibilities of each of the various parties: physicians, hospitals, purchasers, and patients. The key issues relate to the procedures for setting rates and paying claims, utilization review, the scope of benefits, termination rights, and the mechanism for resolving disputes.

The legal issues affecting utilization review include liability for harm allegedly arising as a consequence of UR decisions, the process for conducting the review, maintenance of confidentiality, and whether the deliberations are privileged.

CONCLUSION

The increasing concern on the part of purchasers of health care services over the rising costs of health care and the growing competition for patients on the part of both practitioners and hospitals is stimulating providers of health care services to explore alternative health care delivery systems as a means for maintaining their patient bases and prompting payors of health care services to participate and sponsor HMOs and PPOs as a means of controlling health care costs. In the rush to achieve greater control over costs and greater accountability over the services rendered, it must be remembered that the ultimate beneficiary of the system is the patient. Successful HMOs and PPOs are those that provide quality health care to satisfied patients. It is possible to provide quality care at an affordable price.

Of all the parties involved in these arrangements, it is the professional providers who have the fiduciary duty to act in their patients' best interests. Consequently, the responsibility for maintaining the integrity of the health care system as we know it and of its values lies primarily with physicians.

NOTES

1. Shouldice, R. G., and K. H. Shouldice. 1978. *Medical Group Practice and Health Maintenance Organizations*. Washington, D.C.: Information Resources Press. P. 10.
2. Mackie, Dustin L., and Douglas K. Decker. 1981. *Group and IPA HMOs*. Rockville, Md.: Aspen Systems Corporations.
3. Luft, Harold S. 1980. "Assessing the Evidence on HMO Performance." *Milbank Memorial Fund Quarterly* 58 (Winter):501.
4. Enthoven, Alain C. 1978. "Cutting Cost without Cutting the Quality of Care." *New England Journal of Medicine* 298:1229.
5. *Ibid.*
6. *Ibid.*
7. *Ibid.*
8. *Id.* at p. 1232.
9. The Physicians Health Plan of Minnesota. 1980. *A Case Study of Utilization Controls in an IPA*. Washington, D.C., United States Department of Health and Human Services. Public Health Service. Office of Health Maintenance Organizations. DHHS Publication No. (PHS) 80–50128.
10. Iglehart, John K. 1984. "Health Policy Report, HMOs (Fort-Profit and Not-for-Profit) on the Move." *New England Journal of Medicine* 310 (18, May 3):1203–1208.
11. *Ibid.*
12. Iglehart, John K. 1984. "Health Policy Report: The Twin Cities' Medical Marketplace." *New England Journal of Medicine* 311 (5, August 2):343–348.
13. *See* generally Cowan, Dale H. 1984. *Preferred Provider Organizations: Planning Structure Operation*. Rockville, Md.: Aspen Systems Corporation.
14. *Arizona v. Maricopa County Med. Soc'y,* 102 S.Ct. 2466 (1982).
15. *In re Brunswick Corp.,* 94 F.T.C. 1174 (1979).
16. Adapted from Proger, P. 1983. *Antitrust Primer*. Washington, D.C., National Health Lawyers Association.
17. Baxter, William. Speech to National Association of Manufacturers, 5 CCH Trade Reg. Rep. 50,447 (May 10, 1983). Cited by C. Weller, "Antitrust Aspects of PPOs," in Cowan *supra,* n. 13.

18. Bradley, Joseph F. 1982. Joint Ventures and Antitrust Policy'' *Harvard Law Review* 95:1521–26; Bork, Robert. 1978. *The Antitrust Paradox*. New York: Basic Books. Business review letter from Department of Justice to Health Care Management September 21, 1983), Ohio A J Memorandum (17 Nov. 1983).

19. *Deeson v. Professional Golfers, cert. denied,* 385 U.S. 846 (1966).

20. *U.S. v. Realty Multi-List, Inc.*, 629 F.2d 1351, 1375 (5th Cir. 1980).

21. *See,* e.g., *Hahn v. Oregon Physician's Service,* 689 F.2d 840 (9th Cir. 1982); *New Jersey Chiropractic Society v. Radiological Society of New Jersey,* 383 A.2d 140 (1980).

22. *Jefferson Parish Hospital Dist. No. 2 v. Hyde,* 80 L. Ed.2d (1984).

23. *St. Bernard General Hospital v. Hospital Service Association* CCH Trade Reg. Rptr. 65565, 1983–2 Trade Cases.

24. *Bartholomew v. Virginia Chiropractors Ass'n,* 612 F.2d 812 (4th Cir. 1980), *cert. denied,* 446 U.S. 938 (1980); FTC Advisory Opinion letter to the American Podiatory Ass'n (18 Aug. 1983).

25. *Union Labor Life Insurance v. Pireno,* 102 S.Ct. 3002 (1982).

26. *St. Bernard General Hospital v. Hospital Service Association, supra* n.23; *Trident Neuro-Imaging Lab. v. Blue Cross,* 568 F.Supp. 1474 (D.C.S.C. 1983); *Patino v. Blue Shield,* CCH Trade Reg. Rptr. 65641 (4th Cir. 1983).

27. *Hospital Building Co. v. Trustees of Rex Hospital,* 691 F.2d 678 (4th Cir. 1982).

Index

About the Editor

Dr. Wecht received his B.S. at the University of Pittsburgh, his M.D. at the University of Pittsburgh School of Medicine, his LL.B. at the University of Maryland School of Law, and his J. D. at the University of Pittsburgh School of Law. He is a Clinical Adjunct Professor of Pathology at the University of Pittsburgh Schools of Medicine and Dental Medicine. He is both a physician and an attorney, and is well-versed in medico-legal issues. In addition to his position as Adjunct Professor of Law at Duquesne University School of Law, he is the President and Director of the Pittsburgh Institute of Legal Medicine and a Charter Diplomate of the American Board of Law in Medicine. A Past President of the American College of Legal Medicine and the American Academy of Forensic Sciences, Dr. Wecht is the author or editor of over 230 publications, including a well-known three volume work entitled *Forensic Sciences*.

www.ingramcontent.com/pod-product-compliance
Ingram Content Group UK Ltd.
Pitfield, Milton Keynes, MK11 3LW, UK
UKHW020802290926
15470UKWH00003B/900